THE COOKING OF SOUTH-WEST FRANCE

Also by Paula Wolfert

Couscous and Other Good Food from Morocco
Mediterranean Cooking
Paula Wolfert's World of Food

THE COOKING OF SOUTH-WEST FRANCE

A COLLECTION OF
TRADITIONAL AND NEW
RECIPES FROM FRANCE'S
MAGNIFICENT RUSTIC CUISINE
AND NEW TECHNIQUES TO LIGHTEN HEARTY DISHES

PAULA WOLFERT

Drawings by Jerry Joyner

PERENNIAL LIBRARY

Harper & Row, Publishers, New York
Cambridge, Philadelphia, San Francisco
London, Mexico City, São Paulo, Singapore, Sydney

For My Mother and Father
and for Bill

A hardcover edition of this book was originally published in 1983 by The Dial Press. It is hereby reprinted by arrangement with Doubleday, a division of Bantam, Doubleday, Dell Publishing Group, Inc.

Parts of this book appeared originally in slightly different form in *International Review of Food and Wine, Bon Appétit, Cuisine, Travel & Leisure, Pleasures of Cooking, House & Garden,* and *Cooking.*

First PERENNIAL LIBRARY edition published 1988.

LIBRARY OF CONGRESS CATALOG CARD NUMBER: 88-45367
ISBN: 0-06-097195-9 (pbk.)

88 89 90 91 92 RRD 10 9 8 7 6 5 4 3 2 1

CONTENTS

ACKNOWLEDGMENTS

Many wonderful, generous people helped me with this book, and I hope every one of them will find his or her name in the various lists below, arranged alphabetically within each region.

There were three people who particularly influenced and helped me in special and major ways. If this book is unique, different from others published in its field, then their collective assistance must be the reason.

The first is André Daguin. This extraordinary Gascon chef opened the doors of Aquitaine for me and delivered the entire South-West. He sent me everywhere, to all the corners of the region, to meet, talk, eat, and learn. And then, too, he and his wife, Jo, gave me my own little room under the roof of their home in Auch, overlooking the top of *Cathedrale Ste.-Marie* and the plains that spread from the Gers River. Here I sorted out papers, studied my notes, and read books loaned to me from the library downstairs, and if I had a question, André was always there to answer it. He is an exceptional chef—original, controversial, always experimenting, applying new concepts and techniques to traditional Gascon food. He was the first to show me how to update classic regional cuisine. Daring, intelligent, generous-spirited, he is a Gascon's Gascon.

Lucien Vanel of Toulouse opened the kitchen of his restaurant and all the "secrets" of his mother's famous *cuisine Quercynoise.* It has been said of this kind and unpretentious man that he has done for country cooking what the brothers Troisgros have done for *cuisine bourgeoise* and the restaurant Taillevent has done for *haute cuisine*; he has updated it without losing the strengths, subtleties, and depths of what had gone before. He takes simple country food and gives it extraordinary lightness and flavor. He and his two sous-chefs, Jean Tillot and Luc Zwolinski, left nothing of the Périgord, Toulouse, Bordeaux, and the Quercy unturned. They *wanted* me to learn it all, and if I missed anything, that's my fault and not theirs.

The third is André Guillot, who is not from the South-West. The foremost cooking teacher in France, Guillot truly and viscerally loves the culinary arts, to which he brings a keen and probing intelligence. I think he is the only teacher I have ever met who seems to exist *within* his subject and, simultaneously, outside it. To listen to him is to bask in culinary wisdom and to catch his own passion for the subject. Among the most important things I learned from Guillot is that there need be no incompatibility between great food and good health—that I have a responsibility toward my readers to think of their health as well as their delight—and that one *can* lower the quantity of fat in a dish without sacrificing any of its flavor. A recipe is a blueprint. The cook need not act as slave to the recipe; we have each of us our own interpretation, and it is the quality of our individual spirits that is the essence of finesse.

I am sincerely grateful to Alain Dutournier for allowing me to work in his kitchen and for giving generously of his time and knowledge.

With thanks to Pepette Arbulo, Noël and Michel Baris, Jean-Pierre Capelle, Maurice Coscuella, Bernard Cousseau, Jo Daguin, Louis Darmanté, Roger Duffour, Robert Garrapit, Christine and Michel Guérard, Robert and Fabienne Labeyrie, Claude Laffitte, Gustav Ledun, Huguette Melier, Jean-Louis Palladin, Jacques Pastour, Maïté Sandrini, Marie-Claude

Soubiran-Gracia, Marylyse and Dominique Toulousy, and Monique Veilletet for recipes and notes on Gascony and the Landes.

With thanks to Firmin Arrambide, André Canal, Robert Casau, André Darraidoü, Pierre LaPorte, Geneviève and Rosalie Muruamendiaraz, and the Urguty family for recipes and notes on the Basque country and the Béarn.

With thanks to Jean-Marie Amat, Christian Clément, Jean-David Dickson, Isabelle Dussauge, Francis Garcia, Jean Ramet, Pierre Veilletet, and Jean-Pierre Xiradakis for recipes and notes on Bordeaux.

With thanks to Max Ambert, Madame Ambert-Molinier, Monique Darras, Vivienne Gautier, Pierrette Lejanou, and Jacques Rieux for recipes and notes on the Languedoc.

With thanks to Pierre Escorbiac, Georgie Géry, Madame "Marthou," Madame Danièle Mazet-Delpeuch, Robert Meyzen, René Mommejac, Albert Parveaux, Jacques Pébeyre, Jean-Pierre Pébeyre, the Rougié family, Paul Turon, and Lucienne Vanel for recipes and notes on the Lot, the Corrèze, and the Dordogne.

With thanks to all those who worked with me here in America: William Bayer, Patricia Brown, Ariane Daguin, Hallie Donnelly, Suzanne Hamlin, Barbara Kafka, Annick Klein, Susan and Robert Lescher, Frances McCullough, Leslie Newman, Anne Otterson, Carol Robertson, Carl Sontheimer, Ronnellie van der Merwe, James Villas, and Roger Yaseen.

A special thank-you to Bill Otterson for his wonderful word processor, Lexor, which helped me put the whole thing together with a lot less labor and a lot more joy than I thought possible.

I owe a particular debt to Ariane and Michael Batterberry for sending me to the South-West of France in the first place. Particular thanks to Gloria Adelson and Jerry Joyner, who made this book look so appealing.

A NOTE ON ATTRIBUTION

A woman chef I know, who takes herself very seriously as a feminist, made the point to me that since the cooking of South-West France is really women's cooking, it was odd that I was collecting and publishing so many recipes obtained from men. My response was that I wanted to write a living cookbook, a book that encompassed the traditional recipes of the region as well as the new ones adapted from the old. Any recipe that appealed to me was worth considering for inclusion. And then I said that as far as I was concerned, one could no longer draw the line of gender in the kitchen; it must be the result, the food, that is the point, and not the man or woman who produced it.

Still, of course, recipes generally have a source, and we food writers must be scrupulous about assigning credit. I've developed my own way of acknowledging sources, a system that is used throughout this book. If a recipe bears no attribution at all, then it is my version of a new or traditional dish belonging to no one, a dish in the common domain. I don't invent recipes, at least not for a regional book like this. When I develop a recipe, I base it on my various tastings of the dish, the literature and oral lore that surrounds it, and my own amalgam of methods and techniques, most taught to me by various cooks through the years. If a recipe bears this line at the end: *"Inspired by a recipe from _____,"* then, in fact, that is just what happened—I've taken a recipe taught or imparted by a specific individual and made *definite* changes in it. These changes include not just substituting ingredients more available in the United States, but also making simplifications or improvements that would better serve my readers. Finally, if a recipe bears the name of a specific individual in its name or is fully attributed in its introduction, then that is the recipe as it was given to me, and I am imparting it with *some* changes, having tested it in this country and adjusted it for a good result.

FOREWORD BY
BARBARA KAFKA

For me, writing about Paula Wolfert is an almost guilty pleasure. Our minds have marched for several years in such tight and sympathetic cadence that it is almost as if I were flattering myself. We are bound together by an interest in discovering not only the recipe, but also, and perhaps more important, why it works or why it does not. It is only this knowledge that satisfies our curiosity and permits us to continue to learn and create. For many years my students have asked me what books I would recommend to give them more "whyfor" information. Frankly, there have been few. Now, with Paula's book, there is, finally, a superb book to recommend. We do not always agree, but the thrust of our inquiries is similar and the search is always passionately pursued. The disagreements are often the most fun, for they provide the basis for good discussions and further inquiry. Along the way there have been many good meals and lots of laughter.

Being privy to the evolution of this book over a five-year period has been an exciting privilege. Paula became interested first in the food of South-West France and then in those cooks who were busy both preserving the traditional recipes and at the same time updating and lightening them so that they would be appealing to contemporary tastes. During numerous trips to the area she became friendly with these chefs and learned their recipes. Pleased though she was, she wanted something more: to understand and conceptualize intellectually what was being done—with these great recipes. She took what her cooks were doing several steps further to create, on her own, new concepts and new versions of traditional recipes. It is this rich multiplicity of understanding, clearly explained, that makes *The Cooking of South-West France* a brilliant addition to the culinary literature. Bravo, Paula, and thank you.

It is not French, not Austrian, not European even: it is the country of enchantment which the poets have staked out and which they alone may lay claim to. It is the nearest thing to Paradise this side of Greece. Let us call it the Frenchman's paradise, by way of making a concession. Actually it must have been a paradise for many thousands of years. I believe it must have been so for the Cro-Magnon man, despite the fossilized evidences of the great caves which point to a condition of life rather bewildering and terrifying. I believe that the Cro-Magnon man settled here because he was extremely intelligent and had a highly developed sense of beauty. I believe that in him the religious sense was already highly developed and that it flourished here even if he lived like an animal in the depths of the caves. I believe that this great peaceful region of France will always be a sacred spot for man and that when the cities have killed off the poets this will be the refuge and the cradle of the poets to come. I repeat, it was most important for me to have seen the Dordogne: it gives me hope for the future of the race, for the future of the earth itself. France may one day exist no more, but the Dordogne will live on just as dreams live on and nourish the souls of men.

HENRY MILLER, *The Colossus of Maroussi*

INTRODUCTION

To paraphrase Charles de Gaulle, I once had a "certain conception" of the cooking of South-West France—ducks, foie gras, goose fat, and cassoulet, with Michel Guérard working alone in the wilderness, practicing cuisine minceur. I knew the food was good down there; nearly every French person told me so. But the impression persisted of an overly rich, hearty peasant cooking, a rustic change, perhaps, from the elegance and excitement of the culinary scene in Paris, but nothing that could possibly tempt me to spend half a decade writing a book.

Indeed there are ducks, foie gras, goose fat, and cassoulet; the purpose of my first serious trip, in fact, was to seek out the perfect cassoulet. But on that journey I caught sight of something else: a magnificent peasant cookery in the process of being updated. The food was modern, honest, yet still close to the earth—a true *cuisine de terroir*, "of the soil," barely touched upon by other commentators. Here was the cuisine I'd been searching for; it struck a resonance with certain beliefs that had been quietly growing within me for years.

These ideas seemed contrary to the spirit prevailing at the time, and so I kept them to myself. They had to do with a love of logic in recipes in which a dish is built, step by step, inexorably toward a finish that is the inevitable best result of all the ingredients employed. They had to do with simplicity and healthiness and the pleasures of dining upon foods that bear natural affinities, as opposed to wild experimentation, gratuitous gestures, complexity for its own sake, and striking dramatic contrasts and effects. I found that my favorite restaurants in Paris were not the citadels of haute cuisine or the laboratories of nouvelle, but rather Alain Dutournier's Trou Gascon in a working-class area on Rue Taine, and Antoine Magnin's Chez l'Ami Louis in the third arrondissement. Dutournier updates and lightens great regional specialties, most of them from South-West France. Magnin takes traditional country dishes and elevates them to exquisite bliss.

As I explored the South-West, I found many chefs doing the same sort of thing: first trying to reproduce the regional dishes they remembered from childhood, then working to refine them. If good country "Mother's cooking" can rival the finest bourgeois cuisine (and I think a strong case can be made for this), then sophisticated versions of "Mother's cooking" might just be the very best cooking around.

When I returned from my first expedition and began to teach South-West cooking to my classes, I found my students reacting just as I had. They were seduced by its succulence, its deep taste as opposed to its dazzle, and like me, they could not get enough. And so, to satisfy our mutual desire for more, I launched a series of trips. What had started out as a simple venture to supply material for a few articles and classes turned into a passionate long-term enterprise.

Now let me tell you what is in this book and also what is not. Here is a personal collection of favorite South-West regional specialties, most of them updated by chefs, home cooks, or myself. There is country food here and bourgeois food, but no haute cuisine. Some of these dishes are very modern, while some are purely traditional. You'll find "Mother's cooking" and adaptations of "Mother's cooking."

There is a sampling of the cooking of regional chefs. It is not an attempt at a definitive work or at encompassing everything. The criteria for inclusion were that first of all, the dish had to be very good to eat; second, it had to be practical to prepare here in the United States; and third, it had to interest me on account of something special in the recipe, a unique touch—a *truc*, or secret, as the French like to say—or, as I prefer, an element of finesse. From time to time there are comments on these *trucs* at the end of the recipe, called "Notes to the Cook."

This book does not cover the geography or history of the South-West, or the customs and folklore. It is a cookbook first and foremost, a book of recipes, and the recipes are detailed, sometimes even long. This lengthiness does not necessarily connote difficulty. Rather, it stems from needs I've felt since I've begun to teach: to be as precise as I possibly can; to answer as many questions as I can anticipate; and to impart those elements of finesse that can turn the preparation of food into a joyful art. Truly lengthy recipes are presented with advance warning.

One could write a rich and anecdotal book about the region, the people, and the land, the sights and smells and moods. I've tried to put some of that sensibility into this book, but my primary intention has been to describe the making of food. I want to show you ways to actually bring the South-West into your home in the form, for instance, of a rich oxtail daube or a satiny and delicate wild mushroom flan, a deeply aromatic dish of chicken and garlic with Sauternes, or a haunting croustade containing apples, orange flower water, and Armagnac. The idea is that you, too, can possess the South-West not merely in words, but in that most tangible and sensuous necessity of people's lives: the wonderful food they eat.

Most cooks were generous with me. I never found a professional cook who was not willing to demonstrate a dish. The days when chefs gave out recipes but forbade observation of their cooking because the recipes left out something essential now seem to be past. The tendency toward secretiveness is still prevalent, however, among some of the older, bony-faced "mothers" in the tight black hats who, staring about a marketplace, can tell the difference in taste between two chickens squawking at their feet. I thought at first it was me, the American, with whom they didn't want to share. But one day, on a train between Cahors and Brive-la-Gaillarde, I happened to witness an encounter between two such women, and I have never heard such recipe-dangling in my life. Each would begin to tell the other how she made a certain dish. Her voice would start off clear, then she would begin to mumble, and then the description of the recipe would peter out. They took turns torturing each other this way, smiling as they did it. I was fascinated. Was this some kind of ritual? Perhaps, but not in the way it seemed. Those old women of the South-West hold a certain matriarchal power over the region by virtue of controlling the preparation of its food. I felt a flood of sympathy for them: their secrets were their usefulness. To give them up would be to diminish themselves, their glory, and their honor. So sometimes it was their daughters or their sons who showed me those famous *trucs*, those special touches. These touches always have a purpose, and they can elevate a dish to excellence: to cut mushrooms into matchsticks so that they will expose more surface and thus absorb more liquid from a sauce; to wipe the moisture off the bottom of a cover when cooking a potato cake so that it will not drip back and make the cake soggy instead of crisp. It is these little details that I call the "finesse of cooking," which to me is its joy.

Finally, I wish to draw your attention to two special sections in this book: the section on cooking with fats that follows this introduction, and my recipes for pastry doughs that appear at the end. The great cliché about the dishes of the South-West is that they are good but heavy and therefore not healthful. I disagree emphatically, and I have made a special effort in this book to include recipes that have been lightened. Please read what I have to say about "fighting fat with fat" and about "double degreasing" principles. I have applied these techniques to nearly every *traditional* dish, with a few obvious exceptions such as cassoulet, whose very essence is its richness and which, if lightened, would simply not be the same. As for the pastry recipes, they represent a long-term effort to develop ways of making first-class pastry in a food processor, so as to enable the home cook without a "pastry hand" to achieve consistent and professional results.

A HEALTHY APPROACH TO COOKING WITH POULTRY FATS, LARD, BUTTER, CREAM, AND CRÈME FRAÎCHE

One does not live by how one eats, but by how one digests.
—SOUTH-WEST SAYING

I've had a feeling for some time that much of the so-called new food served up to us by the "innovative" chefs is really "front of the mouth" food. By this I mean that though these dishes may appeal to the tips of our tongues, there is no real depth to them, and not much desire to eat them again.

That's why I am less interested in novel or revolutionary dishes than in new renditions of old favorites, what I like to call "evolved dishes," recipes that show us how to cook the foods we love in simpler ways with lighter, more contemporary results. The innovations displayed in such recipes do not come out of thin air; they are rooted in historical traditions, natural taste affinities, and the eating needs of healthy people. They are, in short, recipes displaying the logic that should lie behind every good thing we cook and eat.

The recipes in this book are examples of updated South-West French dishes that I feel have logic behind them. They employ many of the new techniques we've learned over the last fifteen years, but they do not depart from qualities traditional to the area. Classically, the cooking of France has been broken down into three culinary zones—torrid, temperate, and frigid—each with its corresponding cooking medium: olive oil, animal fats, and butter. The South-West is considered a temperate zone, and its cooking media are goose, duck, and pork fat. It is important to understand how to cook with these so-called temperate media to obtain good-tasting results without fear of ingesting too many saturated fats, which may in turn produce high cholesterol levels.

"*Sans beurre et sans reproche,*" said Curnonsky of Périgord cooking—"without butter and above reproach."* He meant it as a compliment. It's a cliché, and a false one, that South-West food is greasy and heavy. It can be, in careless hands, but at its best, good South-West food is merely enhanced by the fats in which it is cooked. I often use these animal fats for taste, the way I use a cinnamon stick in a red-wine compote of fruits: I add it for flavor in the cooking, but take it out before the fruits are served. I want goose, duck, or pork fat to give flavor to a sauce, but I almost always remove it so that the food, when served, is relatively fat-free. This is possible because, according to our latest scientific knowledge, the ingredients that give the actual flavor to fats are in fact water-soluble—they can be separated from the fat itself. The techniques I'm about to describe are not only applicable to this particular cuisine; once you understand them, you can substantially reduce the amount of fat in all your meat dishes without sacrificing flavor.

In addition, the temperature at which one uses fats can make the difference between a dish that is heavy or light, greasy or velvety, succulent or bland. For instance, if you eat toast spread with cold butter, digestion will be relatively easy. But if you eat sautéed brains cooked with the same amount of bubbling *beurre noisette*, your stomach will feel somewhat leaden.

Meat braised at a very low temperature is very tender. The cooking fats mingle but will not bind with the wine and juices, and thus will be easy to remove by degreasing after cooling the dish. Moreover, the sauce will retain the *flavor* of the fats and yet will not be greasy. For example, in Crushed Meat Daube for Early September, a lean piece of beef is sliced, layered with seasoned ground pork fat, slowly simmered in wine, then thoroughly degreased before reheating; each slice lifted out of the pot is moist, tender, flavorful, yet virtually fat-free.

*Curnonsky, the famous French food writer, was playing with the old adage *Sans peur et sans reproche.*

Chef Lucien Vanel of Toulouse is the creator of the recipe for the Compote of Rabbit with Prunes, a dish that employs culinary alchemy. The richness of this tender, moist compote is an illusion. Its flavor is deep, since the meat is cooked with chunks of pork fat, but afterward the fat chunks are removed and the dish is carefully degreased. Though the meat is shredded and thus similar in texture to rillettes, the difference in fat content is enormous. Most rillettes are 50 percent fat. But this recipe is virtually fat-free except for a small amount of fresh cream added at the end to round out the flavor. I call this technique of extracting the flavor of fat, degreasing, and then adding a tiny amount of fat at the end "fighting fat with fat."

DOUBLE DEGREASING FOR ADDED FLAVOR IN STEWS

If you remove absolutely all the fat from a dish, there will indeed be a loss of flavor. To compensate, I often degrease, then add *more* fat for more flavor, cook the dish some more, then degrease again. I call this technique "double degreasing."

A good example is the recipe for Oxtail Daube. I use the natural fat of the oxtail to enhance its flavor, totally degrease, then add some pork fat for more flavor, and degrease again before the dish is served. The result is a really tender, meaty, flavorful daube of incredible lightness. The secret is long, slow cooking in a closed pot. The meat must *not* be moved, and the juices must *never* be allowed to boil rapidly until they are thoroughly degreased. (If they do boil, the fat binds with the wine; the sauce becomes muddy and the meat mushy.) The best way to thoroughly degrease is to allow a stew or soup to stand overnight in the refrigerator so that the fat solids rise to the surface and congeal. It is then easy to see and remove the fat. (Of course, there will always be a little fat left in the nooks and crannies of the meat.) Luckily, most stews and soups improve with *slow* reheating (and sometimes multiple reheating), so this chilling process has the additional benefits of enhancing flavor and permitting advance preparation. As in a long-simmered soup, the nutrients will be in the liquid.

There is another way to degrease thoroughly when a dish is to be served the same day it is cooked. Meat and sauce are separated. The sauce is left for a short time so that most of the fat surfaces and can be carefully spooned off. Meanwhile the meat is kept warm in a very low oven. Then the sauce is placed in a heavy saucepan and set half over a stove burner. The heat is adjusted so that the side over the heat slowly boils and the fat and any other impurities in the sauce rise on the cooler side. This process takes about 20 to 30 minutes, with frequent skimming, to remove all the fat and impurities in the sauce. The resulting sauce is clear and shiny.

SAUTÉING WITH LESS CHOLESTEROL-RICH FAT WHILE ACTUALLY IMPROVING FLAVOR

An interesting fact I discovered in a U.S. Department of Agriculture publication— Handbook 8-4 (revised, 1979)—is that rendered poultry fat (goose, duck, and chicken) contains 9 percent cholesterol and lard contains 10 percent compared with butter's 22 percent. Since one needs less poultry fat, oil, or lard than butter to sauté meat or vegetables, one will ingest far less saturated fat if these cooking media are used instead of butter. One needs less of these because butter breaks down and burns at high temperatures whereas poultry fat, lard, and oil do not. Many cooks recommend a mixture of oil and butter to avoid this burning. My suggestion is either to use poultry fat alone or to mix it with oil, especially for browning meat and poultry. Flavor is actually improved if poultry fat (even chicken fat!) is used instead of the standard butter-and-oil combination when browning beef for a stew.

I use grape-seed oil† for high-heat searing for lamb or beef sautés, or for pan roasting (as in Fillet of Beef with Roquefort Sauce and Mixed Nuts). Since this oil has a slightly odd taste, I dilute it with poultry fat in a ratio of 2:1.

BUTTER AND CREAM IN SOUTH-WEST FRENCH COOKING

Until World War II, butter was rarely used in sauces in most parts of the South-West. André Daguin told me that when rationing took place, butter was allotted in huge amounts compared to what the South-Westerners were used to, and as a result some of the cooks started using butter in their cooking. In the Pyrenees, on the other hand, dairy products were always used in sauces, though not to the degree common in Normandy. For example, in the recipe for Artichokes and Potatoes au Gratin, raw churned milk is used to create a creamy-textured dish.

Some dishes simply are not good without the addition of cream or butter, and so a number of dishes in this book employ them as thickening agents. Sauces bound with cream and butter are very easy to prepare and, when used in *small* quantities, give the illusion of lightness (unfortunately, they are also fattening). The principle behind sauces bound with butter is simple: a flavorful liquid is reduced to a few tablespoons, butter is whisked into it, and it is brought quickly to a boil. The resulting sauce will carry the original flavor in a suspension just thick enough to lightly coat a dish. Butter is fragile and breaks down easily, becoming oily and heavy when allowed to boil. The technique described in the recipe for Hot Oysters with Vegetables and Foie Gras and that for Asparagus with Asparagus Sauce deals with this problem successfully.

In this book a few traditional South-West dishes have been "updated" and "lightened" with butter, thus eliminating some of the long simmering for which people no longer have time. All you need for these quickly made dishes is a large batch of demi-glace or a well-reduced meat and/or poultry stock sauce base. Basically, then, it's a trade-off; you either take the time to make a long-simmered dish, or save time by using a demi-glace plus cream or butter but pay the price with extra calories.

AN ARGUMENT IN FAVOR OF FLOUR-BASED SAUCES

It has been fashionable for the past ten to fifteen years to scoff at flour-thickened sauces. I'm not sure all this scoffing has been terribly helpful to fine cuisine. The

†Grape-seed oil breaks down at a higher temperature than other oils, and of all the vegetable oils and animal fats, grape-seed oil and safflower oil have the lowest levels of saturated fat.

process of multiple slow reheating and chilling for some South-West stews and daubes can result in a loss of flavor. Here is where something can be said on behalf of the currently much despised flour-based sauces: they can help to hold the flavor through these multiple rounds. A good example is the traditional recipe for Duck Legs Cooked in Red Wine, a dish with a flour-based sauce that is smooth, rich, light, and delicious. If it is properly prepared so that the flour taste is cooked right out of the sauce, the flavor will be stronger and better than that of the same dish prepared without flour.

MAKING SAUCES BY STRATIFICATION

The concept of stratification was developed by the brilliant teacher-chef André Guillot, who is not as well known in the United States as he should be. Stratification is simple; with it you can make sauces without the usual thickening agents (flour, arrowroot, or egg yolk) by a series of rapid reductions. You start off with an acid—as, for example, in Caramel Vinegar Sauce—which you reduce in a deep saucepan to intensify its flavor. Then you add a protein-rich stock, deep in flavor, that will harmonize with the acid. In the case of caramelized vinegar, you would add a duck-flavored demi-glace with a background hint of red wine. Next you add heavy cream and, without whisking, allow the sauce to boil vigorously until many bubbles appear on its surface. From time to time you stir this bubbling mixture with a wooden spoon until you catch a glimpse of the bottom of the pan. When you see the bottom, your sauce is finished and will adhere lightly to meat or fish (in this instance, to Duck Liver Flans). Basically, this is what has happened: the water in the cream has evaporated, allowing the remaining butterfat, in the presence of protein and acid, to bind the sauce and make it silky. "The faster the evaporation, the better the coagulation" is the rule for creating a sauce by stratification. It takes less than 10 minutes to complete the entire process in a heavy-bottomed pan, and the sauce will hold for quite a while.

BROILING WITH CRÈME FRAÎCHE

Crème fraîche is a cultured heavy cream that you can easily make yourself with a starter of lactic bacteria. It works marvelously as a basting medium for broiling.

When you broil foods with a coating of homemade crème fraîche instead of butter, you cut down the butterfat by more than 50 percent. Homemade crème fraîche using starter and 36 percent butterfat-rich heavy cream is *still* only 36 percent rich in fat. Since broiling is a dry-heat process, there is always some evaporation of moisture from meats, poultry, vegetables, or fish, but by using crème fraîche you can keep poultry and fish moist. As the crème fraîche warms up under the broiler, its butterfat (36 percent) browns while its whey creates a thin protective layer that prevents the juices from evaporating and at the same time bastes the poultry or fish. Normally the moisture that evaporates during broiling is the natural moisture of the food. In this case, however, it is the water in the crème fraîche that evaporates, leaving the food full of its natural juices. Yet you cut down on the amount of butterfat that the food would absorb if it were basted with butter. (Large pieces of chicken should not be broiled too close to the source of heat, but boneless chicken pieces and fish may be placed closer for better color.) When a French recipe calls for cooking with crème fraîche, never substitute sour cream or yogurt, which break down under high heat.

CRÈME FRAÎCHE AS A TENDERIZER

The lactic acid in crème fraîche tenderizes poultry. Unlike lemon juice or vinegar, often used to tenderize food, crème fraîche does not overpower the natural flavors. Marinating poultry in crème fraîche (as in Chicken with Garlic Pearls and Sauternes Wine Sauce) is a process similar to the Indian method of using yogurt or buttermilk as a marinade. Actually, even milk has a tenderizing effect on chicken and keeps it extremely moist (see recipe for Chicken Breasts with Mussels and Asparagus Flans).

For the recipe for Crème Fraîche and further information, see the Appendix.

DEFINING THE SOUTH-WEST

To my surprise I have found that food commentators disagree about just which areas are encompassed by the term "South-West France." I've seen texts that ignore the Ariège portion of the Pyrenees, that omit every part of Languedoc, and that delineate Gascony as a special and separate culinary zone. Certainly each province has its own specialties, but there is a land the French call *Sud-Ouest*, which can be gastronomically defined. As drawn on the accompanying map, it is the land of preserved meats—*confits*—a preparation that unifies such diverse regions as the Basque country, the Béarn, the Quercy, the Gers, and the western portions of the Languedoc.

You will be reading often of these regions in this book, and also of the Landes, the Rouergue, the Tarn, and the Périgord, so I suggest we take a brief tour of the whole area to catch a glimpse of each subdivision, to meet the people, and to gain a notion of what they eat.

As often as I was told that "one eats well in the South-West," I was also told about how kind the people were, how warm and generous-spirited. Indeed, both assertions turned out to be true; the people are as wonderful as their food. From the proud Basques and the zany Catalans to the earthy Périgourdins and Quercynois, from the gentle Landais and Tarnais to the sophisticates of Bordeaux, the gallants of Gascony, and the sunny-tempered people of Toulouse, I never failed to find help and encouragement, a special kindness or a smile. These are not the sort of provincial French who eye you with suspicion, nor do they behave falsely, only pretending to be your

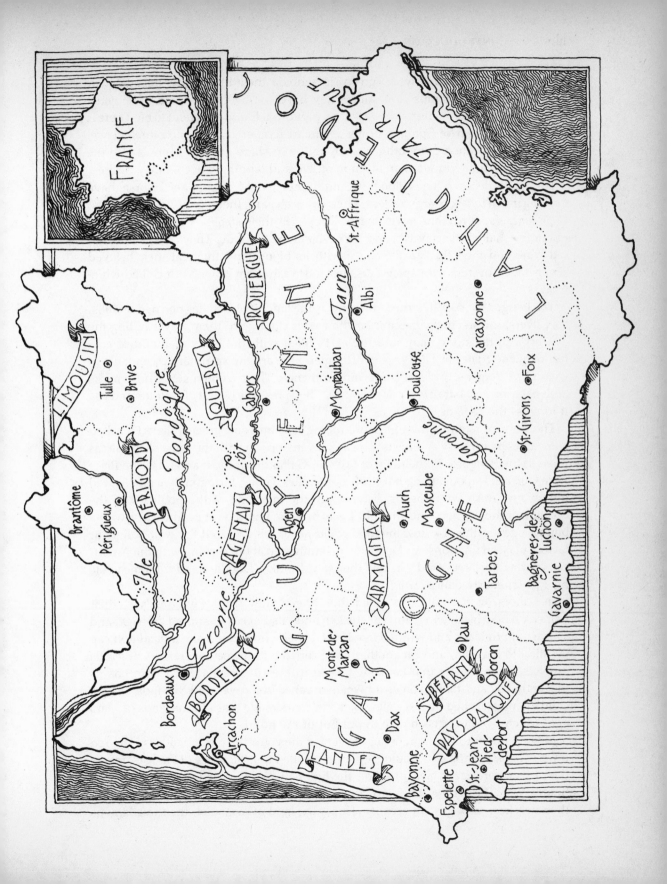

friend. Their friendship, when given, is serious; their hospitality, despite their relative poverty, generous to a fault. They have not been corrupted by *le grand tourisme*, nor are they xenophobic, as many provincial Europeans tend to be. There is more than a touch of Spanish honor in them, tempered by French intelligence, decency, forbearance, sympathy, and an ability to share humor. There is also the spirit of the Mediterranean, an attitude of live and let others live as they desire.

For the Bordelais, wine is blood; without it they would be poor and, worse, have nothing much to talk or argue about. Their city is elegant, their life-styles are serious, their tempers sturdy but never mean. They grill their steaks over vine cuttings, honor the shallot, the crayfish, and the caviar of the Gironde. They cook lamprey in red wine and then thicken the sauce with its blood, and they eat their beloved silver-tinged oysters with spicy sausages and wash them down with chilled white Graves.

The Périgord, also called the Dordogne, is the land of old castles perched on hills, lazy rivers, forests, rocky precipices with towns clinging to them, caves hiding the artwork of prehistoric man, and the earth filled with the black diamond of gastronomy, the *truffe noire de Périgord*. The men here are the spiritual descendants of Cyrano de Bergerac, at least concerning romance. Their women stuff goose necks and make the best hare *à la royale* in France. They press the oil out of walnuts and use it to dress their salads.

The Corrèze reminds me of Britain: rolling hills and soft green valleys, touched sometimes by mystery and mists. The houses are topped with the same black tiles as those in the Périgord. In the town of Brive-la-Gaillarde, at the marketplace on Place de la Guierle, I stood among boxes of chanterelles, cèpes, tarragon, live rabbits, red plums, and fresh white beans, listening to the quacking of the poultry and the cackling of the women, and thought I was in some paradise of produce, for with a bounty such as this, I knew, the food could never fail. I visited the walnut liqueur factory of a certain Monsieur Denoël who reminisced about serving with the Americans during the First World War, and then sang "Yankee Doodle Dandy" for me while he spontaneously danced a jig.

In Cahors, in the Lot, also called the Quercy, they drink *vin de Cahors*, their namesake inky black wine, and eat chicken and salsify *tourtes*, stuffed cabbage, and sausages both black and white. Here I met a chef whose dog wore a plaid golf cap identical to his own, and on another day I dined with three generations of truffle growers on an omelet that contained more truffles than eggs. Each farm has its pigeon house and its personalized weather vane. In a cave in Pech-Merle I saw a child's hand stenciled on the wall, a personal mark made tens of thousands of years ago, which I've never been able to put out of my mind.

Moving down to the Languedoc, we enter the country of troubadours. The red town of Albi, birthplace of Toulouse-Lautrec, called the "Florence of France," marks the place where garlic meets shallot, the link between the Mediterranean and the South-West. The people of the Tarn are rightly known for their stability as well as for their peaches, sausages, and *confits*. This is the land of cassoulet, the three famous versions of Toulouse, Carcassonne, and Castelnaudary, and also of a certain pastel blue tint (locally called *coca)* employed in the church frescoes that gives this area the name *pays de cocaigne*.‡

To the west is Gascony, a land of rolling hills studded with farms and *bastides*, red-roofed, fortified towns. This is the country of D'Artagnan, and it's no coincidence that the local chefs have banded together and now call themselves *la ronde des mousquetaires*. Their monthly dinners at one another's restaurants reflect the sharing quality of Gascons: laughter and fellowship and exchange of information, including the trying out of new dishes—there are no secrets here. They eat their grilled duck breasts bloody rare, use foie gras and truffles as if they were mere condiments, adapt their menus to the availability of wild game, and turn cabbage soups, called *garbures*, into glorious cuisine.

Things are calmer in the Landes, a sandy land of swamps and brooks and pine forests so thick they darken the midday sun. The people here are truly sweet; their idea of a burning issue is whether one should put white wine or red in a wild mushroom ragout. The local summer pastime is the *course Landaise*, a modified, less cruel version of the *corrida* of Spain (the bull is never killed). The people of the Landes are specialists in *gavage*, the force-feeding of ducks and geese to produce the delicacy foie gras. I visited one home in a town where the country-born grandmother conducted her force-feeding in a garage filled with geese.

The Basques are known for their code of silence, their stoic acceptance of life, their pride, and their dishes enriched with *pipérade*. On the Atlantic coast one finds the famous ham of Bayonne. Back in the hills, in villages of timbered white stucco houses, one is apt to be served garlicky sausages called *louquenkas*, followed by hake, asparagus, and peas, then a cake stuffed with black cherries or pastry cream.

When I think over my memories of the South-West I am struck by how varied the country is. I recall the smell of cheese that permeates the town of Roquefort-sur-Soulzon; the pilgrims lighting candles before the grotto at Lourdes; the oil-rich people of Pau, France's answer to Dallas; a market day in late October in Mirande in the Gers, where a car drove up with a fattened turkey nestled in straw strewn over the backseat. The turkey was to be sold for Christmas dinner.

One day my friend André Daguin sent me to the half-abandoned town of Poudenas in Lot-et-Garonne so that I could interview a well-known Gascon restaurateur. She received me graciously, talked food with me for hours, then telephoned the château on the hill above the village to see if I could spend the night there, since there was no local hotel. "Yes," said the count, "of course she may stay, and she should come up right away since she is interested in food. I am serving a very typical dinner." I hurried up the hill. The hunting party guests were assembling for dinner. People from all over the South-West were arriving, from Casteljaloux, Gimont, Mont-de-Marsan, Sarlat, and Bordeaux. The *chasse* was to be for stag, hunted from horses in the forests at dawn, and there was an aura of excitement, a

‡Actually, most dictionaries translate this as the land of plenty or the land of milk and honey.

sense of a purposeful adventure about to be undertaken. Local wines were served, and then a feast consisting of fresh foie gras, duck breasts grilled rare, an intensely flavored daube of onions cooked in red wine, fresh goat cheese whipped with young Armagnac and sugar, and a croustade, a closed flaky pastry filled with apples and pears. The guests began to sing hunting songs, which they all seemed to know, sipped from their glasses of Armagnac, and occasionally rapped the table with their fists. This delirium went on for hours. I felt myself entranced. At one point a young man turned to me. "You want to know about the South-West?" he asked. I looked up at him and nodded. "Welcome," he said, gesturing with his hand. "You are here. This is it."

A NOTE ON PLACE NAMES

There is a quadruple overlapping of place names in South-West France that may require some explanation. The entire area encompassed by this book is sometimes thought of as two distinct regions: the Aquitaine, whose most important city is Bordeaux, and the Midi-Pyrénées, whose "capital" is Toulouse. Additionally, cutting across these two regions are the two old duchies of Gascony (Gascogne) and Guyenne, Gascony consisting of the Landes, Gers, and some other parts; Guyenne consisting of the Bordelais, the Dordogne, parts of the Quercy, and the Rouergue. But now the real confusion begins: there are names for the old provinces and names for the new *départements*; and the borders of the provinces and *départements* do not always precisely coincide. Still, one can make up a table of place names that are more or less equivalent. Thus traditionally one can speak of the Périgord, Quercy, and Rouergue while contemporaneously speaking of the Dordogne, the Lot, and the Aveyron.

What to do with all this confusion? One approach would be simply to go with the old provincial names and leave out words for regions such as Gascony. What I have done instead is to speak of these places as the people of the South-West speak of them. So if Lucien Vanel tells me a certain dish is "Quercynoise," that is how I identify it. If André Daguin speaks of an "old Gascon recipe," I have so recorded it. But if I am limiting my discussion to that area of Gascony called Gers, that is the place name I use. A little complicated, perhaps, but I feel serious readers will soon come to appreciate the intent behind these usages and will find a visual guide on the map.

CHAPTER 1

THE TASTE OF
THE SOUTH-WEST

FOIE GRAS

"Our cuisine does not begin in our kitchens," I was told by a young woman from the Landes. "It begins with our fathers and brothers hunting birds; our neighbors raising pigs; whole families gathering wild mushrooms in the fall; our mothers and sisters fattening up ducks and geese." An eloquent statement, and yet, I assure you, one hears a great deal of eloquence in the South-West when the subject turns to food. These people have an almost mystical appreciation of it and of the many ways it derives from the bounty of their land.

The production of foie gras—the term refers to the fattened liver of a force-fed goose, also called *foie gras d'oie,* while *foie gras de canard* is the fattened liver of a force-fed duck—is one of the most important cottage industries of the rural South-West. It is women's work, as the caring for poultry has generally been. The force-feeding is called *gavage,* and the women who do it are called *gaveuses.* When I visited the famous foie gras market in Mirande, I was surprised to find women of all ages there, not just the cliché ruddy-complexioned old women one would expect, but young ones, too.

Mirande is a Gascon town known for its poultry, candied fruits, and *confits* (preserved poultry or pork). Like other foie gras market towns, it holds a fair late in the winter where the *gaveuses* compete to see who has produced the best enlarged livers. I talked to many of the women there and found them full of pride. They gently ridiculed the notion that their work was cruel. In fact, they claimed to adore their birds even as they fattened them to be killed. "It is their destiny to provide us with livers," one of them said.

Richard Olney wrote a fine paragraph on this in his wonderful book *Simple French Food:*

> I once listened in amazement to a Périgord farmwife describing—in what was intended to be a vehement denial that the raising of geese destined to produce *foie gras* involves cruelty to animals—the tenderness and gentleness with which the birds are treated and, with mounting enthusiasm and in the most extraordinarily sensuous language, the suspense and the excitement experienced as the moment arrives to delicately slit the abdomen, to lovingly—ever so gently—pry it open, exposing finally the huge, glorious, and tender blond treasure, fragile object of so many months' solicitous care and of present adoration. One sensed vividly the goose's plenary participation, actively sharing in the orgasmic beauty of the sublime moment for which her life had been lived.

Some *gaveuses* claim secret feeding formulas: moist corn, dry corn, corn mixed with salt, and so on. And they talk amusingly of birds with which force-feeding just doesn't seem to take. The Rougié firm, which packages enormous quantities of foie gras, raised one goose that was force-fed three times and still didn't produce an enlarged liver.

Foie gras is expensive, worth more than ten times all of the rest of the bird. The last time I was in the South-West, duck livers were selling for forty dollars a kilo and goose livers for sixty dollars. But the rest of the bird, called the *paletot*, does not go to waste. One finds the breasts sealed in vacuum-packed bags ready for grilling, and the other parts on sale for use in *confits* and stews. The gizzard and other innards are sold separately, as is the blood, used in a South-West specialty called *sanguette* for which it is coagulated into a round cake, then fried in goose fat and served with garlic and parsley.

Foie gras d'oie is about twice the size of and softer than the flatter *foie gras de canard*. The goose liver weighs about 2 1/2 pounds; the duck liver, about 1 pound. Because these livers are perishable they are usually subjected to some kind of preservation. Sometimes they are canned, sometimes just barely cooked (*mi-cuit* or *semi-cuit*) and vacuum-packed, which will keep them fresh for about a month. (The expression *mi-cuit* does not mean half-cooked in the sense that more cooking is necessary; it means the liver has been cooked sufficiently for eating within a month.) On some farms in the South-West, foie gras is cooked and then preserved under a thick layer of fat for as long as three or four months.

Each Christmas and New Year (the traditional time in France for those who can afford it to indulge their desire for foie gras) the sales of canned foie gras fall and those of *mi-cuit* start to rise. This is because the taste and color of *mi-cuit* are preferable to those of the canned varieties. But there are people who claim that foie gras aged in the can achieves a special and desirable flavor, as do wine, sardines, and pâtés when matured. A canned goose liver reaches its peak about six to eight months after canning. Formerly packers aged their canned livers before sending them out to the stores.

Raw top-grade foie gras has a certain suppleness and a slight resistance when pressed gently with the thumb. Some experts say it should have the consistency of cool butter, that the thumb should leave a slight impression; a tiny amount of fat should ooze out, too. Touch is one of the most important tests when purchasing a raw fresh liver, a consideration that is somewhat irrelevant in the United States, into which it is illegal to import raw duck and goose livers.

Though it is doubtful that you will ever cook a fresh foie gras, I should tell you that even in the South-West many people are insecure about how best to do it. A foie gras is an extremely delicate piece of meat that can be totally destroyed if overcooked. If the fat runs out, the foie gras will nearly melt away, so it must be cooked carefully for the least amount of shrinkage, and so that the final result is not too dry. South-Westerners talk endlessly about this. The Petrossian family, so famous for its caviar, now uses the traditional method of wrapping the foie gras in a towel before steaming it. Others, like Monsieur Escorbiac, previously of La Taverne Restaurant in Cahors, claim they poach theirs in a solution called *la mère*, a combination of sweet white wine, Madeira, herbs, and the fatty liquid from previous poachings, which endows the foie gras with a richness of flavor and a texture as fine as silk.

Foie gras is never cooked in aluminum, which tends to alter its color. André Daguin has developed ways of preparing fresh raw foie gras too numerous to mention here, but I did observe one unusual method. He poached the liver for 2 minutes in very hot liquid, then placed it in a scooped-out elongated yellowish green pumpkin, which he set in the oven to braise. The moistness inside the pumpkin and the thickness of its skin helped the foie gras cook evenly. Later, served cool directly from its "terrine," it had a marvelous flavor indeed.

The people of the Périgord say that their corn used in the force-feeding is a deeper shade of yellow and thus gives the livers a richer flavor. On the other hand, the Gascons force-feed with a whiter corn that they believe gives their livers a "rounder" flavor. (Actually, I think the differences reside more in color than in taste; the Périgord livers do have a more yellowish hue.) The taste of goose liver is finer and the texture smoother than the taste and texture of livers from the duck. Goose livers feel exceptionally silky to the tongue; I prefer them slightly chilled, served with a chilled Sauternes. Duck livers taste more rustic and feel firmer, and I like them either hot or cold.

Perhaps the best chilled foie gras I ever ate in Paris was at the restaurant Chez l'Ami Louis. It was presented in overlapping slabs like thick slices of black bread; it was delicately veined, colored pink-beige, with just a drop of blood in the center that someone in the kitchen had not extracted, presumably because he did not wish to mar the perfection of the shape. This foie gras was not cold but somewhat cooler than room temperature. I nibbled it slowly, letting it literally melt in my mouth, an extraordinary experience.

There are more than a hundred hot and cold goose and duck foie gras preparations, including ones with sauerkraut, seaweed, and capers. I have eaten foie gras with shallots (a sort of luxurious version of liver and onions), garlic, port wine, prunes, scallops, green pepper sauce, and celery root. And I believe it is worth a special trip to Magescq in the Landes just to eat it smothered in green grapes. André Daguin may be the master matchmaker between foie gras and other foods. One of his greatest triumphs involves sautéing some slices of lightly smoked *foie gras de canard* and serving it with a lukewarm truffle vinaigrette. Of course, the most famous combination is foie gras and truffles. As the Bordelais say, "To put a truffle in a foie gras is to give it a soul." The fat of foie gras also enhances the taste of the truffles, but too often the portion of truffle used is so small it doesn't do all that much for the liver. For this reason I greatly prefer to eat my truffles and foie gras separately.

In some American cities it is possible to find *foie gras mi-cuit*, especially around Christmas, when more than the limited supply usually reserved for restaurants is flown in from France. Be aware that Daguin advises strongly against freezing foie gras. He says, "It tastes like soap, feels like soap, and the only thing it doesn't do is foam up like soap!" The alternative to *mi-cuit* is canned foie gras, and here you should take great care. Legislation has recently been enacted in France that helps to simplify the choice, and checking the wording on the label can let you know what you are buying:

Appellation: Foie Gras d'Oie Entier or *Foie Gras de Canard Entier*. These are the best livers, pure and natural. The word *entier* is the key: it means one is buying whole livers, although, since not all livers weigh the same, sometimes smaller pieces are molded to the larger lobes or packed with them in the can or jar.

Appellation: Foie Gras or *Foie Gras de Canard*. These second-best types will be 90 percent pure *foie gras entier,* since the new legislation allows 10 percent fat wrapping.

Appellation: Bloc de Foie Gras or *Bloc de Foie Gras de Canard*. This is the third grade. It refers to pieces pressed together to form a block. By law the block need be no more than 50 percent chunks of goose liver or 35 percent duck. The remainder is puréed foie gras used to hold the block together. Ten percent forcemeat or fat wrapping is permitted.

Appellation: Parfait de Foie Gras or *Parfait de Foie Gras de Canard*. This is ground-up 100 percent foie gras. Obviously the best-quality foie gras is not used for this parfait; but still, it is foie gras.

Appellation: Purée de Foie Gras or *Purée de Foie Gras de Canard*. No thickener is permitted in the first four classes, but foie gras labeled in this way can be 50 percent foie gras finely blended with pork, veal, or poultry. (If you see a can of pâté, purée, or galantine with a label that reads *de foie* without the *gras,* that is exactly what you are getting: liver that was not force-fed.)

I don't really recommend using canned foie gras or *mi-cuit* in hot dishes except for stuffings, or when the liver is simply rewarmed gently in the oven or in a skillet. These preparations are already cooked, and additional cooking detracts from their charm. Slice foie gras with a thin-bladed knife, dipped in warm water. Wipe the knife clean between each cut. The proper amount to serve each person is 1 3/4 to 2 ounces.

For mail-order sources in the United States for foie gras, see the Appendix.

TRUFFLES

Here is Colette on truffles, the most eloquent voice yet heard on this wondrous subject:

> If you love her, pay her ransom regally, or leave her alone. But, having bought her, eat her on her own, fragrant, coarse-grained, eat her like the vegetable that she is, warm, served in sumptuous portions. She will not give you much trouble; her supreme flavour scorns complexity and complicity. Soaked in a good very dry white wine, not over-salted, peppered discreetly, she will cook in the covered black pot. For twenty-five minutes she will dance in the constant bubbling, trailing behind her in the eddies and foam—like Tritons playing around a black Amphitrite—some twenty pieces of larding bacon, half-fat, half-lean, which fill out the stock. No other spices! Your truffles will come to the table in their court bouillon; take a generous helping, the truffle stimulates appetite, aids digestion. As you crunch this jewel of impoverished lands, imagine, those of you who have never been there, the desolation of its realm. For it kills the wild rose, saps the strength of the oak, and ripens beneath barren rocks. Imagine harsh Peri-gordian winters, the grass whitened by the hard frost, the pink pig trained to its delicate prospecting. . . . [*Paysages et Portraits*]

There is a famous saying about truffles: "Those who wish to lead virtuous lives had better abstain." Something so magnificent must, inevitably, corrupt. Well—truffles *will* ruin your bank account; as for your virtue, they may ruin that, too.

What is all the fuss about? What can taste so good that it can sell for upward of $700 a pound? After all, it's only some strange kind of underground fungus that must be sniffed out by pigs and dogs. Yes, and if you've just tasted a little bit in a pâté or a sauce you may well have cause to wonder. But if, at least once in your life, you take Colette's advice and eat a truffle as a vegetable, then you, too, may begin to rhapsodize.

I ate my first at the Château de Castel Novel in the Corrèze, the very place where Colette spent some of her latter days. It was baked in a salt crust and served on a doily. The waiter cracked it open with a small mallet, releasing the powerful, penetrating bouquet. I sliced the truffle myself and ate it on toast, with a light sprinkling of walnut oil and a pinch of salt. As I ate I sipped a glass of Médoc from a bottle that had cost less than five dollars.

That truffle seemed to me like earth and sky and sea. I felt at one with nature, that my mouth was filled with the taste of the earth. There was a ripeness, a naughtiness, something beyond description. A gastronomic black diamond, it was utter luxury and earthiness combined.

Another time I ate a whole truffle raw, the way one eats radishes and butter. I sliced it thin, spread salted country butter on the slices, and gobbled it up. Such a feast, of course, costs a fortune; it was an experience I doubt I shall ever have again.

Truffles range in size from as small as a pea to as large as a small melon. They range in color from black to white; they can be as fleshy as a mushroom or as firm as a nut. The taste will vary greatly: some are bland, others taste almost like garlic, and the best taste faintly nutlike, yet not like any ordinary kind of nut.

I went to Cahors to visit Jacques Pébeyre, one of the leading harvesters of truffles in France. A tall, trim, balding man with large blue eyes, he comes from a family of famous *trufficulteurs*. His land, studded with craggy oaks, is perhaps the richest truffle ground in the area.

It was too early in the year to watch a truffle hunt, but just a look at that land was a revelation. The area surrounding each gnarled oak was absolutely bare to a radius of twenty feet—a bit like a baseball mound. "You always know where the truffles are," Pébeyre explained. "They eat up all the vegetation around the roots, so that if there are truffles, you won't even see a weed around the tree."

Some twenty-five varieties of truffle grow in his fields, but the only good ones, the ones he harvests, are *Tuber melanosporum*, the famous black truffles of Périgord. "It is humble work," he says. "I plant a tree and wait ten years and often the truffles will not come." And then, when they do come, he still needs trained dogs or pigs to find them. The animals smell them out, then are given something to distract them while the hunter scoops them from the earth. Another way to find truffles is to look closely at the ground to see if any golden flies are hovering around, since they, too, are attracted by the truffle smell. If a man just digs around looking for truffles himself, he will disturb and break up those too young for harvest and thus waste a precious commodity.

Truffles are hunted every day during the season. In this way, they are collected at just the moment they are ripe. If they are too ripe, they turn soggy and cannot be sold. A good truffle must be firm and not gnawed by insects.

An expert truffle-buyer goes by the aroma. The best market is in Périgueux in January, though in December there is an important market in Sarlat. If you buy canned Périgord truffles (a generic term—Quercy actually produces more truffles than Périgord), look for the ones marked *surchoix* or *I*er *choix* (the latter tend to be irregular in shape).

Monsieur Pébeyre is quite angry about so-called summer truffle breakings (*Tuber aestivum*), which have barely any taste or aroma and yet are frequently palmed off as the real thing. These second-rate truffles are sold at $40 a pound, as opposed to the 1981 price of $650 for *Tuber melanosporum*. They are exported in large quantities to America, where, unfortunately, many restaurants use them and people purchase them because they seem to be a "buy." They are black on the exterior, but white and yellow inside; at the great truffle markets in France, truffles are notched so that the purchaser can see they are black through and through.

Truffle peelings are often sold separately, but they have little taste. If you don't want to spend too much, a can of bits and pieces is probably best. In the winter fresh truffles are flown here to be used by fine restaurants and are sold in fancy food stores. Truffles in jars are also available by mail order from Petrossian, Inc. (see Appendix).

For dreamers and truffle "rustlers," here is a dish to remember all your life.

BAKED WHOLE TRUFFLES IN SALT
Truffes au Gros Sel

SERVES 4

ACTIVE WORK: 10 minutes
BAKING TIME: 15 to 25 minutes

> **4 small whole raw truffles, of similar size, or substitute 4 cooked truffles, preferably *I^{ère}cuisson* (first cooking)**
> **4 paper-thin slices pork fatback, blanched if salted**
> **3/4 pound coarse (kosher) salt**
> **2 large egg whites**

1. ABOUT 35 MINUTES BEFORE SERVING, preheat oven to 425° F.
2. Wrap each truffle in a slice of fatback.
3. Line 4 brioche molds with aluminun foil.
4. Mix salt and egg whites in a bowl. Make a layer of the salt mixture about 1/2 inch deep in the bottom of each mold. Place a truffle in each and spoon salt mixture around the sides of each truffle, pressing mixture with fingertips to pack. Spoon at least a 1/2-inch layer of salt mixture over tops of truffles. Press firmly with palm to completely seal truffles in salt. Flatten salt so that when it's turned out, the casing won't wobble. *Can be prepared 1 to 2 hours ahead up to this point.*
5. Bake 25 minutes for medium-sized raw truffles, 15 minutes for canned (cooked). Remove from the oven; turn out and remove the foil.
6. Place each truffle on a serving dish. Crack each casing lightly and remove the truffle. The truffles will not be salty. In fact, you will probably need to season them with a pinch of salt. Serve along with a cruet of imported walnut oil and a good bottle of Médoc.

NOTES TO THE COOK

1. To preserve truffles raw or once you've opened the can, place the unused quantity in an airtight bottle with a light olive oil to cover. The truffles will keep for a month. Truffles pass on their aroma to fats and oils better than to alcohol. (Often people store truffles in Madeira or port or Cognac, but Monsieur Pébeyre advises against this, calling it wasteful.) You can get good use from the olive oil afterward in salads, on cold cooked leeks flavored with fresh mint, or simply on some blanched thin slices of celery root.

2. To preserve whole fresh truffles, keep them packed in raw rice for 1 to 2 weeks in the freezer or refrigerator. (The rice can later be used in a wonderful risotto.) Freezing for long periods is not a good idea, since truffles tend to dry out. If you do freeze them, do not defrost. Use them straight from the freezer just as you do herbs.

CÈPES

Cèpes, to use the Gascon word for the wild mushroom *Boletus edulis*—called *cèpes* or *king boletes* in the United States—are the cheapest and simplest way to put a South-West flavor in your cooking.

Fresh cèpes are found in all parts of the United States; each fall more of them are appearing in our markets. Wild mushrooms should not be gathered unless you know how to identify them or are with a group that specializes in mushroom gathering.

Recently, in the Landes, I was served very fresh, very firm, and very small raw cèpes, thinly sliced and dressed with lemon and oil. They were truly delicious. But South-Westerners insist that cèpes require long, slow cooking to bring out their deep woodsy flavor and to become digestible. Many types of *Boletus* mushroom are naturally filled with water and need to go through three stages of cooking: a drying out in a slow oven to rid them of excess moisture; a slow stewing in oil; and finally a sautéing to develop a deeper flavor. The careful regional cook doesn't hesitate to add a few tablespoons of boiling water to the skillet if the stewing liquid cooks off too fast.

Ads for real estate in France often include the line *terrain à cèpes,* an indication that cèpes sprout on the land in autumn, which makes the property more valuable. People who love wild mushrooms and forage for them often have secret places— called *nids,* or nests—where they find them year after year. If you gather cèpes, never pull them out by the stalk (unless you are going to use them for identification), but cut them off at ground level with a knife, so that they can sprout again next year.

If you do find a nest of cèpes or other choice boletes, and an expert in mushrooms has approved their edibility, then here is what to do. Choose only the young, firm mushrooms, carry them home in a paper bag (not plastic), and check for insects. If the stalk is firm but tender, peel it and cut it lengthwise to check for insects; set aside. Hard and fibrous stalks should be discarded. Wet, spongy, soft undersides of the caps should also be removed and discarded. Brush caps clean, or quickly run under cool water and press out moisture, or dry out in a slow oven.

Then prepare the very traditional dish of *cèpes à la bordelaise*—cèpes sautéed in oil with garlic—a dish that retains the sweet, delicious flavor best. The less fuss the better to enjoy their nutty flavor. (See the recipe for Wild Forest Mushrooms Sautéed in Oil in the Style of Bordeaux.)

There are many kinds of bolete in France, many shapes and sizes and colors, but the best and most coveted is the *cèpe de Bordeaux*, with its firm, blackish head. It has a superb earthy flavor and the aroma of the woodlands. Even one ounce of dried cèpes of this type mixed with a pound of fresh cultivated mushrooms will give an extraordinary quality to a dish.

The *cèpe de Bordeaux* grows as far north as the Périgord and as far south as Spain, but there are many other fine cèpes to be foraged for in the autumn, beginning in

October, in oak and chestnut forests. I first gathered the *cèpe de Bordeaux* in the woods of St.-Jean-de-Marenne in the Landes. We were a group of American cooking teachers; our guide and mushroom expert was the local pharmacist; and our host, the owner of the woods, was an impoverished baron. From his château on the high ground we descended into the woods, where strange animals called *pottoks* wandered about at will. These are the descendants of prehistoric horses, harmless creatures often depicted on the walls of caves by ancient man. There were many kinds of mushroom in the woods, including three varieties of cèpe and an orange look-alike called *Lactarius deliciosus*, which, to the Catalans, is the best wild mushroom to be found. Its cup is chalice-shaped, and its taste slightly resinous. A Catalan makes sure it's the right mushroom by squeezing the stalk. If carrot-colored juices come out, he grabs it and takes it home, since even one specimen of *Lactarius deliciosus* will make a fabulous omelet. On this same outing we found the sought-after *coulemelles* and the somewhat less exciting russulas, as well as a vast number of various other mushrooms that were either unpleasant or dangerous to eat.

For more information on cèpes, see the Appendix.

ARMAGNAC

On market day in Eauze, one of the great centers of commerce in Gascony, you can see the men buying and selling Armagnac the old way: opening the bottle, rubbing a few drops into their palms, cupping their hands, sniffing, looking for extraordinary depth and aroma, the signs of a great Armagnac.

The connoisseurs use vivid words—"ripe plums," "crushed hazelnuts," "prunes," "violets," "sun-ripened peaches"—the comparisons spin out. But the words I like best come in phrases more simply grasped: "taste of the earth," "dancing fire," "velvet flame." For one does not merely drink Armagnac. One sips it, sniffs it, and literally breathes it in. The initial excitement comes at the first inhalation. It is here that one first senses the *goût de terroir*, or taste of the earth. The glass, warmed in the hand, causes fumes to rise from the liquid. And at their first contact with the tongue, one is touched by the "dancing fire." The Gascons are more than happy to instruct you: inhale the Armagnac as you *chew* it, and you will experience the "dancing fire," followed shortly by the "velvet flame." Don't wash the glass afterward, they say, and it will keep its bouquet for another day, a phenomenon called *fond de verre*.

My friend the chef Roger Duffour, proprietor of the Relais de l'Armagnac in the Gascon town of Luppé-Violles, once competed in a double-blind tasting of Armagnacs and was the only connoisseur to get all the bottles right—twice! Considering how many different vintage bottles circulate in the Gascon countryside, this was considered an amazing feat. He is my authority on the subject. I find his collection astounding—many of his bottles are more than a hundred years old. He offered me a drink from one, and I experienced the classic sensations from the red-black brandy: the dance of fire on my tongue followed by the velvet flame, a definable perfume of violets, and a slight pepperiness as well.

Vintage is not so important as blend in Armagnac, but the blend may well include some of these very old vintage brandies; old ones from the 1920s and 1930s will cost well over a hundred dollars a bottle. Actually, quality in Armagnac is based on four things: the grapes, the distillation process, the length of time the liquid is aged in oak casks, and the brilliance of the cellar-master's blend. Vintage Armagnacs are not imported into the United States, but there are many good brands available: Marquis de Caussade, Larressingle, Clés des Ducs, De Montal, Marquis de Monod, Marquis de Montesquiou, Samalens, and Sempé.

In the old days, Armagnac was distilled on practically every Gascon farm, in traveling stills hauled about by oxen. These were strange contraptions of potbelly stove and copper pipes operated by an expert who would listen to the puffs and gurgles and make adjustments as he saw fit. Copper is still used in the stills, which today are mostly owned by farmers' cooperatives. The special hand-hewn barrels in which the raw fermented firewater is aged and smoothed are beautiful objects in themselves and often last a hundred years in service.

The question most often asked about Armagnac is how it differs from the better-known Cognac, produced in ten times the quantity 150 or so miles to the north. The Gascons are quick to give you answers ranging from the very technical (the distillation process is different) to the far more poetic. Here are three I have collected.

From Alain Dutournier, chef-proprietor of Le Trou Gascon in Paris: "Cognac is dependable, but Armagnac, like the Gascons who make it, is more forceful, more complicated—even excessive at times—and more exciting."

From Georges Samalens, Armagnac producer and author of an authoritative book on the subject: "Cognac gains its distinction by finesse, while Armagnac gains its distinction by its power. We are a bit rougher, but we are closer to the soil, and as a result we need more age."

From a Gascon friend who prefers to remain anonymous: "Cognac is a pretty girl in a freshly laundered smock carrying a basket of wildflowers; she pleases you by the sight of her. Armagnac is a tempestuous woman of a 'certain age,' someone you don't bring home to Mother, someone who excites your blood."

Armagnac is wonderful to cook with—perfect in daubes, poultry dishes, and desserts. It can be used in sherbets, to preserve fruits, to cut the richness of a sauce of wild mushrooms, to perfume and flavor apples and pears. It will add depth to a sauce as well as a mellowness, a rich soft quality obtainable by no other means. Only the strongest condiments, such as mustard, capers, and vinegar, do not blend well with it. A touch of Armagnac added to a cassoulet can give that famous dish extra finesse.

CONFITS/PRESERVED MEATS AND POULTRY

"A Gascon will fall to his knees for a good *confit*," goes the saying. The citizens of Gascony may be the most extreme devotees of this splendid food, but they are not alone in their passion. You may prove the point by going into any traditional home from Périgord to the Pyrenees—farmhouse, town house, or château. Descend to the cellar and inspect the wines, then ask to see the storeroom. You will find shelves lined with stoneware or glass jars embellished with handwritten labels and containing preserved fruits, jams, and above all *confits*, virtually the signature of South-West cooking.

Confits—from the French *confire*, "to preserve"—are simply preserved meats (duck, goose, pork, hen, wild birds, turkey, rabbit, or whatever) that have been salted to draw out the moisture, then cooked in and ultimately put up in fat. But to preserve a meat is to make it into something quite different, to create an entirely new taste and texture. *Confit* is a phenomenon that really has no close counterpart in the rest of French cuisine. The nearest parallel I know is the Moroccan *khelea,* spiced dried beef or lamb that is cooked in and subsequently sealed in oil and rendered fat. I believe that the central culinary role of *confit* in far-flung areas of the French South-West is only one particularly telling clue to the importance of the North African influence throughout this part of France over many centuries.

In its French translation, the method came to be applied most often to the splendid duck, goose, and pork of the South-West. *Confit* is truly the foundation of this region's cooking. It is as fundamental as truffles and foie gras and a lot more likely to be found in the average kitchen. So clearly has it left its stamp on great reaches of the South-West that one could construct an accurate map of culinary boundaries simply by the presence or absence of *confit*. Where there is *confit*, you will find a whole constellation of other ingredients and approaches adding up to a style—the rich, vigorous style of the South-West, to be confused with no other.

As the name indicates, *confit*-making is basically a technique of preserving, devised so that the local poultry and pork butchered in the late autumn could be enjoyed throughout the year. In past generations it was an intrinsic and thrifty part of the farm kitchen routine, a way of making use of every part of the animal, from good pork shoulder and meaty duck legs to such humble odds and ends as duck and goose gizzards, wings, and necks, or the tongue and ears of the pig. One advantage of knowing how to make *confit* is that the process enables you to transform just such bits of meat and poultry into the stuff of innumerable traditional or new dishes, some of which, incidentally, can be produced in minutes once you have *confit* on hand. When large quantities are involved, *confit*-making also provides by-products such as crackling and rillettes, as well as generous amounts of good cooking fats.

Confit is one of those unique ingredients that permanently enlarge your awareness of flavor, and is one of the few things that can accurately be said to add another dimension to any dish in which they are used. Those who have tasted some of the great South-West classics will know how telling its presence is. To many South-Westerners, cassoulets are not worthy of the name unless they contain a piece of *confit*. *Confit* also often appears in that magnificent regional dish called *garbure*, a soup that is based on salt pork, cabbage, and beans and has innumerable local variations enriched with other meats and vegetables.

The secret of a great *confit* lies in a fortuitous combination of factors: the choice of meat; the time spent in marination; the choice of seasoning; the temperature at which the fat and meat are cooked; the length of time the meat is left to ripen; and the method of reheating. Freshly cooked *confit* can be superb; one-month-old *confit* is even better. As time passes, the flavor deepens. You can keep *confit* up to three or four months in the refrigerator.

Despite the large amounts of rendered fat used in the preparation and storage of *confit*, there is nothing fatty—or dry, salty, or stringy—about the effect of properly made *confits*. Rather, they are nutty, silky, delicate, and almost fat-free. One secret is gentle heat and patient cooking. Traditionally *confit* was cooked in an earthenware crock or iron pot set in the dying embers of the hearth. Slow methods are still the best. A good principle to follow—one taught to me by Alain Dutournier—is to gradually raise the temperature of the fat along with the pieces of meat, let the *confit* cook evenly, and then cool it in the fat as slowly as it heated.

The slow initial heating allows much of the fat under the skin to melt out, the slow cooking inhibits stringiness, and the slow cooling prevents the meat from falling apart or losing its shape. (Incidentally, it is the meat of mature rather than young and tender animals that makes the best *confit*; it is firmer and less likely to break down in cooking.) When handled with this kind of care, the rendered fat used in *confit* can be reused for several more batches. (It stores well in the refrigerator or freezer and is also excellent for sautéing and braising vegetables.) But like all animal fats, *confit* fats are fragile and burn much faster than oil. Once the fat gets hot enough to smoke, it is "spent" and is not usable in cooking again. To duplicate the best qualities of the ember method and keep the fat at a gentle simmer, use a Crock-Pot or cook the *confit* in a very low oven.

One would think that the different tastes and aromas of different *confits* would be enhanced if each was cooked in its own fat, but, surprisingly, this is not the case. If goose, duck, and pork are cooked together in a mixture of duck and pork fat (and goose fat, too), they will be all the better, and the fat will be tastier.

Though the versions of *confit* presented in this book are really intended to be kept refrigerated, the method itself long predates refrigeration. In the South-West, *confit* has traditionally been kept in heavy stoneware jars in cool dry cellars or storage rooms. If you have a storage area that will remain *at a constant low temperature without fluctuation*, you may let the *confit* ripen naturally, embedded in fat in tall stoneware containers, for a few months. But be sure you have not overlooked anything—I know of one batch of *confit* that was ruined because the cook had forgotten about the heat of the basement furnace!

Refer to the index for recipes for *Confit* of Duck, *Confit* of Goose, and *Confit* of Pork, and for instructions on Rendering Pork Fat.

JAMBON DE BAYONNE/BAYONNE HAM

There is a famous anecdote about a wet nurse from the Béarn who went to the Louvre to visit her former charge, now the grown-up King Henri IV. Noticing that there were no hams hanging from the ceiling, a sign of wealth in a Béarn home, the nurse exclaimed, "Henri, my Henri, my love, you must be so hungry. I'll send you ham as soon as I get back home!"

Ah, the Basques and the Béarnais and their *jambon de Bayonne!* It has been famous since the Middle Ages; on the portal of the Église Ste.-Marie in Oloron I saw sculptures of a man killing a pig and then preparing ham from its legs.

We eat Bayonne ham raw, but the Basques like it best cut into thick slices and sautéed. A favorite Basque dish consists of eggs fried in goose fat served with sautéed ham sprinkled lightly with vinegar. The taste of ham permeates many dishes in the Landes, the Béarn, and the Pays Basque. Often dishes are accented by the addition of a regional version of *hachis,** a mixture of hand-chopped raw garlic, chopped fresh parsley, and chopped-up fatty bits of Bayonne ham, simply strewn over the food. The bone of a Bayonne ham is so highly regarded that it is used again and again to flavor soups and stews.

My friend Maurice Coscuella, a Gascon chef, once remarked to me in his enigmatic way, "You know, there are some salts that don't actually salt." He went on to explain that some are much saltier than others, and some are merely salty and taste flat, while others have an actual flavor. I bring this up because the justified fame of Bayonne hams depends upon the use of two different salts, each with its own special properties.

The first is the famous salt from Salies-de-Béarn, reputed to have been discovered by accident by a boar hunter in the eleventh century. This salt is rubbed into the pork legs for three days, preserving the meat, imbuing it with an extraordinary flavor, and giving it color as well. The second salt is a gray crystal variety called *sel de Bayonne*, which is used in the giant salt boxes where the hams are kept while being cured. They are then lightly rubbed with pepper and air-dried.

You will not find true Bayonne ham in America, as it is illegal to import it. The real stuff is most carefully labeled *Marque Déposée Véritable Jambon de Bayonne*. Many imitations are sold that lack the special subtlety and flavor of the original. You will find some delicious approximations, however, in stores in some Basque

---

*Other *hachis*: in the Languedoc—bacon, garlic, and parsley; in the Périgord—garlic and parsley. In the Landes, it is the same as in the Périgord but is called *persillade*.

neighborhoods, especially in northern California, where the local Basque-Americans have imported the special salts required.† Contrary to what has been written about Bayonne ham in many source books, it is not smoked—it is a salt-cured country ham dried over a period of five to six months. The best substitute hams I have come up with for my recipes have been the mildly smoked Citterio and John Volpi brands of prosciutto and the German Westphalian ham, which is readily available.

CHEESES OF THE SOUTH-WEST

I was twenty years old before I ate proper Roquefort cheese, and I shall never forget the experience. It was my first meal at Brasserie Lipp in Paris, and when the cheese was brought out, it was a revelation: not dry and crumbly as it had always been in the United States, but creamy-soft and spreadable. Roquefort is, of course, one of the greatest of all cheeses, certainly the most important cheese manufactured in South-West France. Like the names of great wines, the name Roquefort is now controlled to the extent that lawsuits have been filed against producers of other blue cheese who have tried to sell their products as "Roquefort."

For me, one of the best desserts imaginable is a wedge of Roquefort, some plump black mission figs, and a glass of chilled estate-bottled Sauternes. The combination of the rich, nectarlike wine, the sweet ripe fruit, and the pungent, salty, creamy cheese is as perfect a trio of taste affinities as one is likely to encounter on this earth.

Roquefort is made from ewe's milk and matured in the famous limestone caves of Combalou upon whose cliffs the town was built. These caves are remarkable in that they maintain a constant temperature and humidity year-round. This is perfect for the maturation of the *Penicillium roqueforti* mold, the source of the blue veins that give Roquefort its special taste. (The story of the shepherd who accidentally left behind some ewe's milk in a cave and, returning to fetch it, discovered Roquefort has been told all too many times.)

Roquefort is always salty, but some of the exported brands seem too salty to me. (The salt is added for flavor, of course, but also to inhibit the spread of molds other than the desirable *Penicillium roqueforti*.) I suggest tasting for saltiness as well as condition before buying. To deserve its title as "the King of Cheeses and the Cheese of Kings," Roquefort should be spreadable and moist at the center. If it's a little hard, it can ripen in the refrigerator vegetable crisper. Eat it at room temperature.

The most famous South-West goat's milk cheese is the tangy Cabecou of Quercy. Goat cheeses do not keep well, and change as the weeks pass. They go through three different stages, each with its own special qualities; South-Westerners, being frugal and despising waste, have developed different styles of treating goat's milk cheese depending on its stage.

---

†See under "Ham" in the Appendix for sources of American-made *jambon de Bayonne*.

At first these cheeses are very soft, fresh like milk, silky, and sometimes a little cottony, too. At this stage they are best served with a coating of crème fraîche and a light sprinkling of chopped chives. If a first-stage Cabecou is not available, a good substitute might be a creamy Sainte-Maure from Touraine, a very fresh Montrachet from Burgundy, or a fresh goat cheese from California or New Jersey sold under the Chevreese label.

As a goat cheese begins to firm in texture, it enters the second stage, when it is called *affiné*. It becomes piquant and almost fruity, more intense than in stage one, with a yellowish rind beginning to form, but it is still silky at the core. Now it can be cooked to great advantage, first brushed with a little walnut or olive oil, then set under the broiler to crust. Or it can be stored brushed with oil and folded in aromatic leaves or flavored with herbs. Broiled goat cheese served on toasted rounds of French bread with a crisp green salad dressed with a smattering of walnut oil is one of the great simple delights. Again, if you cannot find Cabecou, substitute a dry Montrachet or any other goat cheese that has reached this tangy stage but whose interior is not yet chalky or dry.

It is at the third and final stage that one must begin to tamper with the elderly goat cheese—now just dried-out disks resembling shriveled silver dollars. Soak them in *eau de vie de prune* and white wine with pepper, as they do in Rocamadour, then wrap them in chestnut leaves for several days before serving them with thin slices of walnut bread. My friend Georgie Géry, a great South-West gastronome, instructed me *never* to throw out a dying goat cheese unless it smelled of ammonia, in which case it would be truly dead.

There is a fresh goat cheese called Chèvre Frais from Poitou available all year round in many cheese stores in the United States. It is sold in a crock, tastes light and fresh, and is so mild that in Gascony it is whipped with white rum or Armagnac and flavored with sugar until it becomes *fromageon*, ready to be spread on dried bread and served to children after school as a snack.

In the Landes there is a jar-fermented sheep cheese, Poustagnacq, which, in the Basque country, is flavored with coffee essence.

The cheeses of the Pyrenees are interesting and good. Names to look for among the semifirm varieties are Tomme des Pyrénées, especially if it is from the Ossau Valley; the mildly peppery cow cheese Crottin du Poivre; the Pyreneean version of Manchego; the aged and full-flavored Prince de Navarre; and the 100 percent sheep's-milk Ardi-Gasna.

The proprietor-chef of Le Bistro d'Hubert, on the Place du Marché-St.-Honoré in Paris, who cooks and writes about cheese under the single-name by-line "Hubert," describes, in his book *Moi, le Fromage et Vous*, the lore of cheese-making by the shepherds of this lonely region. Their ten-pound cheeses are marked with their initials, and Hubert knows them all. He likes the production of the shepherd whose mark is *P*, complains about the high cost of Bethmale cheeses from another valley, and deeply regrets the passing of a poetic shepherd in a third valley who made an extraordinary goat cheese flavored with the wild herbs upon which his flock was prone to munch.

Though I have touched little in this book on the cooking of the very poor region called the Rouergue, where the food is oriented toward the cuisine of the Languedoc, I must mention two extraordinary Rouergue cheeses: Cantal and its farmhouse brother, Laguiole. There are some French gastronomes who place Laguiole from Aveyron so high that they are willing to say it's nearly as good as their beloved Roquefort. And when Laguiole and Roquefort are put together in *le gatis*, then you will have an extraordinary experience. (See the recipe for Cheese in Brioche, where I have had to substitute the more available Cantal.)

WALNUTS FROM THE PÉRIGORD

The South-West concept that everything should be used, that no part of any ingredient should go to waste, is summed up beautifully in an aphorism one hears around the Périgord: "Nothing is lost of the walnut," a peasant's wife will tell you, "except the noise when it is cracked!"

We shall see this imaginative economy later when we get to the duck—how no part of it is ignored, including the tail feathers, which can be used for applying fat. Since walnuts are foraged for, they must be used particularly carefully, as if the labor of their gathering cannot otherwise be justified. The shells are ground up and used for fuel. A *digestif* is made from the tender walnut leaves by infusing them with old red wine, sugar, and some marc. Another drink is made by macerating fresh walnuts in 90 proof *eau de vie*. (This is an excellent aperitif, by the way, served over ice, and is also used to flavor an interesting ice cream.) The walnuts themselves are used in salads, cakes, and candies, with green beans and fish, and joined with Roquefort on endives. In the Corrèze, which neighbors the Périgord, I once ate an extraordinary dish of sautéed duck in which the pan juices had been deglazed with the black juices of unripened walnuts.

In the Périgord there is a class of elderly women who specialize in shelling walnuts. Called *les énoiseuses*, they travel from house to house, village to village, during the walnut harvest season, bringing their special wooden mallets and the round wooden boards upon which they rhythmically crack open the nuts, five to the minute, without ever smashing one to powder.

Many people prefer their walnuts peeled, since they believe the skins are indigestible. This is done by pouring some boiling water directly over the nuts, or by placing them in a slow oven, after which the skins may be easily slipped off.

One of the great by-products of walnuts is their extraordinary oil—"all of the Périgord in a bottle," in the words of Zette Guinaudeau-Franc—soft, fragrant, green-hued, and strong-tasting. This oil, delicious on salads, should always be diluted, since it is so very strong. The addition of two parts olive oil or French peanut oil to one part walnut oil is a popular dilution formula.

Try a few drops of walnut oil on white beans, or add some to a cassoulet, the "secret" of many cooks who pride themselves on their renditions of this quintessential South-West dish. And if you get to the South-West, consider making a visit to a walnut oil mill. I especially recommend the hundred-year-old one in St.-Nathalène outside Sarlat.

For more information on walnuts, including mail-order sources, see under "Nuts" in the Appendix.

CHESTNUTS

It was in the Dordogne that I first experienced the pleasures of grilling and cleaning fresh chestnuts. It was in a country house in a region where nearly everyone has a chestnut tree in the garden, and it was during chestnut-gathering and -eating weather, one of the first cold days of autumn.

The procedure was this: a small knife with a short curved head was used to slit each chestnut on its rounded side. The nuts were then thrown into a special long-handled skillet with about a dozen holes in its bottom. The skillet was shaken every so often, and the nuts stirred about. They were cooked when one could smell their sweet aroma. A cooked chestnut is firm but mealy throughout. As soon as the nuts were roasted they were placed in a basket lined with a heavy cloth soaked in wine to keep them moist and warm. (Cold chestnuts are *impossible* to peel.) The next step was the most laborious, but you can munch as you work. I was taught to squeeze each nut with my fingers so that the shell cracked open and the moist, mealy nut slithered out, then to peel off the bitter inner skin with a small knife. The French have a vulgar nickname for this squeezing procedure—*técot*—which is the local slang word for the nipple of a breast when it is full of milk and ready to be pressed. Finally, a most important part of the ritual: as one eats, one washes down the chestnuts with a sweet young wine, usually a *vin nouveau*—a tradition that dates back to the days of Charlemagne.

Much as I enjoyed my lesson in slitting, roasting, and peeling chestnuts, I also learned that chestnuts once played a crucial role in the lives of the very poor peasants who inhabited the rocky, poverty-stricken region of the Cévennes. Before they learned to cultivate potatoes in their poor soil, chestnuts were their staple. One spoke of a chestnut tree as *l'arbre à pain* ("the bread tree"), since everyday bread was necessarily made of chestnut flour. Just as we sometimes speak of a subsistence diet as being one of "bread and water," so the people of the Cévennes are often referred to as those who "live on chestnuts and water."

For further information on purchasing, peeling, and cooking chestnuts, see the Appendix.

OTHER PRODUCTS

One cannot leave out the many other specialties of the South-West and the many splendid wines of this region; you will find them discussed later on in the Appendix.

CHAPTER 2

Basic Preparations: Stocks, Sauce Bases, and Bread

Someone once said that "England has three sauces and sixty religions while France has three religions and sixty sauces." In fact, there are far more sauces than that in the famous catalog of Austin de Croze.

Most of the sauces for the dishes in this book are included with the recipes. But I am adding a few base preparations here: an all-purpose chicken stock; an all-purpose demi-glace; a duck stock; a duck and wine demi-glace; and a fish stock and a fish fumet.

You may notice that my Demi-Glace does not require browning the bones. The reason is that when you make most modern sauces, you are reducing to such an extent that there is the possibility of a bitter taste from well-browned meat and bones. On the other hand, I do caramelize the vegetables so that their flavor will be strong and the sauce will have good color. Color is also the reason I suggest

30

blackening an onion over flames or under the broiler, a process that will also offset any possible bitterness.

I particularly like my all-purpose Demi-Glace; it keeps up to a year in the freezer, takes up hardly any room, and is available in an instant to enhance and sometimes even save a dish.

To avoid spending a good deal of time skimming, I often cover the bones of veal and chicken with warm water and quickly bring to a boil. After 3 minutes of boiling, I drain, rinse, and start cooking the bones in clear water. This procedure removes most of the scum. It does not remove protein or taste; the nutrients and flavor of stock come from long simmering.

CHICKEN STOCK
(FOR SOUPS, POT-AU-FEU, AND SOME STEWS)
Fond de Volaille

MAKES 2 QUARTS
ACTIVE WORK: 25 minutes
UNATTENDED SIMMERING TIME: 4 to 5 hours
REDUCING TIME: 30 minutes

> 5 pounds chicken necks, backs, and wings, plus leftover cooked or roasted carcasses, if available
> 2–3 chicken gizzards
> 1 veal shank and/or a few marrowbones (optional)
> 1 onion stuck with 2 cloves
> 1 medium onion, halved
> 1 carrot, halved
> 2 cloves garlic, unpeeled
> 2 small ribs celery, halved
> 2–3 leeks (green parts only)
> Peel and seeds from 2–3 medium tomatoes (see Note) or 1 small tomato, quartered

1. Place chicken parts and veal shank and marrowbones (if using) in pot. Cover with warm water and quickly bring to a boil. Boil vigorously 3 minutes. Drain; rinse bones and place in large deep pot.

2. Cover with 6 quarts cold water; slowly bring to a boil. Skim off scum that surfaces until only a small amount of foam rises to top. Add remaining ingredients and bring back to a boil. Lower heat, partially cover pot, and simmer slowly, without disturbing, 4 to 5 hours.

3. Ladle stock through a colander into a deep bowl. Remove solids.

4. Rinse a large piece of cheesecloth and line a fine strainer with it. Ladle stock through cheesecloth into another bowl.

5. Chill, degrease carefully, and return to a heavy saucepan. Bring to a boil. Set saucepan half over the heat. Cook at a slow boil, skimming, 25 to 30 minutes, or until reduced to 2 quarts.

NOTE TO THE COOK
Peel and seeds from fresh tomatoes will flavor the stock as well as attract scum. Use the best part of tomato for some other purpose.

DEMI-GLACE (ALL-PURPOSE REDUCED MEAT AND POULTRY SAUCE BASE)
Demi-Glace

MAKES 2 1/2 CUPS
ACTIVE WORK: about 30 minutes
SIMMERING WITH OCCASIONAL SKIMMING: 5 hours
REDUCING WITH OCCASIONAL SKIMMING: 1 hour

8–10 pounds veal bones
 2–3 pounds chicken carcasses, plus 1 heart and 1 gizzard
     Fatty pieces of veal (optional)
    3 tablespoons poultry fat or butter
    2 ounces fatty cured ham, chopped (optional)
    2 medium carrots, chopped
    2 medium onions, chopped
    1 leek, split and sliced (white and green parts separated)
    1 small rib celery, sliced
 5–6 sprigs parsley
    1 bay leaf
    1 onion, halved
    1 head garlic, halved and unpeeled
    2 large tomatoes, halved, with skin and seeds
 1/4 teaspoon grated nutmeg

1. Crack veal bones and chicken carcasses with a cleaver into very small pieces or have butcher do this for you. Place them in deep pot, cover with warm water, and quickly bring to a boil. Boil hard 3 minutes. Drain; rinse and return to the pot.
2. Cover bones with 6 quarts cold water. Add fatty pieces of veal, if using. Slowly bring to a boil over medium heat; skim and simmer 1 hour.
3. Meanwhile, in a wide skillet, heat fat or butter; add ham, carrots, and chopped onions. Cover and cook over low heat 10 minutes, or until moist beads appear on surface of vegetables. Remove cover; add white parts of leek and celery. Slowly brown all the vegetables, stirring, about 15 minutes. Caramelize cut sides of the

onion by placing them close to burner flames or under broiler and allowing surfaces to blacken.

4. When bones have simmered 1 hour and liquid is clear, add the browned vegetables, caramelized onion, leek greens, and remaining ingredients. Bring back to a boil; reduce heat and simmer slowly at least 4 hours, skimming from time to time. Do not stir.

5. Strain through a colander into a deep bowl, discarding solids. Line a sieve with a damp piece of cheesecloth and set over another deep bowl. Ladle the stock through.

6. Chill, degrease carefully, and return to a heavy saucepan. Bring to a boil. Set saucepan half over the heat. Cook at a slow boil, skimming, 1 hour, or until reduced to 2 1/2 cups. (Demi-Glace will just lightly coat a spoon.)

DARK RICH DUCK STOCK
Fond de Canard

A good duck stock can be the basis for a slew of stews, ragouts, sauces, and soups. If you do not have sufficient duck pieces, use a mixture of duck and chicken bones. If you have cooked duck or chicken carcasses, use them, too.

MAKES 1 1/2 QUARTS
ACTIVE WORK: 30 minutes
UNATTENDED SIMMERING WITH OCCASIONAL SKIMMING: 4 hours
REDUCING TIME: 25 minutes

> **Carcasses, necks, and wing tips of 4 ducks**
> **1 large onion, halved and peeled**
> **1 large tomato, halved, with skin and seeds**
> **1 1/2 cups cubed carrots**
> **1 cup coarsely chopped onions**
> **2 leeks, trimmed, halved, and cut into 1-inch pieces (white and green parts separated)**
> **1 cup red wine vinegar**
> **1/2 cup dry red wine**
> **12 whole black peppercorns, lightly cracked**
> **2 cloves garlic, unpeeled and smashed gently**
> **Herb bouquet: 8–10 sprigs parsley, about 3/4 teaspoon thyme leaves, and 1 bay leaf, tied together in cheesecloth**

1. Preheat oven to 450° F.

2. Break up or crack carcasses, necks, and wing tips with a cleaver or mallet. Spread out pieces in a large, deep roasting pan and place in the hot oven. Brown

bones, turning them once or twice. This should take about 15 minutes.

3. Meanwhile, place onion and tomato halves, cut sides up, in a shallow pan; place under preheated broiler and broil until browned, or brown separately in the hot oven.

4. When bones have browned, remove and place in a deep pot. Add fresh cold water to cover and slowly bring to a boil.

5. Meanwhile, pour off all but 2 tablespoons fat from roasting pan. Scatter carrots, chopped onions, and white parts of leeks in pan; toss to coat lightly with fat. Return to oven for 30 minutes to brown, turning vegetables from time to time.

6. Transfer vegetables to side bowl. Deglaze pan with vinegar and wine, scraping up brown bits that cling to bottom and sides of pan. Reduce to 3/4 cup. Scrape into bowl with vegetables.

7. When water in pot has reached the boil, begin skimming until only a little foam is left on the surface. Add contents of bowl and remaining ingredients and simmer, partially covered, 4 hours, skimming whenever necessary. (If at any time the bones and vegetables are not covered with liquid, add enough water to cover.)

8. Ladle the stock into a strainer set over a tall, narrow container, gently pressing the solids in the strainer to extract all possible liquid. Discard all solids. Chill, degrease carefully, and return to a heavy saucepan. Bring to a boil. Set saucepan half over the heat. Cook at a slow boil, skimming often, 25 minutes, or until reduced to 1 1/2 quarts.

DUCK DEMI-GLACE
Demi-Glace de Canard

When duck stock is reduced, the result is a concentrated sauce base that can be used in the sauces of many dishes or to add flavor to pâtés, stews, and duck liver flans.

MAKES ABOUT 2 CUPS
REDUCING WITH OCCASIONAL SKIMMING: about 45 minutes

1 1/2 quarts Dark Rich Duck Stock

1. Carefully degrease duck stock. In a heavy saucepan, boil steadily, uncovered, over half the heat until reduced by about half, skimming often.

2. Strain into a small, heavy saucepan. Slowly reduce to 2 cups. *Do not reduce further;* deeply browned bones often make a bitter glaze.

DUCK OR GAME RED-WINE-FLAVORED DEMI-GLACE
Demi-Glace de Canard au Vin Rouge

Use this for Duck Liver Flans with Caramel Vinegar Sauce for Duck Legs Cooked in Red Wine, or for enriching red wine sauces for game.

MAKES ABOUT 1 1/2 CUPS
☆ Begin 2 days in advance
   ACTIVE WORK: 25 minutes
   UNATTENDED SIMMERING TIME: 3 hours
   SIMMERING WITH OCCASIONAL SKIMMING: 2 to 3 hours

> **2 duck or game carcasses** *with all fat and skin removed*
> **1 bottle full-bodied red wine, such as Petite Sirah or a Côtes-du-Rhône**
>   **Herb bouquet: 8 sprigs parsley, about 3/4 teaspoon thyme leaves, and**
>   **1 bay leaf, tied together with a string or wrapped in cheesecloth**
> **1 carrot, sliced**
> **1 onion, sliced**
> **1 leek, white and green parts, sliced**
> **1 quart Chicken Stock or Dark Rich Duck Stock, degreased**

1. 2 DAYS IN ADVANCE, crush the bones of the carcasses into very small pieces. (This permits the marrow in the bones to be released and enrich the sauce.) Place pieces in a deep, noncorrodible saucepan or earthenware crock. Cover with red wine and let soak overnight.

2. THE FOLLOWING DAY, add herb bouquet and bring to a boil, then reduce heat to very low and cook slowly until reduced to a glaze, about 3 hours. (A Crock-Pot set on medium is perfect here.)

3. Add vegetables and stock. Bring to a boil, lower heat, and reduce slowly by half, about 2 to 3 hours, skimming (see Note).

4. Ladle contents of pan into a strainer. Set over a tall, narrow container, pressing the solids in the strainer to extract all possible liquid. Discard all vegetables and bones. Cool completely, then chill. Remove surface fat. Spoon out only the clear jellied sauce, leaving bottom scum in the container. Discard scum. Reduce if necessary, boiling sauce half over the heat, to 1 1/2 cups, skimming often. Can be stored in the refrigerator 1 week or frozen up to 3 months.

VARIATION

To make a quick duck-wine sauce, slowly reduce red-wine-soaked carcasses to a glaze. Add 2 cups Demi-Glace and simmer 15 minutes, skimming. Strain and degrease. Use at once or keep refrigerated up to 1 week. It can also be frozen.

Inspired by a recipe from Jean-Louis Palladin.

FISH STOCK AND FISH GLAZE
Fond de Poisson

It's a sad fact of American culinary life that it's nearly impossible to obtain fish bones for stock except in coastal areas. Still, the motivated cook will manage to make up fish stocks somehow, for they are indispensable for numerous sauces and soups.

Bottled clam juice does *not* make a good substitute, though mussel broth or *fresh* clam broth will do. There is a rather expensive commercial frozen concentrate of fish and lobster essence (Saucier brand) available in some fancy food stores that is adequate. But the best method is to save up fish heads plus frames and tails from any nonoily fish, then keep them frozen to be used to make your own stock, which is a simple procedure that takes only 35 minutes.

A rather desperate method but one that works is to purée a few oysters or mussels and shrimp in a food processor and cook them in chicken stock for 30 minutes, then strain it carefully; you will come up with a satisfactory stock.

Fish glazes or concentrates are merely fish stocks that have been greatly reduced. If you want to boil down a stock into a glaze, I suggest you do it in the oven, to contain most of the strong fish odor. Fish glazes are easier to store than stocks and can be kept almost indefinitely in the freezer. Though their odors are strong, they can be most helpful when stretched with cream and butter *plus* other flavorings; they can give body and deep background flavor to a sauce.

I like to use red snapper frames and heads for my stock, but you can just as easily use the frames of sole, sea bass, halibut, whiting, or a mixture of these. The heads and bones are important, for they give a stock good body. Frozen fillets of sole and flounder don't give sufficient body. Twenty-five minutes of slow simmering is ideal; longer simmering won't release any more gelatin and taste from the bones and has the negative effect of making the stock somewhat bitter and "fishy-tasting."

Finally, in regard to white wine, I urge you to use a good, tasty wine such as Chablis or Riesling, and not something called "cooking" wine. Rather than substituting a cheap white wine, I suggest no wine at all.

MAKES 3 QUARTS STOCK OR
2 CUPS GLAZE
     ACTIVE WORK: about 10 minutes
     UNATTENDED SIMMERING WITH OCCASIONAL SKIMMING: 25 minutes

> **6 pounds fish bones, heads, and tails, with gills removed**
> **1 leek, halved and cut into 1-inch pieces**
> **1 rib celery, cut into 1-inch pieces**
> **4 cloves garlic, halved but unpeeled**
> **5 sprigs parsley**
> **1/2 bay leaf**

Pinch of crumbled thyme leaves
1/2 tablespoon lightly crushed black peppercorns
1 medium carrot, sliced
1 small onion, sliced
1 1/2 cups good white wine

1. With a knife, cut the fish trimmings to remove any traces of blood, liver, intestines, and eggs.

2. Wash the trimmings under cold running water until water runs clear. Place them with 6 quarts water in a stockpot or deep kettle, preferably enameled or stainless steel (aluminum tends to discolor stock but doesn't affect it otherwise). Bring to a boil and skim carefully 2 to 3 minutes. Add remaining ingredients, lower heat, and simmer 25 minutes, skimming when needed.

3. Strain the stock. Reduce, if necessary, boiling it down to 3 quarts. Cool, then chill. The stock can be refrigerated or frozen. As it cools, fat will rise to the top and can be easily removed. This recipe can easily be halved or quartered and can also be increased.

4. To make Fish Glaze, boil 3 quarts of Fish Stock until reduced to 2 cups.

FISH FUMET
Fumet de Poisson

This is a short concentrated base used to flavor sauces.

MAKES 1 CUP
ACTIVE WORK: about 20 minutes
SIMMERING WITH OCCASIONAL SKIMMING: 25 minutes
REDUCING WITH OCCASIONAL SUPERVISION: 20 minutes

1 1/2 tablespoons unsalted butter
1/2 medium onion, chopped
1 rib celery, chopped
1 small carrot, chopped
1 leek (white part and half the green), well washed and thinly sliced
   Herb bouquet: 5 sprigs parsley, 2 sprigs thyme, and 1 small bay leaf, tied together
2–3 pounds fish heads and frames from nonoily fish, washed and cut into small pieces
1 1/2 cups dry red or white wine

(continued)

1. Melt the butter in a wide saucepan or deep skillet. Add the onions, celery, and carrots. Cover and cook over low heat 5 minutes.

2. Add the leek, herb bouquet, and fish heads and bones. Cook, uncovered, 5 minutes longer, stirring.

3. Add 2 quarts cold water and slowly bring to a boil. Skim 2 to 3 minutes.

4. Reduce heat and simmer, uncovered, 25 minutes, skimming whenever necessary.

5. Strain the liquid, cool, and skim off fat.

6. Add wine and reduce over medium heat to 1 cup.

NOTE TO THE COOK
To avoid excessive fish odors in your kitchen, bring liquid to a boil, set in a 375° F. oven, and reduce to 1 cup.

COUNTRY-STYLE BREAD
Tourte

La tourte is a round, dense loaf of bread found in the Périgord and Quercy, made with either rye or whole wheat flour mixed with bread flour. It makes a perfect all-around bread upon which to spread country pâtés and rillettes, and a perfect stuffing for chicken; its slices are good in thick soups.

It's been difficult up to now to obtain a crackly, golden brown exterior on this bread using a typical home oven, but since I've started using a wonderful new piece of equipment, the crusts of my *tourtes* have vastly improved. The device is called La Cloche, a sort of instant brick oven, a bell-shaped top of unglazed stoneware fitted over a shallow baking dish. This is available by mail from Williams-Sonoma (see Appendix).

MAKES 1 LOAF
☆ Begin 1 to 2 days in advance to make the starter
ACTIVE WORK FOR STARTER: 5 minutes

ACTIVE WORK: 25 minutes
FIRST RISING TIME: 1 to 2 hours
SECOND RISING TIME: 1 to 2 hours
FINAL RISING TIME: 1 to 2 hours
BAKING TIME: 50 to 60 minutes

Starter

> 1 1/2 teaspoons active dry yeast (see Note 1)
> 3/4 cup lukewarm water
> 1 cup bread flour or unbleached all-purpose flour with 13 percent protein (gluten) content
>
> 1 1/2 cups lukewarm water
> 4 1/2 teaspoons fine sea salt
> 1 cup whole wheat flour
> 5 1/2 cups (1 1/2 pounds) bread flour or unbleached all-purpose flour with 13 percent protein (gluten) content
> Cornmeal

1. 1 TO 2 DAYS IN ADVANCE, make the starter. In a bowl or pint measuring cup, mix the yeast with the 3/4 cup lukewarm water and the 1 cup flour until well blended. Cover with plastic wrap and let stand in warm place. (If starter is left for 2 days, some liquid will rise to the top; stir it in before using.)

2. The day you plan to make the *tourte*, dump the starter into a mixing bowl. Add the 1 1/2 cups lukewarm water and the salt. Stir to blend well. Add the 1 cup whole wheat and 5 1/2 cups bread flour by cupfuls, mixing thoroughly and allowing each cupful of flour to be absorbed before adding the next. (You can use an electric mixer with a dough hook, set on slow.) Scrape down sides of bowl from time to time. If dough is tacky after all the flour has been added, add 1 to 2 tablespoons more flour. By hand, knead dough 20 minutes. If using mixer, knead 10 minutes on slow. If dough becomes too cumbersome for mixer, halve dough and knead in 2 parts. Turn out and knead by hand for 1 minute to achieve proper consistency—a smooth, elastic, somewhat soft dough.

3. Lightly grease a mixing bowl. Transfer dough to bowl, cover with plastic wrap, and let rise in a warm place free from drafts for 1 to 2 hours, or until double in volume. Punch down dough and turn out onto a work surface. Knead 2 minutes, then return dough to bowl and cover. Allow a second rising, 1 to 2 hours, or until doubled in bulk. Punch down again, then prepare for the last rising.

4. Rub plenty of flour into a linen or heavy cotton cloth and line a round 8-inch bread rising basket (see Note 2), or use an 8-, 9-, or 10-inch shallow basket or shallow bowl. Turn dough into basket or bowl, cover with overlapping cloth or another cloth, and set in a warm place to double in bulk, 1 to 2 hours. Dough is ready when you poke it gently with your finger and it doesn't spring back.

5. Preheat oven to 450° F. Place a baking sheet on middle oven shelf to heat up or set baking tiles in place.

6. Turn dough round upside down onto another, cornmeal-sprinkled baking sheet. With a razor blade, slit surface of bread in a crisscross. Just before placing bread in the oven on top of first baking sheet, mist the hot oven with 5 to 10 spurts from an atomizer filled with plain water; this will help make a crunchier crust. Lower

oven temperature to 400° F. Immediately place bread in oven to bake 50 to 60 minutes. At this point mist interior of the oven again with 2 or 3 spurts. The bread is done when it sounds hollow when tapped on the bottom. Remove from oven and transfer bread to rack to cool. Loaf will keep fresh 3 to 4 days.

If using the domed La Cloche, shape and bake in the following manner: Preheat oven to 450° F. Do not soak the dome or bottom part of La Cloche in water. Lightly grease bottom part of oven mold for the last rising of the dough. Cover with the dome and let stand until dough is doubled in bulk. Slash top of loaf deeply with a razor blade 3 or 4 times. Cover again and bake 50 minutes without removing cover. Misting oven is not necessary. If your oven heats unevenly, halfway through baking turn the mold around for even cooking. Uncover and remove to a rack to cool. As soon as possible, with a wide spatula, lift the loaf from the bottom of the *cloche* and continue cooling on the rack.

NOTES TO THE COOK
1. Different brands of yeast produce different qualities of bread. I have used Red Star, Fleischmann's, and Engedura with good results. Engedura, available by mail from Williams-Sonoma (see Appendix), produces the best bread of all.
2. A special reed basket called a *banneton* can be used for raising dough. This is also available by mail from Williams-Sonoma (see Appendix).

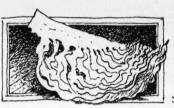

CHAPTER 3

Soups, Pot-au-feu, and Garbures

"Faire bien la soupe!" ("Make a good soup!") That's what mothers teach their daughters in South-West France. If France is a country of soup-eaters, the South-West is the land of soup-*lovers*. Soup is often eaten more than once a day, and very often a fine, rich soup will constitute an entire evening meal.

The soups of the South-West range from very simple to extremely hearty to ravishingly elegant. I believe there are more different soups eaten here than in all the other regions of France. The Périgord cooks are the most famous soup-makers in the region, and their soups are rich in nutrients, medicinal qualities, and the fortifying powers attributed to the classic chicken soup of Jewish mothers.

Most of these soups, of course, are never made the same way twice. The ingredients change from season to season, there is much room for improvisation, and each cook makes her own adjustments, "feeling" her soup as she goes along. All great makers of soup have their special secrets. One uses her mother's old earthenware *tupino* (the belly pot that sits in the chimney) for soup and nothing else. She cleans it once a year on Ash Wednesday, she told me. She'll cook everything else on her modern stove, but "never a soup," she says. Another cook always adds a few ribs of swiss chard to give her soups a certain indefinable smoothness. Another swears by an old iron kettle, and still another contends that a *fricassée* (the Périgord habit of browning a portion of the *cooked* vegetables* in fat and then returning them to the kettle) is her secret. And still another says all the vegetables *must* be raw, but says it in such a way that one knows she has still another secret, a secret within her revealed "secret," which she will *never* reveal.

There are quick soups such as *tourains*, which can be made in half an hour, hardly longer than it takes to open up a can and heat its contents. And then there are soups that must be mothered for two or three days. *Tourains* are the mainstay of most evening meals in the South-West except for the Béarn and Bigorre areas, where heartier garbures are served nearly every night. Evening soups—garbures, their Périgord variations called *sobronades*, and their Basque variations, *saldas*—are often so thick that a spoon will remain upright if placed in them. And to finish off the soup, *faire chabrot* (or in the Béarn, *faire la goudale*). This means that after all the bread on the soup plate is gone and there is only a spoonful or two of soup left, the diner pours some red wine into his plate, mixes the wine and the soup, raises the plate to his mouth, and drinks the mixture. This is considered either restorative or quaint, depending on one's point of view.

There are assorted soups of wild greens, and herbal soups made only in the spring. There are garlic soups to be eaten at eight in the morning after having picked grapes off the vines, beginning at 4 A.M.

Fifty years ago a wedding night in the South-West was unthinkable without a heavily peppered soup on hand for the bride and groom. (In the Landes it was often served in a chamberpot!)

And then there is a soup that was used to warm both the stomach and the bed. It was made in the evening, left in the dying embers to cook during the night, reheated to boiling in the morning, then placed under the covers of the bed to keep the bedding warm during the day. At noon a piece of bread was left to soak in it, so that by nightfall the soup had turned into one big *panade*. It was then devoured for the evening meal, and a new soup was put into the embers to provide the next night's nourishment and to keep the bed warm during the cold winter day.

The Basque and Landais coasts provide a number of extraordinary fish soups, and then there are the inevitable pot-au-feu ranging from simple "rich broth" soups served in the Landes, to *poule au pot* versions served in the Béarn, to the rich, thick, garbure-like pot-au-feu of Albi.

What follows is a sampling of some of the more unusual and best soups I know.

---

*A mixture of chopped turnips, carrots, cabbage cores, onions, leeks, and wild greens. In the Quercy it is called a *fleuri*; in Gascony, a *sabous*.

CABBAGE AND DUMPLING SOUP
Soupe aux Miques et aux Choux

It was in the old capital of the Black Périgord, in the town of Sarlat, that I first heard about *miques*—enormous dumplings poached in a soup to give added substance to a meal. *Miques* are traditional peasant fare in the Périgord, Quercy, and Corrèze and are therefore considered a homey accompaniment to soup.

They can be made with stale bread, or a mixture of cornmeal and flour leavened with yeast, or a type of brioche dough mixed with garlic, parsley, and pork cracklings. A *mique* is like bread, served after the first helping of broth, along with the meat and vegetable portion of the soup. In the Périgord it is usually moistened with broth, while in the Corrèze the brioche-style *mique* is generally served dry. Leftover *mique* is saved, sliced, and fried the following day either with bacon and eggs or sprinkled with sugar and served as dessert.

I've eaten *mique*, brioche-style, with chicken in red wine, with a *civet* of rabbit, and even, in one home, simply doused with tomato sauce. My hostess, rather than cut the *mique* with a knife, or with a string the way you might cut polenta, actually broke up the *mique* with two forks to show how light it was.

The *mique* is a good way to approach an understanding of the earthy country cooking of South-West France, a perfect example of its purpose, which is, of course, to fill the diner up. The *mique* of Sarlat, fondly nicknamed *nuages pesants* ("heavy clouds"), is made from stale bread, bacon bits, and eggs, and leavened with baking powder. It is served with a sparerib soup and assorted vegetables, and if the pot is big enough and the family prosperous enough, a veal knuckle or a chicken may be added, too.

I asked a friend who was born in St.-Cyprien (a neighboring town to Sarlat) to find someone who could teach me a local *mique*. She took me to a woman who taught local cooking to city people who owned vacation houses in the region, and here I confronted the classic difficulty of a food writer conducting field research in provincial France. Madame X had a pointed chin and pointed ears, a tiny mouth, short-cropped hair, high cheekbones, and a typical square Périgourdin face. She was a quintessential peasant woman who loved to talk about cooking, worked hard for very little money, and was fiercely loyal to her family. On the other hand, she was obsessed with the notion that she must guard her "culinary secrets," suspicious of my interest in her knowledge, and totally confident in her ability to deceive. She did try to hide the "secret" of her *mique* and got caught in her own trap. Though her soup was delicious, her *mique* barely rose (*miques* generally double in volume). Her own family, sitting there at the table, complained about its size and less than marvelous good taste. She pretended not to hear one word and gobbled up her portion.

Still, the experience was fascinating, an insight into the cult of "secrets" and into the life-style of a peasant family. The kitchen was in a wonderful stone building with a fireplace in the center. While we waited for the soup to cook and the *mique* to rise, we grilled chestnuts over the fire. Her husband came in and washed up—he had just finished force-feeding a dozen geese. One by one the children came home from school, changed their clothes, and proceeded to do chores around the house. During this time, while we were together, Madame X bombarded me with a confusion of advice, all sorts of theories about temperatures and cooking times, her subterfuge sprinkled with a little bit of peasant feminism. Actually it was fun to fence with her and to watch her cook—she was really very good.

When the dough was ready to be cooked, she removed the chicken from the soup, explaining she had to make room for the *mique*, give it space to expand. I liked the way she slipped the *mique* into the pot along with the floured tea towel in which it was wrapped. She then pulled the towel out gently, covered the pot, and let the dough cook in the simmering liquid. After about 25 minutes she turned the *mique* over and let it cook some more.

The recipe presented here is not Madame X's, since her *mique* did not turn out particularly well. My friend from St.-Cyprien went about finding another "teacher" for me. This time it was a lovely lady in her late seventies, Madame "Marthou," who quietly prepared this wonderful cabbage, sparerib, and *mique* soup. The *mique* is a stale-bread dumpling with bacon, garlic, and herbs, flavored as is the custom in St.-Cyprien.

SERVES 6 TO 8
  ACTIVE WORK: 45 minutes
  UNATTENDED SIMMERING TIME: 3 1/2 hours

The Soup (Meat)

    1 1/2 pounds streaky salt pork
    2 pounds meaty spareribs
    1 small veal knuckle
    1 onion, halved, 1 half stuck with a clove
       Herb bouquet: 6 sprigs parsley, 2 sprigs fresh thyme, and 1 small bay
         leaf, tied together with string

The Mique

    4 eggs
       Salt
    1/2 pound stale French, Italian, or Country-Style Bread, torn into small
         pieces by hand or cut into small cubes (crusts are included) to make
         3 loosely packed cups
    4 strips bacon

    3 tablespoons milk
    3 tablespoons reduced soup liquid (for full flavor)
    2 tablespoons mixed chopped fresh herbs: parsley and chives
 1/4 teaspoon finely minced garlic
     Freshly ground pepper to taste
    1 cup all-purpose flour
1 1/2 teaspoons baking powder
     Vegetable oil

The Soup (Vegetables)

    1 pound savoy or green cabbage, halved and cored
    5 carrots, scraped and left whole
    4 medium turnips, peeled and left whole
    1 clove garlic, halved
    3 leeks (whites with pale green shoots), washed well and tied in a bundle

1. ABOUT 4 HOURS BEFORE SERVING, cover the meats with water. Quickly bring to a boil; boil 5 minutes and drain. Refresh and drain.

2. Place all the meats, the onion, and the herb bouquet in a deep, wide-topped kettle. Add fresh water to cover and slowly bring to a boil. Skim off any scum that surfaces, then partially cover and simmer 1 1/2 hours.

3. Break eggs into a shallow bowl. Sprinkle just enough salt over the yolks to create a thin veil (about 1/2 teaspoon). (This is Madame Marthou's *truc* for adding just enough salt to a stuffing.) Beat eggs to combine. Set aside.

4. Place bread cubes in a large wide bowl.

5. Dice bacon and place in a skillet. Add 2 tablespoons water and gently cook 5 minutes, or until all the water has evaporated and the bacon has rendered its fat and is half crisped.

6. Reserve bacon and fat separately. Deglaze skillet with milk and reduced soup liquid, and scrape into beaten eggs. Add bacon fat and beat lightly to combine. Mix in herbs, garlic, and pepper to taste. Pour around the bread cubes; mix gently but thoroughly.

7. Have flour and baking powder ready in a strainer set over a plate. Shake one third of flour mixture over moistened cubes. Swirl bowl so cubes toss with flour and become coated evenly. Repeat with second third and swirl to combine. Sprinkle bacon over cubes. Add remaining third, swirling to keep the mixture as light as possible.

8. Fold large piece of cheesecloth (24 × 36 inches) in half. Lightly brush one side with oil. Gently press mixture into a mound and place on double layer of cheesecloth, oiled side touching the *mique*. Wrap up loosely because the *mique* almost doubles in size when cooked. Tie ends with string.

(continued)

9. Set on a plate and refrigerate at least 30 minutes to allow bread and flour to absorb moisture.

10. When meats have cooked 1 1/2 hours, remove from heat. Allow to cool so that excess fat can be easily removed. (If this is not done, soup will be too greasy.) *Can be prepared ahead up to this point.*

11. Bring meats to a boil. Add vegetables and simmer, partially covered, 1 hour.

12. ABOUT 1 HOUR BEFORE SERVING, remove 1 cooked carrot and 1 turnip from kettle; cut into slices and brown in a little hot fat in a small skillet, about 5 minutes. Return this *fricassée* to the soup.

13. Slide *mique*, still loosely wrapped in cheesecloth, into soup. The *mique* should be submerged in boiling liquid. Add a little boiling water if necessary. Cover and simmer over medium-high heat 45 minutes. Do not uncover while *mique* is cooking.

14. Lift out *mique* onto a plate. Drain off any cooking liquid and let rest 10 minutes. Remove cheesecloth. Halve, then cut into slices.

15. Slice and arrange meats and vegetables in individual, heated wide soup bowls. Add a thick slice of *mique* to each plate and moisten with a little cooking broth. Serve at once with a grainy mustard and French cornichons.

NOTE TO THE COOK
The cooking liquid is not served as a separate soup.

THICK MIXED MEATS AND BEAN STEW
Garbure

There always comes a point while people are talking seriously about French gastronomy when someone quotes Curnonsky, the so-called Prince of Gastronomes active in French culinary circles earlier in this century. And usually when he is quoted people nod their heads, believing that if Curnonsky said something, it *must* be true. Indeed, he seems to have been a legendary figure, and among his most famous statements is the one in which he listed the four great regional dishes in France: *choucroute garnie,* bouillabaisse, cassoulet, and garbure. Almost everyone has heard of the first three; very few (including many French people) know anything of the last. I myself am not too sure about some of the pronouncements of Curnonsky, but I have to admit that garbure in the right hands is most assuredly a great dish. Basically it is a soup, a relatively simple one at that, made up of salt pork, cabbage, and beans. But, of course, like many "simple" peasant dishes, garbures are not as simple as they seem. It is in the embellishments, the variations, that the really great garbures come about.

Garbure is the very symbol of Béarnais cookery, but it is eaten widely in Gascony, the Landes, and the Pays Basque, too. It's usually served as the evening meal, one of those soups that is a meal in itself. Preferably cooked in an earthenware *toupin* (a high, round-bellied casserole), garbure has all kinds of variations, depending on local ingredients. The best garbures are made in spring with the second shoots of young cabbages (*broutos*). In the late fall, grilled chestnuts are added; and in the Landes during the summer, cooks add roasted red pepper strips instead of beans. Some cooks will add a *fricassée* of onions and vegetables fried in goose fat during the last hour or so of cooking; others will add swiss chard to make the soup more succulent, and still others will serve it as a gratin with layers of bread and cheese. On the average weekday night a cook will often add a *sahit* (a minced mixture of aged pork fatback with garlic and herbs) and perhaps a spoonful of goose fat. But a truly luxurious Sunday garbure requires a *trébuc*—a final embellishment of *confit.*

Here is a little story about *confit* and garbure that sums up, in an amusing way, the mystique of the "secret" in South-West French cookery. A gastronomic reporter asked a famous local cook just precisely *when* she added the leg of goose *confit* to her deservedly famous garbure. The cook replied that first she took the preserved goose leg in her hand and stirred it around in the soup. She kept stirring and stirring until all the surface goose fat melted off and flavored the soup. Then she stirred some more until she could actually feel the *confit* imparting its wonderful flavor to the liquid. "I keep stirring," she said, "and stirring . . . and stirring . . . and then finally I let it drop in."

"Yes, yes," said the impatient gastronomic reporter, "but explain to me precisely when."

(continued)

There was a long silence, and then the cook whispered her "secret": "When my hand gets too hot to keep holding it," she said.

SERVES 6 TO 8
ACTIVE WORK: 1 hour
UNATTENDED SIMMERING WITH OCCASIONAL SKIMMING: 3 1/2 hours

6 thigh-drumstick portions *Confit* of Duck, or 3 thigh portions *Confit* of Goose
1 pound dried white beans, such as Great Northern (see Note)
1 fresh ham hock, 2 pounds unsmoked picnic shoulder, or 2 pounds pork butt
1 pound unsmoked pork belly or lean salt pork with rind, blanched 5 minutes in boiling water and drained
1 duck or goose carcass, cut up, or bone from country ham (optional)
1 onion stuck with 2 cloves
3 medium onions, sliced
2 leeks, trimmed, split, and carefully rinsed (white plus 2 inches of green leaves)
2 medium turnips, peeled and quartered
5 cloves garlic
   Herb bouquet: 3 sprigs parsley, 1 sprig thyme, 1 bay leaf, and 1 sprig marjoram, tied together in a bundle
   Salt and freshly ground pepper to taste
   Cayenne pepper to taste
1 medium head green cabbage, trimmed, and quartered
3 sprigs fresh parsley
2 slices smoked bacon
3 medium boiling potatoes (about 1 pound), peeled and cut into 1-inch chunks
1 pound French garlic sausage or *cotechino*, cooked 15 minutes in simmering water, drained (optional)
6–8 thin slices stale French bread or Country-Style Bread, dried in slow oven
   Cornichons and pickled hot peppers as accompaniments

1. 4 HOURS BEFORE BEGINNING MAIN PREPARATION, set out crock of *confit*, in warm room or pan of warm water, to soften fat.

2. Pick over beans and soak in water to cover for 1 1/2 hours.

3. When beans have soaked 15 minutes, place ham hock, pork belly, and duck carcass or ham bone (if using) in a large kettle. Add 3 1/2 quarts cold water and bring to a boil. Reduce heat to low; simmer, partially covered, 1 hour, skimming frequently.

4. When beans have soaked 1 1/2 hours, drain them, put them in a 4- or 5-quart

heavy pan, cover with tepid water, and slowly bring to a boil.

5. Boil beans for 5 minutes and drain immediately, then slip them into simmering meat liquid. Add the onion stuck with cloves. Simmer, uncovered, 1 hour, continuing to skim as necessary.

6. While soup simmers, melt 3 tablespoons of the fat from the *confit* in a heavy medium-size skillet over moderate heat. Add sliced onions and leeks; cook, tightly covered, 3 minutes to "sweat" vegetables until softened but not browned. Add to soup kettle along with turnips. Heat to a slow boil, uncovered, over medium heat.

7. Mince 3 of the garlic cloves; add to kettle along with herb bouquet. Season lightly with salt, pepper, and cayenne, and cook at a slow boil, uncovered, 45 minutes. If poultry carcass was used, discard at this point. *Can be prepared ahead up to this point.*

8. 40 MINUTES BEFORE SERVING, in medium-large kettle of boiling salted water, blanch quartered cabbage, uncovered, about 10 minutes. Drain and chop coarsely; set aside.

9. Remove pieces of duck *confit* from softened fat. Scrape off fat clinging to pieces; reserve 1 tablespoon for later addition to the soup, if desired.

10. Finely chop or process parsley, bacon, and remaining 2 cloves garlic to a purée. Add to kettle along with *confit* pieces, cabbage, potatoes, and sausage (if using); heat over medium-high heat to boiling. Reduce heat to medium-low; simmer slowly, uncovered, 30 minutes.

11. JUST BEFORE SERVING, remove meats to a warmed platter; moisten with a few tablespoons soup liquid and cover loosely with aluminum foil to keep warm. Check consistency of soup; it should be thick enough so a wooden spoon stands up straight in center. If too thin, boil down. Add 1 tablespoon reserved *confit* fat, if desired; taste and correct seasoning.

12. For first course, place a slice of bread in each bowl and serve soup over it. For second course, slice meats and serve accompanied by cornichons and pickled hot peppers.

NOTE TO THE COOK

Beans can be soaked overnight. Discard any that are shriveled. Blanch 5 minutes, drain, and add to simmering meat liquid. Also see entry on Beans in Appendix.

VARIATION

To make a gratinéed variation, layer many slices of Country-Style Bread, the boned meats, and the vegetables in a deep ovenproof or earthenware bowl. Pour over the cooking juices, sprinkle with grated cheese such as dried Gouda or mild Cheddar, and set in a preheated 350° F. oven to bake until the top is crusty and brown, about 45 minutes.

BOILED MEATS DINNER
Pot-au-Feu à la Faouda

This is a delicious family pot-au-feu from the Languedoc. It is a little different from most in that it includes a small stuffed breast of veal (the *faouda*) cooked in a rich broth along with the various soup meats and vegetables. To make the dish even more substantial, you can serve it with green beans and new potatoes flavored with a light vinaigrette. The Fresh Tomato and Caper Sauce that follows is a lovely accompaniment.

SERVES 4 TO 6

ACTIVE WORK: 1 hour
UNATTENDED SIMMERING WITH OCCASIONAL SKIMMING: 3 1/2 hours

1 1/4–1 1/2 pounds veal knuckle
    1 beef shin (1 3/4 pounds) with marrow "soup bone"
1 3/4–2 pounds lean beef brisket, thick-cut, trimmed of fat
    1 tomato, halved
    1 onion, halved
    1 onion stuck with 2 cloves
    1 small head garlic
    1 tablespoon coarse (kosher) salt
    Herb bouquet: 4 sprigs parsley, 1 bay leaf, 2 sprigs thyme, 2–3 celery leaves, and 4 leek greens tied together in cheesecloth

La Faouda

    1/2 veal breast (1 3/4–2 pounds), with pocket for stuffing
    8 ounces pork sausage meat
    2 slices bread, crumbled, soaked in milk, and squeezed dry
    2 cloves garlic, finely chopped
1 1/2 ounces (1 1/2 thin slices) baked ham, chopped
    2 shallots, finely chopped
    1 egg
    1 tablespoon chopped fresh parsley
    1/4 teaspoon Quatre Épices
    Salt and freshly ground pepper to taste

    4 large carrots, scraped
    2 turnips, peeled, and halved if large
    2 large leeks, well washed, trimmed, and tied in a bundle
    Mustard, gherkins, and coarse (kosher) salt for garnish
    Fresh Tomato and Caper Sauce

1. Place veal knuckle and beef shin bone in a large pot. Add 4 quarts cold water and slowly bring to a boil. Simmer 15 minutes, skimming. Add brisket; bring back to a boil and simmer 45 minutes longer, skimming often.

2. Meanwhile, place tomato and onion halves under the broiler. Remove tomato when just slightly blackened and soft. Remove onion when the cut side is totally black. Set aside.

3. When meats have simmered 1 hour, add the tomato and onion halves, onion stuck with cloves, head of garlic, salt, and herb bouquet. Simmer 1 hour.

4. Make the stuffing for the veal breast: combine the sausage meat, bread, chopped garlic, ham, shallots, egg, parsley, and seasonings; blend well. *Can be prepared in advance up to this point.*

5. ABOUT 2 HOURS BEFORE SERVING, stuff the pocket and sew up to secure. Add veal breast, carrots, turnips, and leeks to the pot. Partially cover, return to a boil, and cook over medium heat 1 1/2 hours.

6. 20 MINUTES BEFORE SERVING, remove the vegetables for garnish, beef, and veal breast. Carefully strain the cooking liquid and degrease. Discard onion stuck with clove and any debris.

7. Reheat the meats and vegetables in one quarter of the cooking liquid. (Remaining liquid should be saved for soups and sauces.) Adjust seasoning of the liquid. Cut the veal breast into thick slices. Arrange meats and vegetables in clumps attractively on a warm serving platter. Meanwhile, boil down the cooking liquid (in which meat and vegetables were reheated) even further, to intensify flavor. Sprinkle meats and vegetables with the liquid to moisten. Serve hot.

8. Pass grainy mustard, gherkins, coarse salt, and the Fresh Tomato and Caper Sauce.

ANOTHER PRESENTATION

Serve a slice of veal breast in each individual shallow soup bowl; add meat and vegetables. Reduce 6 cups well-degreased cooking liquid by one half. Swirl 4 to 5 tablespoons butter into cooking liquid to enrich it. Spoon 1/2 cup liquid over each serving; sprinkle with fresh snipped chives and parsley.

Fresh Tomato and Caper Sauce
Sauce Tomate aux Câpres

This is a light and tasty sauce. It cannot be made successfully in a food processor, but it can be made many hours in advance and refrigerated.

MAKES 1 CUP

  1 hard-boiled egg
  1 tablespoon finely chopped shallots
  1 tablespoon finely chopped fresh parsley
  3 tablespoons strong red wine vinegar
  1/2 cup peeled, seeded, and finely chopped red-ripe tomatoes*
  1/3 cup olive oil
  1 tablespoon nonpareil capers, drained but not rinsed
    Salt and freshly ground pepper to taste

*In winter, use Italian egg (plum) tomatoes.

1. Crush the egg. Mix with the shallots, parsley, vinegar, and tomatoes in a mixing bowl.
2. Whisk in the olive oil in a slow steady stream.
3. Fold in the capers. Adjust seasoning with salt and pepper. Serve at room temperature.

BOILED MEATS IN THE STYLE OF ALBI
Pot-au-Feu à l'Albigeoise

This version of pot-au-feu, the famous boiled dinner of meats and vegetables served with assorted condiments and beef marrow, is a specialty of Albi, the beautiful red-brick city on the Tarn River sometimes called the "Florence of France." In this variation the addition of *confit* gives this nationally popular dish a distinctly South-West character. During the winter months, the cooks of the city add beans as well—at times, one suspects that the Albi pot-au-feu might almost be called garbure! Sometimes the Albi cooks will also add stuffed *confit* of goose neck.

Pot-au-feu can be a no-win situation. If you start the meat cooking in cold water, you end up with slightly bland meat and a great broth; if you add the meat after the water has come to a boil, the meat will be delicious (because of the quick sealing in of the juices), but the broth will be so-so. In this recipe, however, you can win both ways: the broth is made in advance with chicken and beef bones, and the meat is cooked the next day in the hot broth.

The secret of a great pot-au-feu is complete skimming of scum and foam. *Do not let the pot boil and do not stir,* as agitation clouds the liquid. Add cold water whenever necessary.

SERVES 10 TO 12
☆ Begin 1 day in advance
   ACTIVE WORK (DAY 1): 30 minutes
   UNATTENDED SIMMERING WITH OCCASIONAL SKIMMING (DAY 1): 3 to 4 hours
   ACTIVE WORK (DAY 2): 45 minutes
   UNATTENDED SIMMERING WITH OCCASIONAL SKIMMING (DAY 2): 3 1/4 hours

   Marrow from 8 (3-inch) pieces beef marrowbone (bones reserved and added to Chicken Stock)
   4 quarts (double recipe) Chicken Stock
   4 to 6 thigh-drumstick portions *Confit* of Duck
   2 1/2 pounds beef shin or brisket, in 1 piece
   3 pounds beef top round, in 1 piece
   1 small head garlic
   Herb bouquet: 3 sprigs parsley, large pinch thyme, and 1 bay leaf, tied together in cheesecloth
   2 1/2 teaspoons salt
   1/2 teaspoon freshly cracked peppercorns
   2 pounds meaty veal shank, sawed crosswise into 2-inch pieces
   Tomato Sauce (recipe follows)
   4 medium carrots, trimmed, scraped, and cut into large chunks
   3 small turnips, peeled and cut into large chunks
   8 small leeks, trimmed, split, carefully rinsed, and tied in a bunch
   1/2 small head green cabbage, cored
   8 small boiling potatoes
   1 pound French garlic sausage or *cotechino*, cooked 45 minutes in simmering water and drained
   10–12 thin rounds French bread, lightly toasted
   2 tablespoons salted butter, softened
   Freshly ground pepper to taste
   1 1/2 tablespoons chopped fresh parsley
   Cornichons
   Coarse (kosher) salt
   Coarse-grained mustard

1. 1 DAY IN ADVANCE, extract marrow from bones by soaking them in lukewarm water until marrow can be pried out easily. Soak marrow, refrigerated, in salted icy water, until ready to prepare and serve with first course of pot-au-feu.

(continued)

2. Make a double quantity of Chicken Stock, using emptied marrowbones for added richness. To reduce constant skimming, blanch all bones 5 minutes; drain and return to a clean stockpot. Simmer 3 to 4 hours, skimming whenever necessary. Strain, cool, and chill overnight.

3. THE FOLLOWING DAY, ABOUT 5 HOURS BEFORE SERVING, set out crock of *confit* in warm room or deep pan of warm water to soften fat.

4. WITHIN 1 HOUR, begin to cook soup. Degrease prepared stock and bring to a boil. Slip all the beef into the pot and bring back to a boil. Skim off scum as it rises to the surface. Lower heat and simmer slowly (liquid should quiver rather than boil), uncovered, until no more scum rises, about 15 minutes.

5. When scum has just about disappeared, add garlic, herb bouquet, the 2 1/2 teaspoons salt, and the peppercorns. Partially cover; continue to simmer very gently 1 1/2 hours, skimming if necessary.

6. Add veal shank to soup; increase heat to keep the simmer and continue to cook, partially covered, 1 hour, skimming often.

7. Meanwhile, make Tomato Sauce.

8. When soup has simmered a total of 2 1/2 hours after initial rising of scum from beef, add carrots, turnips, leeks, and cold water as required to cover; return to a boil, then reduce heat and simmer, partially covered, 30 minutes.

9. 30 MINUTES BEFORE SERVING, cook cabbage in a separate pot of boiling salted water over medium-high heat for 15 minutes. Remove *confit* pieces from softened fat; scrape off most of the fat clinging to *confit*. Divide thigh-drumstick pieces at the joints; add with potatoes to cabbage. Return to a boil; reduce heat once more and simmer 15 minutes.

10. Cut sausage on the diagonal into 8 equal pieces; add to cabbage and simmer a minute longer to heat through.

11. Remove *confit* pieces to warmed dish; keep warm and moist under a tent of aluminum foil. Check to see whether vegetables are tender; remove to warmed bowl as they are done. Moisten with a few tablespoons hot cooking liquid; keep warm and moist under foil tent. Remove sausage from cabbage cooking liquid and keep warm. Keep other meats warm.

12. Prepare the marrow toasts to serve as part of the first course. Have ready the lightly toasted rounds of French bread, buttered with the salted butter. Place marrow pieces in small saucepan of simmering salted water; poach gently for a few minutes, removing pieces with slotted spoon as soon as they turn pinkish gray. Divide marrow among buttered toast rounds, mashing lightly on each slice. Reserve. Heat the broiler.

13. TO SERVE THE FIRST COURSE, remove herb bouquet and garlic head from soup and discard. Ladle enough of the soup to serve as the first course through a fine sieve into a soup tureen or other container. Carefully degrease surface; taste and adjust seasoning. Run toast rounds under broiler for a few seconds, or until marrow is heated and glistening. Lightly sprinkle with pepper and serve at once, very hot, on a separate platter with the soup.

14. TO SERVE THE SECOND COURSE, slice or chunk meats, and arrange on warmed large platter; surround with vegetables. Sprinkle lightly with parsley; season to taste with salt and pepper. Serve accompanied by Tomato Sauce, cornichons, coarse salt, and coarse-grained mustard.

Tomato Sauce
Fondue de Tomates

Pot-au-feu is a spectacular winter dish, and a highly seasoned thick tomato sauce is a very popular accompaniment; it rounds out the flavor of boiled meats and blends well with the usual sharp accompaniments to the dish. Unfortunately, it is not the time of year to find a fresh, juicy, red-ripe tomato. The following recipe has been developed to bring out the flavor of winter tomatoes as they do in France. Imported canned tomatoes can be substituted with excellent results.

MAKES ABOUT 1 1/2 CUPS
ACTIVE WORK: 10 minutes
UNATTENDED SIMMERING TIME: 30 minutes
REDUCING TIME: 10 minutes

   1/2 cup chopped onions
    1 tablespoon olive oil
    2 cups seeded, cubed tomatoes (there is no need to peel tomatoes; sauce will be strained after cooking)
      Pinch of sugar
      Salt and freshly ground pepper to taste
      Herb bouquet: 4 sprigs parsley, 2 sprigs thyme, and 1 small bay leaf, tied together
    1 clove garlic, halved
1 1/2 cups stock or liquid from the pot-au-feu
      Cayenne pepper to taste

1. In a small, heavy enameled casserole, cook onions in oil until soft but not brown. Add tomatoes, sugar, salt, pepper, herb bouquet, and garlic.

2. Bring to a boil; cover tightly and cook 30 minutes over very low heat, or until well reduced.

3. Add the stock and reduce to 2 cups. Sieve, then reduce by boiling to 1 1/2 cups. If too thick, thin with a little water or stock. Adjust seasoning. Add cayenne to taste.

NOTE TO THE COOK
If you wish, Tomato Sauce can be made up to a day ahead; add about half the discarded skins and seeds to the soup pot for added flavor.

TWO EVENING SOUPS: FROM THE CORRÈZE

AND FROM THE QUERCY-PÉRIGORD

Tourains

A *tourain* is a soup made with onions or garlic or tomatoes, or a mixture of two or three of these. It is sometimes called a *tourin*, a *tourri* in the Pyrenees area, or an *ouliat* in the Béarn. Most *tourains* are thickened at the last minute with a mixture of egg yolks and vinegar, and sometimes beaten egg whites are stirred in, too. *Tourains* are very typical of South-West France and are much beloved there.

   Below are two versions: a *tourain* from the Corrèze, which has a light aroma of garlic and onions, and another from the Quercy-Périgord, which is long-simmered and flavored with *confit*.

EVENING GARLIC SOUP IN THE MANNER
OF THE CORRÈZE
Tourain à l'Ail Comme en Corrèze

A typical evening meal would continue with assorted slices of pâté, a terrine, some pickled fruits, crusty bread, and a salad; dessert could be Preserved Spiced Pears in Red Wine with Armagnac.

SERVES 4 TO 5
   ACTIVE WORK: 15 minutes
   UNATTENDED SIMMERING TIME: 30 minutes

       1/4 **cup thinly sliced garlic from about 10 large cloves (not elephant garlic)**
   1 1/2 **cups minced onions**
   2 1/2 **tablespoons poultry fat or 3 tablespoons unsalted butter**
       1 **tablespoon all-purpose flour**
   4 1/2 **cups poultry or meat stock, degreased and heated to lukewarm**
       2 **eggs, separated**
       4 **teaspoons red wine vinegar**
         Salt and freshly ground pepper to taste
    8–12 **thinly sliced rounds of French bread, toasted lightly, dabbed with**
         goose fat (if available), and sprinkled lightly with black pepper

   1. In a heavy-bottomed 3- or 4-quart saucepan, cook the garlic and onions in fat over medium-high heat until golden but not brown, about 5 minutes. Lower heat; add the flour, stirring, and cook until it turns a straw-beige color. Remove from heat.
   2. Gradually add 4 cups of the stock, stirring to avoid lumps. Return to heat. Bring

to a boil and simmer, uncovered, 30 minutes. *Can be prepared ahead up to this point; cool and refrigerate.*

3. 10 MINUTES BEFORE SERVING, lightly beat egg whites with a fork in a small bowl or pitcher until frothy but not foamy. Add remaining 1/2 cup stock and mix to blend. Set aside.

4. In a second bowl, whip egg yolks with a fork to break them up, then beat in the vinegar.

5. Reheat soup to boiling. Ladle 1 cup of the hot soup into the yolks and vinegar. Beat to combine and set aside.

6. Bring soup back to a boil, then remove from heat. Pour in the egg-white mixture in a thin, steady stream, gently whisking with a wire whisk in order to form strands. Return soup to low heat, stir in the egg-yolk mixture with a spatula, and simmer gently, stirring, until soup is creamy. Do not allow soup to boil or eggs will curdle and strands will harden. Adjust seasoning and serve at once. Pass the bread rounds.

VARIATION

Omit the egg whites.

THE ARCHBISHOP'S *TOURAIN* WITH *CONFIT* OF DUCK
Tourin d'Archevêque

SERVES 4 TO 6
    ACTIVE WORK: about 15 minutes
    UNATTENDED SIMMERING TIME: about 1 hour

    2–3 wings and necks plus 2 thigh-drumstick portions *Confit* of Duck
    3–4 tablespoons fat from *confit*
      3 medium onions, chopped (about 2 cups)
      1 large fresh ripe tomato, peeled, seeded, and coarsely diced, or 2/3 cup
          drained imported canned peeled tomatoes
      1 teaspoon chopped garlic
        Salt and freshly ground pepper to taste
      2 jumbo egg yolks
      1 tablespoon red wine vinegar, preferably a strong-flavored variety
    4–6 thin slices Country-Style Bread or good-quality seedless rye

1. ABOUT 4 HOURS BEFORE BEGINNING MAIN PREPARATION, set out crocks of *confit* in warm room or in deep pans of warm water to soften fat.

2. Remove *confit* pieces. Carefully scrape off fat. Place 2 tablespoons fat into flameproof 4-quart casserole; reserve remainder in bowl. Heat fat in casserole over

medium heat to rippling. Set thigh-drumstick pieces aside; add onions and neck and wing *confit* to hot fat. Cook 5 minutes, stirring often.

3. Add tomatoes and garlic; cook 2 to 3 minutes. Add 5 cups warm water and heat to boiling. Skim any foam from surface. Season with pepper and a little salt. Reduce heat to low; simmer, partially covered, 30 minutes.

4. Divide each thigh-drumstick piece in two at the joint. Add to soup; simmer 30 minutes. Strain soup through sieve; skim fat from surface. Set duck pieces aside. Return liquid to casserole, still on low heat. When duck pieces are cool enough to handle, pull out bones, remove skin, and return meat to strained soup. *Can be prepared ahead up to this point.*

5. 10 MINUTES BEFORE SERVING, whisk egg yolks with vinegar in a small bowl until thoroughly blended. Over very low heat and stirring constantly, slowly pour egg-yolk mixture into soup; continue to stir until slightly thickened. Do not allow soup to boil. Remove from heat; let stand, covered, a few minutes before serving. Taste and correct seasoning. Spread slices of toasted bread with a thin layer of *confit* fat and sprinkle with freshly ground pepper; place a slice in each warmed individual soup bowl and pour soup over. Serve immediately.

VARIATION

Spread bread slices with a thin layer of *confit* fat; sprinkle with freshly ground pepper. Toast bread on baking sheet in preheated 450° F. oven until glistening, about 3 minutes. Otherwise, at the last minute, toast bread in a toaster and spread with *confit* fat; sprinkle with pepper and serve at once.

Inspired by a recipe from Zette Guinaudeau-Franc's Les Secrets des Fermes en Périgord Noir.

OLD-FASHIONED RABBIT SOUP
Soupe de Lapin à l'Ancienne

This is a simple soup from the tiny village of Poudenas in the Lot-et-Garonne. It is delicious and worth making whenever you intend to cook rabbit. Since the front legs and rib cage of rabbits have little meat but are very flavorful, they are better used for soup. The saddle and hind legs should be reserved for sautés. Hare can be substituted with terrific results.

SERVES 4 TO 6
ACTIVE WORK: 30 minutes
UNATTENDED SIMMERING TIME: 5 hours
REDUCING TIME: 10 minutes

Rib sections as well as tail bone, loose skin and fat, spine, and forelegs
   of 2 young, tender rabbits, or 1 stewing rabbit (see Note)
Salt and freshly ground pepper to taste
1 tablespoon olive oil
1/2 pound carrots, pared, halved, and thinly sliced (about 1 1/2 cups sliced)
1 leek (white and pale green parts), well washed and thinly sliced
1 tablespoon finely chopped shallots
2 quarts unsalted Chicken Stock, degreased
1 clove garlic, peeled
Herb bouquet: 4 sprigs parsley, 2 sprigs thyme, 1 small bay leaf, tied
   together in cheesecloth
1 cup heavy cream
1 tablespoon snipped fresh chives

1. With a cleaver, chop rabbit into 1-inch pieces. Sprinkle with salt and pepper; set aside.

2. In a 4-quart casserole, heat olive oil; add carrots, leeks, and shallots. Stir once, then cover and cook gently for 5 minutes so that the vegetables become soft but do not brown.

3. Add the rabbit pieces; cover and cook 5 minutes. Uncover the casserole and cook the vegetables and rabbit pieces about 10 minutes, or until they are lightly browned on all sides.

4. Add stock, garlic, and herb bouquet; bring to a boil. Cover with buttered waxed paper and a cover, and simmer very gently 5 hours. (You can also cook the soup in a preheated 250° F. oven.)

5. Cool soup slightly; skim off all fat and strain into a bowl. Pick over the solids to remove the bones. Discard the herb bouquet. Press the solids through the fine blade of a food mill so that all the liquid and the vegetables are puréed. Press on the rabbit meat to extract as much flavor as possible. Discard the fibrous solids. Rinse out the casserole and return the soup to it. *Can be prepared ahead up to this point.*

6. 15 MINUTES BEFORE SERVING, bring soup to a boil and reduce to 5 cups. Add cream; adjust seasoning with salt and pepper. Garnish each serving with snipped chives.

NOTE TO THE COOK
If using frozen cut-up rabbit, buy 2 boxes; use bony pieces for soup. Rewrap meaty portions and save for Rabbit Stew with Preserved Pear and Ginger. If you have a whole, skinned rabbit, you can include the head for added richness. Ask the butcher to split the head in half and chop it into small pieces. Freeze the brains and use in dishes calling for calf's or lamb's brains.

Inspired by a recipe from Marie-Claude Soubiran-Gracia.

OYSTER VELOUTÉ WITH BLACK CAVIAR
Velouté aux Huîtres et au Caviar

This fine luxurious soup is not an "invented" recipe, as you might assume, but one based on traditional cooking in the South-West.

Caviar has been taken from the Gironde River since the Russian Revolution; according to the story, the owner of the famous Parisian fish restaurant Prunier employed Russian refugees to help him extract and preserve caviar from the sturgeon of the Gironde. The eggs obtained were of excellent quality, comparable to the best Iranian caviar. Unfortunately, parts of the Gironde are now quite polluted and caviar production is down, but you can sometimes find the local variety in certain restaurants in Bordeaux. According to J.-E. Progneaux in his *Recettes et Spécialités Gastronomiques Bordelaises et Girondines*, the *caviar de Gironde* (as it is known locally) is sold in Paris under the Volga label.

Fat, juicy oysters of Japanese origin are raised in the bay of Arcachon. Oysters have been raised in these waters since Roman times. The oldest were the flat, common European oyster that was wiped out in the 1920s. Portuguese oysters, much like our bluepoints, are still raised in the bay, but are being replaced by the more resistant Japanese oyster. The oysters are puréed in a food processor or electric blender and are added near the end. As a result, they are not overcooked and retain their natural taste.

If you garnish this velouté with a fine caviar, it becomes an extremely elegant soup course. Lumpfish eggs, too, make a nice garnish, but whatever type of caviar you choose, be sure to add it at the last minute to avoid possible discoloration.

SERVES 6 TO 8

ACTIVE WORK: 20–25 minutes
MOSTLY UNATTENDED SIMMERING TIME: 20 minutes

     2 shallots, peeled and finely chopped
     3 tablespoons unsalted butter
     3 tablespoons all-purpose flour
     3 cups unsalted Fish Stock
     3 cups unsalted Chicken Stock, fully degreased
   3/4 teaspoon sea salt
 12–15 oysters, shucked, plus their clear liquor (or, if you buy them shucked,
          about 1 1/3 cups including liquor)
        Pinch of cayenne pepper
     3 large egg yolks
 3/4–1 cup heavy cream
   1–2 drops fresh lemon juice
   2–3 tablespoons black caviar

1. In a heavy-bottomed 4-quart saucepan, preferably of copper, soften the shallots in the butter without browning. Blend in the flour and cook over low heat, stirring often, 10 minutes. The mixture—called the *roux*—must be very smooth and not darken beyond the color of yellow straw. If necessary, use an asbestos or metal pad to control the heat. This mixture must cook slowly so that the flour proteins will absorb liquid and thicken properly.

2. In a second saucepan, combine the stocks (see Note) and heat to lukewarm. Gradually add stocks to the roux, stirring constantly, and bring to a boil over medium heat. Reduce heat and simmer gently 20 minutes, skimming off scum that rises to the surface. Add *half* the salt.

3. Strain oyster liquor to remove any traces of shell and sand. Purée oysters in a food processor or electric blender. Add puréed oysters and strained liquor to soup. Simmer, partially covered, 5 minutes. Add cayenne. Rub soup through a fine strainer set over a large mixing bowl, pressing down hard with the back of a spoon to extract as much oyster pulp as possible. *Can be prepared ahead up to this point.*

4. 5 TO 10 MINUTES BEFORE SERVING, reheat soup. Combine egg yolks and 3/4 cup heavy cream in a small mixing bowl; whisk them together. Gradually whisk in 1 cup of the hot soup in order to raise the temperature of the egg yolk–cream mixture and prevent curdling. Stir egg-yolk mixture into soup, and continue stirring constantly, over low heat, until soup has thickened slightly. Bring soup almost, but not quite, to the boiling point. Remove from heat at once. Taste for seasonings and adjust. If necessary, add a bit more cream. Sprinkle caviar with lemon juice. Ladle soup into individual soup plates and top each with a teaspoon of black caviar. Serve at once.

NOTE TO THE COOK

The mixture of equal amounts of fish and chicken stocks is important to this dish; it provides good body and background taste without overpowering the flavor of the oysters.

VARIATION

To serve the soup cold, chill quickly over cold water or ice, then refrigerate. Thin with half cream and half milk before serving.

FISH SOUP BASQUAISE
Ttoro

This is a modern interpretation of the classic onion and pepper fish soup of Bayonne.

It is moderately spicy on account of the hot red pepper flakes. The Basques have a fondness for their home-grown *piment d'Espelette,* which gives a rounder, deeper pepper taste to the soup than ordinary cayenne pepper or flakes.

I attended the pepper festival in the village of Espelette, where they grow and cure hot red peppers. This festival is held each year in late October to celebrate such wonderful hot peppers—spicier, meatier, and richer in flavor than rival peppers from rival towns. Peppers are everywhere—strings of them hang from buildings, and like everyone else, I wore a string of them around my neck!

Espelette isn't the only Pyrenees town that likes to promote its produce. Biarritz sets aside a day to celebrate its bounty of shellfish; Bayonne honors its ham; Hendaye (on the coast near Spain) boasts its delicious tiny eels; St.-Gaudens fetes its excellent fat white beans served in garbure; and in Ste.-Croix-du-Mont the grape pickers toast the fruity wine called Irouléguy—so good that it makes the girls dance.

SERVES 4
>   ACTIVE WORK: 30 minutes
>   COOKING TIME: 10 minutes

>   1/4 **cup olive oil**
>   1/2 **cup finely diced onions**
>   1/2 **cup finely chopped celery**
>   1 **large clove garlic, finely sliced**
>   1/4 **teaspoon red pepper flakes, or 1/8 teaspoon cayenne pepper (or more to taste)**
>   **Pinch of paprika**
>   1/2 **cup diced red bell peppers**
>   1/2 **cup diced green bell peppers**
>   3/4–1 **pound mixed boneless fish fillets, cubed: red snapper, halibut, monkfish, hake, and/or cod (see Note 1)**
>   2 1/2 **tablespoons chopped fresh herbs: parsley, basil, chervil, a few leaves of rosemary and/or sage**
>   1/2 **cup peeled, cubed, and seeded red-ripe tomatoes**
>   1 **dozen large mussels, steamed with 1/2 cup dry white wine (see Note 2), or substitute 12 small littleneck clams (see Note 3); shelled, with liquor reserved**
>   3 **cups Fish Stock or water, heated**
>   1/2 **cup cooked crab meat (optional)**
>   **Fresh lemon juice**
>   **Salt and freshly ground pepper to taste**

1. 10 MINUTES BEFORE SERVING, in a large skillet, heat olive oil; add onions, celery, garlic, pepper, paprika, and red and green peppers. Cook over medium heat 2 minutes, swirling to blend flavors.

2. Add fish, herbs, tomatoes, and mussel or clam liquor. Bring pan juices to a boil. Add hot stock or water, and simmer 5 to 7 minutes, swirling the pan often. Skim off foam that rises to the surface.

3. Add mussels or clams, crab meat (if using), a dash of lemon juice, and salt and pepper to taste. Cook 2 minutes over low heat.

4. Lift out fish and mollusks, and place in individual soup bowls. Pour over liquid and serve at once.

NOTES TO THE COOK

1. The earliest recipes for this dish call for using grated potatoes to thicken the water in which salt cod has been cooked. Today the procedure is quite different and involves a fast sauté of various fish, depending upon your choice. The fish must not be allowed to disintegrate, so avoid fluke, flounder, and sole; stick to firm-fleshed, delicately flavored, white-meat fish such as bass, red snapper, hake, halibut, cod, scrod, monkfish, and sea eel.

2. Directions for cleaning and steaming mussels are given under the heading "Mussels" at the beginning of Chapter 8.

3. If using clams, scrub well and soak in icy *salted* water for several hours to purge them of sand and other impurities. A handful of cornmeal is often added to the water to help them expel sand.

VARIATION

To make the soup more substantial, garnish it with garlic croutons: brown slices of French bread in hot olive oil; drain on paper towels. While still hot, rub each slice with a cut piece of garlic and sprinkle with salt. If making the croutons in advance, reheat in a warm oven before serving. Pass with the soup.

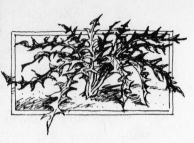

CHAPTER 4

SALADS

There are some who think that the little composed salads so popular now as a first course—those containing foie gras, sautéed duck breasts, and bitter greens—are the inventions of the new young chefs. In fact, these salads are variations on the regional practice of combining the rich pork and duck *confits* (hot or cold) with foods that are both refreshing and slightly acidic. They can also be thought of as luncheon dishes or late supper dishes.

All of the salads have been "composed" for a pretty presentation, but unlike a lot of so-called pretty dishes, they have more than a merely decorative effect. The principal flavors sparkle with their own identity. They blend with hot or cold accompaniments for a striking appeal to the taste buds and to the eyes.

COLD *CONFIT* OF PORK WITH GREEN BEANS AND CABBAGE
Salade de Confit de Porc aux Haricots Verts et aux Choux

This recipe shows off the special succulence of pork *confit* browned in a little of its own fat. The amount of pork *confit* can be increased as desired, depending on whether you plan to serve this salad as an appetizer or a luncheon or supper dish.

Confit of Pork is much more aromatic and delicious than a simple cold roast pork, and is definitely worth having on hand. It is extremely easy to make.

SERVES 4 TO 6

ACTIVE WORK. 30 minutes

> **4–6 pieces *Confit* of Pork**
> **1/2 head white cabbage, finely shredded (about 5 cups)**
> **1 pound tender fresh young green beans**
> **Coarse (kosher) salt**

Creamy Dressing

> **2 tablespoons tarragon-flavored white wine vinegar**
> **3/4 teaspoon salt**
> **1 level tablespoon Dijon mustard**
> **3 tablespoons olive oil**
> **2 1/2 tablespoons walnut oil**
> **5 tablespoons Crème Fraîche or heavy cream**
> **3 tablespoons snipped fresh chives**
> **1 tablespoon finely chopped shallots (chopped by hand—see Note 1)**

1. ABOUT 4 HOURS BEFORE SERVING, set out *confit* crock in warm room or deep pan of water to soften fat. When softened, carefully remove the pork without breaking the pieces. Scrape off the fat. Sauté slowly in a little fat to glaze the outsides. Cool completely.

2. Soak the shredded cabbage in ice water 2 to 3 hours.

3. Clean the beans by removing the tips and strings, if any. Soak in ice water 30 minutes (see Note 2).

4. Bring water to a boil in a deep pot (not aluminum). Add 2 tablespoons coarse salt for 2 1/2 quarts water. Return to a boil. Drain the beans and add in small lots so water does not stop boiling. Boil, uncovered, until just tender (timing depends upon the quality of the beans). Immediately scoop out and drain on a kitchen terry towel. Cool to room temperature. (Do not refresh beans in cold water.)

5. To make the dressing, bring the vinegar and 3/4 teaspoon salt to a boil in a noncorrodible saucepan; stir to dissolve salt. Have ready a small bowl with the mustard in it. Pour boiling vinegar over and whisk to combine; the mustard must completely dissolve. Gradually beat in the oils. Fold in the cream and chives. Mix with the green beans and the well-drained cabbage. Let stand 1 hour. Sprinkle with shallots.

6. Thinly slice the *confit* on the diagonal. Arrange overlapping slices on a serving plate. Serve with the salad.

(continued)

VARIATION

Sliced cabbage can be blanched 10 minutes, drained thoroughly, then rolled in a kitchen terry towel to dry. Fluff strands. Sprinkle with 2 to 3 tablespoons tarragon-flavored vinegar and 1/2 teaspoon salt, and let stand 3 to 4 hours. Serve as a side dish with the *confit* of pork and the string beans dressed with a reduced amount of the Creamy Dressing.

NOTES TO THE COOK
1. I believe that whenever shallots are used *raw* in a dish they must be hand-chopped at right angles. This method of chopping ensures that the shallots will be milder in flavor and less acrid to the taste buds. To hand-chop at right angles, use a small sharp paring knife. Peel the shallot, leaving the root end attached. Hold the shallot by the root end and lay it flat on the chopping surface; if necessary, halve the shallot so it will lie flat. With the knife pointing at the stem end, make small nicks downward about 1/8 inch apart. Then use the knife to make thin slices across the grain and finally to slice downward crosswise. The shallots will be in perfect tiny cubes, much "pinker" in color, and have a far more subtle flavor.
2. The green beans are hardened by soaking them first in ice water so that they will "sear" when they hit the boiling water in batches; thus no flavor will be lost to the pot. The raw cabbage is soaked in ice water so that it will remain crunchy, even after it has been marinated in a creamy dressing.

DUCK BREAST AND WILD MUSHROOM SALAD
Salade Landaise

The original recipe calls for the use of the two very small fillets behind each whole duck breast, the "filets mignons." These pieces are so small that only at a restaurant where numerous fresh ducks are served can enough of them be accumulated for this salad. Since this really isn't possible in the home, the following recipe can be made with the entire duck breast, which, though not quite so tender and fine as filets mignons, will work very well. Cook the legs for *confit* if the duck has been defrosted, or use in any of the duck recipes in this book. See Chapter 10 for How to Cut Up a Duck.

This is an easy first course and is one of my favorites using canned cèpes. It is not advisable to substitute dried mushrooms. (If you have 2 or 3 fresh cèpes available, see Note 1 for cooking directions.)

SERVES 4 TO 6
ACTIVE WORK: 10 minutes
COOKING TIME: 10 minutes

1 whole duck breast, boned, skinned, trimmed of fat, and cut into long
    thin julienne strips
Coarse (kosher) salt
1 can (9 3/4 ounces) cèpes or *steinpilze*, whole or in chunks
Juice of 1/2 lemon
3 tablespoons extra virgin olive oil or Wild Mushroom-Scented Oil
1 teaspoon finely minced shallots
2 teaspoons mixed fresh herbs: finely chopped parsley, chervil, and
    chives
Salt and freshly ground pepper to taste
2 bunches mixed slightly tart greens such as arugula, chicory,
    watercress, radicchio, etc.
2 1/2 tablespoons rendered goose or duck fat, or 3 tablespoons unsalted
    butter
2 thin slices stale, crustless French bread, cut into 3/8-inch dice
1 clove garlic, peeled and halved

1. EARLY IN THE DAY, sprinkle the duck pieces with 1/2 teaspoon coarse salt (see Note 2). Spread out on a plate, cover, and refrigerate until 10 minutes before serving.

2. Drain canned cèpes and cut into very thin slices. In a small bowl, combine lemon juice, olive oil or Wild Mushroom-Scented Oil, shallots, herbs, and a light sprinkling of salt and pepper; blend well. Pour over cèpes and refrigerate until ready to serve.

3. Wash greens; trim away thick stalks, and dry well. Wrap in paper towels and allow to crisp in the refrigerator. *Can be prepared ahead up to this point.*

4. 10 MINUTES BEFORE SERVING, remove duck breast strips from the refrigerator. Pat dry with paper towels to remove moisture and salt. Heat half of the fat or butter in a small skillet, and when it just begins to foam throw in the cubes of bread and the garlic. Fry until golden brown on all sides, stirring constantly so that they don't burn but just brown evenly. Drain; discard the garlic and cooking fat.

5. Mix greens and cèpes; arrange on individual serving plates.

6. In the same skillet, quickly sauté duck strips in remaining hot fat or butter, stirring, about 3 minutes. Drain duck on paper towels, then season with salt and plenty of black pepper. Scatter duck strips evenly over prepared salad, top with warm croutons, and serve at once as a first course.

NOTES TO THE COOK

1. If you have just 1 or 2 fresh cèpes, brush caps dry with a damp cloth. Don't soak them or they will become waterlogged and tasteless. If they are very dirty, quickly wash under running water. (If they feel soggy or waterlogged, it is a practice in the Landes to dry them out in a slow oven for 10 minutes before cooking.) Remove their stalks and peel them. Slice the stalks into rounds and set aside. Heat 1 tablespoon goose or duck fat or oil in a skillet. Add the caps, the stalks of the cèpes, and a split garlic clove when the fat or oil is hot; cook over high heat 1 minute, stirring. Lower

heat, cover, and cook 10 minutes without disturbing them. Uncover, turn over each cap and cook, uncovered, 5 to 10 minutes over medium-high heat to reduce liquid. They are done when the fat or oil turns clear. Drain off fat and reserve for mixing with the marinade. Use the remainder for browning the bread cubes. Allow cèpes to cool, then slice and marinate as directed above.

2. Marinating the duck meat in salt helps to tenderize it. It is even better to do this one day in advance.

Inspired by a recipe from Robert Garrapit.

Wild Mushroom-Scented Oil
Huile de Cèpes

This is a delicious woodland flavoring to make in the early fall. Use it with cultivated mushroom and duck salads, and as a basting marinade for lamb and pork.

MAKES 1 1/2 CUPS
ACTIVE WORK: 5 minutes
MELLOWING TIME: at least 1 month

   1/3 cup dried cèpes, in large pieces
1 1/2 cups green-hued olive oil such as the French Puget
  12 (5-inch) sprigs fresh thyme
   2 bay leaves, preferably imported

1. Wash the cèpes under running water, rubbing them with your fingers to rid them of grit and dirt. Pat dry on paper towels.

2. When they are absolutely dry, place them in a jar with the remaining ingredients. Leave at least 1 month before using.

CHICKEN OR DUCK LIVER SALAD WITH APPLES AND WATERCRESS
Salade Cressonnière aux Foies de Volaille

Another very easy first course. The beauty of this particular dish is that the livers are sautéed gently until they obtain a consistency reminiscent of foie gras, then arranged atop a lightly dressed salad. The salad can be further enhanced with Duck Cracklings, if desired.

I usually serve this dish whenever I spot a few very pale-colored chicken livers at the meat counter. "Blond" chicken livers have a very delicate flavor, which is necessary to make this dish distinctive.

Another good time to make this salad is when you are cutting up ducks for *confit*.

SERVES 4

ACTIVE WORK: 10 minutes
COOKING TIME: 3 minutes

4 chicken or duck livers, pale-colored and picked over for bile, fat, and strings
Milk
Coarse (kosher) salt
1 1/4 cups picked-over watercress leaves with tender stems only, well washed, dried, and kept crisp in the refrigerator
1 tasty red apple, unpeeled
2 tablespoons strained fresh lemon juice
1 tablespoon sherry wine vinegar
1 tablespoon imported walnut oil
2 1/2–3 tablespoons olive oil
Salt and freshly ground pepper to taste
2 tablespoons unsalted butter
2 thin slices garlic-flavored sausage such as Genoa salami, cut into thin julienne strips
1 leek, trimmed, split, washed, cut crosswise into hair-thin julienne strips, and kept in iced water

1. AT LEAST 3 HOURS BEFORE SERVING, place livers in a bowl to soak in lightly salted milk to cover.

2. 10 MINUTES BEFORE SERVING, place watercress in mixing bowl. Halve the apple, slice thinly, and sprinkle with 1 tablespoon lemon juice. Add to watercress.

3. Mix vinegar, remaining lemon juice, and oils. Season with salt and pepper.

4. Rinse livers under running tap water until water runs clear. Drain, but do not pat them dry (the slight amount of moisture will keep them soft as they cook, rather than allowing them to harden at the edges).

5. Heat butter in a small skillet and cook livers gently 1 1/2 minutes per side. Set on a plate to rest 2 minutes before slicing each liver thinly on the diagonal.

6. Toss watercress and apple with dressing; arrange on four plates. Add the livers, dividing them equally. Grind additional pepper over each salad and scatter with the julienned salami and drained leek. Serve at once.

SALAD OF COLD DUCK *CONFIT* WITH RED CABBAGE, CHESTNUTS, AND WATERCRESS
Salade Cévenole

This makes for a very pretty presentation, but unlike a lot of so-called pretty dishes, it has more than a merely decorative effect. The principal flavors—*confit*, vegetables, nuts, and vinaigrette ingredients—blend together brilliantly; the visual appeal is equally striking.

It is very important to use roasted chestnuts, not the type packed in syrup or brine. If you don't roast your own, in winter you can often buy fresh-roasted chestnuts from street vendors; or use the plain vacuum-packed variety.

SERVES 4 TO 6 AS A FIRST COURSE
ACTIVE WORK: 20 minutes
PEELING ROASTED CHESTNUTS: 15 minutes

- 4–6 thigh-drumstick portions *Confit* of Duck
- 8 ounces roasted chestnuts, fresh or vacuum-packed (see Note)
- 3 1/2 ounces (1 scant cup) walnut halves
- 1 1/2 teaspoons sugar
- 4–5 tablespoons fat from *confit*
- 2–3 tablespoons grape-seed oil or peanut oil
- 1/4 cup red wine vinegar, preferably a strong-flavored variety
- 2 tablespoons red wine
- 2–3 tablespoons fresh lemon juice, or to taste
- 3 tablespoons walnut oil
- 1 tablespoon French peanut oil or olive oil
- Salt and freshly ground pepper to taste
- 1 small head red cabbage, trimmed, quartered, cored, and thinly sliced with a stainless steel knife
- 2 bunches watercress, stems removed, or mixture of watercress and several large handfuls of tender chicory
- 2 young carrots, scraped
- Cracklings (optional)

1. 4 HOURS BEFORE SERVING, set out crock of *confit* in warm room or deep pan of warm water to soften fats.
2. Peel roasted chestnuts and cut into dice. You should have about 3 cups.
3. Heat oven to 350° F.
4. Spread walnuts in small baking pan; sprinkle with 1/2 teaspoon of the sugar.

Toast until lightly browned, 5 to 8 minutes. Remove from oven; let cool. *Can be prepared ahead up to this point.*

5. When fat has softened, remove 4 to 6 *confit* pieces. Carefully scrape fat from 2 to 3 pieces into a large, heavy skillet with a tight-fitting lid; add half the grapeseed or peanut oil. Pull out any loose bones from *confit*. If skillet is not nonstick or well seasoned, add another tablespoon of fat from crock. Heat fat and oil over medium-high heat to rippling. Add 2 to 3 pieces of *confit*, skin side down. Cook, tightly covered, 2 to 3 minutes. During cooking, remove lid 2 or 3 times and carefully wipe off surface moisture clinging to underside. Shake pan to make sure *confit* is not sticking. When skin is well browned, remove skillet from heat; let stand, tightly covered, 30 seconds. Uncover, pour off and discard fat. Let *confit* pieces crisp a second longer, then turn each piece skin side up and set on a wire rack or brown paper bag to drain. Repeat with remaining fat, oil, and *confit*. Let cool while you make the salad. (If *confit* skin loses its crisp quality, return to greased skillet, skin side down, and crisp for 30 seconds.)

6. Make dressing by combining vinegar, red wine, remaining 1 teaspoon sugar, lemon juice, oils, and salt and pepper to taste in small mixing bowl. Toss dressing with sliced cabbage; let stand at room temperature 30 minutes to develop flavor.

7. At serving time, toss marinated cabbage in salad bowl with chestnuts, watercress, and walnuts. Taste and correct seasoning, adding drops of lemon juice to taste. Using a citrus zester or swivel-bladed vegetable parer, sliver carrots directly into salad bowl over other ingredients. Serve salad accompanied by *confit* and cracklings.

NOTES TO THE COOK
1. Roasted whole chestnuts, vacuum-packed in jars, are available by mail from Williams-Sonoma (see Appendix).
2. If using fresh chestnuts, roast as follows: With sharp knife, slit an X on the round side of each chestnut. Place in 1 layer on baking sheet; roast 30 minutes. Remove from oven, and while still hot, peel. When cool, cut into dice. You should have about 3 cups.

SALAD WITH GARLIC CROUTONS
Salade en Chaponnade

Try to preserve a balance of flavors when choosing greens for this salad. Be sure there is a slightly bitter leaf such as chicory, as well as a tangy one like sorrel and a peppery one like arugula.

SERVES 4 TO 5
ACTIVE WORK: 10 minutes

> 1/4 loaf French bread, split lengthwise if thin or quartered if fat, left to dry out
>   2 cloves garlic, peeled and halved
> 1/8 cup walnut oil
> 1/8 cup olive oil
>   1 tablespoon sherry wine vinegar or very sour *verjus* (see Appendix)
>   Salt and freshly ground pepper to taste
>   2 tablespoons rendered poultry fat, preferably goose or duck fat
>   3 cups torn mixed greens such as chicory, escarole, sorrel, arugula, radicchio, and young dandelion leaves, well washed and spun dry
>   Fresh herbs such as parsley, chives, chervil, and thyme, snipped (not chopped)

1. Rub the bread crusts with the cut garlic cloves until they become shiny in appearance.

2. Combine walnut and olive oils. Drizzle 1 tablespoon oil over the bread. Let stand at least 30 minutes.

3. Finely chop the garlic *by hand*. Mix remaining oil with vinegar or *verjus*. Season dressing with salt and pepper.

4. Break or cut the bread into small pieces (about 1 1/4 cups). Sauté in hot poultry fat until golden on all sides. Toss while hot with the greens, dressing, and chopped garlic. Sprinkle with herbs.

CATALAN SALAD WITH TOMATO-SCENTED BREAD CRUSTS
Salade à la Catalane au Pain à l'Huile

Marie-Thérèse Carreras in her book on Catalan food describes the Catalan salad as follows: "It is like a Spanish inn. It accepts everyone and everything it can hold."

On a large flat serving plate mix piles of anchovy fillets, shredded bitter greens, sliced red onions, grilled and sliced peppers, tomato chunks, chopped walnuts, diced cheese, scallions, celery, and any other cooked vegetables. Toss in mayonnaise with fresh chopped garlic. Top with sliced hard-boiled eggs, serrano ham, and sausage.

Prepare *tartines*—long, narrow pieces of lightly toasted French bread lavishly rubbed with fresh tomato pulp and green fruity olive oil and sprinkled with coarse salt, or spread with sun-dried tomatoes from Italy along with their marinating oil (available in fine food stores under the San Remo label).

Serve with piles of green and black olives and salami slices.

TOMATO AND ARTICHOKE SALAD WITH ROASTED BREAD, ANCHOVY-OLIVE DIP, AND SALMON RILLETTES
Salade de Tomates et d'Artichauts à la Rôtie et à la Tapenade de Toulouse, et aux Rillettes de Saumon

The four recipes that make up this salad are really just a sequence of steps, most of which can be completed in advance. This isn't a composed salad but an informal assembly of good things to eat together. Robert Courtine, a French food writer, recently wrote, "There is no new cuisine; there are no inventions, but there is research and the discovery of natural affinities among different foods." This dish is served by Lucien Vanel at his restaurant Vanel in Toulouse.

To serve, let each person arrange his or her own plate with a sampling of the Tomato and Artichoke Salad and a scoop each of the Salmon Rillettes and Anchovy-Olive Dip to accompany the hot bread.

(continued)

Tomato and Artichoke Salad
Salade de Tomates et d'Artichauts

SERVES 8

ACTIVE WORK: 35 minutes
COOKING TIME: 35 minutes

> 5 large artichokes
> 1 lemon halved
> 1 medium yellow onion, sliced
> 1 carrot, sliced
> 1/2 cup olive oil or French peanut oil
> 3 tablespoons fresh lemon juice
> 3 tablespoons milk
> 1 1/4 teaspoons salt
> 1/8 teaspoon freshly ground pepper
> 5 large ripe tomatoes, peeled
> Sugar
> 2 tablespoons red wine vinegar
> 1 tablespoon Dijon mustard
> 5 tablespoons Crème Fraîche or heavy cream
> 3 tablespoons chopped fresh chives
> 1 tablespoon finely chopped shallots (chopped by hand)

1. Snap off artichoke stems and tough outer leaves. Trim away green nubs from bottom with stainless steel paring knife. Using a stainless serrated knife, cut off and discard top third of artichoke. With a thin-bladed, very sharp stainless steel knife, remove the leaves one by one, using a seesaw motion behind each leaf. The knife should cut off the leaf, leaving the fleshy part attached to the artichoke bottom. Repeat all around until the artichoke is cone-shaped and pale green. Cut off this cone about one third of the way down. Pare the bottom and sides of each artichoke to remove any tough green exterior. Rub cut surfaces with lemon as you work. As you prepare them, drop the artichoke bottoms into a pan of acidulated water (1 tablespoon of vinegar or lemon juice to 2 cups water).

2. Combine drained artichoke bottoms, 2 cups water, onions, carrots, 2 tablespoons of the oil, the lemon juice, milk, 1/2 teaspoon of the salt, and the pepper in a large, heavy, noncorrodible saucepan. Heat to boiling; cover saucepan with waxed paper and tight-fitting lid. Reduce heat to low; simmer until artichoke bottoms are tender when pierced with knife, about 30 minutes.

3. Meanwhile quarter tomatoes, stem to tail. Remove entire inside of each quarter; save for stock or juice. You should have 4 "petals" from each tomato. Sprinkle each petal with a pinch of salt and sugar; let drain 30 minutes, cut side down, on a plate lined with paper towels.

4. Drain artichoke bottoms on kitchen terry towel. When cool, cut into 1/2-inch cubes, cover with plastic wrap, and reserve.

5. Cut drained tomatoes into 1/2-inch cubes.

6. Heat vinegar and remaining 3/4 teaspoon salt to boiling in small noncorrodible saucepan. Place mustard in medium heatproof bowl; pour vinegar mixture over mustard. Whisk until mustard dissolves. Gradually beat in remaining 6 tablespoons oil.

7. JUST BEFORE SERVING, whisk Crème Fraîche or cream, chives, and shallots into vinaigrette. Add tomatoes and artichokes; gently toss to coat with dressing. Serve at room temperature.

Anchovy-Olive Dip
Tapenade de Toulouse

This is a mixture of the Provençal *tapenade* which is a black-olive-based spread, and the Languedoc version of *anchoïade* that uses anchovies as its base. It is perfect on crusty "roasted" bread.

MAKES ABOUT 3/4 CUP
ACTIVE WORK: 10 minutes

> 1 (2-ounce) can anchovy fillets packed in oil, drained, or two salt-packed anchovies (see Note)
> 18 pitted oil-cured or salted black olives, soaked overnight in olive oil with slivers of garlic
> 1 tablespoon Dijon mustard
> 1 egg yolk
> 2/3 cup fruity olive oil
> 1 tablespoon fresh strained lemon juice
> Cayenne pepper

1. Place anchovies in small bowl with cold water to cover; let soak 20 minutes; drain.

2. Combine anchovies, olives, and mustard in workbowl of food processor fitted with metal blade or in electric blender; using on-off motion, process until coarsely chopped, scraping down sides of bowl as necessary.

3. Add egg yolk; blend thoroughly until smooth. With machine on, add oil in a slow, steady stream. Add lemon juice; season to taste with cayenne. Spoon into 1-cup crock. *Tapenade de Toulouse* can be refrigerated, covered, up to 3 days.

NOTE TO THE COOK
If using salted anchovies, soak them in cold water 2 hours. With a small knife, remove fillets; rinse thoroughly and pat dry. Use all 8 fillets.

(continued)

Roasted Bread
La Rôtie

This is delicious and quite unusual as an accompaniment. You will make this bread often to serve with goat cheese, salad, Red Pepper Mousse, and, of course, with this salad.

Herbes de Provence is a popular seasoning in the Languedoc as well as in Provence. It is used to flavor *confit* of goose, breads, and salads. It includes bay leaves, thyme, rosemary, basil, coriander, nutmeg, lavender, savory, cloves, and white pepper. (Available by mail from H. Roth and Williams-Sonoma; see Appendix.)

In some parts of the Languedoc (principally in Gard) a similar mixture called Herbes de la Garrigue is more common. Wild herbs such as lavender, sage, savory, thyme, and fennel, as well as rosemary and mint, are gathered, blended, and kept in closed jars. The mixture following the recipe gives a captivating, robust flavor to grilled meats and to slices of roasted bread.

ACTIVE WORK: 5 minutes
BAKING TIME: 5 to 6 minutes

8 stale 1/2-inch-thick slices of coarse Country-Style Bread
3 tablespoons fruity olive oil
1 tablespoon herbes de Provence or Herbes de la Garrigue

1. Heat oven to 450° F.
2. Brush both sides of bread slices with olive oil; sprinkle 1 side of each evenly with herbs.
3. Place herb side up on ungreased baking sheet; bake until bread is golden brown and crisp, 5 to 6 minutes.

Herbes de la Garrigue

1 bay leaf
2 teaspoons summer savory
1 teaspoon dried sweet basil
1 tablespoon thyme
2 teaspoons marjoram
1 1/2 teaspoons fennel seed
1/4 teaspoon sage
3/4 teaspoon dried mint (optional)
1/2 teaspoon dried lavender (optional)
3/4 teaspoon rosemary

Crumble herbs; blend well. Keep the mixture in a tightly capped jar. Finely crush amount needed in a mortar or electric spice mill just before using.

Salmon Rillettes
Rillettes de Saumon

This dish improves with age; keep it up to 1 week under a layer of clarified butter. It is perfect starting on the third day. Try it with mixtures of fresh and smoked eel, trout, or mackerel as an appetizer. These rillettes also go well with a salad of roasted red peppers, thin green beans, and tender lettuce leaves. Follow with a doubled recipe for The Priest's Omelet, and Poached Figs in Raspberry and Red Wine Sauce.

SERVES 8 (ABOUT 4 TABLESPOONS EACH)

☆ Prepare at least 3 days in advance
  ACTIVE WORK: 30 minutes
  COOKING TIME: 4 minutes

> 1 **skinned fresh boneless salmon fillet (1/2 pound), cut into 4 pieces**
> 1/4 **teaspoon ground sea salt**
> 9 **tablespoons unsalted butter**
> 1 **large shallot, minced**
> 1 **tablespoon dry white wine**
> 1/4 **pound lightly smoked salmon, in one piece, cut into 1/4-inch dice**
> 2 **tablespoons light olive oil**
> 1 **egg yolk**
> 1 **tablespoon fresh lemon juice**
> 1/8 **teaspoon freshly ground pepper**
> **Pinch of freshly grated nutmeg**
> 1/4 **cup clarified butter (see Index)**
> **Salt to taste (if necessary)**

1. Sprinkle salmon with salt and let stand at room temperature 20 minutes (see Note). Bring butter to room temperature.

2. Meanwhile, in a wide saucepan slowly cook shallot in 1 tablespoon butter until soft but not brown. Pat salmon dry with paper towels.

3. Add salmon pieces and white wine in 1 layer; cover with waxed paper and tight-fitting lid. Cook, turning once, until center of fish is opaque, 3 to 4 minutes. Remove from heat; allow to cool, uncovered. Remove salmon to side plate. Reduce pan juices and pour over fish. Flake salmon with fork; mix well with cooked shallot.

4. Pound remaining butter with wooden mallet or end of rolling pin until soft and smooth but not greasy. Cut butter into small pieces; place in the workbowl of a food processor fitted with the plastic blade, along with cool cooked salmon and smoked salmon cubes. Chop, using on-off motion, until combined.

5. With machine on, quickly add olive oil, egg yolk, and lemon juice. The mixture should have a gritty texture. Transfer to small bowl; add spices and salt to taste.

6. Pack rillettes into a small 2 1/2- to 3-cup crock; pour clarified butter over surface. Refrigerate 3 days before serving. Serve at room temperature. If rillettes are partially used, reseal with clarified butter.

CHAPTER 5

APPETIZERS

COLD APPETIZERS

RED PEPPER MOUSSE
Mousse de Piments Doux

Sweet red peppers cooked as in this recipe, rather than roasted over embers or flames or broiled, have an intense flavor. Lightly spooned into a tall crock and served with Roasted Bread, the mousse makes an unusual and delicious accompaniment to drinks. It is also excellent with cold *Confit* of Pork and Duck Breasts Baked in Salt.

SERVES 4 TO 6
☆ Begin 1 day in advance
  ACTIVE WORK: 15 minutes
  COOKING TIME: 25 minutes

       1 teaspoon unsalted butter
       4 fleshy red peppers, cored, seeded, and cut into 1/4-inch dice
       1 medium clove garlic, thinly sliced

Pinch of crumbled thyme leaves
1 tablespoon white wine vinegar
2/3 cup heavy cream, chilled
Salt
1/4 teaspoon freshly ground white pepper

1. ONE DAY IN ADVANCE, melt butter in heavy medium-size saucepan over medium-low heat. Add peppers, garlic, and thyme. Cover and cook, stirring occasionally to prevent burning, about 20 minutes.

2. Add the vinegar, increase heat, and cook uncovered until all liquid has evaporated. Transfer mixture to food processor or electric blender and purée 30 seconds.

3. Press through a sieve to remove skins. Discard skins and return purée to the sieve to drain and cool. Discard any liquid. Cover and keep refrigerated overnight.

4. THE FOLLOWING DAY, in a chilled bowl with chilled beaters, beat the cream until stiff. Gently fold cold pepper purée into whipped cream and chill thoroughly. Just before serving, season mousse with salt and pepper.

VARIATION

Molded Pepper Mousse: If you wish to serve this mousse molded in baby savarin or timbale molds, here is how to do it.

1. Cook the peppers as described above, but do not add the vinegar.

2. Soften 1 scant teaspoon unflavored gelatin in 1 tablespoon white wine vinegar. Combine purée and gelatin in a saucepan and heat *without boiling*. Stir to dissolve gelatin completely. Remove from heat and cool over ice mixed with some salt and water.

3. Meanwhile, whisk 3/4 cup cold heavy cream to soft peaks. Combine peppers and cream, mixing gently but thoroughly. Season with salt and pepper.

4. Use a spatula to fill 6 oiled miniature savarin or timbale molds. Chill 3 hours.

5. JUST BEFORE SERVING, turn out on individual serving plates lined with shredded greens. Serve with lukewarm *Confit* of Duck and slices of Roasted Bread. Sprinkle the mousse with a fruity olive oil, preferably flavored with thyme. Good as part of an antipasto-like salad.

COMPOTE OF RABBIT WITH PRUNES
Compote de Lapin aux Pruneaux

This unusual and heavenly compote is Lucien Vanel's version of an old French dish—shredded rabbit and plump prunes set in aspic. In the South-West the word "compote" can be applied to any sort of stewed shredded meat or poultry.

One of the problems with rabbit is that it often comes out tasteless and dry. In this dish, however, the flesh is tender and moist, and when shredded gives the compote the texture of rillettes. The main difference between this compote and rillettes is lightness—instead of enriching it with duck, goose, or pork fat, Vanel's recipe calls for a small amount of fresh cream. The tangy, piquant touch of sorrel rounds out the dish, and the rich, plump prunes make a sweet counterpoint.

This must be made 2 to 3 days in advance so the compote has time to mellow. It is wonderful on thin slices of lightly buttered toast.

SERVES 6 TO 8
☆ Begin 3 days in advance
ACTIVE WORK: 45 minutes
COOKING TIME (MOSTLY UNATTENDED): 4 1/2 hours

    1 mature, skinned stewing rabbit or fryer (about 3 pounds), fresh or frozen

Marinade

    2 cups dry white wine
    3 medium yellow onions (about 12 ounces), peeled, halved, and thinly sliced
    1/2 cup sliced carrots
    2/3 cup olive oil
    1 shallot, sliced
    1 clove garlic, halved

    5 ounces lean salt pork or mild-flavored bacon, blanched 3 minutes and refreshed and drained dry
    2 1/2 tablespoons vegetable oil
    2 teaspoons Dijon mustard
    4 cups unsalted Chicken Stock
    Herb bouquet: 3 sprigs parsley, 1/4 teaspoon dried thyme or 3 fresh sprigs, 1/4 teaspoon dried rosemary or 1 sprig, and 1 bay leaf tied in cheesecloth
    Salt and freshly ground pepper to taste

1/2 teaspoon Quatre Épices (recipe below)
2 tablespoons Armagnac, flamed and cooled

1. Preheat the oven to 300° F., or heat Crock-Pot to simmer, or high setting.

2. Trim all fat and skin from the ducks, and chop into small pieces. Place skin and fat in a 3-quart pan. Add 3 tablespoons water. Render the fat; strain. Measure 1 1/2 cups liquid fat and reserve in the refrigerator. (This barely "cooked" fat is the secret to a light and easily digestible compote of shredded duck.) Leave remaining fat in the pan.

3. Meanwhile, with a mallet or cleaver chop the legs and thighs of the duck into 1-inch pieces. Chop the carcasses, wings, and backs. Add to the pan or Crock-Pot along with the pork. Season with 1 teaspoon each salt and pepper. Add the stock, wine, herbs, garlic, shallots, and Quatre Épices. Cook, uncovered, in the oven or in the Crock-Pot 4 to 5 hours, or until the meat is falling off the bones. Stir from time to time to prevent sticking. (The liquid in the pan will evaporate, and the meat pieces will be cooked slowly in the remaining fat.)

4. Strain pork and duck through a colander set over a deep bowl. Let cool 10 minutes. Pick out lean meat, including the sweet morsels of duck flesh on the carcass and around the wings, and discard the skin, bones, and gristle. Set aside 1/2 cup flavorful fat.

5. Transfer duck meat and pork to the workbowl of a food processor fitted with the plastic blade. Process on and off 4 to 6 times, or until the fibers are broken down. Add the reserved 1 1/2 cups chilled fat, the cooked garlic and shallots, and the Armagnac; process 10 seconds, stopping twice to scrape down bowl. The mixture should have a shredded texture. Taste for seasoning, adding more salt, plenty of pepper, thyme, and Quatre Épices to taste. It should be very peppery.

6. Lightly pile the rillettes into clean stoneware crocks, leaving about 1/2 inch at the top. Tap to settle. Cover rillettes with reserved flavorful fat. Use within the week.

NOTES TO THE COOK

1. If time permits, marinate duck and pork pieces with seasonings and white wine overnight before cooking.

2. To keep the rillettes 2 to 4 weeks, it is necessary to cook the reserved fat at a simmer until it becomes clear (about 15 minutes), skimming as needed. When the water and impurities have been removed from the fat, use as directed above. When fat has solidified, melt 1/2 cup lard and spoon over each filled crock to within 1/4 inch of the top. Cool to solidify. Cover tightly. Chill and keep refrigerated.

Spice Mixture for Pâtés and Stews
Quatre Épices

Despite its name, Quatre Épices is a mixture of more than four spices: pepper, allspice, cinnamon, cloves, coriander, and others. You can create your own mixture to taste.

(continued)

MAKES 1 TABLESPOON

    10 cloves
     1 tablespoon white peppercorns
     1 cinnamon stick (preferably the thicker and more pungent cassia
        cinnamon)
   2/3 teaspoon ground Jamaica ginger
   3/4 teaspoon freshly grated nutmeg

1. Grind all ingredients in a spice mill until powdery.
2. Sieve and store in a tightly capped jar.

NOTE TO THE COOK

I prefer to make up small batches of this mixture, since ground spices lose their punch in a short time.

OLD-FASHIONED DUCK TERRINE
Terrine de Caneton à l'Ancienne

When you serve this terrine, pass a small bowl of homemade Sweet and Sour Prunes as an accompaniment.

SERVES 10
☆ Prepare 3 to 4 days in advance
  ACTIVE WORK: 30 minutes
  BAKING TIME: 2 hours

    1 (4 1/2-pound) duck
    8 ounces pork liver
    1 carrot, cut up
    1 turnip, cut up
    1 onion, cut up
    1 tomato, cut up
     Herb bouquet: 3 sprigs parsley, 2 sprigs thyme, 1 bay leaf, 1 leaf of fresh
       celery, tied in cheesecloth
     Salt and freshly ground pepper to taste
    4 eggs, lightly beaten
    2 tablespoons heavy cream
    2 cloves garlic, peeled and finely chopped
    4 shallots, finely chopped
    1 tablespoon chopped parsley

1/4 teaspoon (or more) Quatre Épices
1 black truffle, chopped (optional)
2 ounces (4 tablespoons) Armagnac

1. Bone the duck or have your butcher do it for you. (To prepare duck for this terrine, see Note 2.) Set aside the meat. Save the bones, liver, and skin. Discard the sinews. In the workbowl of a food processor fitted with the metal blade, purée all the fat and a 4×5-inch piece of skin. Set aside.

2. Cut the pork liver into small pieces. Using the medium blade of a food chopper, grind the duck meat and pork liver. Set aside.

3. Crack duck bones into small pieces and brown lightly in bits of duck fat in a medium-size skillet. Drain off any fat. Add the cut-up vegetables, 2 cups water, and the herb bouquet; bring to a boil, skimming as needed. Lower heat and reduce liquid to 2 tablespoons glaze; this will take about 45 minutes. Scrape glaze into a small bowl to cool; discard solids in skillet.

4. Meanwhile, in a large bowl combine ground pork liver and duck meat, puréed skin and fat, 2 1/2 teaspoons salt, 10 grinds of pepper, the eggs, cream, garlic, shallots, parsley, Quatre Épices, and truffle; blend well.

5. Fold in the 2 tablespoons duck glaze. Pat mixture into a bowl and spread Armagnac on top. Let stand, uncovered, 2 to 3 hours at room temperature or, covered, overnight in the refrigerator (but let mixture come to room temperature before next step).

6. Preheat oven to 300° F.

7. Stir mixture to loosen. Pack into a 1 3/4-quart terrine or loaf pan. Smooth it down, cover with foil, and set in a larger pan of hot water (a bain-marie). Place on middle oven shelf and bake 1 1/2 hours. Remove the foil covering, lower oven temperature to 225° F., and bake 30 minutes longer.

8. Remove terrine from the oven and let cool 30 minutes. Cover the top with foil and weight it with a heavy object such as a 2-pound can. Allow to cool. When completely cold, refrigerate. Remove the weight the following day. Reseal completely. Serve after 3 to 4 days.

This will keep a week if well covered with fat. Serve slices straight from the terrine, at room temperature.

NOTES TO THE COOK
To skin and bone a duck for terrines and pâtés:
1. Follow directions in duck chapter for How to Cut Up a Duck.
2. To bone the thigh and leg portions: Locate the thighbone on one side of the duck and run your fingers along the flesh from the exposed end to where it connects with the drumstick. With the tip of a sharp knife, starting at the exposed joint, cut parallel to the bone so the entire bone is exposed. Scrape the meat from the bone at the joint connecting the thighbone to the leg bone, cutting through the joint with the knife

point. Lift out the bone, scraping away any remaining meat or ligaments. Pull the drumsticks out from under the meat and cut completely around the bone and through the skin, meat, and ligaments about 1 inch from the end.

With two fingers, hold the end of the exposed leg bone and cut completely around the bone just below the knob, making certain to release not only the meat but also the thin white ligaments which hold the meat to the bone. Using the edge of the knife, scrape the meat down the bone. Lift out the bone. Repeat with the other thigh and leg.

Inspired by a recipe from Claude Laffitte.

TERRINE OF PORK AND BRAINS
Terrine de Porc aux Cervelles

This is one of the most interesting pâtés that I know. The delicate brains are imbued with the flavors of port wine and spices, and are kept moist and succulent enrobed in a well-flavored pork-and-veal casing.

This terrine should be made at least four days before you intend to serve it in order to give it time to ripen. Serve with your own Sweet and Sour Cherries or use those imported from France.

SERVES 10 TO 12
☆ Prepare at least 4 days in advance
ACTIVE WORK: 45 minutes
BAKING TIME: 1 hour 40 minutes

1 1/4	pounds veal, beef, or lamb brains
	Salt
2	teaspoons red wine vinegar
	Freshly ground black pepper
10–12	ounces unsalted pork fatback in thin sheets
10	ounces unsalted pork fatback, cubed
10	ounces boneless fresh lean pork, cubed
9–10	ounces boneless lean veal, cubed
1	large clove garlic, peeled and halved
2	large shallots, peeled and halved
1	chicken or duck liver
2	eggs
2 1/2	tablespoons port wine
3	tablespoons flour
1/4	teaspoon Quatre Épices

1. Wash the brains, pull off the membranes, and soak the brains in salted cold water for 1 hour. Rinse and check that all the blood and membranes have been removed. Place in a 2- to 3-quart saucepan, cover with cold water, bring to a boil, *then remove at once.* Slip the brains into a bowl of cold water to stop the cooking. Drain well; sprinkle with vinegar, salt, and pepper and set aside to cool.

2. Line a 1 1/2-quart terrine with thin slices of pork fatback, allowing a 1 1/2-inch overhang around the sides. Set in the refrigerator to keep cold.

3. Preheat the oven to 375° F.

4. In the workbowl of a food processor fitted with the metal blade, coarsely grind the cubed pork fatback, pork, and veal in batches. Transfer to a mixing bowl. In the same workbowl, purée the garlic, shallots, and liver. Add to the ground meats and fat. Fold in the eggs, port wine, flour, Quatre Épices, 2 teaspoons salt, and 3/4 teaspoon pepper and mix thoroughly.

5. Pack the prepared terrine with half the meat mixture. Spread the brains on top and sprinkle with their juices. Cover with the remaining meat mixture, filling the terrine to the top. Fold the pork fatback strips over the filling. Cover tightly with a sheet of foil and the lid. Set the terrine in a pan filled with enough hot water to reach two thirds of the way up the sides of the terrine. Bake 1 hour and 10 minutes. Remove the foil; bake 30 minutes longer, or until the top is nicely browned. Remove the terrine from the oven and let stand 10 minutes. Re-cover with foil, weight the terrine with 2 or 3 heavy cans, and allow to cool. Remove the cans, cover the terrine with the lid or foil, and chill 3 to 4 days to ripen. Serve cool—not cold—with Sweet and Sour Cherries.

Inspired by a recipe from Lucien Vanel.

AIR-DRIED DUCK BREAST
"Jambon" de Magret

Fresh (not defrosted) duck breasts can be treated in the same manner as one cures a ham. The breasts are rubbed with salt and pepper, and are left to hang until firm and dry but not hard, about 8 to 10 days. The salt draws out the moisture that would harbor bacteria, and the air drying keeps it from deteriorating. In the South-West, the duck breasts are twice as large as those in the United States, so the process takes longer—12 to 15 days. The resulting "ham" is very flavorful and prosciutto-like in texture. It is served very thinly sliced with fresh figs, melon wedges, or a platter of antipasto-type vegetables.

The recipe is a creation of Jean-Louis Palladin. Many cooks have tried variations on this technique, such as smoking the breast after curing. I have a Catalan friend who makes a spicier version. He combines paprika, cayenne pepper, oil, and vinegar to make a thick paste he rubs on the flesh.

(continued)

SERVES 6 TO 8
☆ Prepare about 2 weeks in advance
ACTIVE WORK: 20 to 30 minutes
CURING TIME: 8 to 10 days

> **1 whole fresh duck breast, with skin (each *magret* weighs about 5 ounces)**
> **1 1/2 teaspoons coarse (kosher) salt**
> **1/2 teaspoon finely cracked peppercorns**

1. See duck chapter for How to Bone a Duck Breast. Use the legs for some other purpose.

2. Gently rub the flesh and skin side of each breast half with salt and pepper. Place on a noncorrodible plate and refrigerate, uncovered, 24 hours.

3. THE FOLLOWING DAY, wipe each breast dry and wrap it in 3 or 4 double folds of clean, dry cheesecloth. Tie each end tightly with string and suspend the breasts in a cool, dry, airy place (but not the refrigerator) 8 to 10 days.

4. AFTER 5 DAYS, turn them upside down.

5. The duck breasts are ready when the fleshy sides feel very firm and the skin sides feel firm but there is some "give" when they are pressed.

6. Refrigerate in a suspended position until ready to unwrap. (They keep up to 1 week.) Slice the fleshy side on the diagonal, like smoked salmon. Serve as part of an antipasto, thinly sliced in a cold consommé with cubed melon balls, or with warm asparagus dressed with a light walnut oil vinaigrette. Odds and ends of the "ham" can be chunked and used like bacon or duck cracklings in a green salad.

VARIATION

Fresh goose breast can be substituted. Adjust salt, using 2 teaspoons for every 3/4 pound boned meat. Air-dry 2 weeks.

NOTE TO THE COOK
I suggest that city dwellers hang their wrapped duck breasts about 3 feet in front of a fan or air conditioner in such a way that the breasts don't touch each other and swing free.

HOT APPETIZERS

HOT OYSTERS WITH VEGETABLES AND FOIE GRAS
Huîtres Chaudes au Foie Gras

The traditional way to eat oysters in Bordeaux is to follow each one with a piece of spicy, warm sausage and a glass of white Graves. The idea is to cleanse the taste buds of salt from the oysters so as not to interfere with the flavor of a good wine. In this recipe, Bordeaux chef Jean-Marie Amat "plays back" this Bordeaux tradition with cool irony: he serves the oysters warm and the foie gras chilled. The harmony is marvelously sophisticated. The dish should be accompanied by a sweet wine such as a Sauternes or a Barsac.

Ideally, buy imported *foie gras mi-cuit* or a good-quality canned foie gras (a block or pieces, not pâté)—brands such as Labeyrie, Petrossian, Rougié, or Bizac. If canned foie gras is unavailable, use a top-quality imported liver mousse or pâté.

SERVES 6
ACTIVE WORK: 20 minutes

> 1/4 cup julienned carrots (1 1/2 × 1/16-inch strips)
> Salt
> 12 tiny, tender green beans, split lengthwise, or 6 larger green beans, quartered lengthwise
> 1/2 pound *foie gras mi-cuit,* or 1 can (7 1/2 ounces) foie gras, chilled or substitute a liver mousse or pâté
> 12 shucked oysters, with 1/2 cup of their liquor
> 3 tablespoons heavy cream
> 7 tablespoons unsalted butter
> 1 tablespoon strained fresh lemon juice
> Pinch of white pepper

1. Blanch carrots in boiling salted water for about 30 seconds until crisp-tender. Remove and refresh to stop the cooking; drain.

2. Blanch green beans in boiling salted water for about 30 seconds. Refresh to stop the cooking; remove to kitchen terry towel to drain. Reserve vegetables for garnish.

3. Remove congealed fat from foie gras. Using a thin, sharp knife dipped in hot water and wiped dry, cut the foie gras into 3/8-inch slices. Arrange the slices in 6 individual 2/3-cup porcelain ramekins. Keep refrigerated. *Can be prepared ahead to this point.*

4. 15 MINUTES BEFORE SERVING, remove foie gras from the refrigerator. Gently reheat

vegetables with 2 teaspoons water in a small saucepan; drain thoroughly and keep warm.

5. Strain the oyster liquor through a double thickness of damp cheesecloth into a small saucepan. Bring to a simmer over moderate heat; add oysters and poach 15 seconds, until they are just cooked (opaque, with their edges just beginning to curl). With a slotted spoon, remove oysters and place 2 on top of each portion of foie gras.

6. JUST BEFORE SERVING, boil the oyster liquor over moderately high heat to reduce it quickly to about 1 tablespoon. Add the cream and reduce to 1 1/2 tablespoons. Whisk in the butter 1 tablespoon at a time. Bring to a boil, whisking constantly, then let the butter foam up for 5 seconds without stirring. Immediately pour into a small bowl. Add the lemon juice and the pepper. Season with salt, if necessary.

7. Spoon the warm sauce over the oysters and foie gras. Garnish with carrots and green beans and serve at once.

SAUTÉED DUCK HEARTS WITH GREEN GRAPES
Coeurs de Canard Poêlés aux Raisins Verts

In an effort to use up every part of the duck, here is a quick meal for one, a special treat for the fatigued cook who has just cut up three or four ducks. Do not substitute chicken hearts.

SERVES 1

ACTIVE WORK: 20 minutes (if you peel the grapes)

> **3–4 duck hearts**
> **1 tablespoon duck fat or unsalted butter**
> **Salt and freshly ground pepper**
> **1/2 cup Rich Dark Duck Stock or 1 cup poultry stock reduced by half**
> **20 green grapes (peeled, if you like)**
> **Red wine vinegar**
> **A piece of toasted crusty bread, lightly rubbed with garlic**

1. Rinse the duck hearts; pat dry.

2. In a small skillet, gently sauté the duck hearts in hot fat about 1 minute, stirring occasionally. Sprinkle with salt and pepper. Blot away the fat.

3. Add the stock, cover, and simmer gently 5 minutes. Boil down, uncovered, until pan juices are reduced by half. Add the grapes, toss the ingredients, and cook 3 or 4 seconds to heat through. Swirl in a few drops of vinegar and serve at once with crusty bread.

DUCK LIVER FLANS WITH CARAMEL VINEGAR SAUCE
Flans aux Foies de Volailles, Sauce de Vinaigre
Caramélisée

This dish, taught to me by Jean-Louis Palladin, is one of the most popular I have presented in my classes. Many other versions have cropped up elsewhere since I began teaching in 1978, but this is the original.

You can substitute chicken livers for duck livers, or mix duck, goose, and chicken livers together. Do not be tempted to mix the eggs, milk, and cream in a food processor; the resulting flans will not be as silky and tender. Also be sure to cook the flans at a low temperature to avoid unsightly holes.

SERVES 5 TO 6

ACTIVE WORK: 20 minutes
COOKING TIME: 20 minutes

> 4 duck livers, or 5 blond chicken livers, cleaned and soaked in milk a minimum of 3 hours
> Salt and freshly ground white pepper
> 1 teaspoon Armagnac or Madeira
> 1 1/2 teaspoons unsalted butter
> 1 tablespoon Duck Demi-Glace or Game Red-Wine-Flavored Demi-Glace
> 1 small clove garlic, peeled
> Pinch of freshly grated nutmeg
> 1 egg yolk at room temperature
> 3 whole eggs at room temperature
> 1 1/2 cups milk, heated and kept warm
> 1/2 cup heavy cream

Caramel Vinegar Sauce

> 1 cup red wine vinegar
> 3 1/2 tablespoons sugar
> 1 1/4 cups Duck Demi-Glace or Game Red-Wine-Flavored Demi-Glace
> 1/2 cup heavy cream

1. Drain livers; rinse under cold running water until water runs clear. Pick over the livers to remove green bile, fat, and sinews.

2. Marinate livers 1 to 2 hours in a mixture of 1/4 teaspoon salt, 1/8 teaspoon pepper, and the Armagnac or Madeira.

3. Lightly butter 5 or 6 (1/2-cup capacity) porcelain ramekins or molds. Arrange

them in a shallow pan lined with 2 or 3 layers of newspaper (slit newspaper in center to avoid swelling when wet). Set aside.

4. Preheat the oven to 325° F.

5. Place livers in the workbowl of a food processor fitted with the metal blade. Add Duck Demi-Glace, garlic, 1 teaspoon salt, 3/4 teaspoon pepper, and a sprinkling of nutmeg. Process 2 minutes. Transfer to a strainer set over a bowl; add egg yolk, whole eggs, milk, and cream. Strain; discard stringy egg albumen and any liver strands.

6. Boil water to be poured into baking pan for a bain-marie. Carefully ladle equal amounts of flan mixture, stirring after each addition, to not quite fill each ramekin or mold. Place bain-marie on center oven rack. Remove one mold and carefully pour enough boiling water in baking pan to come halfway up the sides of the molds. Return mold. Bake 20 minutes or until flans feel firm when lightly prodded with two fingers. If the flans are not set, turn off heat and let stand in the oven 5 to 10 minutes longer. (Different-shaped molds and cups require different cooking times.) Remove the bain-marie from the oven and let molds stand in the water 10 minutes longer before turning out. *Can be prepared 2 to 3 hours ahead up to this point* (flans can be gently reheated in the molds in a bain-marie).

7. Meanwhile make the sauce. In a heavy, deep 2-quart saucepan (not aluminum), cook vinegar and sugar to a caramel over medium heat. Swirl in the red wine sauce or the Demi-Glace; bring to a boil. Add the cream, but do not stir (the cream will be "swallowed up" by the sauce). Boil vigorously 5 minutes, or until the surface is full of tight bubbles—avoid overspills. Stir gently until you can catch a glimpse of the bottom of the pan; remove from heat at once.

8. Season to taste with pepper and a shot or two of vinegar; sauce should be more acidic and peppery than sweet. Spoon hot sauce around turned-out flans (sauce can be kept hot in a double boiler to avoid hardening).

NOTES TO THE COOK

1. This sauce is delicious on Broiled Duck Breasts.

2. To turn out all the molds onto a single warmed serving platter: place a wide spatula over the first mold; with spatula holding the flan in place, invert mold over serving dish. Slip the spatula from underneath, leaving the flan and mold in place. Lift off the mold. Repeat with remaining molds. Serve warm.

STUFFED DUCK NECK IN BRIOCHE
Cou de Canard Farci en Brioche

This is my own version of the South-West classic stuffed goose (or duck) neck, usually stuffed with ground pork, truffles, and foie gras.

You can transform two pair of raw duck legs and thighs or one pair of duck breasts into this delicious variation. In this Gascon-inspired recipe, the stuffing is wrapped in the neck skin, roasted, and cooled. Then it is skinned (the skin is too tough when served this way, but it can be sautéed and used as cracklings in a salad) and wrapped in brioche. With the red wine sauce, this makes a most distinctive first course dish.

Instead of enclosing the stuffed duck in pastry, you can cook it the way you do for *confit* of duck by poaching in rendered goose or duck fat to cover. (You can do this at the same time you are cooking other *confits*.) See variation below.

SERVES 6
☆ Begin the brioche 1 day in advance
ACTIVE WORK: 1 hour
ROASTING TIME: 1 1/2 hours
BAKING TIME: 40 minutes

   3/4 **pound Brioche Dough**
     2 **pair duck legs with thighs, or 1 pair duck breasts**
     6 **ounces boneless pork (about 70 percent lean), cut into 1-inch cubes**
     1 **medium shallot, peeled and sliced**
     1 **clove garlic, peeled and halved**
       Salt and freshly ground pepper
       Pinch of crumbled thyme leaves
  1/4 **small bay leaf, crumbled**
     1 **egg**
     1 **tablespoon Armagnac or Cognac**
     1 **can (4–5 ounces) purée de foie gras or top-quality liver pâté**
     1 **medium carrot, cut up**
     1 **medium onion, halved**
     1 **cup full-bodied red wine such as a Petite Sirah or Côtes-du-Rhône**
       Egg glaze (1 whole egg mixed with 1 teaspoon milk or cream)
       Flour
     1 **cup Demi-Glace**
     4 **tablespoons unsalted butter plus extra for buttering the mold**

(continued)

1. Make the Brioche Dough 1 day in advance. Allow to rest overnight in the refrigerator.

2. Remove skin in large pieces from the duck parts and cut away all excess fat. (Sprinkle with salt, pepper, and Armagnac if planning to use this recipe without the brioche wrapping.)

3. Bone the duck legs and thighs, or the breasts. Trim off all excess fat as well as the tendons.

4. In the workbowl of a food processor fitted with the metal blade, chop duck meat and pork cubes with a few quick on-off turns. Add shallots, garlic, 3/4 teaspoon salt, 1/4 teaspoon pepper, and herbs. Process until the mixture is coarsely but evenly ground.

5. With the machine on, add the egg and 1 tablespoon Armagnac or Cognac.

6. Turn off the machine, add the purée de foie gras, and process on and off 2 or 3 times, scraping down the mixture in between processing. *Can be prepared ahead (even a day in advance) up to this point;* cover mixture and refrigerate.

7. Spread out the duck skins, with the outer side down, in a large rectangle. Sew pieces together if necessary with kitchen string. Pile the ground mixture in a cylinder shape down the center. Wrap mixture completely with duck skins; cut away excess skin. Skewer and/or tie the roll with kitchen string.

8. Preheat the oven to 350° F. Crack the duck bones into small pieces and scatter in a small roasting pan along with the carrots and onions. Place the duck roll, seam side up, on a rack above the bones and roast 1 1/2 hours, basting the roll with the pan juices to keep it moist. Remove and allow to cool. Remove and discard the skin.

9. Pour off the duck fat from the roasting pan; add the wine and deglaze. Add 1/2 cup water and cook slowly on top of stove or in the oven 30 minutes, stirring occasionally.

10. Strain the pan juices into a heavy saucepan; discard the bones and vegetables after pressing down to extract all their juices. Remove fat that surfaces. Bring pan juices to a boil. Place half over a stove burner to cook and reduce 20 minutes. Adjust heat so that the side over the heat slowly boils and the fat and any other impurities in the sauce rise on the cooler side. Skim frequently. Reduce to 1/4 cup. *Can be prepared ahead early in the day up to this point.*

11. ABOUT 3 1/2 HOURS BEFORE SERVING, roll out the cold Brioche Dough into a rectangle large enough to enclose the duck roll. Brush the cold duck roll with egg glaze and dust lightly with flour. Brush the dough with egg glaze.

12. Place the duck roll in the center of the dough and bring the sides of dough up around to cover; press edges together to seal. Roll out the dough at each end to lengthen. Fold the two end flaps over the seam and press the ends together so that they are joined. There should be much more dough on top than around the sides or bottom. (The duck roll sinks when cooking.) Invert into a well-buttered 9×5-inch loaf pan. Let the dough rise in a warm (about 85° F.) place away from drafts until it rises to the top of the pan and feels light and puffy, about 2 to 2 1/4 hours.

13. 1 1/4 HOURS BEFORE SERVING, preheat the oven to 450° F. Place a baking sheet on the lower middle oven shelf.

14. Brush dough with egg glaze and draw lines crosswise with snips from a pair of scissors, going 1/8 inch down into the dough. Let stand 5 minutes. Set the prepared loaf pan on the hot baking sheet and bake 10 minutes. Lower oven temperature to 375° F. and bake 30 minutes longer, or until the brioche is cooked and beautifully browned. If the top browns too fast, cover loosely with a sheet of foil. If it rises unevenly, poke a skewer into the puffy side.

15. Remove from oven; let rest 10 minutes before turning out onto a rack. Let rest an additional 10 minutes before cutting.

16. Meanwhile reheat the pan juices; add the Demi-Glace and simmer 5 minutes, stirring. Remove from heat and whisk in the 4 tablespoons butter, bit by bit. Correct seasoning.

17. Cut the pâté into slices, using a serrated knife. Spoon a few tablespoons of sauce around each slice. Serve the pâté while still warm.

Preserved Duck Neck with *Sauce Périgueux*

Preserved stuffed necks can be used for pot-au-feu (in which they are sensational) or may be crisped brown in hot fat in a covered skillet, to be served hot or cold in winter with a bitter green salad with a walnut oil dressing, and in summer with romaine and soft lettuce seasoned with fresh herbs. Other accompaniments can be Puréed Sorrel, sautéed potatoes and tart apples, or a traditional *Sauce Périgueux* (recipe below).

1. Prepare stuffing as in preceding recipe.

2. Make a patchwork of duck skins and sew them together to make one large piece. Roll stuffing in skin and sew to enclose completely. Slip roll into melted poultry fat to cover and cook until it rises to the surface, usually 30 to 45 minutes. Remove and drain.

3. If using a goose neck, singe the skin over an open flame. Peel the skin from the neck in one piece without tearing. Fill with stuffing, sew, and cook in fat until the neck rises to the surface. Preserved stuffed duck or goose neck can be stored in fat.

Sauce Périgueux

This is a light, elegant sauce, a wonderful accompaniment to a fine beef roast or *confit* of duck neck. The truffle enhances the flavor of this very simple version of the famous sauce.

MAKES 1 1/2 CUPS (SERVES 6)
ACTIVE WORK: 15 to 20 minutes
UNATTENDED SIMMERING TIME: 50 minutes

(continued)

        2 cups dry white wine
        1/4 cup finely chopped cured ham such as *jambon de Bayonne*, prosciutto,
            or Westphalian ham
        1/4 cup crumbled dried cèpes
        2 tablespoons finely chopped shallots
        2/3 cup Madeira wine
    1 1/2 cups Demi-Glace flavored with 2 tomatoes, degreased
        1 medium canned truffle and the liquor
      2–3 tablespoons unsalted butter, cut into small pieces
            Salt and freshly ground pepper

1. In a noncorrodible saucepan combine wine, ham, cèpes, and shallots; bring to a boil. Lower heat and reduce to a glaze, about 30 minutes.

2. Add 1/2 cup of the Madeira and boil down to a glaze. Add the Demi-Glace and simmer 15 to 20 minutes to blend flavors.

3. Strain through several layers of cheesecloth, pressing down on the ingredients to release all their flavor. You should have about 1 1/3 cups sauce base. (Can be chilled and kept 1 to 2 days in the refrigerator or frozen at this point.)

4. Reheat sauce base to a simmer. Finely dice the truffle; add truffle, truffle liquor from the can, and remaining Madeira. Simmer 1 to 2 minutes without boiling. Remove from the heat and swirl in the butter. Add salt and pepper to taste and serve.

SNAILS

The snails of the South-West are quite different from the fat snails of Burgundy we associate with French cuisine. They are smaller, like our own native garden snails, and South-West gastronomes consider them tastier than the Burgundian variety because they have feasted on the berry bushes of the Pyrenees.

I have seen some imported snails from Morocco on sale in New York's Chinatown that resemble the *petits gris* of the South-West. If you buy fresh snails you have to purge them of any toxic plants and fatten them up on aromatic herbs mixed with cornmeal for two weeks while keeping them in a closed box. Then they should be washed many times in salted, vinegar-tinged water, and rinsed well before cooking. An easier solution is simply to buy canned snails—all you have to do is drain them.

Snails are taken very seriously in the Catalan country where they are called *cargols*. In the late spring they are eaten at a kind of picnic called a *cargolada*. About eight days before, hundreds of *petits gris* snails are gathered after a rain, stored in cages made from vine cuttings, and left to starve for eight days to rid them of impurities. Long tables are set up outdoors, and everyone invited takes part in the cooking. Some people scrub the snails, others arrange them open side up on wire grills over a fire made from dried vine cuttings (which will impart a special fragrance), and still others season them at their openings, midway in the cooking, with salt and crushed chili pepper called *pebrina*. Literally hundreds of snails are cooked this way over smoldering embers, face up to the sky. As the snails cook, they sizzle, crack, and spit as someone sprinkles a few drops of melted hot pork fat into each shell to keep the snail meat moist. After ten minutes or so the snails are taken off the grill, removed from their shells one by one with tiny skewers, and eaten with country bread smeared with *aïoli*, a garlic mayonnaise. The snails are usually followed by grilled lamb chops and sausages, washed down with a great amount of full-bodied snoozing wine.

SNAILS WITH COUNTRY HAM AND GARLIC
Escargots à la Caudéran

This is a superb dish, happily free of all the problems usually associated with snails: heaviness, toughness, and the excuse to eat garlic, since, the myth goes, snails have no taste of their own. Snails *do* have flavor, though they do also need seasoning. But they needn't be overwhelmed, and they should certainly not be boiled in garlic butter; boiling toughens them, butter makes the dish too heavy, and too much garlic obscures the flavor of the snails instead of enhancing it.

This recipe from Bordeaux takes all these problems into account. The result is a tender, succulent dish of snails enrobed in a gentle garlic-shallot sauce, lightened with *un*cooked butter, scented with Pernod, garnished with bits of country ham, and sprinkled with herbs.

SERVES 4 TO 6
ACTIVE WORK: 10 minutes
COOKING TIME: 15 to 18 minutes

> 1 (7 1/2-ounce) can French or Taiwanese snails (24 large snails)
> 2 teaspoons rendered pork fat or butter
> 1 1/2 tablespoons finely chopped *jambon de Bayonne,* prosciutto, or Westphalian ham
> 2 tablespoons finely chopped shallots
> 1/2 cup dry white wine
> 1/2 cup well-reduced meat or poultry stock
> 1 teaspoon crumbled fresh thyme or 1/4 teaspoon dried
> 1 tablespoon finely chopped garlic (chopped by hand, not with a food processor)
> Salt and freshly ground pepper
> 1 tablespoon chopped fresh parsley
> 1 red-ripe tomato, peeled, seeded, and cubed
> 2 teaspoons Pernod
> 6 tablespoons unsalted butter, at room temperature

1. Drain the snails; rinse in fresh water and set aside to drain.
2. Heat the fat in a skillet. Add the ham and the shallots and cook over medium-low heat 5 minutes without browning. Tilt the pan; press on the ham and shallots

with a slotted spoon and mop up the exuded fat with a paper towel. Deglaze the pan with white wine and boil down to a glaze.

3. Add the stock, thyme, and garlic; simmer, covered, 10 minutes. *Can be prepared 1 to 2 hours ahead up to this point;* uncover and set aside, then reheat gently.

4. Add the snails; cover and allow to heat through. Do not allow the cooking juices to boil or the snails will toughen.

5. Add the pepper, parsley, tomato, and Pernod. Cook, stirring, 1 minute. Adjust seasoning; "snails like salt," but remember that the ham can be salty. Swirl in the butter both on and off the heat, and serve at once with French bread.

SNAILS WITH WALNUTS
Escargots aux Noix

Walnuts can be a problem because so often they're either dry or old. French housewives have two tricks for reviving them: they soak them in sugared water or hot milk overnight, or they gently toast them in a skillet to release their natural oils.

SERVES 4
ACTIVE WORK: 10 minutes
COOKING TIME: 5 to 10 minutes

1 cup Crème Fraîche or heavy cream
1 7 1/2 ounce can French or Taiwanese snails (24 large snails)
3 tablespoons dry white wine
4 tablespoons unsalted butter, softened
2 tablespoons chopped *fines herbes* (see Note)
2 tablespoons fresh lemon juice
3/4 teaspoon salt
1/8 teaspoon freshly ground pepper
Pinch of freshly grated nutmeg
1/2 cup coarsely chopped walnuts

1. Place Crème Fraîche in a funnel lined with coffee filter paper and let drain until reduced to 3/4 cup, about 3 hours. Or reduce heavy cream by boiling to 3/4 cup. Refrigerate until ready to use.

2. Drain snails and toss with wine in a small bowl. Cover and refrigerate.

3. Place 3 tablespoons of the softened butter in a shallow bowl; cream with a wooden spoon. Gradually work in *fines herbes*, lemon juice, salt, pepper, and nutmeg; reserve. *Can be prepared ahead up to this point.*

4. 20 MINUTES BEFORE SERVING, remove snails from refrigerator.

5. 5 MINUTES BEFORE SERVING, melt remaining butter in medium skillet over medium heat; stir in walnuts and reduce heat to low. Toss walnuts until aromatic, about 3 minutes. Stir in Crème Fraîche or heavy cream. Increase heat and bring to a boil, stirring constantly. Add snails and wine; stir until mixture almost boils. Remove from heat.

6. Swirl in reserved seasoned butter mixture, 1 tablespoon at a time, until sauce is thick and well blended. Return skillet to low heat to reheat gently, 15 to 20 seconds (overheating will separate sauce). Taste and correct seasoning, adding salt and pepper if necessary.

7. Spoon 6 snails into each of 4 hot ramekins; divide sauce equally among them. Serve immediately.

NOTE TO THE COOK
Fines herbes is a mixture of fresh parsley, chives, tarragon, and chervil. At least 2 of the herbs should be fresh and the others can be dried if fresh are not available.

Inspired by a recipe from Lucien Vanel.

ASPARAGUS WITH ASPARAGUS SAUCE
Asperges, Sauce Coulis d'Asperges

This recipe was inspired by an asparagus sauce served with a grilled *foie gras de canard* that I ate at Michel Guérard's restaurant at Eugénie-les-Bains in the Landes. There the sauce was made with lukewarm puréed asparagus mounted with vinegar and oil in an electric blender. My recipe, a purée of asparagus skins mounted with butter and served warm over freshly cooked large asparagus spears, can be used to coat a mixture of other springtime vegetables such as baby carrots, turnips, mushroom caps, and, of course, the tips of young asparagus.

To peel or not to peel. A lot of people discard half of large asparagus spears because they find them tough and stringy. The solution, of course, is to peel the skin off the spears, but many people find this too much work. To those, I propose my dish; you will be able to make something out of the peelings that will enhance the taste of your asparagus, and at the same time you'll salvage the good vitamins that are concentrated in the peels.

A vegetable peeler really won't work very well when you peel asparagus; because of the tapering shape of the spears, you need to remove more skin from the bottom than from the top. There are two solutions to this problem: you can invest fifteen or so dollars in an asparagus peeler, or you can make a knife guide for your paring knife for fifteen cents. I am grateful to André Soltner of the restaurant Lutèce in New York for teaching me how to make this simple knife guide.

(continued)

To make the wire knife guide that can easily slip onto any thin-bladed knife, purchase a 15-inch length of 16-gauge wire. The wire should just bend with a small amount of pressure. Using your two index fingers, twirl each end toward the center, leaving about 1 1/4 inches of straight wire between two concentric circles (see diagram). If you are right-handed, slip the circles onto the blade so that the straightened wire is above and in front of its sharp side. There should be about a 1/8-inch margin between blade and wire to be adjusted as necessary to fit the thickness of the asparagus stalk. Lefties should fasten the circles so that the wire is below and in front of the blade.

SERVES 6

ACTIVE WORK: 25 minutes
COOKING TIME: 15 minutes

> **2 bunches fat, fresh asparagus, about 36 spears**
> **Salt**
> **1/2 cup (1 stick) unsalted butter, cut into small pieces (see Note)**
> **Freshly ground pepper**
> **Fresh lemon juice**
> **Pinch of sugar**

1. Line up the asparagus and cut away the tough bottoms—about 1 inch. (Breaking at the tender part of the asparagus is for pencil-thin types, which are not peeled.) Place one asparagus on work surface and, starting at the end, using the knife and guide, peel toward the tip. (Some people find it easier to work from the tip to the base of the spear.) The guide should just skim the top surface while the knife cuts away the thick peel. You will notice that the knife takes less peel as you near the tip. Peel on all sides. Drop into water to wash. Tie into bunches when all are peeled and wrap in a moist towel until ready to cook. If you prepare asparagus in advance, soak in ice water with 1 teaspoon salt and 1 teaspoon sugar to each 4 cups.

2. To make the sauce, cook the peels in boiling salted water until very soft (10 minutes). Drain, refresh, then purée until perfectly smooth in an electric blender, or push through the fine blade of a food mill. *Can be prepared ahead up to this point.*

3. In a small saucepan bring 3 tablespoons water to a boil and reduce by half. Quickly whisk in the butter, piece by piece over medium-high heat. The butter will

appear foamy. *It must not turn to oil*. When all the butter has been added, bring to a fast boil, whisking constantly, then let it boil 5 seconds. Immediately pour into a small bowl. Stir in the puréed asparagus peels and season with salt, pepper, and lemon juice to taste. A pinch of sugar will intensify the flavor and counteract any bitterness. The sauce can stand about 15 minutes. Reheat very gently.

4. To cook the asparagus, heat 1 1/2 inches of water in a deep, wide skillet. Add salt and bring to a boil. Slip in the bundles of asparagus and simmer 3 to 5 minutes, or until the asparagus are barely cooked. To test if they are done, lift out one bunch with a pair of tongs; if the ends fall slightly limp, they are ready to be transferred to a terry-cloth towel to drain. Cover with another towel. Set aside until ready to serve.

NOTE TO THE COOK

To ensure success when making the sauce, be sure to use AA-quality butter, which has a low water content.

VARIATIONS

In the Périgord, scrambled eggs cooked in goose fat are served with the thin asparagus that grow wild in the spring. The cultivated purple spears are cooked and served lukewarm with a walnut oil vinaigrette dressing. After cooking the spears, dry on towels, pressing lightly to extract excess water. Let marinate 10 to 15 minutes before serving.

In the Languedoc, cooked but still crunchy spears are served with a lovely and very simple dipping sauce held in an eggshell set in an eggcup. It is made with 3 1/2-minute eggs. For each serving, a freshly cooked egg is broken up and mixed with 1 tablespoon melted (but not cooked) fresh butter and seasoned with salt and pepper. Small warmed porcelain ramekins can easily be substituted.

CHEESE IN BRIOCHE
Le Gatis

A specialty of the town of St.-Affrique, this mixture of Cantal and Roquefort cheeses is served melting hot in a brioche crust. I love the rustic quality of this dish, delicious with a green salad, a slivered marinated red cabbage, soup, or as an accompaniment to fresh fruit. Serve it surrounded with slices of fresh pears and pineapple, green and black grapes, and small strawberries. Cantal is a French cheese from Auvergne; Canadian extra-old (9 months) Cheddar is a good substitute because it cooks well and doesn't draw threads, grates easily, and blends well with the buttery, blue-veined Roquefort to make a tasty filling.

(continued)

SERVES 4 TO 6
☆ Begin the brioche 1 day in advance
ACTIVE WORK: 20 minutes
RISING TIME: 2 hours
BAKING TIME: 20 minutes

    1 1/4 pounds Brioche Dough
          Flour
    5 1/2 ounces Cantal, aged Canadian Cheddar, or Monterey Jack cheese
    2 1/2 ounces Roquefort* with appellation of origin on package (a red oval mark with a sheep in the middle, "Roquefort" above it, and "France" below it)
          Egg glaze (1 whole egg mixed with 1 teaspoon milk)
          Unsalted butter

*If Roquefort is excessively salty, decrease the amount by one fourth.

1. Make the Brioche Dough 1 day in advance and allow to ripen and harden in the refrigerator.

2. Grate the Cantal or substitute cheese; set aside 2 tablespoons grated cheese.

3. Crush the Roquefort with a fork and blend with all but 2 tablespoons grated cheese.

4. ABOUT 2 3/4 HOURS BEFORE SERVING, roll out half the dough on a cold, lightly floured work surface to make a 7-inch round or square. Butter a 6-inch shallow earthen or metal pan (round or oval). Place the brioche dough in the pan. Crumble the combined cheese evenly over the dough, leaving a 3/4-inch margin all around.

5. With the remaining dough, make golf-ball-size balls and flatten each with the palm of your hand. Brush the edges of the dough in the pan with egg glaze. Arrange the flattened brioche rounds over the cheese side by side; press around the edges of the dish only. It does not matter if there is a little space between some of the rounds on the top; they will come together during the rising and baking. Cover loosely with buttered foil and set in a warm humid place for 2 hours, or until the dough has become light and springy.

6. Preheat the oven to 425° F. Set a baking sheet on the lower middle oven shelf so that it will become very hot. (This is not necessary if you have a stone tile permanently positioned on the shelf, as I do, which evens out the oven heat and also helps to sear the bottom of dough placed directly on it.)

7. Brush egg glaze over the brioche and scatter the reserved grated cheese on top.

8. Place the brioche on the hot baking sheet or tile and bake 10 minutes. Lower oven temperature to 350° F. and bake 10 minutes longer. Serve hot, in or out of the baking dish.

CHAPTER 6

LIGHT SUPPER DISHES

GREEN CHICKEN
Poule Verte

Whenever a chicken is stuffed (and it is *always* stuffed when poached whole in the South-West), enough extra filling is made to fill a basketball-shaped construction of overlapping cabbage leaves. Such a fabrication is called a *poule verte* or "green chicken." It is extremely popular in South-West France, where it may often be seen in the family kitchen bobbing like a big dumpling in a simmering pot of soup.

The *poule verte* is just further proof of the love of stuffings in this area of France. The best stuffings are made of stale bread that is half wheat, half rye. Cream is added for moisture, eggs for body so the stuffing can be sliced. And for firmness and extra flavor, pork or ham and veal are added along with a medley of herbs and spices.

SERVES 6
☆ Begin filling 1 day in advance
  ACTIVE WORK: 20 to 30 minutes
  COOKING TIME: 2 1/4 hours

(continued)

Filling

> 1/2 **pound dried bread with crust (about 3 cups torn pieces)**
> 3/4 **cup milk or cold stock**
> 5 **ounces lean pork, finely chopped**
> 4 **ounces fatback, puréed in food processor**
> 1/2 **pound lean veal, finely chopped**
> 1 **large shallot, finely chopped**
> 3 **cloves garlic, finely chopped**
> 1 1/4 **teaspoons salt**
> 1/2 **teaspoon freshly ground pepper**
> 8 **allspice berries, crushed**
> 1/4 **teaspoon grated nutmeg**
> 2 **tablespoons chopped fresh parsley**
> 1 1/2 **tablespoons chopped fresh chives**
> 3 **tablespoons heavy cream**
> 2 **eggs**
> 1 **tablespoon Armagnac**
>
> 1 **savoy or green cabbage**
> 5 **quarts of water and 2 chicken bouillon cubes or 5 quarts Chicken Stock**
> **Salt and freshly ground pepper**
> 24 **small potatoes**
> 4 **carrots, scraped and cut into 1-inch pieces**
> 6 **tablespoons unsalted butter, at room temperature**
> 2 **tablespoons snipped fresh chives and parsley, mixed**

1. 1 DAY IN ADVANCE, mix in a bowl all the ingredients for the filling except the Armagnac; blend well. Spread the Armagnac over the top; cover and refrigerate overnight to allow flavor to develop.

2. THE FOLLOWING DAY, carefully remove and discard the outer leaves from the cabbage, then cut out the core and discard. Drop whole cabbage into a pot of simmering salted water and cook 15 minutes or until the leaves separate easily; drain. Cool, then pull back leaves and separate. Trim away all hard ribs. (This makes it easier to shape the *poule*.)

3. Line a deep mixing bowl with damp cheesecloth or netting or a washed string shopping bag. Line with half the leaves, overlapping. Place the filling in the center and cover with the remaining leaves to completely enclose. The *poule verte* should have the shape of a basketball. Tie up the cheesecloth or netting. *Can be prepared a few hours ahead up to this point;* cover and refrigerate.

4. 2 1/2 HOURS BEFORE SERVING, bring *poule* to room temperature if refrigerated. In a very large wide-mouthed pot, bring 5 quarts water or stock to a boil. Add the

bouillon cubes if using them. Lower the *poule verte* into the liquid. The liquid must cover it completely. If it doesn't, add boiling water to cover. Cover pot, lower heat, and simmer 1 1/2 hours.

5. After *poule* has simmered 1 1/2 hours, transfer 4 cups of the cooking liquid to a 3-quart saucepan. (Continue simmering the *poule* in remaining liquid 30 minutes.) Quickly degrease, then cook the potatoes and carrots in it until tender. Reduce this cooking liquid to 3 cups. Adjust the seasoning.

6. Check *poule* after simmering 2 hours. To tell if it is fully cooked, stick a larding needle or thin metal skewer into the center and leave 1 minute. Remove and place the point of the needle on your palm. If the point is burning hot, the *poule verte* is fully cooked. Remove *poule* and set in a colander over a bowl to drain. Keep moist and warm until ready to serve.

7. Cut the *poule* into wedges and place a wedge in each individual serving dish. Garnish with carrots and potatoes. To each dish, add 3/4 cup of the reduced cooking liquid in which the carrots and potatoes were cooked, and 1 tablespoon soft butter. Sprinkle with fresh herbs and serve at once.

CROUSTADE OF DUCK *CONFIT* WITH APPLES
Croustade de Confit de Canard aux Pommes en l'Air

The pastry used for this and similar dishes in South-West France is much like strudel dough; it is called *voile de mariée* or bridal veil. Phyllo leaves can easily be substituted. In this particular pie, the rich flavor of the *confit* goes beautifully with the astringent taste of tart green apples. If your apples are too sweet after sautéing, add a few drops of vinegar or lemon juice to reestablish the proper balance of flavors. (In the South-West, the home cook will add *verjus*, the juice of crushed sour grapes.) For a version made without the pastry crust see the recipe for Duck *Confit* with Sautéed Apples.

SERVES 4 TO 6
ACTIVE WORK: 30 minutes
BAKING TIME: 25 to 30 minutes

> 4 thigh-drumstick portions *Confit* of Duck
> 2 tablespoons fat from *confit*
> 4 tart green apples, such as Granny Smith or Pippins
> Freshly ground pepper
> Salt
> 1/3 cup clarified butter
> 6–8 leaves phyllo dough, thawed slowly in the refrigerator if frozen, and
>   kept covered with damp towel

1. AT LEAST 4 HOURS BEFORE BEGINNING MAIN PREPARATION, set out crock of *confit* in warm room or deep pan of water to soften fat.

2. When fat is softened, remove thigh-drumstick pieces. Carefully scrape off fat clinging to pieces; reserve 2 tablespoons.

3. In steamer basket over boiling water, steam duck pieces, covered, 10 minutes. Set pieces aside to cool.

4. Pare and core apples; cut into 1/4-inch slices. Heat the 2 tablespoons reserved *confit* fat in heavy medium skillet over fairly high heat to rippling. Add apple slices; sauté, tossing to coat well with duck fat, 2 to 3 minutes. Season with pepper and a very little salt. Set aside to cool.

5. Remove skin, bones, and any gristle from duck pieces. Cut meat into chunks; season with pepper. Reserve.

6. Brush a deep 9-inch quiche pan or medium-deep 9-inch round cake pan with a little of the clarified butter. Working with one phyllo leaf at a time and keeping remainder covered with damp kitchen towel, line pan with 5 to 7 phyllo leaves arranged in an overlapping pattern, with half of each leaf hanging over edge of pan on one side like a piece of tissue-paper wrapping, the other half evenly covering bottom of pan. As each leaf is arranged in the pan, drizzle with a little clarified butter before adding next one. Reserve one leaf, covered with damp kitchen towel.

7. Spread duck pieces evenly over phyllo leaves in pan; drain apples and arrange over duck. Fold overhanging half-leaves over top of pie to cover and enclose filling. Brush with clarified butter. Place reserved leaf on top; brush all over with more clarified butter. Tuck neatly around outer rim; lightly brush top with butter. Carefully pour any remaining butter around edges. *Can be prepared 1 to 2 hours ahead up to this point;* cover and refrigerate.

8. Preheat the oven to 400° F.

9. Bake 15 minutes. Remove pan from oven; shake to loosen pie. Pour off excess butter; invert onto large buttered baking sheet. Pierce top in two or three places with fork to allow steam to escape. Return to oven; continue baking 10 to 12 minutes, or until crisp and golden brown. Invert onto serving plate and serve hot, lukewarm, or cold, accompanied by a salad.

DUCK *CONFIT* WITH SAUTÉED APPLES
Confit de Canard aux Pommes en l'Air

An excellent version of the preceding recipe can be made without the pastry.

SERVES 4 TO 6
ACTIVE WORK: 20 minutes

> **4 tablespoons grape-seed or peanut oil**
> **1 tablespoon wine vinegar**

1. Follow directions for removing *confit* pieces from crock and sautéing apples (Steps 1, 2, and 4); do not steam duck as in Step 3. Arrange apples in serving dish and keep hot.

2. In large, nonstick skillet with a tight-fitting lid, heat 2 tablespoons *confit* fat and 2 tablespoons grape-seed or peanut oil over medium-high heat until rippling. Add 2 *confit* pieces, skin side down. Cover tightly; cook 3 minutes. During cooking, remove lid 2 or 3 times and carefully wipe off surface moisture clinging to underside, and shake pan to make sure *confit* is not sticking. When skin is well browned, remove skillet from heat; let stand, tightly covered, 30 seconds. Uncover, turn each *confit* piece skin side up, and cook, uncovered, over moderate heat about 30 seconds longer. Remove to wire racks or brown paper bag to drain. Pour off fat from skillet. Add 2 tablespoons *confit* fat and remaining oil to skillet and repeat with the remaining *confit* of duck.

3. Place drained *confit* pieces over sautéed apples slices. Pour off all but 1 tablespoon fat in skillet. Add 1 tablespoon wine vinegar to fat remaining in skillet; boil quickly over high heat to blend. Season with freshly ground pepper; pour over hot *confit* pieces and apples just before serving.

CABBAGE CAKE WITH SAUSAGE
El Trinxat Cerda

This recipe is from a Catalan cookbook—it's made with white butifarra sausage composed of lean pork, fat pork belly, and flavored with cinnamon, nutmeg, cloves, marjoram, and cayenne. Toulouse Sausage seasoned with the same aromatics substitutes well, and so does fresh sausage from the butcher. Double blanching makes the cabbage lighter and easier to digest. The cake is perfectly cooked when the outside is crusty and the inside soft, like a purée.

MAKES 1 10-INCH CAKE (SERVES 6)

TOTAL PREPARATION TIME: 1 hour

> 3 **pounds savoy cabbage**
> **Salt**
> 1 **bay leaf**
> 1 **tablespoon coarse (kosher) salt**
> 1/4 **cup homemade rendered lard or clarified butter**
> 1/4 **pound thick-sliced bacon, cut into 1/2-inch cubes**
> 8 **ounces fresh sausage**
> 1/2–1 **teaspoon freshly ground pepper**
> **Red wine vinegar**
> **Thin-sliced country rye or whole wheat bread**

1. Discard outer leaves of cabbage. Wash cabbage, quarter, and discard inner core. Bring plenty of water to a boil in a large saucepan over high heat. Add cabbage, return water to a boil, and cook 5 minutes. Drain cabbage well.

2. Bring fresh water to a boil. Add bay leaf, salt, and drained cabbage; cook 10 minutes, then drain. Rinse cabbage under cold running water and drain again. Squeeze cabbage thoroughly dry and chop coarsely.

3. Heat half the fat or butter in skillet over medium-high heat. Add bacon and cook until lightly browned. Add cabbage and toss to coat thoroughly. Set aside.

4. Prick sausage with a fork. Combine sausage and 1/3 cup water in a medium saucepan over medium heat. Cover and steam 10 minutes. Drain sausage well and let cool. Cut diagonally into 1/3-inch slices and set aside. *Can be prepared ahead up to this point.*

5. Place cabbage mixture over medium heat and cook until heated through, about 5 minutes. Add sausage and pepper and mix well. Press mixture into flat cake. Cover skillet and fry 10 minutes, shaking pan often to avoid sticking.

6. Wipe inside of cover dry, grease lightly, then slide cake, crisp side down, onto the greased lid and hold for an instant. Meanwhile add remaining fat to the pan and raise heat. Then return the cabbage cake, crisp side up, to the pan and fry, uncovered, until bottom is crisp and golden, about 10 minutes. Lightly sprinkle with vinegar just before serving. Serve warm with slices of bread.

BASQUE RICE
Riz Gachucua

The word *gachucua* means "pretty to look at" in Basque. This is a wonderful, light supper dish to be served with grilled meat and a crisp salad. Make it ahead and reheat, but don't add the fresh tomatoes, parsley, and vinegar until ready to serve.

SERVES 3 TO 4
ACTIVE WORK: 15 minutes
COOKING TIME: 30 minutes

> 2 tablespoons mixed poultry fat and olive oil
> 1 cup long-grain rice
> 1 cup chopped yellow onion
> 1/2 cup chopped carrot
> 2 1/4 cups unsalted meat or poultry stock, hot
> 1 teaspoon finely chopped and crushed garlic
> 1/4 pound Spanish chorizo or Hungarian paprika sausage, in 1 piece
> 1/4 teaspoon salt
> 3 ounces thick-sliced smoked bacon, cut into tiny lardons (thin strips)
> 1 1/2 cups cubed Italian frying peppers or substitute bell peppers
> 1 1/2 tablespoons finely cubed hot red chili pepper, cored and seeded, or 2 tablespoons finely cubed fresh Hungarian-style hot pepper, cored and seeded
> 1 red-ripe tomato, seeded and cubed
> 1 tablespoon chopped fresh Italian parsley
> White wine vinegar (optional)

1. Preheat oven to 350° F.

2. Heat half the fat and oil in a 3-quart casserole or heavy saucepan. Add onions and carrots. Cover and cook slowly 5 minutes, then uncover and cook, stirring frequently, until beads of moisture evaporate.

3. Add rice and swirl to coat the grains. Add hot stock and bring to a boil, stirring.

4. Add garlic, sausage, and 1/4 teaspoon salt. Cover and bake in the oven 20 minutes.

5. Meanwhile cook the bacon over medium heat in the remaining fat and oil 2 to 3 minutes. Add the peppers and cook 10 minutes, tossing. Drain off fat.

6. Remove chorizo from rice and set aside. Lightly cover the rice with foil. Cut chorizo into thin slices. Fluff rice; add sliced chorizo, bacon bits, and peppers. *Can be prepared up to 1 hour ahead to this point.*

7. Scatter cubed tomato on top. Toss and reheat in oven 3 to 4 minutes. Serve hot with sprinkling of chopped parsley and, if desired, a very light sprinkling of vinegar to balance the richness of the dish.

THE PRIEST'S OMELET
L'Omelette du Curé

This is a wonderful dish to serve for lunch with a strong green salad. In South-West France, a "priest's omelet" seems to be an omelet made from odds and ends, undoubtedly inspired by the austere life-style of the local priests. In Lucien Vanel's Toulouse kitchen, however, the odds and ends are cèpes, chicken livers, veal kidneys, and truffles, making this simple dish one of the most expensive on his menu. Because of the obvious expense involved, truffles are not included in this recipe. However, if you do happen to have a truffle but would rather not use it in an omelet, Vanel suggests placing the truffle with the eggs, in their shells, in an airtight sealed box overnight. The truffle flavor will permeate the egg, and your truffle will remain unscathed.

SERVES 3 OR 4
ACTIVE WORK: 30 minutes
COOKING TIME: 20 minutes

>   2 **duck livers or 3 chicken livers**
>   1/3 **cup milk, lightly salted**
>   1/2 **cup unsalted Chicken Stock, degreased**
>   1/2 **ounce imported dried cèpes, porcini, or 3/4 cup sliced canned cèpes (see Appendix)**
>   **Salt**
>   1 **veal kidney (about 10 ounces) or 2 small kidneys**
>   6 **large fresh eggs, at room temperature**
>   3 **tablespoons olive oil or rendered poultry fat**
>   1/4 **teaspoon finely chopped garlic**
>   2 **teaspoons finely chopped fresh parsley**
>   **Freshly ground pepper**
> 3 1/2 **tablespoons unsalted butter**
> 1 1/2 **tablespoons Madeira or white port wine**
>   **Freshly grated nutmeg**

1. 3 HOURS BEFORE MAIN PREPARATION (OR THE DAY BEFORE), place livers in a small bowl; pour lightly salted milk over livers. Refrigerate, covered, at least 3 hours or overnight.

2. Place Chicken Stock in small saucepan; bring to a boil. Boil until stock is reduced to 2 tablespoons. Reserve.

3. Drain livers; discard milk. Remove tough connecting tissue with scissors or small knife. Rinse livers under cold water until water runs clear; pat dry with paper towels. Cut livers into 1-inch pieces.

4. Place dried mushrooms in small bowl. Cover with 2/3 cup hot water mixed with a pinch of salt; let soak until soft, about 30 minutes.

5. Peel membrane from kidney; cut lengthwise into quarters. Remove as much of fatty central core as possible. Cut each quarter into 3/4-inch pieces. Reserve.

6. Beat eggs in mixing bowl with fork until light, about 30 seconds. *Do not overbeat.* Strain eggs to remove strands of albumin.

7. Drain mushrooms through sieve lined with coffee filter paper; reserve liquid. Rinse mushrooms under cold running water to remove any grit; pat dry with paper towels. Cut off thick woody stems (discard or use for stock). Chop mushrooms into 1/4-inch pieces; reserve in medium bowl.

8. Heat 1 tablespoon oil or fat in heavy 10-inch skillet over medium-high heat until it begins to ripple. Add mushrooms; sauté, stirring constantly, 30 seconds. Reduce heat to medium-low; cook until all liquid evaporates, 2 to 3 minutes. Remove skillet from heat.

9. Stir in garlic and parsley. Season to taste with salt and pepper. Scrape into small bowl; reserve.

10. Heat 1 tablespoon butter in same skillet over medium-high heat. When foam subsides, add livers. Sauté, stirring, until livers are seared on all sides but remain pink inside, about 2 minutes. Scrape into bowl with mushrooms.

11. Heat 1 tablespoon butter in same skillet over medium-high heat. When butter "sings," add kidney pieces, a pinch of salt, and 2 grinds of pepper. Sauté over high heat, tossing frequently, until kidney pieces are seared on all sides but still pink inside, about 1 1/2 minutes. *Do not overcook.* Drain kidney pieces in small sieve; discard their juices. Wipe skillet dry with paper towels but do not wash it.

12. Heat Madeira or port in same skillet over medium heat. When wine is hot, carefully hold a long wooden kitchen match close to surface of wine until alcohol ignites. When flames are extinguished, add reserved mushroom liquid and reduced stock. Heat to boiling; boil until liquid is reduced to 3 tablespoons, about 4 minutes. Pour over mushrooms and livers. Add kidney pieces; toss to coat.

13. Fold eggs into kidney mixture. Season with salt, pepper, and nutmeg to taste. *Can be prepared 1 hour ahead up to this point.*

14. 3 TO 5 MINUTES BEFORE SERVING, heat heavy 10-inch skillet over medium-high heat. Add remaining 2 tablespoons oil or fat and heat to rippling. Pour in egg mixture; shake skillet back and forth to prevent sticking. Cook egg mixture, stirring with fork, 15 seconds. Continue to cook omelet until bottom and sides begin to congeal but top remains moist. Remove from heat. Cut remaining 1 1/2 tablespoons butter into small pieces and scatter on top of omelet; press in with back of fork. Slide half the omelet onto a large warm serving platter; using a large spatula as a guide, flip remaining half over it. Serve at once.

(continued)

Omelet with Dried Wild Mushrooms
Omelette aux Cèpes Secs

One of the most popular omelets is made with fresh cèpes. When only dried cèpes are on hand, a very fine variation can be made by following the recipe for Cèpes in the Style of Gascony. Blend eggs and cèpes together and let stand 30 minutes before cooking to allow flavors to mingle.

TRUFFLED SCRAMBLED EGGS
Oeufs Brouillés aux Truffes

In this dish the truffle is not merely decorative, nor is its purpose to convey a sense of luxury and ostentation. Gently heated with the eggs, it endows them with a fragrant taste and aroma.

These scrambled eggs have a creamy, almost curdless consistency, since they are cooked in the top of a double boiler or in a heatproof bowl set over simmering water. Almost a tablespoon of butter per egg makes for a rich dish, but served in small quantities in little porcelain ramekins, these eggs make a mouth-watering light supper dish or first course.

Be sure to cut the truffles into very small cubes so that you can eat a little bit with each spoonful of scrambled egg. And remember the Quercy tradition "The truffle is a delicate lady"—apart from salt, no other seasoning except a hint of pepper is needed when teaming it up with rich food.

SERVES 6 TO 8
ACTIVE WORK: 15 to 20 minutes

    2 canned black truffles, peeled if necessary
  10 jumbo eggs
6–8 tablespoons unsalted butter
1/2 teaspoon fine salt
    Pinch of white pepper
    2 tablespoons heavy cream

1. 1 HOUR BEFORE SERVING, dice 1 truffle. Cut the other into 8 or 10 thin slices and reserve.

2. Break the eggs into a fine wire sieve set over a bowl. Gently crush yolks with the back of a wooden spoon. Let them drip (takes about 1 hour).

3. Lightly butter the insides and bottom of the top of a double boiler or a 2-quart heatproof glass or porcelain bowl set over a saucepan half filled with simmering water. Add the eggs and 2 tablespoons of the butter. Cook, stirring constantly with a rubber or wooden spatula, over barely simmering heat 1 to 2 minutes.

4. Add salt and pepper and cook, stirring, 7 to 8 minutes longer, being sure to move the spatula along the sides and bottom of the pan where the eggs tend to settle. Rather than stirring in circles all the time, make a figure eight through the eggs. Gradually add the remaining butter, tablespoon by tablespoon. Add the truffle liquid.

5. When the eggs begin to hold together with as few curds as possible but are still very creamy, stir a little faster. Whisk in the cream and the diced truffles. Cook 1 minute longer.

6. Spoon equal amounts of egg into 6 to 8 small warmed ramekins. Garnish each serving with 1 truffle slice.

VARIATION

These scrambled eggs are so delicious you might want to try them without truffles. Substitute for the truffles 1/3 cup of 1/4-inch croutons made from crustless white bread. Make them golden brown by dropping them into 1/2 cup very hot clarified butter in a small skillet. Fry 30 seconds or until golden. With a slotted spoon, remove at once and drain on paper towels.

NOTES TO THE COOK
1. Straining the eggs removes the white strands of albumen.
2. To keep the eggs hot, cover them with a buttered sheet of waxed paper. Set the pan in a bowl of warm water lined with a kitchen towel (it works as insulation). Eggs will keep warm 10 to 15 minutes.

LEEK AND MUSHROOM PIE
Tourte de Poireaux et Champignons

This rustic pie is perfect for a light luncheon entrée served along with a piece of pork or duck *confit*. Or better yet, it can be a good first course before grilled or roasted meat or poultry.

SERVES 6 TO 8
ACTIVE WORK: 45 minutes
BAKING TIME: 1 hour

>   7–8 **medium-size leeks (about 1 1/2 pounds)**
>   8 **tablespoons (1 stick) unsalted butter**
>   2/3 **cup Crème Fraîche or heavy cream**
>   **Salt and freshly ground pepper**
>   1/2 **pound mushrooms, trimmed and thinly sliced**
>   1 **recipe Pastry for Country-Style *Tourtes* and *Tourtières***
>   **Flour**
>   **Egg glaze (1 egg yolk beaten with 1 teaspoon water)**

1. Trim off the roots and dark green portions of the leeks; discard. Split the white and pale green portion lengthwise and wash carefully in cold water. Cut in half again lengthwise and thinly slice crosswise.

2. In a medium-size heavy saucepan, melt 2 tablespoons of the butter over moderate heat. Add the leeks and cook, stirring frequently, about 2 minutes. Add 3 tablespoons of the butter and 1/4 cup water. Cover, reduce heat to low, and cook the leeks, stirring occasionally, 15 to 20 minutes, or until tender. Uncover the pan and cook until moisture has evaporated, 5 to 7 minutes. Set aside to cool.

3. Place Crème Fraîche in a funnel lined with coffee filter paper and let drain until reduced by half, about 2 hours. Or reduce heavy cream by boiling gently until reduced by half, about 20 minutes. Stir it into the leek mixture; add salt and pepper to taste. Set aside to cool.

4. In a medium-size skillet, melt remaining butter over high heat. Add the mushrooms and sauté, tossing, until they are lightly browned, about 5 minutes. Season with salt and pepper to taste. Drain in a colander and set aside to cool.

5. Divide the pastry dough in half. Between sheets of lightly floured waxed paper, roll one half into a 12-inch round (the dough will be *very* thin). Transfer to a lightly buttered pizza pan or sheet.

6. Leaving a 1-inch margin all around, arrange the cold leek mixture over the pastry, packing the leeks so that the edge is round and the surface level; the mixture should be at least 1/2 inch deep. Spread the cold mushroom mixture over the leeks.

7. Roll out the remaining half of the pastry dough between sheets of lightly floured waxed paper into a round about 13 inches in diameter.

8. Brush the margin around the bottom of the *tourte* with some of the egg glaze. Place the 13-inch pastry round over the top and, with the tines of a fork, crimp all around to seal the edges. Trim away any excess dough.

9. Brush the top with the remaining glaze. With the point of a knife, make shallow lines crisscrossing the pastry. *Can be prepared ahead up to this point.* Cover and refrigerate until ready to bake.

10. 1 1/2 hours before serving, preheat the oven to 400° F.

11. Bake the *tourte* 15 minutes on the lowest oven shelf. Lower oven temperature to 350° F. and bake 35 to 40 minutes longer, or until golden brown and crisp. Remove the *tourte* from the oven, let it stand for about 20 minutes, and then cut into wedges to serve.

Inspired by a recipe from Marie-Claude Soubiran-Gracia.

SORREL OMELET
Omelette à l'Oseille

The secret is to barely cook the sorrel leaves so they will retain their fresh, bitter-sharp, lemony taste. Cut them with scissors *(don't chop them in a food processor)*, then add them to the eggs just before cooking. Be sure the pan is hot when adding the eggs.

For a more authentic version, use good-quality rendered duck or goose fat instead of butter.

SERVES 2 TO 3
ACTIVE WORK: 10 minutes
COOKING TIME: 3 minutes

> 6 **large eggs**
> 1/3 **teaspoon salt**
> 1/4 **teaspoon freshly ground pepper**
> 2 **dozen young sorrel leaves, deribbed, washed, dried, and cut into shreds (about 2/3 cup)**
> 2 **tablespoons unsalted butter, or 1 1/2 tablespoons rendered duck or goose fat**

1. In a small bowl, combine the eggs, salt, pepper, and 2 tablespoons water with a fork for 30 seconds. Strain, if desired. Stir in the sorrel.

2. Heat the butter or poultry fat in a 10-inch omelet pan or well-seasoned skillet over high heat. When the foam begins to subside and the pan is hot, pour in the egg mixture.

3. With one hand shake the pan back and forth to keep the eggs from sticking. With a fork in the other hand, flat tines down, stir the eggs for 1 or 2 seconds. Tilt the pan and lift the omelet at the edges to let the top, uncooked part run beneath. As soon as the eggs begin to set but the center is still slightly runny, roll, fold, and slide onto a warm serving dish. Serve at once.

SAUCE BASQUAISE WITH EGGS AND HAM
Pipérade

Pipérade has been misunderstood in the United States. For years I've seen it pictured in food magazines as a plate of scrambled eggs served with a chunky sauce of cubed green and red peppers with a twist of ham perched on the top. It makes for a pretty picture that way, but the picture gives a false impression. The real *pipérade* of the Basque country isn't chunky at all and is not poured like a sauce on top of the eggs, but is blended with them. The great South-West French chef X. Marcel Boulestin wrote a definitive description in his 1931 book *What Shall We Have Today?*: "It is a kind of egg dish, and some people make it either like scrambled eggs or like an omelette. But this is not right, and when finished it should be impossible to see which is egg and which is vegetable, the aspect being that of a rather frothy purée."

So—*pipérade* is a creamy, soft egg-and-vegetable mixture better served in a shallow bowl than on a plate. The *Sauce Basquaise* that is combined with the eggs is ubiquitous in the Basque country, where it is served on top of nearly everything and is even thinned by some cooks who then serve it as a soup.

SERVES 10

ACTIVE WORK: 20 minutes
COOKING TIME (MOSTLY UNATTENDED): 1 1/2 hours

> 5 **pounds red-ripe tomatoes, cored, seeded, and chopped, or substitute imported canned Italian tomatoes**
> 5 **tablespoons olive oil or rendered goose fat**
> 1 **cup chopped yellow onions**
> 2 **large cloves garlic, finely chopped**
> 3 1/2 **pounds Italian frying peppers, cored, seeded, and cut into 1-inch chunks (about 4 cups)**
> 1 **tablespoon salt**
> 1/4 **teaspoon cayenne pepper (or more to taste), or** *piment d'Espelette*
> 1 **tablespoon sugar (if tomatoes are too acid)**
> 4 **teaspoons tomato paste (for color, if desired)**
> 10 **large eggs, lightly beaten and strained**
> 10 **thin slices** *jambon de Bayonne* **or prosciutto or Westphalian ham**

1. Stew the tomatoes in 1 tablespoon of the oil or fat in a 4- to 5-quart casserole over medium heat about 10 minutes, stirring frequently.

2. Add the onions, garlic, and peppers; simmer until peppers are soft and sauce has thickened, about 1 hour. Season with salt and pepper; add sugar if necessary. Stir in the tomato paste, if desired.

3. Press mixture through a food mill to make a smooth sauce. Return to the casserole and reduce to 6 cups. Cool the *Sauce Basquaise* completely. *Can be prepared 2 days ahead up to this point;* cover and refrigerate.

4. 5 TO 10 MINUTES BEFORE SERVING, heat remaining oil or fat over high heat in a deep, heavy 12-inch skillet. Add *Sauce Basquaise* and bring to a boil, stirring constantly. Lower heat to just below boiling.

5. Gradually pour eggs into skillet in circular motion, starting at edge of skillet and working toward center. Cook, stirring with a wooden spoon, until eggs are almost firm but still very creamy.

6. Meanwhile, in a second skillet fry ham slices in their own rendered fat. Serve the eggs at once under a blanket of fried ham.

CHAPTER 7

VEGETABLES

SARLAT POTATO CAKE
Gâteau de Pommes de Terre à la Sarladaise

This recipe is a lesser-known version of the famous and much beloved *pommes à la sarladaise,* in which slices of potatoes are sautéed in goose fat in a skillet, seasoned with salt and pepper, sprinkled (sometimes) with thin slices of black truffle, and served hot. It's especially good with crisp duck or goose *confit*.

This variation is equally delicious, and because it does not require truffles, you will be able to make it more often. It is a marvelous half-crisp, half-soft potato dish, served hot and sprinkled with a *hachis* (a mixture of chopped garlic and parsley).

SERVES 4 TO 6
ACTIVE WORK: 25 minutes

    3 tablespoons rendered duck or goose fat, or fat scraped from a duck
        confit
    2 pounds red potatoes (waxy potatoes are best for this dish)

   2 teaspoons finely minced garlic (minced by hand)
1 1/2 tablespoons minced fresh parsley
   Salt and freshly ground pepper

1. 30 MINUTES BEFORE SERVING, peel and wash potatoes. Cut into 1/8-inch slices. *Do not wash the slices.*

2. Heat the fat in a well-seasoned 10-inch skillet over high heat. Add the potatoes and let them brown for an instant. Cook, turning them with a spatula to coat well and avoid sticking, about 2 minutes. Lower heat to medium. When some of the slices begin to brown, press the potatoes with a spatula to form a flat round cake. Reduce heat to medium-low, cover the skillet with a tight-fitting lid and cook 7 minutes.

3. Raise the lid to allow steam to escape. Toss the potatoes gently so that the crisp bottom pieces will mix with the rest of the potato slices. Gently press down with a spatula to reshape; cover and cook 7 minutes longer, shaking the skillet to keep the potatoes from sticking.

4. Uncover, toss, and reshape by pressing down; cover tightly a third time and cook 7 minutes.

5. Remove from heat without uncovering and let stand 30 seconds. Lift the cover off, moving it to the side quickly so that the moisture does not fall onto the potatoes. Wipe the inside of the cover dry. Tilt the skillet and spoon off any excess fat; reserve.

6. Cover the skillet and invert so that the potatoes rest on the lid. Return the fat to the skillet and heat; slide in the potatoes so that the second side can crisp, uncovered. The "cake" should be puffy, crisp, and golden. Slide onto a heated serving platter, sprinkle with garlic, parsley, salt, and pepper. Serve at once while still hot.

NOTES TO THE COOK

If the skillet is not seasoned properly, potatoes may stick. To season, wash skillet; rinse and dry thoroughly. Wipe 2 tablespoons vegetable oil over inside surface of skillet. Heat over medium heat until very hot, about 5 minutes. Let cool; wipe surface dry and repeat once more. Never use detergents or a stiff brush on the skillet. Coarse salt and damp paper towels are all that is necessary to scrub a skillet clean. I have a restaurant-style steel skillet that I use only for sautéing potatoes (available by mail order from Dean & DeLuca; see Appendix). It has served me well for twenty years!

If good-quality waxy potatoes are unavailable, Idaho potatoes can be substituted—carefully rinse off the starch and dry each slice before cooking.

POTATOES IN THE STYLE OF QUERCY
Pommes de Terre à la Quercynoise

These chunks of Idaho potatoes cooked until crusty-brown in goose fat make a hearty but not heavy or greasy dish. You will notice, after you've cooked the potatoes, that when you pour off the fat and measure it, you have recaptured *almost* all that you've put in.

SERVES 4
ACTIVE WORK: 10 minutes
BAKING TIME: 2 1/4 hours

> 1 1/2 **pounds Idaho potatoes, peeled and cut into 1 1/4-inch chunks**
> 3 **tablespoons rendered goose or duck fat**
> **Coarse (kosher) salt**
> 1 **tablespoon chopped fresh parsley**
> 2 **teaspoons chopped garlic (chopped by hand)**

1. 2 1/2 HOURS BEFORE SERVING, preheat oven to 300° F.
2. Cook potatoes in boiling salted water 3 minutes. Drain completely and shake dry in a colander.
3. Melt the fat in a baking dish and add potatoes in 1 layer. Bake 2 hours, turning potatoes in the fat from time to time. Allow all sides to turn crusty-brown.
4. Raise oven temperature to 375° F. for the last 15 minutes of baking. Just before serving, sprinkle with salt, parsley, and garlic.

NOTE TO THE COOK
During the first hour of baking, the potatoes will remain colorless. Do not attempt to raise oven temperature during this time.

POTATO, CELERY ROOT, AND CORN PANCAKES
Galettes de Pommes de Terre au Céleri-Rave et Maïs

If you go to the Basque country in the fall, you will see a spectacularly beautiful land carpeted with russet-colored ferns and seemingly endless fields of corn. Basque sailors brought corn to France sometime in the sixteenth century, and the Basques have been eating it in a variety of ways ever since. Cornmeal has always been a staple, but it has only been in the past decade that chefs have started to use fresh Indian corn too. Pierre Laporte of the Café de Paris in Biarritz serves these little fried cakes with mustard-coated veal chops. They go marvelously with beef or duck as well.

MAKES EIGHT 3-INCH CAKES
(SERVES 4 TO 8, DEPENDING UPON
OTHER VEGETABLES SERVED AT THE
SAME TIME)

ACTIVE WORK: 10 minutes
COOKING TIME: 20 minutes

> 1 small celery root (about 3/4 pound)
> 1/2 pound Maine or Eastern potatoes*
> 1/2 cup fresh or defrosted corn kernels, dried thoroughly
> 2 tablespoons snipped fresh chives
> 1 teaspoon salt
> 1/4 teaspoon freshly ground pepper
> 1/8 teaspoon freshly grated nutmeg
> 1/3 cup clarified butter

*On the West Coast, do not use "white rose" potatoes; use russets and rinse lightly—don't remove all the starch.

1. Thickly peel the celery root; grate using the grating blade of a food processor. Arrange 2 layers of paper towels on baking sheet. Spread celery root on towels in a single layer; press out extra moisture.

2. Peel potatoes, grate, and squeeze gently to remove excess moisture. Transfer to large bowl. Add celery root, corn, chives, salt, pepper, and nutmeg; blend well.

3. To make individual galettes, butter 8 individual brioche or tartlet molds. Divide mixture evenly among prepared molds, pressing firmly.

4. Heat butter in extra-large skillet (preferably nonstick) over medium heat. One by one invert the molds onto a wide spatula. Slide filled molds upside down into skillet, leaving molds in place. Repeat with all filled molds. Fry potato mixture until golden and crisp, moving molds often to prevent sticking, about 10 to 12 minutes.

5. Slip tip of knife or fork between mold and cake to remove mold. Repeat with remaining molds. Invert cakes with spatula and fry uncovered until cooked through, about 5 to 7 minutes. Drain on paper towels. Keep hot in warmed oven, turned off. Do not stack.

NOTE TO THE COOK

If desired, the celery root can be grated a few hours in advance. To prevent discoloration after grating it must be dried out in a turned-off medium-hot oven. Spread out on kitchen towels and set in oven to dry 20 minutes. Roll up in the towel and set aside until needed.

STRAW POTATO CAKE STUFFED WITH BRAISED LEEKS
Paillaisson de Pommes de Terre aux Poireaux

This golden, crisp potato cake filled with creamed leeks is one of the most popular in my classes. In the South-West, leeks are always cooked until silky and soft, never crunchy like string beans or broccoli. The creamed leeks act as a glue to hold the cake together.

SERVES 6

ACTIVE WORK: 20 minutes
COOKING TIME: 40 to 45 minutes

> **1 pound leeks (white part plus 1 inch of green) roots trimmed, split, washed well, and dried**
> **5 tablespoons unsalted butter**
> **1/2 cup heavy cream**
> **Salt and freshly ground pepper**
> **1 3/4–2 pounds boiling potatoes, peeled**
> **1/4 cup clarified butter**

1. Slice the leeks by hand or in a food processor fitted with the medium slicing disk (makes 5 cups).

2. In a medium-size heavy-bottom saucepan, melt 2 tablespoons butter. Add the leeks and cook, stirring, 2 minutes. Add remaining 3 tablespoons butter. Cover and cook, without browning, 20 minutes.

3. Stir in the cream and boil down to thicken. Season with salt and pepper to taste. Cool, uncovered. *Can be prepared up to 1 day ahead to this point;* cool, cover, and refrigerate.

4. Fit the workbowl of a food processor with the julienne blade. Cut the potatoes to fit the feed tube and process the potatoes into julienne strips, or cut the potatoes by hand into very thin matchsticks (makes about 3 cups). Rinse the potatoes in several changes of water; drain.

5. Spread potatoes out on a kitchen towel to dry. Roll the towel and potatoes up and squeeze tightly to extrude all excess water. Potatoes will keep in this state for 1/2 hour.

6. 20 TO 25 MINUTES BEFORE SERVING, heat the clarified butter in a large seasoned or nonstick skillet. Spread half the potatoes to cover the bottom of the skillet. Top with the braised leeks, leaving a 1-inch margin around the edge. Cover with remaining potatoes and pat to form a cake about 10 inches in diameter. Cover and cook 5 minutes over medium heat, shaking pan often to keep potatoes from sticking. Lift the cover off to allow steam to escape. Wipe the inside of the cover dry. Cover and cook 5 minutes longer, shaking the skillet to keep the potatoes from sticking.

7. Carefully remove the cover so that the moisture on it does not drip back onto the

potatoes. Wipe the cover dry. Tilt the skillet and spoon off any excess butter; reserve.

8. Cover the skillet and invert so that the potatoes rest on the lid. Return the butter
olden-brown side up.
, or until the
ith salt, and

MICHEL GUÉRARD'S PURÉED CELERY ROOT WITH APPLES

Purée de Céleri-Rave aux Pommes

This is an incredibly delicious vegetable, and to my taste is the best of the purées. Serve with Broiled Duck Breasts and deep-fried celery leaves.

SERVES 4 TO 6
ACTIVE WORK: 10 minutes
COOKING TIME: 20 minutes

> 1 pound celery root
> 1 quart milk
> 3/4 pound Delicious apples
> 2–3 tablespoons heavy cream
> Salt and pepper

1. Peel celery root and cut into chunks, using a stainless steel knife. In a noncorrodible saucepan, simmer, covered with milk, 10 minutes.

2. Meanwhile peel, core, and quarter the apples. Add to the celery and cook together 10 minutes, or until celery root is tender. Drain.

3. Purée celery root and apple quarters in batches in food processor until smooth. Add the cream if necessary to loosen the mixture. Season with salt and pepper to taste. For a perfectly textured purée, push the puréed mixture through a fine wire sieve. *Can be prepared several hours ahead.* Cool, cover, and refrigerate. Reheat gently before serving.

NOTE TO THE COOK
The apples replace the more commonly used potatoes, resulting in a more silky, moist purée. The flavor of the apples is hardly noticeable, yet it heightens the flavor of the celery root. The very moist quality of the apple eliminates the need for large quantities of butter and cream.

Adapted from a footnote in Michel Guérard's La Cuisine Gourmande.

STEWED FOREST MUSHROOMS
Sauce de Cèpes

The adapted Landais recipe presented here employs white wine and a mixture of dried cèpes and fresh cultivated mushrooms enriched with tomatoes and ham. This dish is best made a day in advance, then gently reheated before serving. It is served alone as a first course in the Landes, but I like it with roast chicken or grilled meats. Fresh garlic and parsley chopped together can be strewn on top if desired.

A rich and particularly succulent *civet de cèpes au vin de Cahors* was described to me by Monsieur Pierre Escorbiac, formerly of the La Taverne restaurant in Cahors in Quercy. Shallots and onions are softened in duck fat, then beef marrowbones, blanched pork skins, and pig's feet are added along with the cèpes. The mixture is covered with the red wine of the region, which is the inky thick *vin de Cahors*. The mixture is hermetically sealed in an earthenware casserole and allowed to cook slowly in embers for 3 to 4 hours. The marrow is then removed from the bones, the pork skins are cubed, and the pig's feet boned, ground up, then returned to the casserole to thicken the sauce, a procedure similar to that used in my recipe for Oxtail Daube. (If you do this version, be sure to make it one day in advance so that all fat can be removed. Reheating will only make it better.)

SERVES 5 OR 6
ACTIVE WORK: 30 minutes
BAKING TIME: 2 to 2 1/2 hours

> 1–1 1/2 **ounces dried imported cèpes**
> **Coarse (kosher) salt**
> 1 1/2 **pounds fresh, firm cultivated mushrooms, trimmed (if very large, cut in half)**
> 1/4 **cup duck or goose fat or olive oil**
> 2 1/2 **ounces** *jambon de Bayonne*, **prosciutto, or Westphalian ham, chopped**
> 2 **large shallots, minced**
> 1 1/2 **teaspoons finely chopped garlic**
> 3/4 **cup soft and fruity white wine, such as Saumur or a Chenin Blanc**
> 1 **small red-ripe tomato, peeled, seeded, and chopped, or 1/4 cup canned tomatoes, drained**
> **Freshly ground pepper**
> 1 **tablespoon finely chopped fresh parsley**
> **Fresh lemon juice**
> 4 or 5 **rounds of toasted French bread rubbed with 1/2 clove garlic (optional)**

1. Preheat the oven to 300° F.

2. Soak dried cèpes in hot water with 1/2 teaspoon salt for 30 minutes. Drain, reserving soaking liquid. Rinse cèpes under cool running water to eliminate any grit

or sand. Strain soaking liquid through coffee filter paper or several layers of damp cheesecloth and set aside.

3. Wipe caps of fresh mushrooms with damp cloth and a little coarse salt. Set aside.

4. In a large skillet, heat the fat or oil over medium heat. Add the cèpes and their soaking liquid and cook until all liquid in the pan has evaporated. Add the ham, shallots, and garlic and cook, stirring, 1 minute. Add the fresh mushrooms and cook, stirring, over high heat until all moisture has evaporated. Pour the wine over the mixture and boil down to a glaze.

5. Add 1/2 cup hot water and the tomato. Cook, stirring, over gentle heat for an instant, then add 1/2 teaspoon salt, 1/4 teaspoon pepper, and the parsley.

6. Scrape into an earthenware or enameled cast-iron casserole with a tight-fitting lid. Cover with waxed paper and the lid; cook slowly in the oven 2 to 2 1/2 hours. Uncover and cool completely. Refrigerate, covered.

7. Reheat slowly. Adjust seasoning with a few drops of lemon juice, salt, and pepper. Serve with toasted rounds of French bread, if desired.

NOTE TO THE COOK

If you can obtain fresh cèpes, eliminate Step 2, and also substitute cèpes for the cultivated mushrooms. Dry them out in a moderately low oven for 10 to 15 minutes before cooking if they have been washed.

Inspired by a recipe from Monique Veilletet.

CÈPES IN THE STYLE OF GASCONY
Cèpes à la Gasconne

It was less than a hundred years ago that the fashionable Café Anglais first introduced *Cèpes à la Bordelaise* to Paris, a dish in which these wild forest mushrooms and garlic (not shallots) were cooked in oil. This was before the interest in provincial cookery, and the special combination of cèpes and oil was not particularly appreciated by the gourmets of the capital. Instead, the chefs starting cooking the cèpes in butter, a tradition still carried on today. Parisians also cook them with shallots. The classic recipe Cèpes Sautéed in Oil in the Style of Bordeaux, which follows this one, uses garlic. The following recipe uses olive oil, garlic, and cured ham, and mixes dried wild mushrooms and cultivated fresh mushrooms.

Auguste Colombié, the great nineteenth-century cooking teacher, once said, "The gourmets eat cèpes with butter; the fanatics eat them with oil." His recipe calls for the cèpes to be cooked twice, first in oil and then in butter!

SERVES 4 TO 6

ACTIVE WORK: 10 minutes
COOKING TIME: 25 minutes

(continued)

        1 ounce dried cèpes
        4 tablespoons French olive oil or a light Italian olive oil
        1 teaspoon finely chopped garlic
        2 tablespoons *jambon de Bayonne*, prosciutto, or Westphalian ham,
           finely chopped
        1 pound fresh cultivated mushrooms, quartered or sliced
           Salt and freshly ground pepper
     1–2 tablespoons strained fresh lemon juice
        2 tablespoons chopped fresh parsley

1. Soak the dried cèpes in a bowl in 2 cups lukewarm water for 30 minutes. Drain by lifting them out of the liquid without stirring up the sediment at the bottom of the bowl. Rinse the cèpes under cool running water. Drain well by pressing on them lightly. Ladle soaking liquid through coffee filter paper or several layers of fine damp cheesecloth.

2. In a nonaluminum skillet (preferably copper) heat the oil until hot. Add the cèpes; let them "sing" for a second, then lower the heat to medium-high. Add the garlic and ham; cook, stirring, 2 to 3 minutes. As soon as the garlic begins to color slightly, add all the strained soaking liquid and bring to a boil. Slowly cook down to a glaze, about 15 minutes.

3. Add the fresh mushrooms, salt and pepper to taste, and a sprinkling of lemon juice. Cook, tossing over medium-high heat until all the moisture in the pan has evaporated, about 7 minutes. Serve very hot with a sprinkling of parsley. (This dish can be made ahead and gently reheated. After cooking, cool uncovered. Cover and refrigerate until ready to serve.)

NOTE TO THE COOK
If you have fresh cèpes on hand, omit Step 1 and the addition of the soaking liquid. If they have been washed, dry them out in a moderately low oven for 10 to 15 minutes before cooking.

CÈPES SAUTÉED IN OIL IN THE STYLE OF BORDEAUX
Cèpes à la Bordelaise

With as few as one or two fresh cèpes you can make this memorable dish for two people.

SERVES 2
    ACTIVE WORK: 5 minutes
    COOKING TIME: 30 minutes

      2 large fresh cèpes or other boletes
    1 or 2 cloves garlic, chopped

2–3 tablespoons oil (French peanut or light olive oil)
1 teaspoon strained lemon juice
2 teaspoons minced parsley
Salt and freshly ground pepper

1. Chop the stalks and mix with the chopped garlic.

2. Sauté chopped stalks and garlic in oil in a shallow enameled or earthenware pan over low heat until soft (5 minutes).

3. Add caps, whole or sliced. Cook slowly 15 minutes or until all the moisture has evaporated. Turn them over, add a few tablespoons of water, and cook an additional 5 to 10 minutes over low heat. Drain off any excess oil.

4. JUST BEFORE SERVING, sprinkle with lemon juice and parsley. A light sprinkling of salt and a very little pepper will do for seasoning.

NOTE TO THE COOK

Cèpes cooked this way are even better the next day. To keep freshly cooked cèpes a few weeks, simply cook in oil without seasoning, drain, pack in clean jars, sprinkle lightly with salt, and cover with fresh olive oil. Keep covered and cool.

ARTICHOKES AND POTATOES AU GRATIN
Artichauts et Pommes de Terre au Gratin

In the Pyrenees, this dish is made with raw churned milk, rarely found anymore. No matter—it works fine as I've adapted it and is great with roast leg of lamb.

SERVES 4

ACTIVE WORK: 20 minutes
COOKING TIME: 1 1/2 hours

4 large or 5 medium fresh artichokes*
2 lemons
1 cup milk
3 tablespoons unsalted butter
1/2 cup chopped onion
1/2 teaspoon finely minced garlic
2 baking (russet) potatoes (about 1 pound)
2/3 cup heavy cream
Salt and pepper
1/2 teaspoon meat glaze or 1/4 cup meat stock reduced to a glaze (optional)
Crumbled thyme leaves

*Frozen artichoke hearts may be used, but the results are not as tasty.

(continued)

1. Twist or break off the stem from each artichoke. If the stem base is too thick or short, make a small incision around the base of the artichoke and it will twist off easily. This will remove the tough inner fibers of the base.

2. By hand, break off 2 rows of outer tough leaves. With a thin-bladed, very sharp knife, remove the leaves one by one, using a seesaw motion behind each leaf. The knife should cut off just the leaf, leaving the fleshy part attached to the artichoke bottom. Repeat all around the artichoke until the trimmed leaves are tender, cone-shaped, and pale green. Cut off this cone about one third of the way down.

3. Using a swivel vegetable parer, trim the bottom and top of each artichoke to remove any tough green exterior.

4. Rub artichokes all over with half a lemon. As you prepare them, drop the artichoke bottoms into a bowl of acidulated water (juice of 1 lemon mixed with 3 to 4 cups water).

5. In a large pot, bring 6 cups of salted water to a boil. Add remaining lemon half, 1/3 cup milk, and the artichoke bottoms. Cover the pot and cook 3 minutes (see Note 1).

6. Drain the artichoke bottoms well and discard the chokes. Slice them on the diagonal into thin slices; you can use the food processor fitted with a thin (3 mm) slicing disk.

7. Preheat oven to 350° F.

8. In a small skillet, melt half the butter; cook the onion and garlic until soft but not brown. Spread remaining butter on the bottom and sides of a shallow 10-inch baking pan. Scatter the onion-garlic mixture on the bottom of the pan.

9. Peel potatoes and slice as thinly as the artichokes (see Notes 2 and 3). Arrange artichoke and potato slices in rows, overlapping.

10. In a mixing bowl, combine 1/2 cup of the heavy cream, the remaining 2/3 cup milk, 1/2 teaspoon salt, 1/3 teaspoon white pepper, meat glaze (if using), and thyme; blend well. Pour over the potatoes and artichokes. Bake 1 1/4 hours. *Can be prepared 1 hour ahead up to this point*; set aside uncovered.

11. 15 MINUTES BEFORE SERVING, preheat the broiler. Spoon remaining heavy cream over vegetables and run under the broiler until hot and golden brown. Serve immediately.

NOTES TO THE COOK
1. The artichokes are only partially cooked before being layered with potatoes. Cook them just before using to avoid any loss of flavor and oxidation.
2. The potatoes can be peeled in advance and kept covered in salted water in the refrigerator. Do not slice until ready to assemble and bake.
3. The secret of this dish is not to wash the potato slices. Their starch thickens the liquid and creates a creamy texture until the crust is formed. Remember that when you make gratins you must use enough milk or cream to cover the vegetables; otherwise they will shrivel on top, and there won't be sufficient liquid to make them tender. Use more cream if necessary.

ARTICHOKE HEARTS IN RED WINE SAUCE
Ragoût d'Artichauts au Vin Rouge

This is a rich, wonderful dish, but it takes time. The recipe is an old one from the Languedoc; the sauce has extraordinary depth and texture. I originally served the ragout in small, individual brioches, but now I prefer it with grilled lamb or roast veal.

SERVES 6

ACTIVE WORK: 30 minutes
UNATTENDED SIMMERING TIME: 1 3/4 hours

> 6 artichokes or 2 (9-ounce) packages defrosted artichoke hearts
> 4 tablespoons French peanut oil or light olive oil
> 1 cup cubed fatback or blanched lean salt pork
> 1 cup cubed *jambon de Bayonne*, prosciutto, or Westphalian ham
> 1 1/2 cups chopped onions
> 1/2 cup chopped mushrooms
> 2/3 cup minced scallions
> 1 cup sliced carrots
> 2 teaspoons sliced garlic
> 1 bottle full-bodied red wine such as California Petite Sirah or Algerian Medea
> 2 teaspoons tomato paste
> Herb bouquet: 3 sprigs parsley, 1 sprig thyme, and 1 bay leaf tied in a bundle
> 6 peppercorns, lightly cracked
> Salt
> 1 1/2 cups unsalted Chicken Stock, degreased
> Pinch of sugar
> 1 1/2 tablespoons Armagnac or Cognac
> 2 tablespoons unsalted butter
> 1–2 teaspoons minced fresh parsley

1. Prepare the artichokes as described in Steps 1 through 5 of the preceding recipe. Reserve 1 cup trimmings for sauce base. If using defrosted artichokes, chop 2 or 3 hearts into small pieces and set aside.

2. In a noncorrodible large skillet, heat 2 tablespoons of the oil and lightly brown the fatback cubes. Add the trimmings of the artichokes, ham, onion, mushrooms, scallions, carrot, and garlic. Sauté one minute, stirring. Add the wine. Bring to a boil, stirring; skim.

3. Blend in the tomato paste, herb bouquet, peppercorns, and 1/2 teaspoon salt. Reduce heat, cover, and cook gently 1 1/2 hours.

(continued)

4. Meanwhile reduce Chicken Stock by half and reserve.

5. Stir in the reduced stock and simmer 5 minutes.

6. Strain, pressing down on the vegetables to extract all their juices. Degrease. You should have about 2 cups. Adjust seasoning; add a pinch of sugar, if necessary.

7. Quarter the raw artichokes and remove the chokes.

8. In a clean skillet, sauté artichoke quarters in remaining hot oil until lightly browned around the edges. Pour off oil. Add brandy and reduce to a glaze.

9. Add red wine sauce and simmer 15 minutes for raw artichokes, or 5 minutes for defrosted artichoke hearts. Swirl in butter to thicken sauce. Sprinkle with parsley.

EGGPLANT STUDDED WITH GARLIC
Aubergines au Four à l'Ail

An easy and delicious dish. Use the young and most tender eggplants you can find, one per person. A lot of recipes for eggplant call for cooking them in oil—delicious, of course, but sometimes indigestible since eggplants sop up oil like a sponge. In this dish from the Pyrenees, fresh olive oil is added at the last minute and absorption is minimized.

The eggplants are seasoned with a mixture of crumbled dried herbs. You can mix your own or use the mixed herbs from France called herbes de Provence or Herbes de la Garrigue.

SERVES 6

ACTIVE WORK: 10 minutes
BAKING TIME: 30 minutes

3 large or 6 small cloves garlic, peeled and halved
1/2 cup fruity extra virgin olive oil (such as Puget brand)
1/2 teaspoon salt
1/4 teaspoon freshly ground pepper
2 tablespoons herbes de Provence or Herbes de la Garrigue
6 small whole eggplants, each about 5 inches long
1–1 1/2 teaspoons finely chopped garlic (chopped by hand)
2 tablespoons chopped fresh parsley

1. Preheat oven to 400° F.

2. Marinate garlic cloves in olive oil 10 minutes. Remove and dry on paper towels. Cut into long, thin slivers. Mix olive oil with salt, pepper, and herbs. Let steep.

3. Make 4 or 5 holes in each eggplant at equal distances. Slip garlic slivers into holes. Brush eggplants with seasoned oil and wrap each one in a sheet of aluminum foil, enclosing securely. *Can be prepared ahead up to this point*.

4. Set all wrapped eggplants on a baking sheet. Bake on middle oven shelf 30 minutes.

5. To serve, slit eggplants open, spoon a tablespoon of scented oil over each, and sprinkle with garlic and parsley. Serve warm or cold.

RED WINE-COOKED ONIONS
Daube d'Oignons

A long, slow cooking of Spanish onions results in a meltingly sweet, thick sauce, wonderful with grilled squab or calf's liver, braised duck, or on toast rounds with drinks.

MAKES ABOUT 2 CUPS (SERVES 6)
ACTIVE WORK: 20 minutes
PARTIALLY UNATTENDED COOKING TIME: 2 1/2 to 3 hours

> 1/4 cup (1/2 stick) unsalted butter
> 2 1/2–3 pounds Spanish onions, halved lengthwise and thinly sliced
> 1 tablespoon granulated sugar
> 1 1/2 cups full-bodied red wine such as a Petite Sirah or Côtes-du-Rhône
> Salt and freshly ground pepper
> 1 teaspoon or more red wine vinegar

1. Heat butter in a 4-quart saucepan (not aluminum) over low heat. Add onions. Cover and cook, stirring occasionally, 45 minutes.

2. Uncover, increase heat to medium-high, and cook, stirring frequently, until onions are glazed and golden brown (20 minutes). Sprinkle with sugar and boil down, stirring, 2 to 3 minutes to glaze.

3. Reduce heat to low, add wine, and cook, stirring frequently, until onions are very soft and deep mahogany in color, about 1 1/2 to 2 hours.

4. Season with salt and pepper, and add vinegar to counteract any sweetness. Serve hot, lukewarm, or cold. This will keep in refrigerator 2 to 3 days. The onions can be frozen.

NOTE TO THE COOK
If you can't get Spanish onions, increase the sugar to balance acidity; add a little vinegar at the last minute to counteract any excessive sweetness.

SORREL FRITTERS
Beignets de Feuilles d'Oseille

Try this dish in early summer when sorrel leaves are tangy-sour. I wouldn't attempt it in spring when the leaves are young, because their subtle taste will be lost. Serve beignets overlapping on a napkin in a basket with cocktails or with veal, chicken, or fish.

SERVES 6

ACTIVE WORK: 15 minutes

Batter

> 6 ounces (about 1 1/4 cups) sifted unbleached all-purpose flour
> 1 teaspoon fine salt
> 1 egg yolk
> 2 teaspoons vegetable oil
> 2 teaspoons brandy, slivovitz, or Armagnac
> Peanut or corn oil for deep-fat frying
> 2 egg whites
>
> 2 large bunches fresh sorrel leaves (about 45 leaves, washed, patted dry
>   with paper towels)
> Coarse (kosher) salt
> 1 lemon, cut into wedges

1. In a deep mixing bowl combine flour, salt, egg yolk, 1/2 cup plus 2 tablespoons lukewarm water, oil, and brandy. Do not overbeat. Let stand at least 1 hour.

2. ABOUT 15 MINUTES BEFORE SERVING, heat cooking oil to 370° F. in a deep-fat fryer. Preheat the oven to 200° F. Line a baking sheet with a single layer of brown wrapping paper.

3. Beat egg whites until stiff. Gently fold them into the flour mixture, using a rubber spatula.

4. Add half the leaves to the batter. Gently stir them with the spatula. Using tongs or a pair of chopsticks, unfold any folded leaves so that the batter coats them evenly.

5. With tongs or a pair of chopsticks, pick up a leaf of sorrel and scrape it off along the inner edge of the bowl to remove excess batter. Scrape the other side of the leaf on the side of the bowl. Repeat with 4 or 5 leaves. The number of leaves you can fry at once will depend upon the width of your fryer. But drop no more than 4 or 5 leaves into the hot fat at one time.

6. Fry until golden brown, turning once.

7. Remove leaves to the paper. Keep warm in oven. Repeat with remaining leaves.

8. Serve leaves as soon as possible or they will lose their crisp texture. Sprinkle lightly with salt and lemon juice.

LEEKS BROILED OR BAKED IN THEIR OWN JUICES
UNDER A BED OF ASHES
Poireaux Sous la Cendre

There is a town called Mirepoix in the Ariège whose name will be familiar to students of French cooking, since it is also the name of the vegetable base of so many French sauces and stews.

It was near there that I first tasted young leeks roasted in dying embers, then peeled and served with a garlic and herb vinaigrette. These delicious leeks were a revelation of simplicity and pleasure. Their flavor is very intense and a great improvement over leeks boiled or steamed. Serve lukewarm with a garlic, herb, and olive oil vinaigrette.

The recipe has been adapted to enable the reader without a bed of ashes to prepare the dish in the oven or under the broiler.

SERVES 6
>ACTIVE WORK: 15 minutes
>COOKING TIME: 10 to 15 minutes

> 12 **thin leeks**
> **Salt**
> 2 **tablespoons olive oil**
> **Salt and freshly ground pepper**

1. Position broiler rack 4 inches from heat source and preheat, or position rack in lower third of oven and preheat the oven to 450° F., or stoke ashen coals for even, steady heat.

2. Trim all but 1 inch of green leaves from leeks. Remove any remaining tough outer leaves; discard root. Beginning about 1 inch from base, split leeks lengthwise, using thin sharp knife. Wash leeks thoroughly; if very sandy, let stand in bowl of cold water about 10 minutes.

3. Drain leeks and pat dry with paper towels. Arrange in 1 layer on large sheet of heavy-duty aluminum foil. Rub each leek with olive oil. Sprinkle with salt and pepper to taste. Enclose completely in foil, wrapping tightly. *Can be prepared ahead up to this point.*

4. Transfer to broiler pan or baking sheet or outdoor grill. Broil (or bake) 5 minutes, then turn and broil (or bake) 5 minutes more. For outdoor grill, add 5 minutes to each side and shake the "package" from time to time to prevent the leeks from sticking to the foil.

ROASTED GARLIC
Ail au Four

The concept of an entire head of garlic roasted in embers will appeal to all garlic lovers and be the despair of those who fear garlic for its potency. If you are among the latter, you'd probably do well to ignore the following two recipes. I count myself among the garlic lovers of this world, believing that we are, in Stendhal's words, "The Happy Few."

In France the round white garlic of the Limousin and the flatter white variety from Lomague in Armagnac are roasted when the heads weigh about four ounces, and served as a sweet and creamy "vegetable" accompaniment to grilled meats and stews. The restaurateur Huguette Melier roasts them in the embers and serves them with meat and hearth-roasted potatoes. I've eaten them with fresh whipped goat cheese (*fromageon*), and have found them delicious with any kind of peppered cheese and Roasted Bread. The second version below makes a fine lunch served with Corn Cakes and a bitter green salad dressed with a walnut oil vinaigrette.

The best time to make this dish is late spring when plump young tender white garlic bulbs become available. (Avoid using elephant garlic, which does not taste very good when cooked, and also avoid garlic heads that are dried out.)

Roasted Garlic I

ACTIVE WORK: 5 minutes
ROASTING TIME (WITH FREQUENT BASTING): 1 to 1 1/2 hours

1 whole head garlic per person
Coarse (kosher) salt and freshly ground pepper
1 tablespoon butter per person, cut into small pieces

1. To prepare the garlic heads for roasting, carefully cut away the outside paper skins of each head with a small knife, starting from the top and stopping halfway down, leaving just a thin skin around exposed upper portion of each clove so that it will not dry out during roasting.
2. Preheat the oven to 350° F.
3. Place garlic heads in a buttered shallow baking dish just large enough to hold them snugly in 1 layer. Sprinkle with salt, pepper, and chips of butter; place in the oven to roast. When lightly colored (about 20 minutes), add 1/2 cup water and start basting every 10 minutes with the cooking juices, adding hot water whenever necessary. Roast 1 to 1 1/2 hours, depending upon the size of the garlic heads.

Roasted Garlic II

ACTIVE WORK: 10 minutes
ROASTING TIME (WITH FREQUENT BASTING): 1 to 1 1/2 hours

1 whole head garlic per person
1 1/2 ounces fatty prosciutto-type ham per person, finely chopped
1 teaspoon butter per person, cut into bits
2 teaspoons chopped fresh parsley
Coarse (kosher) salt, pepper, thyme, and sugar

1. Preheat the oven to 350° F.
2. Place heads in cold water to cover. Bring to a boil; drain and refresh under cold water. Place again in cold water and repeat; drain. Peel skins back, starting at the top and ending at the root. Use a sharp knife to sever all the papery peels. Only one skin should be left on each clove as protection against the oven heat.
3. Scatter the ham on the bottom of a lightly greased shallow baking pan just large enough to hold the garlic heads snugly. Arrange the garlic heads in 1 layer, root side down; sprinkle with butter, parsley, and a pinch of coarse salt, pepper, thyme, and sugar.
4. Set in the oven to roast, basting every 10 minutes with juices in the pan. Add 1/2 cup water after the first 15 minutes. Roast 1 to 1 1/2 hours, depending upon the size of the garlic heads. Serve with pan juices.

Inspired by an unsigned article in Quercy Magazine *entitled "Les Produits de Nos Terroirs."*

SAUTÉ OF TOMATOES, RED PEPPERS, AND ZUCCHINI
Fricassée de Jardinier

This bright sauté of tomatoes, pimentos, and zucchini is light and easy to make, and goes well with any meat or with braised chicken breasts.

SERVES 4
ACTIVE WORK: 20 minutes
COOKING TIME: 20 minutes

- 2 **red bell peppers (pimentos)**
- 1/3 **cup unsalted butter**
- 1 **cup coarsely chopped onions**
- 1/2 **teaspoon finely minced garlic**
- 3 **large red-ripe tomatoes, peeled, seeded, and cut into 1-inch chunks**
- 2 **young firm zucchini, cut into 3/4-inch chunks**
- **Salt and freshly ground pepper**
- **Cayenne pepper**
- 2 **tablespoons chopped fresh parsley mixed with 1 teaspoon fresh basil**

1. Broil peppers until skins are black and blistered on all sides (about 12 minutes). Cool 10 minutes under a kitchen towel or in a paper bag. Core, seed, and slip off the skins. Cut into 1/4 × 2-inch strips.

2. 20 MINUTES BEFORE SERVING, in a heavy shallow skillet heat 3 tablespoons of the butter; add the onions and garlic. Cover tightly and cook 5 minutes over low heat.

3. Add the tomato and zucchini chunks; cook, covered, 12 minutes, stirring often. Raise heat; uncover pan and rapidly boil off excess moisture, about 4 to 5 minutes. Stir often to avoid burning the vegetables.

4. Fold in pepper strips and allow to heat through. Season with salt, pepper, and cayenne to taste. Off heat, swirl in remaining butter, cut into small pieces. Sprinkle with fresh herbs and serve hot.

SAUTÉED PEPPERS IN THE STYLE OF BÉARN
Piments à la Béarnaise

Serve these peppers with the Calf's Liver as Prepared in the Valley of Ossau, or with thick slices of country-cured ham. In the Béarn they often garnish hot slices of foie gras with fried peppers. Use the green, Italian-style "frying peppers" for this dish; they do not need to be peeled. If unavailable, substitute bell peppers and peel as directed in Note to the Cook at the end of this recipe.

SERVES 4

ACTIVE WORK: 15 to 20 minutes

1 pound Italian frying peppers
1 1/2 tablespoons rendered poultry fat
1 or 2 splashes wine vinegar
Salt and freshly ground pepper

1. Steam peppers 5 minutes. Remove core and seeds.
2. Cut peppers into bite-size pieces. Pat dry on paper towels.
3. 3 TO 4 MINUTES BEFORE SERVING, heat fat in a medium-size skillet over high heat; add the peppers and cook, tossing, 2 to 3 minutes, or until peppers brown slightly around the edges. Remove with a slotted spoon. Sprinkle with vinegar, salt, and pepper. Serve at once.

NOTE TO THE COOK

If using bell peppers, blanch in boiling salted water for 2 1/2 minutes. Drain and use thin-bladed knife to cut away thin peel. Omit steaming and cook the peppers 3 to 4 minutes in hot fat.

FRIED PUMPKIN SLICES
"Chips" de Potiron

There are a lot of pumpkin dishes in South-West France. I found au gratin recipes for pumpkin with or without tomatoes, pumpkin soups that were enhanced with sweet red peppers, and creamy soups served with and without cheese. But of all the pumpkin dishes this was the one I liked best, served very hot with a confettilike sprinkling of hand-chopped garlic and parsley. Serve with veal or lamb roasts, or separately as a snack.

SERVES 4 OR 5

ACTIVE WORK: 10 minutes
COOKING TIME: 8 to 12 minutes

1 (2-pound) wedge fresh pumpkin, preferably the redder-fleshed
variety
3/4 cup milk
1/2 cup flour seasoned with 1/4 teaspoon salt and 1/8 teaspoon freshly
ground pepper
2/3 cup oil for frying
1 tablespoon finely chopped garlic (chopped by hand)
2 tablespoons finely chopped fresh parsley

(continued)

1. Peel and seed pumpkin. Scrape out fibrous lining and discard. Cut pumpkin into slices 1/4 inch thick, then cut slices into 1 × 1 1/2-inch rectangles.

2. Pour milk into large bowl. Dip pumpkin slices into milk and dust with seasoned flour; shake off excess.

3. Heat oil in large, heavy skillet over medium-high heat. Oil is ready when a piece of pumpkin sizzles as it hits the oil. Add half the pumpkin (do not crowd) and cook until crisp and golden (2 to 3 minutes). Turn and cook underside. Remove with slotted spoon and drain on paper towels spread out on a baking sheet. Gently blot pumpkin pieces. Repeat with remaining pumpkin rectangles. Arrange on platter, top with parsley and garlic at the last minute, and serve hot.

CORNMEAL PORRIDGE
Las Pous

Las pous, as it was known in the patois of the Périgord (also called *rimotes*, *milhas* in the Languedoc, *cruchade* in the Landes, *armottes* in Gascony, *broye* in the Béarn, and, frequently throughout the South-West, just simply *millas*), was the true starch of the peasants. For them white bread was a luxury eaten only on Sundays.

Las pous can be made with any of the following additions: garlic, sautéed onions, melted ham fat, any kind of poultry fat, or lukewarm milk or butter. Allowed to cool, cut into pieces and fried, it makes a superb accompaniment to any of the wine-based beef, chicken, or duck stews and daubes in this book. In fact, I highly recommend it as the best possible starch accompaniment to these meat dishes. (I have some reservations, however, about leftover cornmeal porridge flavored with sugar and orange flower water and served as a peasant dessert.)

Fulbert Dumonteil, in *La France Gourmande*, says that the reason this polenta-type porridge is called *las pous* is because, when it is prepared over low heat, its surface sputters and seems to break into a smile, giving forth a great sigh, "*pou*," like a person moving, smiling and sighing in his sleep. I have tried to smile back at *las pous*, but usually to no avail. It requires constant stirring, and sometimes while preparing it I feel like sighing myself. The demanding, almost constant stirring needed to reach the desired consistency can be achieved with an electric polenta machine available from Bel Canto Importers (see Appendix).

One of the most delicious versions of cornmeal porridge was made for me in the town of Cordes in the Tarn. The woman who demonstrated the dish had been showing me how to make goose *confit*. When she finished, there were some meat juices, bits of goose meat, and a tiny amount of goose fat left in the pot. To this she added a few cups of water and some flour and cornmeal, and stirred the mixture to make it smooth. She then proceeded with the recipe as described below.

Another time, in the Pyrenees, on the road to Gavarnie (the local equivalent of the Grand Canyon), I had the rare opportunity to observe a shepherd make a polenta-type porridge *without* stirring! He had spent the summer utterly alone, tending his sheep in the mountains, and had brought some rich sheep's milk down to the inn where I was lunching. He put a quart of this milk into an iron pot set in the fireplace and let it come to a boil. Then he threw in a few handfuls of fine white cornmeal, stirred once in a secretive fashion, then pulled back from the fireplace to reveal that a large skinlike bubble had formed on top of the mixture and that the porridge was cooking within it, in effect within its own steam. At a certain precisely chosen point, he stabbed this dome and scooped out perfectly tender cornmeal porridge. The people who were watching with me were amazed. They did not know this method and could not conceive of making a good cornmeal porridge without the hard labor of constant stirring.

One waitress told me that this shepherd would tell no one his secret, and that when he died it would surely be lost. Then she added with a smile, "Perhaps one day he will marry me and pass the secret along to our son."

SERVES 8

TOTAL PREPARATION TIME: 1 hour

> **1 1/3 cups finely ground yellow cornmeal**
> **2/3 cup unbleached all-purpose flour**
> **3/4 teaspoon salt**
>   **A few tablespoons lukewarm milk, butter, chicken fat, pork fat, ham fat, or cream**

1. In a heavy-bottomed deep saucepan, combine the cornmeal and flour with 2 cups lukewarm water. Stir until completely smooth.

2. In another pan bring 4 cups water to a boil with 3/4 teaspoon salt. Slowly stir the boiling water into the cornmeal mixture. Cook over moderate heat, stirring *without stopping*, using a long wooden spoon (called a *toudeillo*), 15 minutes. *There must be no lumps.* Taste for salt and adjust.

3. Set over extremely low heat and allow mixture to cook gently 30 to 45 minutes; stir from time to time. It is fully cooked when the porridge no longer "smiles" when a spoon is stirred through it, but rather packs itself around the spoon. Stir in lukewarm milk, butter, fat, or cream to loosen the mixture, then immediately pour into a greased serving bowl and serve hot. Or spread it out on a greased flat surface (using a wet spatula) to a 3/4-inch thickness and let cool.

Inspired by a recipe from Monique Darras.

FRIED CORNMEAL PORRIDGE CAKES IN THE STYLE OF GASCONY

Armottes

Cornmeal first appeared in the South-West in the sixteenth century, when corn was brought back from the New World by Basque sailors. It grew well in this region, as did other New World vegetables such as tomatoes, pumpkins, peppers, and beans. I was particularly struck by this dependence on American ingredients when a young Basque in Espelette told me about a flat cornmeal and flour pancake that his mother used to make, called a *taloa*. This pancake, about five inches in diameter, was fried on both sides in a pan greased lightly with ham fat until it showed little black burn spots and puffs on its surface. His mother then filled it with crumbled fresh cheese or crumbled bacon and hot pepper sauce.

This is my favorite accompaniment to all red wine-based stews and daubes.

> **1 recipe for Cornmeal Porridge, spread on a flat surface**
> **Flour**
> **1/2 cup poultry fat, preferably goose, or rendered pork fat or oil and butter**

1. When the Cornmeal Porridge is cool, cover and refrigerate until ready to use. (It can keep 2 or 3 days.)

2. 30 MINUTES BEFORE SERVING, preheat the oven to 300° F.

3. Cut porridge into desired shapes. I like 1 1/4-inch rounds or squares. Dust with flour. Heat fat in a skillet until sizzling. Fry cornmeal shapes in very hot fat until golden brown and crisp on both sides, about 5 minutes.

4. Immediately remove from the skillet; drain on paper towels and finish reheating spread out in 1 layer on a hot baking sheet in the oven. In this way cakes will remain crisp and dry on the outside and somewhat moist within until ready to eat.

NOTES TO THE COOK
1. If the cakes are cold when placed in the hot skillet, they will not absorb as much of the fat but will gain the flavor of the fat.
2. If you are working in batches, let the fat regain its high temperature before continuing with the next batch, or it will be absorbed.

CORN CAKES

Tourteaux

These golden, crusty cakes are an excellent accompaniment to Chicken in Red Wine. They are very similar to the American corn fritter, except that they are cooked in a smaller amount of fat. This is an updated method of combining corn kernels and white flour to make a particularly light version of a rather heavy pancake called *tourteaux*. Other accompaniments that work well are Roasted Garlic II and a sauce of wild mushrooms (see Stewed Cèpes).

MAKES EIGHT 3-INCH CAKES
ACTIVE WORK: 10 minutes
FRYING TIME: 10 minutes

> 2 fresh cobs of corn, or substitute 3/4 cup thawed corn kernels
> 2 tablespoons butter
> 1/4 cup milk
> 3/4 teaspoon salt
> 1/4 teaspoon freshly ground white pepper
> Pinch of grated nutmeg or more to taste
> 1 egg
> 1 egg, separated
> 8 tablespoons all-purpose flour
> 1 tablespoon mixed butter and oil for frying

1. Cut the corn kernels from the cobs. Crush lightly in a food processor fitted with the metal blade. Place corn in a sieve to drain well. Makes 2/3 cup.

2. Cook corn in hot butter in a small nonstick skillet 3 minutes, stirring over medium heat. Lower heat and continue to cook until it no longer tastes raw.

3. Add the milk and immediately remove from heat. Milk should *just* warm up from the receding heat in the skillet. Stir in the seasonings.

4. Meanwhile, in a mixing bowl, combine whole egg and extra yolk until well blended. Gradually stir in warm corn mixture and flour; let stand a minimum of 1 hour so that flour absorbs all liquid and relaxes. *Can be prepared ahead up to this point.*

5. Just before serving, whisk the egg white until stiff; gradually and carefully fold it into the mixture without losing volume.

6. 15 MINUTES BEFORE SERVING, preheat the oven to 250° F. In a large seasoned skillet, heat butter and oil. It should just coat the bottom of the skillet. Fry corn cakes (using a 1 1/2-ounce ladle for measure) in batches until set and lightly browned on the bottom, about 1 1/2 minutes. Turn and brown the other side. Drain on a brown paper bag or paper towels.

7. Transfer to a baking sheet; spread out in 1 layer and keep hot in oven for 5 to 10 minutes.

NOTES TO THE COOK
1. A well-seasoned skillet is critical for cooking these cakes in a small amount of fat. To season your skillet, brush the inside with oil and slowly warm it over gentle heat. Then sprinkle with coarse salt and rub vigorously with paper towels.
2. Corn cakes can be made in advance but they will lose some of their crispy texture. To reheat, spread out cool (not refrigerated) cakes on a baking sheet and place in oven preheated to 375° F.

PURÉED SORREL
Purée d'Oseille

One of the great natural affinities is a plate of rich duck *confit* and lemony puréed sorrel. Sorrel naturally purées itself when cooked, so it is an easy vegatable to prepare. Finding and cleaning enough for large groups is the problem. One pound of fresh young sorrel leaves makes about 1 1/4 cups purée, enough for two servings.

SERVES 2
ACTIVE WORK: 10 minutes
COOKING TIME: 5 to 10 minutes

> 1 pound fresh sorrel leaves
> 3 tablespoons unsalted butter
> 1/2 teaspoon salt
> 1/4 teaspoon freshly ground pepper
> 1–2 tablespoons heavy cream or Crème Fraîche

1. Carefully wash sorrel leaves and remove the stems; drain well. Tear the larger leaves into small pieces. Roll leaves into neat small bunches and cut each roll with a stainless steel knife into thin strips (chiffonnade). Makes about 6 packed cups.

2. Melt the butter in a nonaluminum saucepan over medium-low heat. Add sorrel and salt and pepper. Cover and cook 1 minute to steam leaves. Uncover and cook down until all moisture evaporates and the sorrel is thick. With the back of a stainless steel fork, crush the sorrel to a purée. Set aside until ready to serve.

3. Reheat gently with cream. Adjust seasoning.

NOTE TO THE COOK
If only a handful of sorrel is available, combine with 3/4 pound of spinach, but cook each separately and purée the spinach in the food processor before combining.

CHAPTER 8

SEAFOOD AND FISH

MUSSELS / *MOULES*

Mussels are popular along the entire Atlantic coast of South-West France, where they are served in a number of unusual and delicious ways. I could not imagine a better preparation than the Normandy classic Moules à la Marinière until I tasted the little-known regional specialty Éclade de Moules, particularly famous in the town of Rochefort in the Charente-Maritime.

To prepare *Éclade*, the cooks of the region arrange tightly closed mussels hinge side up on a wooden plank so that the mussels are crammed together and won't easily open despite the pressure of the steam within their shells. The idea here, as opposed to the normal procedure, is to keep the juices *inside*, where they will swell up the mussels and make them succulent. A thick layer (about 5 inches) of partly dried pine needles is placed above the shells and set aflame. When the flames have died, in about 3 minutes, the ashes are brushed away, and the mussels are eaten with ash-blackened fingertips. The taste is intense and the experience a delight, as is any eating experience requiring bare hands.

In the Landes I found a home version of *Éclade*. Pack your mussels together in a deep black skillet or enameled cast-iron casserole with a tight-fitting lid (36 medium-size mussels fit perfectly into a 3-quart dutch oven) hinge side up so that none of them can move. Lay partially dried pine needles on top, cover, and set the skillet or saucepan over medium heat for 3 to 4 minutes. The mussels will plump up from their own steam as they try to force open their shells; the pine needles will impart a delicate flavor and aroma. (But it will not be the smoky flavor of the Charente version.) Some juices may escape, but they are not lost and can be used later for stocks and soups, or simply boiled down to a tablespoon and used to flavor an accompanying bowl of lemon butter.

A few words about the purchasing, cleaning, soaking, and cooking of mussels:

Buying mussels: Purchase about a pound of unshelled mussels per person for a large main-course dish and slightly less if served as a first course. A pound in volume is about 3/4 quart or 16 medium-size mussels. (Sometimes mussels are sold by weight and other times by volume.) Always buy a few extra because some may be cracked or dead. If you buy mussels in a plastic bag, remove them to a bowl as soon as you get home and leave them in the coldest part of the refrigerator. They will keep a few days. Small and medium-size mussels are usually the best buys; I think they are more tender, delicate, and full-flavored. Very heavy, large mussels are apt to be filled with mud. One muddy mussel can ruin a dish, so check each one and discard any that are very heavy in relation to others of similar size. If a mussel refuses to close after a minute or two when tapped with another mussel, soak it in icy water for 10 minutes and check again. If it doesn't close, it is dead and must be discarded.

Cleaning mussels: The standard complaint against mussels is that they're too much trouble to clean. Yes, perhaps, for a large party—but for a small dinner of from four to six people, the work goes as fast as any kitchen chore such as cleaning vegetables. A strong wire brush is the best implement for scrubbing the shells. A small knife or a simple tug will remove the beards.

Soaking mussels: I no longer believe in soaking mussels in water flavored with mustard (the theory is that they will hate the taste and spit out their sand), or in cornmeal-enriched water (the theory is that they will fatten up). Nor do I leave them in milk for 30 minutes (this supposedly cleans out their intestinal systems). I simply swish the mussels around in a large basin of water, drain them by lifting each one up to scrub and rinse, then set them in a bowl of salted water to soak for 45 minutes. I think it's best to cook them as soon as possible after cleaning and soaking, though they can wait (out of the water) another day.

Cooking mussels: Steaming is the most common way. When I am steaming large numbers of mussels, I spread them out in one layer in a wide, covered, turkey roaster with no liquid but some flavorings. In a very hot oven, all the mussels cook evenly in about 8 minutes. When I am steaming a few dozen, I loosely wrap them in cheese-cloth and set them in my couscous cooker (a two-part steamer) to steam over boiling shallot-flavored wine. The mussel liquor passes through the cheesecloth and mixes (sand-free) with the wine. I find this speeds up the making of a sauce. Steaming in a couscous cooker cooks the mussels faster than the normal steaming method of shaking in a deep kettle, leaving them extra plump and not dry.

The absolute best method to cook mussels is to vacuum-pack them in boilable pouches. Flavor, tenderness, and juiciness are all better retained than in any of the methods listed above. Vacuum-pack in batches of 12; seal and immediately immerse the pouch in boiling water. Boil 3 minutes or until mussels begin to open. Remove at once; open the pouch. Use as directed in a recipe. Another simple way to prepare mussels is to grill them over coals, arranged on an iron grill, until they just begin to open, 1 to 2 minutes.

MUSSELS PEASANT STYLE
Moules Paysanne

This is a very simple and quickly made dish to serve as a first course for two or three. It was in the city of Pau, the capital of the Béarn, that I first tasted this dish. What impressed me most, I think, is how well mussels and ham go together despite the fact that both are rather salty. The soft fresh white bread crumbs seemed to swallow up the excess salt and kept the dish light.

One of my favorite menus for spring begins with these mussels. Follow with a *Confit* of Duck with Green Peas and Ham and a dish of Preserved Spiced Pears in Red Wine with Armagnac.

SERVES 2 TO 3
ACTIVE WORK: 10 minutes
COOKING TIME: 15 minutes

> 2 pounds fresh mussels
> 2–3 tablespoons soft fresh white bread crumbs
> 3 tablespoons unsalted butter
> 1 ounce *jambon de Bayonne,* prosciutto, or Westphalian ham, cut into thin matchsticks
> 1 1/2 teaspoons minced shallots
> 1/4 cup dry white wine
> 1/2 teaspoon finely minced garlic (chopped by hand)
> 1 tablespoon chopped fresh parsley
> Freshly ground pepper

1. Preheat the oven to 300° F.
2. Follow instructions for cleaning mussels.
3. Roll bread crumbs in a towel to dry them well. Unroll and fluff them so that they are loose. Set aside.
4. In a nonaluminum skillet, heat 1 tablespoon of the butter. Gently cook the ham and shallots 4 to 5 minutes without browning.
5. Meanwhile, steam mussels. Strain the liquor through several layers of damp cheesecloth and add to the skillet. Add the wine and cook until reduced by one quarter.
6. Remove the upper shell of each mussel and discard. Place the mussels in their

half shells on a shallow heatproof platter. Cover loosely with foil and set in oven to keep warm.

7. Add garlic, parsley, a few grinds of pepper, and the bread crumbs to the reduced cooking liquid. Reduce heat to medium.

8. Cut the remaining butter into small chunks. Add to the skillet; swirl until butter binds with bread crumbs to make a sauce. Pour over the mussels and serve at once. Pass rounds of lightly toasted French bread rubbed with garlic.

Mussels in the Style of Bordeaux
Moules à la Bordelaise

Add 2 red-ripe tomatoes, peeled, seeded, and cubed, a drop of Pernod, and a pinch of cayenne pepper to the shallots and ham in Step 4.

NOTE TO THE COOK
If the ham is excessively salty, blanch it 3 minutes before using.

HOT MUSSEL SALAD
Salade de Moules Chaudes

This is a very pretty first course of mussels, carrots, and shredded wild greens, a variation on the famous *mouclade* of the Charente—a dish often tinted with saffron and curry. A hint of curry with saffron is more common that you might think—especially along the coast where ships from India stopped in at Bordeaux en route to England.

SERVES 4 TO 6
ACTIVE WORK: 35 minutes
COOKING TIME: 15 minutes

    4 pounds fresh mussels (about 3 1/2 quarts)
      Salt
    4 small carrots, scraped
    2 tablespoons finely chopped shallots
  5–6 sprigs parsley
  1/2 cup dry white wine
      Juice of 1 lemon
      Freshly ground white pepper
      Pinch of saffron threads
      Pinch of curry powder
  1/2 cup heavy cream
    5 tablespoons unsalted butter
  3–4 tablespoons snipped fresh chives
    1 bunch tender chicory (curly endive), rolled up and cut into thin strips
      (about 1 3/4 cups)

1. Pick over and discard any mussels that are cracked. Clean as directed.

2. 45 MINUTES BEFORE COOKING, soak the mussels in icy salted water.

3. Preheat the oven to 500° F.

4. With a multihole citrus zester or a sharp small knife, cut the carrots into julienne strips. Cook in boiling water 30 seconds. Refresh and drain. You should have about 3/4 cup. Set aside.

5. Remove mussels, rinse well, and drain. Place side by side on a rack in a large roasting pan. Sprinkle with shallots, parsley sprigs, and 1/2 cup white wine. Cover tightly with foil or a cover; set in the oven to cook 8 minutes for *average-size* mussels. Overcooking will make them tough, so take a peek after 8 minutes. If the shells are *just* beginning to open, leave them 1 minute longer. If they are open and mussels could easily be removed, they are cooked. Remove from their shells over the roasting pan in order to catch their juices. If mussels are very large, remove the black-brown "rubber" band around each of them.

6. Sprinkle mussels with pepper and a few drops of lemon juice. Set aside in a bowl to keep moist and warm while finishing the sauce.

7. Strain cooking liquid through several thicknesses of wet cheesecloth directly into a wide saucepan. If the liquid is extremely salty, remove half and replace with water. Add saffron threads and the curry powder. Bring to a boil and reduce by half. The curry powder should cook in the liquid so that it will not have a raw taste. Add the cream; bring to a boil and simmer until sauce *barely* coats a spoon.

8. Swirl in the butter to thicken the sauce. Throw in the mussels, the carrots, the chives, and the shredded chicory. Swirl over very low heat for about 1 minute to blend flavors and heat the ingredients. *Do not allow the sauce to boil.* Adjust seasoning, adding a few drops of lemon juice if necessary. Serve in warmed soup plates as a first course.

Inspired by a recipe from Francis Garcia, Restaurant Clavel, Bordeaux.

SLICED SALMON WITH FRESH OYSTERS
Escalope de Saumon au Fumet d'Huîtres

This dish is a quintessential demonstration of everything the "new cooking" should be and so often isn't. There is nothing phony about it, nor is there anything decorative for decoration's sake. And, perhaps most important, there is nothing here that is not essential; each part works to create a whole greater than the sum of the parts. Christian Clément taught me this dish. It is his invention and all the nuances are his. The combination brings a wonderful briny taste of the sea to freshly caught freshwater salmon. It is easy and elegant, light and delicious.

SERVES 4

ACTIVE WORK: 15 minutes

> 1 1/4 pounds fresh boneless fillet of salmon, in 1 piece
> 4 large white very fresh mushrooms
> 1 teaspoon fresh lemon juice
> 3 1/2 ounces unsalted butter (AA quality)
> 12 shucked oysters, with 1/2 cup of their liquor reserved
> 3 tablespoons Crème Fraîche or heavy cream
> Salt and freshly ground white pepper
> 3 tablespoons snipped fresh chives

1. Preheat the oven to 300° F.

2. Lay the salmon fillet on your work surface, skin side down. With a very sharp, thin, flexible knife, cut the fillet diagonally (as you would slice a side of smoked salmon) into 4 equal "scallops," about 4 ounces each; discard the skin.

3. One by one, place each mushroom sideways on your work surface; holding it by the stem with one hand, slice the cap into thin rounds, stopping when you reach the gills. Stack the rounds and cut them into thin julienne strips. Sprinkle with lemon juice. Wrap tightly in plastic wrap. *Can be prepared ahead up to this point*. Refrigerate salmon and mushrooms.

4. Lightly oil a baking sheet. Place a large skillet, preferably nonstick, over moderately high heat. When the pan is hot, add 2 teaspoons of the butter. When the foam subsides, add the salmon scallops and cook on one side only for 30 seconds, or until edges are opaque, the center still raw. Season with a light grinding of pepper and *invert* raw side down onto the oiled baking sheet. Set skillet aside.

5. Top each piece of salmon with 3 oysters. Sprinkle with pepper and place in the oven. Cook 3 minutes, or until oysters are warm and salmon is just cooked through.

6. Meanwhile, prepare the sauce. Add the oyster liquor to the skillet in which the salmon was partially cooked; swirl to pick up any pieces stuck to the pan. Add the slivered mushrooms and boil over moderately high heat until reduced to a thick

mass. Add the cream, return to a boil, and continue to cook until liquid is reduced by half, about 1 minute. Swirl in the remaining butter 1 tablespoon at a time. Season with salt and pepper.

7. Use a spatula to transfer salmon to individual heated serving dishes. Coat the salmon and oysters lightly with the sauce. Sprinkle with the chives and serve at once as a first course.

STEAMED SALMON WITH COOKED EGG SAUCE
Saumon Cuit à la Vapeur, la Sauce de Sorges

This delicious sauce, based on cooked eggs and oil, involves the same techniques as hollandaise and mayonnaise. Though the Sorges of the title is a village in the Dordogne, the sauce is quite common beyond the area, where it is generally served with boiled chicken. Traditionally, the eggs are dipped in hot water, dried, and placed to cook under the embers of a fire where they take on a smoky flavor.

Here the sauce has been adapted to accompany salmon that has been seasoned, buttered, and wrapped airtight in heatproof plastic wrap or boiling pouch before cooking. This technique enhances the moist, fresh flavor of the fish.

SERVES 4

ACTIVE WORK: 20 minutes

2 salmon steaks (about 10 ounces each), cut 3/4 to 1 inch thick
Salt and freshly ground pepper
4 teaspoons unsalted butter, cut in 4 even pieces, softened
2 large eggs, set under running warm water for 1 minute
3/4 teaspoon Dijon mustard
2–3 tablespoons fresh strained lemon juice
1/4 cup mild olive oil
1/4 cup French peanut oil
3 tablespoons heavy cream
1 small ripe tomato, peeled, seeded, chopped, and drained (about 1/4 cup)
2 tablespoons chopped fresh parsley
1 tablespoon small nonpareil capers, rinsed and dried
2 tablespoons chopped fresh chives
1 1/2 teaspoons chopped fresh basil leaves (optional)

1. Trim bones and skin from salmon. Season steaks with salt and pepper and coat with thin film of butter. Wrap each steak water- and airtight in 3 or 4 layers of heatproof plastic wrap such as Saran Wrap, or wrap airtight using a vacuum packing appliance (see Notes). Refrigerate until ready to cook.

(continued)

2. TO MAKE THE SAUCE: Cook water-warmed eggs in simmering water 4 minutes. Remove and refresh under cold running water for 1 minute. Carefully scoop out soft-cooked yolks into small mixing bowl or top of double boiler. Set aside whites.

3. Set bowl or top of double boiler over hot *but not simmering* water. Mash egg yolks with spoon until smooth and pastelike. Beat in mustard and 1 tablespoon of the lemon juice, whisking until the mixture thickens. Very gradually add combined oils using a beaker-type container; add 1/4 teaspoon oil at a time, whisking constantly. An emulsion should form—just as it does when you make homemade mayonnaise. Remove from heat if the mixture at any time appears about to curdle. (If this happens, dip the bottom of the pan into a bowl of cold water or quickly whisk in a spoonful of cold heavy cream.) It takes about 5 minutes to add all the oil. Remove from heat and add heavy cream.

4. Press whites through medium sieve with back of a spoon. Fold whites and remaining ingredients into sauce. Season and reserve. Sauce can be prepared early in the day and reheated very gently.

5. TO STEAM THE FISH: Set steamer rack over 1 1/2 inches boiling water in large saucepan. Steam 4 minutes per side. Do not overcook; salmon continues to cook while waiting to be unwrapped. (Salmon can be cooked up to 10 minutes before serving.) Carefully unwrap and place on individual heated serving plates. Top with lukewarm egg sauce.

NOTES TO THE COOK
1. If the sauce begins to separate, you should try to cool it down as fast as possible over a bowl of ice water—just as you do when you first learn to make hollandaise. If that doesn't work, you will need to cook another egg and begin adding the curdled mixture in droplets, just as you do when attempting to save mayonnaise.
2. If you have a vacuum sealer (an electrical appliance available in houseware stores), you can seal the salmon steaks airtight in their special packaging and drop them directly into simmering water to cook 7 to 8 minutes. If the packages float to the top, weight them down with a plate so that the water covers them entirely.

Inspired by a recipe from Lucien Vanel.

SCALLOPS IN TANGERINE SAUCE
Coquilles St. Jacques, Sauce Mandarine

A lovely dish created by Jean-Louis Palladin. The sweetness of the scallops is counterpointed by the astringent taste of the sauce, so intense that very little is needed.

The sauce is based on the theory of stratification expounded by André Guillot. Stratification is a simple method of binding sauces without flour, arrowroot, or egg yolk by a series of rapid reductions. (See "A Healthy Approach to Cooking with Poultry Fats, Lard, Butter, Cream, and Crème Fraîche," in the Introduction.)

SERVES 4

ACTIVE WORK: 10 minutes
COOKING TIME: 20 minutes

- 16 large fresh sea scallops, preferably all the same size (about 1 1/2 ounces each, 1 1/2 pounds total)
- 3 tablespoons fruity olive oil
- 1 tablespoon roughly chopped fresh parsley
- 1 tablespoon roughly chopped celery leaves
- 2 pinches crumbled fresh thyme leaves
  Salt and freshly ground pepper
- 8 heavy tangerines or clementines, enough to make 1 1/2 cups strained juice
- 1/4 cup Fish Glaze, or 1 1/4 cups unsalted Fish Stock reduced by boiling to 1/4 cup
- 2 tablespoons Demi-Glace or 3/4 cup degreased, unsalted Chicken Stock reduced to 2 tablespoons
- 1/2 cup heavy cream, at least 35 percent butterfat
  Fresh lemon juice

1. Rinse scallops; pat dry and toss with olive oil, parsley, celery, and thyme. Season with salt and pepper; let marinate 2 to 3 hours.

2. In a noncorrodible deep saucepan, boil down the tangerine juice to 1/3 cup.

3. Add the Fish Glaze and Demi-Glace. Bring to a boil; add the cream and boil vigorously without stirring 5 to 7 minutes. Large bubbles will appear on the surface as the sauce begins to bind. From time to time, test by stirring with a wooden spoon to see if the sauce has thickened. You should be able to glimpse the bottom of the saucepan for an instant. If the sauce is too sweet, adjust with a few drops of lemon juice and freshly ground pepper to taste. If the sauce turns oily, you have reduced it

too much; in this case add a tablespoon of water and the sauce will immediately smooth out. Sauce can be held over warm water and gently reheated just before serving.

4. 15 MINUTES BEFORE SERVING, heat the broiler. Remove the scallops from the refrigerator and arrange on the broiling rack. Broil the scallops 2 minutes on each side.

5. Meanwhile, spoon 2 tablespoons hot sauce on each individual *warmed* serving dish. Tilt the plate to coat the bottom evenly. Set 4 scallops on each. Serve hot.

NOTES TO THE COOK
1. If sauce is too strong-tasting or too thin, swirl in butter, in bits, on and off the heat.
2. "The faster the evaporation, the better the coagulation" is the rule for creating sauces by stratification. It takes less than 10 minutes to complete the entire process in a heavy-bottomed pan.

BABY EELS
Piballes

Baby eels—called *piballes* in French, *angulas* in Spanish, *guindillas* in Basque, and sometimes called "elvers" in English—are soft, white, slippery little things 1 1/2 to 2 inches long; heaped together, they resemble a mass of cut-up pasta. You should not be put off by their appearance; they are among the best and cheapest foods available along the coasts of Morocco, Spain, Portugal, and France from the Spanish border up to Bordeaux. For years, when I lived in Tangier, I'd anticipate them as I drove forty minutes down the coast to the town of Asilah to Pepe's Café, where they were a famous specialty. And whenever I am in St.-Jean-de-Luz in early winter, I make a point to eat them at Pablo's Restaurant on Rue Mlle. Etcheto, where they are served in a shallow earthenware casserole in sizzling hot olive oil flavored with the piquant *piment d'Espelette* and slivered garlic. At Pablo's one eats them the traditional way, with a wooden fork.

SALT COD
Morue

In inland areas, far from the fresh fish markets along the coast of South-West France, the only saltwater fish to be found in the past were slabs of cod, either salted (*morue*) or wind-dried. At the local grocery stores, beside the barrels of lentils, beans, and other staples were huge tubs where these slabs were piled up on Thursdays. The salt cod would be sold that day in order to be soaked at home under slowly dripping water for 24 hours. The overnight soaking prepared the fish for the traditional Friday lunch.

In the southern part of the Languedoc the great salt cod dish is the famous, delicious *brandade* made with olive oil, creamy milk, and garlic all crushed together to produce a light, creamy substance. Just a bit north, in the Rouergue, they have a variation I like even better; it's made with walnut oil, hard-boiled eggs, garlic, and herbs. In the Lot you will find it prepared with potatoes and drizzled with fresh walnut oil. In Gascony salt cod and beans is a dish to seek out, and in the Basque country salt cod and hot peppers are delicious together.

Once acquired, the taste for salt cod can turn the most sedate individual into a gastronomic savage upon the mere mention of *morue*. The French have a particular way of wetting their lips and rolling their eyes up toward heaven with reverence when they think about the dishes made from this inexpensive, though very nourishing protein-rich, highly digestible, humble creature. Most appealing is the particularly succulent and briny taste, which is extremely delicate and not really salty at all. These qualities make salt cod especially popular in Italy, Spain, Portugal, and Greece—and, until the end of the last century, the United States.

You will find the fish in most Spanish, Portuguese, Greek, and Italian fish markets as well as in large supermarkets. Buy about 4 ounces per person. Look for ivory-colored flesh with a tinge of green or yellow; salt cod should not be snowy white. Your piece should be thick and supple and should feel somewhat smooth. When pressed lightly it should not give off flakes of salt. Cod from Gaspé in Canada is excellent, and so is Icelandic cod. When buying salt cod, do not confuse it with the yellow-hued, wind-dried cod called stockfish, which often has a strong fishy odor (it disappears after soaking, but the taste is still stronger than that of salt cod). Salt cod is sold whole, with skin and bones intact; it requires 24 to 36 hours soaking in several changes of water. It is also sold in fillets, which require less soaking time.

To soak the cod: Cut into large pieces, then place pieces in a wire salad basket or colander so that the salt that leaches out will not repenetrate the fish. Ideally, salt cod should be rinsed under cold running water for 12 hours. Since this is impossible for most readers, the next best thing to do is to set your colander or salad basket into a deep pot filled with cold water, and then change this water 3 or 4 times, or until the water no longer has a salty taste. (Salt cod is not evenly salted and thus some pieces are more salty than others; this fact will affect the number of times you must change the water.) A well-soaked piece of salt cod will sometimes actually require salt in the final dish. The type of salt used to preserve the fish is not particularly good for eating, though the Catalans sprinkle grated, unrinsed dried salt cod on fresh fava beans and radishes to give them a salty flavor.

To cook the cod: When your piece of cod has swollen up from its soaking, it is ready to cook. Poaching and frying are two popular methods.

To poach desalted cod, cover the piece with cold water, or with a mixture of cold water and milk if you want the cod to come out white. Slowly bring it *almost* to the boiling point. (This poaching water can be flavored with herbs or a split, unpeeled whole head of garlic can be added—an excellent idea when you intend to use the same water later to cook potatoes.) When the first white foam appears on the surface of the cooking liquid, remove the pot from the heat, cover, and let stand 10 minutes or so, depending upon the thickness of the fish. (The reason for removing the pot completely from the fire and then letting the dish "cook" in the receding heat is to ensure that the cod never boils, thus preserving its succulence—if cod boils, it becomes leathery.) To tell when the fish is done, stick the point of a sharp knife into the thickest part; if there is little resistance, the cod is ready. Lift the pieces out and let them dry on a kitchen towel. When cool enough to handle, remove the fatty skin and all the bones. Save the poaching liquid if you are making Purée of Salt Cod, Potatoes and Walnut Oil, or for a fish soup.

To fry salt cod, simply drop the pieces into hot oil in a heated skillet with garlic and herbs (see recipe below for Salt Cod with Hot Peppers and Garlic. Another way is simply to dry the fish well, dust the pieces with flour, brush them with egg, then fry in an oiled pan.

Another interesting salt cod dish prepared in the South-West is *Morue Llauna*. It is a Catalan specialty in which a soaked and dried, whole, thick piece of salt cod is oven-roasted in a casserole with garlic, oil, and chopped tomatoes. The fish is sprinkled with bread crumbs for the last 10 minutes of cooking. *Llauna* means a casserole in Catalan.

SALT COD WITH HOT PEPPERS AND GARLIC
Morue Pil-Pil

The Basque expression *pil-pil* means to cook slowly. In this recipe, salt cod is simmered and shaken in a shallow earthenware dish along with garlic and olive oil until the pieces of fish begin to "float" in the resulting emulsification between the olive oil and the exuded white gelatinous juices of the fish. The dish is decorated with chopped fresh parsley and thin strips of red chili pepper. It is traditionally served in the earthenware cooking dish.

When buying the salt cod for this dish, try to get a thick center piece. If the salt cod is packaged, buy a little more than you need, choose the thickest pieces for this dish, and save the thin ends for the Rouergue version of *brandade*—Purée of Salt Cod, Potatoes, and Walnut Oil.

SERVES 4
ACTIVE WORK: 30 minutes

> 1 pound boneless salt cod
> 1 cup milk
> 1/4 cup olive oil
> 4 cloves garlic, peeled and thinly sliced
> 1 small hot red pepper, cut into very thin rings
> 2 tablespoons chopped fresh parsley

1. Soak the cod in cold water to cover for 18 to 24 hours, or until it is swollen. Change the water at least 3 times, adding milk for last soaking.

2. Rinse the cod; cut into 8 pieces of approximately equal size. Pick out bones; remove the scales but not the skin. (The skin has much of the gelatin needed to enrich the sauce as well as to add flavor.) Lay each piece on a kitchen towel-lined plate and keep refrigerated until ready to cook.

3. 30 MINUTES BEFORE SERVING, place the pieces, skin side down, in a shallow 10-inch round earthenware cooking dish, or substitute an enameled cast-iron skillet. Pour over the olive oil, add the garlic, and set over low heat (use an asbestos mat or trivet to protect the earthenware from cracking); cook 30 minutes. During this time shake the dish or skillet often so that juices exuded from the fish mix with the oil. Do not turn the fish pieces over, but do move them around a bit so that they do not stick to the bottom of the pan or skillet. From time to time tilt the pan and spoon the simmering juices over the top parts of the fish.

4. JUST BEFORE SERVING, raise heat and bring almost to a boil. Add the peppers and parsley and swirl the juices in the skillet to combine flavors and lightly reduce the juices. The result should be a smooth, blended sauce. Serve directly from the skillet or transfer to individual serving plates. Serve hot.

PURÉE OF SALT COD, POTATOES, AND WALNUT OIL
Morue à la Rouergate

All food enthusiasts know about the famous *brandade* of Nîmes in which pounded salt cod moistened with olive oil is mixed with boiling milk and served warm with fried garlic croutons. Here is an unusual and heavenly version that uses a little mashed potato, sieved hard-boiled eggs, and fragrant walnut oil. In the original Rouergue version, wind-dried cod (stockfish) is used instead of salt cod.

MAKES ABOUT 4 1/2 TO 5 CUPS
(SERVES 6 TO 8)
ACTIVE WORK: 15 minutes
COOKING TIME: 15 minutes

> 1 1/3 pounds salt cod (1 pound boneless)
> 1 3/4 cups milk
> Herb bouquet: 3 sprigs parsley, 1 sprig thyme, and 1 bay leaf tied together
> 1 onion, quartered
> 1 large clove garlic, halved
> 2 to 3 black peppercorns, freshly cracked
> 3/4 pound floury (baking) potatoes, peeled and cut into chunks
> 1/2–3/4 cup imported walnut oil
> 1 egg
> 1 teaspoon finely chopped garlic
> 2 hard-boiled eggs, peeled and pressed through a strainer
> 1 tablespoon finely chopped fresh parsley
> White wine or sherry wine vinegar, or strained lemon juice
> 24 triangles of crustless bread, toasted or fried in olive oil, then rubbed with garlic

1. ONE DAY BEFORE SERVING, in a large basin soak the cod in cold water to cover for 1 day or until swollen, changing the water at least 3 times and adding 1 cup of the milk for the last soaking.

2. Rinse the cod; cut into 3 or 4 pieces. Place in a large saucepan and cover with fresh cold water. Add herb bouquet, onions, garlic clove, and peppercorns. Heat slowly until the first white foam appears. Remove from heat at once; let stand, covered, 10 minutes.

3. Using a slotted spoon, remove the salt cod pieces to a napkin-lined plate. Reserve the liquid for cooking the potatoes. Carefully remove the bones and hard skin; flake the flesh finely. Keep warm.

4. Meanwhile cook the potatoes in the poaching water. Drain off cooking liquid. (This broth can be used for a soup.) Dry potatoes over low heat, then immediately

mash them until smooth, using a ricer or a potato masher or the wire beaters of an electric mixer. Beat in 2 tablespoons of the walnut oil, the egg, and chopped garlic. Beat until smooth. Keep warm.

5. Meanwhile scald the remaining 3/4 cup milk in a small saucepan and heat the walnut oil in a second saucepan.

6. Place cod and a little of the warm milk in the workbowl of a food processor. Process on and off once. Gradually add the warmed oil and milk alternately without overworking the salt cod. The mixture should feel light but slightly gritty. Scrape into the puréed potatoes, then gently stir in the sieved hard-boiled eggs and the parsley. Gently but thoroughly mix until well blended and light. Adjust the seasoning with white pepper and a few drops of vinegar or lemon juice to taste. Serve warm in a wide dish surrounded with the toast triangles.

NOTE TO THE COOK

The mixture can be made hours in advance. When making it in advance, reserve a few tablespoons warmed milk for the reheating. Mix together over low heat, loosening the mixture as it reheats.

FISH STEAKS WITH GREEN VEGETABLES AND SHELLFISH
Merlu à la Koskera

The first time I tasted this dish I despised it. It was made with a thick slice of two-day-old fish slapped together with canned vegetables. As I traveled about the Basque country, people insisted it was an exemplary dish of the region. Perhaps dishes become favorites because they satisfy our desire for contrasts of texture: a tender slice of fish combined with chewy clams and crisp spring vegetables. I later tried many recipes in Basque cookbooks and found a succession of superb renditions. It is simple to make, delicious to eat, and visually a wonderful dish for the first days of spring.

The fish (which must be absolutely fresh and, according to some authorities, "caught on the line" rather than captured in a trawled net) and the clams cook in their own juices, then combine with the oil at the last minute to make a liaison. The vegetables, too, should be absolutely fresh. The goal with a dish of this kind is to work for total honesty and simplicity. Success with *Merlu à la Koskera* begins at the greengrocer's and the fishmonger's. Either hake, cod, or tilefish may be used since they all release a great deal of gelatinous milky fluid that will make a natural liaison with the clam juice and a small amount of hot oil. The baby clams of the region, called *chirlas*, replace the tiny littlenecks or steamers, or small mussels. It is only in the Basque country that you can find wonderful hake. I like tilefish best as a substitute.

(continued)

SERVES 4
ACTIVE WORK: 20 minutes
COOKING TIME: 10 minutes

    4 fish steaks 1 inch thick (about 1 1/2 pounds):* tilefish, hake, or cod
      Sea salt
    8 fresh asparagus spears
  2/3 cup small fresh green peas
4 to 5 tablespoons fruity olive oil
    2 dozen very small clams (littlenecks or steamers) or very small mussels
    2 large cloves garlic, finely chopped
  1/4 teaspoon red pepper flakes or a good pinch of cayenne pepper
1 1/2 tablespoons finely chopped fresh herbs: parsley, chives, and mint
      Juice of 1/2 lemon

*Do not substitute fillets, because you need the fish to be cut across the grain.

1. Sprinkle the fish with salt and refrigerate for 20 minutes.
2. Peel the asparagus and soak spears in salted and sugared ice water until ready to use. Cook in simmering water 3 to 4 minutes, or until *just* tender.
3. Cook the peas in boiling salt water until *just* tender.
4. Drain both vegetables in a colander lined with a paper towel. Dry out vegetables in empty skillet over low heat; set aside and keep warm. *Can be prepared 1 hour ahead up to this point.*
5. 10 MINUTES BEFORE SERVING, heat 2 tablespoons olive oil in a skillet, preferably one made of earthenware. Add the fish and cook slowly so that the fish just sears on each side, about 2 minutes. Add the shellfish, cover, and cook 3 to 5 minutes, or until the shellfish open. Discard those that refuse to open.
6. Meanwhile, in small saucepan bring the remaining oil to a boil with the garlic and pepper. Add to the skillet, raise the heat, and gently swirl until oil and liquid combine. Decorate with the chopped herbs and the peas and asparagus, either still warm or reheated in a slow oven (reheating in boiling water will only make them watery).

NOTES TO THE COOK
Clams are cleaned differently from mussels. Soak clams in at least 2 changes of salted water, then feed with a sprinkling of cornmeal for a last soaking of at least 8 hours to eliminate all the grit and sand. Clams must not be overcooked or they become tough and rubbery. Discard any that remain closed.

Mussels should be well scrubbed and soaked 45 minutes in salted water. (Follow instructions under "Mussels" at the beginning of this chapter for cleaning mussels.)

Inspired by a recipe from Maïté Escurignan's Manuel de Cuisine Basque.

FISH FILLETS WITH RED WINE
Filets de Poisson au Vin Rouge

Fish such as lamprey, monkfish, eel, trout, and shad are often served with a red wine sauce in Bordeaux. The sauce served with lamprey is thickened with its blood—a very popular spring dish served at the Brasserie de Noailles just across from the Grand Théâtre. Out of season the Bordelais will continue to order it, knowing it comes directly from a can. Many gastronomes prefer it aged in the can! (Georgio DeLuca of Dean & DeLuca in New York tells me he gets many requests for sardines aged at least ten years in the can. He does not stock them.) In the neighboring Landais region the red wine sauce for eels cooked with prunes and leeks is thickened with chocolate, which, though not evident to the taste, deepens its flavor and color. This modern version of that sauce can be used for fillets of any of the fish listed above, as well as for bass or mullet.

SERVES 4

ACTIVE WORK: 20 minutes
PARTIALLY UNATTENDED COOKING TIME: 50 minutes

> 1 1/2 cups full-bodied red wine (see Note 2)
> 2 tablespoons finely chopped shallots
> 1 pound boneless fish fillets (see suggestions above)
>   Sea salt crystals and freshly ground pepper
> 4 leeks (white parts with 1/2 inch of the green), well washed and thinly
>   sliced crosswise
> 4 tablespoons heavy cream
> 1 1/2 cups unsalted Chicken Stock, completely degreased and reduced to 1/2
>   cup
> 1 1/2 cups unsalted Fish Fumet made with red wine and reduced to 1/4 cup
>   glaze
> 8 tablespoons unsalted butter
> 1 teaspoon unsweetened cocoa dissolved in 1 1/2 teaspoons water
> 1 teaspoon red wine vinegar
> 2 tablespoons snipped fresh chives

1. In a nonaluminum saucepan, slowly reduce the red wine with the shallots to 4 tablespoons. This takes about 40 minutes.

2. Cut the fish into 4 pieces of approximately equal size, slicing each slightly on the diagonal. Lightly season with sea salt and pepper. Set aside.

3. In a steamer or the top half of a couscous cooker, steam the leeks until soft (about 12 to 15 minutes). Shake off excess moisture; place in a saucepan and cook away all moisture. Add half the cream and cook, uncovered, until thick. Season with 1/4 teaspoon ground sea salt and a pinch of pepper. Set aside uncovered.

(continued)

4. Add the reduced stock to the red wine reduction and boil down to one half to make a glaze.

5. Add fish glaze to wine and stock. (This is the fish sauce base.) *Can be prepared ahead up to this point.*

6. ABOUT 10 MINUTES BEFORE SERVING, gently reheat the leeks.

7. In a wide, deep skillet, melt 1 tablespoon of the butter; place the fish in 1 layer. For extra moisture, sprinkle with 1 tablespoon water. Cover pan tightly and cook over low heat 2 minutes.

8. Spread the fish sauce base around the fish so that the flavors mix with the pan juices. Cover and cook, basting once over low heat, about 2 minutes, or until just cooked. With a slotted spatula, transfer fish pieces to a warmed serving dish.

9. Quickly bring the pan juices to a boil; add remaining 2 tablespoons cream and boil down to one half. Gradually swirl in the remaining 7 tablespoons butter, cut into chunks, and allow sauce to thicken without boiling.

10. Mix cocoa and vinegar; stir into sauce. Adjust seasoning.

11. Place equal amounts of leeks on individual warm serving plates. Set a piece of fish on each mound. Coat with the sauce and sprinkle with chives. Serve at once as a first course.

NOTES TO THE COOK

1. If a whole fish is purchased (about 2 1/2 pounds), have the backbone and head cut up to use in making the Fish Fumet.

2. The choice of wine is very important because the sauce will be mounted with butter and will lose some of its deep color. The best wines for this kind of sauce are a California Petite Sirah, a French Côtes-du-Rhône, or an Algerian Medea or Dahra, or vin de Cahors. The wine should cook slowly so that it will mellow, and the shallots need long cooking to become soft. If the wine evaporates before the 40-minute cooking time, add a little water and cook down slowly until the shallots are soft, then let the water evaporate.

I prefer using sea salt with fish dishes; to my taste it is "saltier" and brings up the flavor of the fish.

PAN-FRIED TROUT WITH MOUNTAIN-CURED HAM AND BACON
Truites Comme en Sare

The combination of trout and bacon is not unique to camping trips in Oregon; it is also found in Yugoslavia, Italy, and France. There is nothing so wonderful as a freshly caught trout from a clean, cold, swiftly running stream cooked in bacon fat over a slowly burning fire. In this version, from the town of Sare in the Basque countryside, mountain trout about 10 inches long are pan-fried in bacon-flavored oil and garnished with ham, onions, and garlic.

The repertory of trout dishes is not large in the South-West, but the dishes are quite wonderful. In the Dordogne, trout are wrapped in oiled parchment and slowly grilled over juniper-berry-scented embers, then sprinkled with *verjus* just before serving. Larger trout are stuffed with cooked cèpes, herbs, and ham, then grilled. Other regional cooks simply stuff trout with fresh herbs and butter and cook them in a simple white-wine-flavored broth.

Freshly caught trout simply do not need stuffings of salmon mousse, nor need they be smothered in cream sauces or pickled, though of course they take to these preparations wonderfully. Pond-raised trout, on the other hand, "taste as dull and dry as lengths of bandaging gauze" according to Curnonsky. Perhaps that is why there are so many elaborate preparations for them.

SERVES 2

ACTIVE WORK: 10 minutes
COOKING TIME: 7 to 8 minutes

> 2 trout (8–10 ounces each), cleaned but with head and tail left on
> 3 ounces thick-sliced bacon
> 1 tablespoon vegetable oil
> Milk
> Salt (preferably sea salt) and freshly ground pepper
> Cornmeal or flour for dredging
> 1 ounce *jambon de Bayonne,* or prosciutto, or Westphalian ham, diced
> 2 tablespoons chopped onion
> 1/2 teaspoon chopped garlic
> 4 tablespoons red wine vinegar
> 1 tablespoon finely chopped fresh parsley
> 1 good pinch of crumbled fresh thyme leaves (optional)

1. Wash the trout with vinegared water; rinse, drain, and dry.

2. Dice bacon. In a large skillet, preferably oval, slowly cook the bacon with the oil until fat is rendered and bacon is crisp, about 5 minutes. Set bacon aside, leaving fat in the skillet.

3. Dip trout in milk, then roll in cornmeal or flour seasoned with pepper and a tiny pinch of salt. Shake off excess coating.

4. Fry the trout in the skillet in fairly hot fat 4 minutes on the first side. Using two spatulas, turn trout over and fry 2 minutes longer to brown the other side. Tilt the skillet, pour off the fat, and scatter the ham, onion, and garlic around the trout. Lower heat and finish cooking, about 1 to 2 minutes, until *just cooked*. Carefully transfer trout to individual warm serving dishes. Garnish with the contents of the skillet. Add the vinegar to the skillet, bring to a boil, and pour over the trout. Sprinkle with the parsley and thyme and serve at once.

CHAPTER 9

CHICKEN

SQUAB CHICKEN OR ROCK CORNISH GAME HEN WITH LEMON-GARLIC SAUCE
Poussin Rôti à l'Ail au Citron

A sauce of sweet garlic and astringent lemon at first astounded me. It turned out to be one of the most wonderful blends of two ingredients that I have ever tasted. Almost any bird could be served with this sauce; André Daguin used guinea hen when he first demonstrated it to me. Since then I have switched to squab chickens and finally to Rock Cornish game hens that have never been frozen. Any of these birds—or a chicken—makes a succulent foil for the sauce.

Originally this is a Catalan dish that bears the nickname "the poultry dish for the bandits' hideout" (*repaire de bandits Catalans*), perhaps because the garlic is cooked so long it loses its strong aroma and thus cannot give away the location of the hiding bandits!

The dish can be made in two stages: the sauce base the day before, and the cooking of the bird and the assembling just before it is served. Daguin suggests serving it with a garnish of a gratin of sliced summer vegetables: eggplants, tomatoes, and zucchini.

162

SERVES 6

ACTIVE WORK: 1 hour
PARTIALLY UNATTENDED SIMMERING TIME: 1 to 2 hours
ROASTING TIME: 45 minutes to 1 1/4 hours

>   3 large fresh Rock Cornish game hens (1 1/2 pounds each) or 6 smaller
>   game hens (3/4 pound each)
>   Coarse (kosher) salt and freshly ground pepper to taste
>   6 ounces large fresh garlic* (about 1 packed cup cloves)
>   3 large lemons, unpeeled, dipped in boiling water for 30 seconds to
>   remove any foreign matter and drained dry
>   1/2 teaspoon sugar
>   1 1/2 cups light cream or half-and-half
>   3 tablespoons unsalted butter, at room temperature
>   1/4 cup ruby or tawny port wine or dry Madeira wine
>   2 cups unsalted Chicken Stock, degreased and reduced to 1 cup

*Do not use elephant garlic, which has an odd taste when cooked.

1. Rub the hens with salt and pepper; refrigerate, loosely covered, until 30 minutes before cooking.

2. Separate garlic cloves. Blanch garlic in boiling water 2 minutes; drain and peel (makes 1 packed cup).

3. Peel 1 1/2 of the lemons with a vegetable peeler and set peel aside. Remove inner white peel and cut the lemons into thin slices. Discard all seeds. Blanch peel in boiling water 1 minute and drain.

4. In a heavy 3-quart enameled saucepan, combine peeled garlic cloves, lemon peel and slices, sugar, 1 teaspoon salt, and 1 quart fresh water. Bring to a boil; reduce heat and simmer, uncovered, 1 to 2 hours, or until liquid in pan has almost entirely evaporated and garlic cloves are golden brown and meltingly tender. Stir from time to time to avoid burning. (This can be done in a 350° F. oven, in a heatproof glass or earthenware bowl.

5. Add cream or half-and-half and reduce by half, stirring. Strain through a fine sieve, pushing down on solids; discard solids. Sauce base will be thick and will taste slightly acrid. Set aside, uncovered. When cool, refrigerate until ready to use. *Can be prepared 1 day in advance up to this point.*

6. 1 1/4 HOURS BEFORE SERVING, preheat oven to 350° F. Cut remaining 1 1/2 lemons into quarters. Slip 1 or 2 quarters into cavity of each hen. Truss birds and rub with butter.

7. Arrange hens on their sides in a greased roasting pan. Roast 45 minutes to 1 1/4 hours (depending upon size), turning and basting hens every 15 minutes to brown them evenly. To test for doneness, prick the thighs—if the juices run clear, the hens are done. Remove trussing strings and lemon quarters; arrange hens on heatproof serving dish. Cover loosely with foil and return to turned-off oven to keep warm.

8. Discard fat in roasting pan. Deglaze with port or Madeira, stirring to dissolve all

the brown particles that cling to the bottom of the pan. Add stock and reduce quickly over high heat by half. Pour into small saucepan.

9. Halve the larger hens, if using; add any new juices that birds have exuded onto serving dish to the sauce. Let juices stand a few moments so that fat will rise to surface. Skim and discard fat. Stir in reserved garlic cream. Reduce to a creamy sauce, 1 1/3 cups. Adjust seasoning, adding a few drops of lemon juice for perfect balance between sweet and sour. Serve at once.

ROAST CHICKEN STUFFED WITH GARLIC CROUTONS IN THE STYLE OF THE CORRÈZE
Poularde Farcie en Chaponnade Comme en Corrèze

A perfectly roasted chicken can be simplicity itself, elegant in concept and rustic in flavor. Basically, this is just a roasting chicken stuffed with slices of dry country bread (cut from large round loaves called *tourtes*) that have been rubbed with garlic and then sprinkled with salt, thyme, and walnut oil. The bread slices are called *la frotte* in the Corrèze. The special quality of this dish derives from the taste of the barding fat which, when melted, is used as a basting medium, resulting in a rich, flavorful skin as well as a very crisp one. After the chicken is roasted, the pieces of bread are pulled out and allowed to soak up the degreased juices in the pan.

An interesting first course, such as Hot Mussel Salad, can combine with this dish to make a very elegant dinner. Finish with Mint Parfait Stuffed with Chocolate Mousse.

SERVES 6

ACTIVE WORK: about 20 minutes
ROASTING TIME: about 1 1/4 hours

> 1 roasting chicken (5–5 1/2 pounds)
> Salt and freshly ground pepper
> 2 tablespoons imported walnut oil
> 1 1/2 teaspoons finely chopped garlic (not mashed)
> 1 sprig thyme or 1/4 teaspoon dried, crumbled
> 6 (1/2-inch-thick) slices Country-Style Bread, crusts trimmed
> 2–3 thin strips fresh pork fatback, or 1 piece salt fatback, simmered in water
> 3 minutes, rinsed, drained, and thinly sliced
> 2 tablespoons rendered chicken, goose, or duck fat, or 2 1/2 tablespoons
> unsalted butter
> 1 cup chopped onions (about 1 medium onion)
> 1 large carrot, chopped
> 1/2 leek, thinly sliced

1. Position rack on lower oven shelf and preheat oven to 425° F.

2. Remove all the fat from chicken and reserve for rendering, if desired. Trim liver and heart. Peel gizzard and chop into small pieces. Discard skin from neck. Chop neck bone into small pieces. Wipe cavity with moistened paper towel. Season cavity with salt and pepper.

3. In small bowl, combine oil, garlic, 1/4 teaspoon salt, 1/8 teaspoon pepper, and thyme; mix well. Brush each bread slice with garlic mixture. Stuff cavity with bread slices and then liver and heart. Truss chicken loosely. Pat chicken dry with paper towels. Cover breast with thin layer of fatback and tie in place.

4. Melt poultry fat or butter in a 4- or 5-quart pot or casserole over low heat. Add vegetables and cook until softened, about 5 minutes. Add chopped gizzard and neck bones; cook 1 minute, mixing so that contents of pot are coated in fat.

5. Roll chicken in the vegetable and bone mixture. Nestle chicken upside down, scattering some of the vegetables and bones on its back. Transfer to oven and roast, uncovered, 15 minutes.

6. Lower oven temperature to 350° F. Turn chicken onto its side. Cover pot with generously buttered parchment paper, then with a tight-fitting lid; roast 20 minutes. Turn chicken onto other side, cover, and roast an additional 20 minutes. Remove fatback strips from chicken breast. Set chicken breast side up and continue roasting, uncovered, until golden brown, basting occasionally with the juices in the pan, about 20 minutes. (Chicken is done when, on piercing thickest part of thigh with fork, juices run clear—or test thigh with meat thermometer for 160° F.)

7. Remove chicken and keep warm. Quickly strain cooking juices into a tall, narrow container set in a bowl of ice water. Discard vegetables and bones after pressing down on them to extract all their flavor. Degrease cooking juices. Deglaze pot with 1 cup water and bring to a boil, scraping up browned bits that cling to bottom and sides of pot. Return degreased cooking juices to the pot and boil down to about 1 1/4 cups. Taste and adjust seasoning.

8. Untie chicken and remove stuffing from cavity. Transfer both to heated serving dish. Spoon juices over stuffing until completely saturated, using about half the sauce. Carve chicken. Pass remaining sauce separately.

CHICKEN IN A POT
Poule au Pot à la Gasconne

Character and *flavor* are the best words to describe this dish. On farms where chickens still scratch the barnyard earth and are fed on maize, they stew in the pot for many hours before coming to table. I have rarely eaten such a bird since I lived in Morocco, where there was hardly anything else. We cooked these tough birds at least 3 1/2 hours, which resulted in tasty but still chewy flesh. I have adapted this recipe to work with the tender, quick-cooking roasting chickens that are easily available.

In the past, one simmered the vegetables along with the chicken for hours. The flavors mingled, and the chicken, stuffing, stock, and vegetables had both character and old-fashioned good flavor. In this recipe the assorted vegetables for serving are steamed to retain their individual flavor. Serve this with the accompanying tangy Green Sauce.

In the Périgord a similar dish is served, but *sauce de Sorges* (served with salmon in Steamed Salmon with Cooked Egg Sauce) is the typical accompaniment. The true *poule au pot* from the Béarn, the ultimate "mother" version from which all other regional recipes have been derived, always includes a stuffing flavored with marjoram and thyme. Otherwise the dish is exactly the same as one I present. This Gascon version was taught to me by Roger Duffour.

A perfectly cooked stuffed chicken like this is, of course, at its best with a simple salad and a refreshing dessert such as Prunes in Sauternes. I would suggest serving them with some freshly baked Madeleines from Dax.

SERVES 4

STOCK
ACTIVE WORK: 20 minutes
UNATTENDED SIMMERING TIME: 3 to 4 hours

CHICKEN
ACTIVE WORK: 20 minutes
SIMMERING TIME: 1 1/4 hours

SAUCE
ACTIVE WORK: 10 minutes
COOKING TIME: 10 minutes

Stock

- 3 pounds veal bones
- 3 pounds inexpensive chicken parts (wings, neck, backs, and feet)
- 1 large leek, halved, well washed, and cut into 3-inch lengths
- 1 onion, unpeeled, halved, cut side browned on an ungreased griddle or over an open flame
- 2 ribs celery, cut up
- 1/2 bunch parsley stems
- 2 tablespoons coarse (kosher) salt
  Mixed spices—1/8 teaspoon each: nutmeg, black pepper, cloves, and cayenne; pinch of ground ginger
- 1 tablespoon tomato paste
- 1 bay leaf
- 1/4 teaspoon dried thyme
- 6 cloves garlic, whole and unpeeled

Chicken

- 1 whole roasting chicken (3 1/2 to 4 pounds)
- 7–8 ounces *jambon de Bayonne,* prosciutto, or Westphalian ham

1 small onion, quartered
2 shallots, peeled
2 small cloves garlic, peeled
3 chicken livers, picked over
Pinch of sugar
1 tablespoon mixed chopped fresh herbs: parsley, thyme, marjoram,
   chervil, and bay leaf
1 whole egg, lightly beaten
1/2 cup soft, crustless bread crumbs
Salt and freshly ground pepper to taste

Green Sauce

3 eggs
4 teaspoons wine vinegar
1/2 cup olive oil
2 tablespoons chopped parsley
2 teaspoons chopped shallots
Salt and freshly ground pepper to taste

Steamed Vegetable Garnish

4 (3/4-inch-thick) leeks
4 ribs celery
4 large carrots
4 small white turnips
8 new potatoes
1 small green cabbage
Salt and freshly ground pepper to taste

1. Place veal bones and chicken parts in a deep 7- or 8-quart kettle, stockpot, or casserole. Add 5 quarts cold water and bring to a boil. Simmer, uncovered, 10 minutes, skimming often. When all the scum has been removed, add leek, onion, celery, parsley, salt, the mixed spices, tomato paste, bay leaf, thyme, and garlic. Bring back to a boil; lower heat and allow stock to simmer gently, partially covered, 3 to 4 hours.

2. Meanwhile, remove all excess fat from cavity of chicken. Add fat to the stock for added flavor. Process the ham in the workbowl of a food processor fitted with the metal blade until coarsely ground. (Or use a food grinder.) Add onion, shallots, garlic, chicken livers, sugar, and herbs. Process until well blended. Mix in egg and bread crumbs. Add salt and pepper to taste. Stuff the chicken, sew up openings carefully, and truss securely.

3. When stock is full-flavored, remove and discard vegetables and bones, using a slotted spoon. Add enough cold water to make 5 quarts liquid. Slip in the stuffed

chicken. Bring almost to a boil, then lower heat and cook at a simmer, partially covered, 1 1/4 hours, or until chicken is cooked (internal temperature of thigh is 160° F.).

4. To make the sauce, hard-boil the eggs, scoop out the yolks, and discard the whites. Place yolks in the workbowl of a food processor fitted with the metal blade; add vinegar and whirl to blend. With machine on, add oil in a slow, steady stream. Scrape into a small bowl. Stir in parsley and shallots; season to taste with salt and pepper. *Sauce can be prepared hours in advance.*

5. Trim and discard leek roots; split leeks lengthwise, wash well, and cut off green shoots. Trim off celery leaves and hard bases, use a vegetable peeler to scrape off strings, and cut ribs into 3-inch lengths. Peel, trim, and shape carrots, turnips, and potatoes into 1 1/2-inch ovals. Set vegetables aside under a damp kitchen towel.

6. Remove outer leaves of cabbage, cut into quarters, and discard core. In a deep saucepan, blanch cabbage quarters in boiling salted water 10 minutes. Drain well, refresh, and drain.

7. 20 MINUTES BEFORE SERVING, return cabbage quarters to the saucepan; add 1 1/2 cups of the simmering stock (strained), season with salt and pepper to taste, and simmer, covered, 20 minutes.

8. Steam vegetables 10 to 15 minutes, or until just tender. Use either a couscous pot or a collapsible steamer set in a covered saucepan with 1 1/2 cups boiling seasoned water. *The vegetables can be steamed 1 hour ahead of time.* They should then be under-cooked, drained, seasoned with salt and pepper, and left under a damp kitchen terry towel. Steam 5 minutes just before serving to finish their cooking.

9. To serve, cut chicken into quarters, discarding all the strings. Cut away backbone and wing tips. Arrange quarters in the center of a heated serving dish. Slice stuffing and arrange overlapping slices at one end of the dish. Garnish with piles of leeks, celery, carrots, turnips, potatoes, and cabbage. Spoon a few table-spoons hot stock over chicken and vegetables. Pass the sauce.

NOTE TO THE COOK

After the dish has been served, cool the stock and degrease completely. Reduce to 2 quarts. Cool, cover, and refrigerate or freeze for use in other dishes.

CHICKEN WITH RED ONION SAUCE
Poulet aux Oignons de Trébous

In the South-West you will find many dishes—chicken, veal, tuna, or duck—smothered in onions, a residue, possibly, of Moorish influence, since so many Moroccan dishes are structured this way. A Gascon friend told me I could not leave this dish out because it is a typical "Mother's dish," as basic to South-West cookery as beans and franks are to American.

I have spoken in the Introduction of the role played by "Mother's cooking" in South-West France. My friend Pierre Veilletet, a journalist originally from the Landes where Chicken with Red Onion Sauce is much beloved, refers to this kind of matriarchal cooking as *la cuisine ombilicale*. Pierre speaks eloquently of the South-West mothers and their total matriarchal power over everything that enters the mouth. For every problem the mother-cook will offer a culinary solution: garlic bread for worms; soup for every ailment. Her great refrain is, "It's good for you, so *eat!*" Pierre refers to all this alleged knowledge as *la gastronostalgie*.

One thing I like about this dish is its utter simplicity. It requires no stock, just perfectly chosen ingredients: a fine, tasty chicken and a good-quality cured ham to complement the flavor of the red onions. Serve rice or noodles with this, and a tart green salad scattered with roasted walnuts. An unusually refreshing dessert would be Preserved Spiced Pears in Red Wine with Armagnac.

SERVES 4

ACTIVE WORK: 15 minutes
COOKING TIME: about 35 minutes

> 1 chicken (3 1/2 pounds), quartered
> Salt and freshly ground pepper to taste
> 2 tablespoons rendered goose fat, or substitute another poultry fat
> 2 1/2 ounces *jambon de Bayonne*, prosciutto, or Westphalian ham, diced (1/2 cup diced)
> 2 pounds red onions, coarsely chopped (about 3 cups)
> 1/2 cup dry white wine
> 1 tablespoon mixed chopped fresh herbs: parsley and chives

1. Rub the chicken with salt and pepper as soon as you bring it home; cover with plastic wrap and keep refrigerated. Before cooking, remove from refrigerator and allow to stand 30 minutes to come to room temperature.

2. Heat poultry fat in a deep 12-inch heavy-bottomed skillet over medium-high heat. Add chicken quarters, skin side down, and cook until browned, 2 to 3 minutes per side, shaking skillet to keep chicken from sticking.

3. Add diced ham, cover, and allow ham to soften, about 2 minutes. Add onions and cook, covered, over low heat 5 minutes, or until they are soft but not brown.

4. Add wine and bring to a boil; stir to blend flavors. Cover tightly and cook over low heat 20 minutes, turning chicken once in the cooking juices. (Chicken can wait in the skillet with the onions, partially covered, for 30 minutes before serving.)

5. 15 MINUTES BEFORE SERVING, preheat broiler. Remove cooked chicken quarters and arrange them skin side up in a shallow flameproof baking dish; set aside.

6. Meanwhile, slowly boil down onions and cooking liquid in skillet until thick but still saucelike. Adjust seasoning. Run chicken quarters under broiler for 2 to 3 minutes to reheat and crisp the skin; pour onion sauce over and glaze for 30 seconds. Decorate with fresh chopped herbs and serve at once.

CHICKEN WITH GARLIC PEARLS AND SAUTERNES WINE SAUCE
Poulet aux Perles d'Ail Doux et au Sauternes

The original way to do this old Gascon dish is to rub a tasty barnyard hen with garlic and then stuff it with many garlic cloves. The hen is then cooked slowly so that the cloves become soft but do not lose their shape. Later the pan is deglazed with Sauternes (which has a high concentration of sugar), and the cloves are pulled out and left to caramelize in the pan juices. The following recipe is a sophisticated adaptation conceived by Alain Dutournier—more elegant, I think, than the original, and with a deep, rich flavor that is highly seductive. In the Dutournier adaptation, I believe this dish is truly great.

The sauce base and the garlic cloves are prepared ahead of time, and the chicken, quartered, is broiled just before serving. Thus one has an elegant dish with a minimum investment in last-minute work. The sauce is really the key: chopped vegetables and bones are cooked in an open pan; the Sauternes is added gradually and allowed to boil away and caramelize before more is added, so that the color deepens; the taste of the vegetables and bones mellows; and the bouquet of the wine becomes intoxicatingly intense. The garlic cloves, cooked separately, are added at the last minute. This sauce can be made up in quantity and frozen, for use whenever you wish.

A pleasant and unexpected beginning to dinner could be Old-Fashioned Rabbit Soup. Serve the chicken with buttered ribbon noodles. For dessert, I'd serve a crisp, warm Gascon Croustade—a flaky Pastry Cake Filled with Apples and Prunes in Armagnac.

SERVES 4

ACTIVE WORK: 30 minutes
PARTIALLY ATTENDED COOKING TIME FOR SAUCE: 2 1/2 hours
PARTIALLY ATTENDED COOKING TIME FOR GARLIC: 2 hours
BROILING TIME: 20 to 25 minutes

> 1 chicken (3 pounds)
> Salt and freshly ground pepper to taste
> 2/3 cup Crème Fraîche (do not substitute sour cream or yogurt)

Sauternes Sauce

> 2 1/2 tablespoons oil or rendered poultry fat
> 1 3/4 cups thinly sliced onions
> 1 2/3 cups thinly sliced carrots
> 1 leek, split, well washed, and thinly sliced
> 2 pounds meaty veal neck bones or riblets, cut into 1-inch pieces

    1 bottle (750 ml) Sauternes, sweet California Semillon Blanc, or other
       sweet white wine
1 1/2 cups unsalted Chicken Stock, degreased
    Herb bouquet: 3 sprigs parsley, 2 sprigs thyme, 1 celery leaf, and 1 bay
       leaf, tied together

    2 fresh heads garlic (preferably with large cloves, but *not* elephant
       garlic), cloves separated and unpeeled
1 1/2 teaspoons unsalted butter
1 1/2 teaspoons sugar
    2 carrots, scraped
    Salt and freshly ground pepper
  1/3 cup heavy cream
    2 teaspoons (or more) strained fresh lemon juice (optional)
2–3 tablespoons unsalted butter (optional)
    1 tablespoon chopped fresh parsley

1. Cut chicken down the back along both sides of backbone; remove backbone. Cut wings off at second joint. Quarter chicken. Rub with salt, pepper, and Crème Fraîche. Refrigerate until 1 hour before serving. *Can be left to marinate overnight in the refrigerator.*

2. Using a heavy cleaver, chop chicken neck, backbone, and wings into very small pieces. Peel and slice gizzard and set aside. (Reserve liver for another use.)

3. To make the sauce, heat oil or fat in a large deep skillet, preferably copper or enameled cast-iron, over medium heat. Add onions, sliced carrots, and leek. Cover and cook 5 minutes. Remove cover and continue cooking, stirring frequently, until vegetables are lightly browned around the edges, about 15 minutes.

4. Add veal bones and reserved chopped chicken bones. Raise heat to medium-high and cook, stirring often, until bones are evenly browned on all sides, about 10 minutes. Drain off fat and discard.

5. Pour 1 cup wine into skillet and cook until liquid is reduced to a glaze, about 20 minutes. Continue adding remaining wine 1 cup at a time, reducing to a glaze after each addition (bones and vegetables should begin to caramelize and turn orange-brown). Reduce heat to low. Add stock, herb bouquet, and reserved gizzard to skillet. Cover and cook 1 hour.

6. Transfer mixture to a sieve set over a deep bowl and strain, pressing down on vegetables with back of spoon to extract all liquid; discard bones and vegetables. Strain sauce through fine-mesh sieve into a small saucepan. Skim off fat that rises to surface. Bring to a boil and set saucepan half over the heat. Cook at a slow boil, skimming, 10 to 15 minutes, or until reduced to 1 cup. Set aside. *Sauce can be prepared several days ahead up to this point;* keep refrigerated or frozen.

7. Preheat oven to 250° F.

8. To make garlic pearls, bring 3 cups water to a boil in a small saucepan. Add garlic cloves and cook 3 minutes. Drain garlic well; peel off skins. Melt 1 1/2 teaspoons

butter in heavy ovenproof pan over *very* low heat. Add garlic, sprinkle with sugar, and cook in oven, uncovered, until garlic is very soft and golden (but not brown), about 2 hours, shaking pan two or three times—do not stir or garlic will fall apart. *Garlic can be prepared several hours ahead;* set aside at room temperature.

9. Meanwhile, make carrot garnish. Notch whole carrots with lemon zester or stripper; cut into thin flower-shaped rounds. Blanch 30 seconds, then drop into ice water to stop cooking; drain. Cover and refrigerate.

10. Bring reserved chicken to room temperature. Preheat broiler. Lightly coat broiler pan with oil. Arrange chicken skin side down on pan. Broil 10 minutes about 6 inches from heat source. Turn chicken over, baste once with Crème Fraîche marinade and continue broiling until skin is crisp, meat is cooked through, and juices run clear when chicken is pierced with fork, about 5 to 7 minutes for breasts and an additional 10 to 12 minutes for legs.

11. Meanwhile, place reserved sauce over medium heat and bring to a boil. Add cream and continue boiling until sauce is thick enough to coat a spoon, about 10 minutes. Reduce heat to low and swirl in garlic. Taste and adjust seasoning, adding lemon juice to taste if sauce is too sweet. If sauce is thin, swirl in up to 3 tablespoons butter, 1/2 tablespoon at a time. Remove from heat.

12. Cut chicken into serving pieces. Remove as many bones as possible. Arrange chicken attractively on heated platter. Spoon sauce over top. Place carrot rounds in sieve and dip into boiling water for a second to reheat. Garnish with parsley and carrot rounds. Serve at once.

NOTE TO THE COOK

In the recipes for Chicken with Garlic Pearls and Sauternes Wine Sauce and Chicken Breasts with Mussels and Asparagus Flans, an innovative basting medium for broiling is used: crème fraîche. To simulate the crème fraîche so widely used in French cooking, see Appendix.

SAUTÉED CHICKEN WITH RED PEPPERS, TOMATOES, AND BLACK OLIVES
Poulet à la Catalane

There are many ways to do this dish. I think this way is superb. It even makes supermarket chickens taste good, and the touch of cinnamon blends perfectly with everything else. You will want to serve rice with this. For dessert I'd serve a Soufflé Omelet with Fresh Fruits.

SERVES 4

ACTIVE WORK: 20 minutes
COOKING TIME: 30 minutes

1 chicken (3 pounds), quartered
  Salt and freshly ground pepper
2 cups unsalted Chicken Stock, degreased
3 tablespoons olive oil
3 ounces lean salt pork, simmered 3 minutes, drained, refreshed,
    drained, and cubed (1 cup cubed)
3 onions, halved and sliced (2 cups sliced)
8 plump cloves garlic, unpeeled
  Herb bouquet: 3 sprigs parsley, 1 sprig thyme, 1 small bay leaf, 1 small
    piece cinnamon stick, tied together
3 tablespoons dry white wine
2 fresh red bell peppers, roasted and peeled, seeded, and cut into chunks
    or 1 (5-ounce) jar pimentos, drained and cut into chunks
1 1/2 pounds red-ripe tomatoes, peeled, halved, and cut into chunks
  Zest of 1 lemon (see Note)
12 salt- or oil-cured black olives
  Pinch of red pepper flakes
  Chopped fresh parsley

1. Rub the chicken with salt and pepper. Cut away excess fat. Loosely wrap with plastic wrap and keep refrigerated until 1 hour before serving.

2. ABOUT 1 HOUR BEFORE SERVING, remove chicken from refrigerator to bring to room temperature. Dry chicken well. In a small saucepan, reduce stock to 2/3 cup.

3. In a 12-inch *sauteuse* or deep heavy-bottomed skillet, heat 2 tablespoons of the olive oil over medium heat. Add diced salt pork; cover and cook 1 minute. Raise heat; add chicken pieces skin side down, half the onions, and the garlic cloves. Brown chicken 1 minute each side, shaking pan to keep its contents from sticking. Lower heat, cover, and cook slowly 10 minutes.

4. Uncover pan; tilt and degrease the juices. Turn chicken over. Add herb bouquet and white wine; cover and cook slowly 10 minutes longer.

5. Meanwhile, in a separate skillet, cook the remaining onions, the peppers, and tomatoes in remaining 1 tablespoon olive oil 5 minutes, tossing. Add olives and a pinch of red pepper flakes. Tilt pan to remove excess fat and use a paper towel to blot it. Set aside.

6. Remove cooked chicken breast pieces to a side dish; cover and keep warm. Add reduced stock to the skillet containing the chicken legs. Cook legs and garlic, uncovered, 5 minutes, or until legs are cooked. You should have about 4 tablespoons syrupy pan juices, plus garlic and pork. Remove herb bouquet.

7. Cut lemon zest into very thin 1-inch strips. Blanch in boiling water for an instant and refresh in cold water. Drain and set aside for the garnish.

8. Return chicken breasts to pan. Turn each piece of chicken and garlic in the syrupy juices in order to glaze.

9. Raise heat and add contents of second skillet. Swirl over heat to combine for 30 seconds. Remove from heat; adjust seasoning with salt and pepper.

(continued)

10. Arrange chicken, vegetables, garlic, and olives on a platter. Spoon over the sauce, which will be thick. Sprinkle with parsley and the lemon zest.

NOTE TO THE COOK

Remove the lemon zest with a four-holed zester, if you have one. If not, use a swivel vegetable peeler and then cut zest into the very thin 1-inch strips.

CHICKEN WITH PEPPERS, HAM, AND TOMATOES
Poulet à la Basquaise

Another classic dish with a hundred interpretations. Mine is simple to make and good eating. Serve with sautéed potatoes or rice. Make a *clafouti* with the first Italian black plums of the season—Custard and Fresh Fruit Baked in a Skillet—or Fresh Strawberries with Peppercorns and Red Wine would be a delicious dessert.

SERVES 8

ACTIVE WORK: 20 minutes
COOKING TIME: 30 to 40 minutes

> 2 chickens (3 pounds each)
> Salt and freshly ground pepper
> 6 tablespoons aromatic olive oil
> 1 1/2 cups coarsely chopped onions
> 2 cups coarsely chopped mixed green and red peppers, seeds and
>   membranes removed
> 6 small or 4 medium cloves garlic, unpeeled
> 3 ounces *jambon de Bayonne*, prosciutto, or Westphalian ham, diced (2/3
>   cup diced)
> 2 pounds red-ripe tomatoes or 2 (20-ounce) cans Italian tomatoes,
>   drained, peeled, seeded, and cut into large chunks
> 2 teaspoons tomato paste (if using tasteless tomatoes)
> 2 good pinches of sugar
> 1/2 cup dry white wine
> 1/4 teaspoon cayenne pepper or 1 small fresh hot pepper, seeded and cut
>   into extra-thin rings
> Chopped fresh parsley

1. Quarter chickens: set aside backbones, wings, and necks. Rub legs, thighs, and breasts with salt and pepper. Loosely cover with plastic wrap and keep refrigerated until 1 hour before cooking.

2. ABOUT 1 HOUR BEFORE SERVING, remove chicken from refrigerator to bring to room temperature. Dry chicken well. With a cleaver, chop backbones, wings, and necks

into 1-inch pieces. In a deep skillet, brown chopped chicken pieces in 3 tablespoons of the oil.

3. Add onions and brown lightly around the edges. Add peppers, garlic, ham, tomatoes, tomato paste (if using), and sugar. Cover and cook over low heat 15 minutes.

4. Meanwhile, in another skillet over high heat, brown chicken in remaining 3 tablespoons oil on all sides. Lower heat, cover, and cook 5 minutes. Pour off all the fat. Add wine; cover and cook 10 minutes.

5. Remove bones from the sauce and skim off all the fat. Remove garlic cloves; crush and return to the sauce.

6. Add the sauce to the chicken and cook slowly, uncovered, until breasts are tender. Remove breasts and set aside; continue cooking legs until tender. Return breasts to sauce to reheat. Add cayenne or fold in hot pepper rings. Serve garnished with chopped parsley.

CHICKEN BREASTS WITH PINE NUTS, CÈPES, AND HAM *GOUDALIÈRE*
Blanc de Volaille à la Goudalière

This chicken dish, one of the best from the Landes, is garnished with pine nuts, wild mushrooms (cèpes), and country-cured ham. (*Goudalière* is a Landais word for a gastronomic society.) Today the Landes region is filled with pine trees, planted over a hundred years ago to hold back the erosion of marshy areas. It is not surprising, therefore, to find pine nuts in many local recipes—they are used in cookies and cakes, sautéed with grilled wild birds, and, as in this recipe, sprinkled over the dish.

The original version of this dish calls for the use of a harsh local wine named Tursan, which tasted to me like a mixture of vermouth and lemon juice—a combination I have employed for the base of the sauce. A well-reduced Demi-Glace is very important to the success of this dish: the richer it is, the less butter will be needed to thicken the sauce. The method of cooking chicken breasts in a reduced Demi-Glace is an unusual technique, but one that results in an extremely succulent, silky piece of meat.

For a more substantial meal, accompany this dish with Fried Cornmeal Porridge Cakes in the Style of Gascony. For dessert, serve wedges of Croustade with Quince and Prunes—a rich mixture of prunes and quince baked in a pastry and served with a bowl of lightly whipped unsweetened cream. If this seems too rich, try the Red Wine Sorbet and some petits fours straight from the bakery.

(continued)

SERVES 4

ACTIVE WORK: 15 minutes
COOKING TIME: 35 minutes

> 2 ounces dried French cèpes or Italian porcini, or, if available, 1 pound fresh or 1 (10-ounce) can whole or quartered cèpes (see Note)
> 2 large whole chicken breasts (about 1 1/4 pounds each), on the bone, with first wing joint attached, at room temperature
> Salt and freshly ground pepper to taste
> 8 tablespoons unsalted butter
> 1 1/2 tablespoons chopped shallots
> 1 1/2 tablespoons strained fresh lemon juice
> 1 1/2 tablespoons dry vermouth, or substitute dry white wine
> 1 cup Demi-Glace
> 2 tablespoons olive oil
> 3/4 pound fresh mushrooms, quartered
> 1 1/2 tablespoons finely chopped fresh parsley
> 1 teaspoon finely chopped garlic (chopped by hand)
> 3–4 ounces *jambon de Bayonne,* prosciutto, or Westphalian ham, cubed (2/3–3/4 cup cubed)
> 3 tablespoons pine nuts, toasted
> 1 tablespoon Cognac

1. Cover dried mushrooms with hot water. Let stand 30 minutes.

2. Set rack on lowest oven shelf and preheat oven to 300° F.

3. Cut chicken breasts in half. Pat dry with paper towels. Sprinkle with salt and pepper.

4. Melt 3 tablespoons of the butter in a 12-inch ovenproof skillet over medium-high heat. Add chicken breasts, skin side down, and cook just until browned, about 3 minutes. *Do not turn chicken.* Tilt skillet and remove excess fat. Add shallots, lemon juice, and vermouth. Continue cooking over medium-high heat until juices are reduced to a glaze. Add 1/4 cup of the Demi-Glace. Cover skillet tightly, transfer to oven, and cook until chicken is just firm to the touch, 15 to 20 minutes. (Breasts are not turned over at any time.)

5. Meanwhile, drain cèpes in sieve set over small bowl. Strain soaking liquid through coffee filter paper or several layers of damp cheesecloth. Set aside. Rinse cèpes with cold water to remove any remaining dirt or sand. Drain dry.

6. Heat olive oil in a 10-inch skillet over medium heat. Add cèpes and fresh mushrooms and sauté 5 minutes. Add reserved soaking liquid and cook until reduced to a glaze, about 12 minutes. Add parsley, garlic, and salt to taste. Toss lightly until well blended. Transfer mushroom mixture to a small bowl.

7. Add ham cubes to same skillet. Place over low heat and cook 2 to 3 minutes, covered, in own fat. Return mushroom mixture to skillet and toss. Set aside.

8. Remove chicken breasts to a work surface; set skillet aside. Use a thin-bladed

knife to lift each breast off the bones in one piece. If breasts are not fully cooked, return to cooking liquid to poach gently, 1 to 2 minutes, or until done. Place skin side up on work surface. Slice each breast into 4 slices diagonally against the grain. Arrange chicken slices on heated serving dish, overlapping them slightly.

9. Discard fat from cooking liquid. Add remaining Demi-Glace. Place skillet over medium-high heat and cook until liquid is reduced by half, about 5 minutes. Remove sauce from heat and swirl in remaining butter 1 tablespoon at a time to thicken the sauce. Taste and adjust seasoning with salt and pepper. Stir in Cognac, blending well (do not heat further, or sauce will separate).

10. Strain sauce over chicken. Place mushroom and ham mixture over medium-high heat and warm until heated through. Garnish chicken with mixture. Sprinkle pine nuts on top and serve.

NOTE TO THE COOK
If using canned or fresh cèpes, omit Steps 1 and 5. Drain and dry canned cèpes. Dice the stems and quarter the caps. For Step 6, heat 2 to 3 tablespoons olive oil in a skillet until very hot. Add caps and stems; simmer 10 minutes for canned or 20 minutes for fresh cèpes. Cook until oil is clear. Then add parsley, garlic, and salt to taste.

Inspired by a recipe from Bernard Cousseau.

CHICKEN WITH SALSIFY IN PASTRY
Tourtière du Périgord aux Salsifis

This is a wonderful-tasting ragout of chicken legs and salsify wrapped in pastry. It is a specialty served around Mardi Gras in the Corrèze, the Périgord, and the Quercy. Originally it was prepared in a special three-legged iron or unlined copper pot (called a *tourtière*) placed in the fireplace and surrounded by embers.

Black salsify, black in color and also called *scorzonera*, is the most flavorful variety but the least digestible. Many people describe the taste as faintly like the meat of a coconut. Usually this *tourtière* is made with white salsify, also called oyster plant, which tastes to some like oysters and to others somewhat like asparagus with lemon. It is sometimes available in Italian markets in late winter and early spring. But other root vegetables can also be used. See the Notes to the Cook on how to substitute fresh parsnips. In the Périgord some cooks substitute quickly sautéed chanterelle mushrooms tossed with garlic and parsley, or cubed ham and peas.

On a cold day start with an Evening Garlic Soup in the Manner of the Corrèze made with onions and garlic and lightly enriched with eggs. A crisp salad is all you need as an accompaniment. Farmhouse Crêpes with South-West Fragrance, which are tender, thin, and particularly good, are served still warm. Just lightly sugar and serve with a squeeze of lemon juice and some slightly warmed Green Fig and Walnut Jam.

(continued)

SERVES 6

☆ Begin 1 day in advance
    ACTIVE WORK (DAY 1): 1 1/2 hours
    ACTIVE WORK (DAY 2): 20 minutes
    BAKING TIME: 1 hour

> 1 recipe Pastry for French Country-Style *Tourtes* and *Tourtières*
> 2 pounds chicken thighs, fat removed (about 8 thighs)
>   Salt and freshly ground pepper
> 1 clove garlic, halved
> 1 1/2 lemons (3–4 tablespoons strained fresh juice)
>   Pinch of crumbled thyme leaves
>   Pinch of ground bay leaf
> 3 ounces lean salt pork
> 2 tablespoons vegetable oil
> 1 cup thinly sliced onions
> 1 1/2 tablespoons aromatic vinegar such as sherry wine
> 2 1/2 cups unsalted Chicken Stock
> 3/4 cup heavy cream
> 2 bunches firm salsify (about 1 pound), or 1 (14-ounce) jar or can cooked salsify
> 4 tablespoons softened unsalted butter
> 3 tablespoons mixed snipped fresh herbs: chives and parsley
> 1/4 teaspoon finely chopped garlic
>   Egg yolk beaten with 1 teaspoon water

1. Make the pastry dough; refrigerate overnight.

2. Rub chicken with salt, pepper, and half a garlic clove. Sprinkle with the juice of 1/2 lemon (about 1 1/2 tablespoons), thyme, and bay leaf, and let marinate in the refrigerator at least 3 hours. Remove from refrigerator 30 minutes before cooking.

3. Blanch salt pork in plenty of water 3 minutes. Drain, rinse, and cut into 1/4-inch dice. In a large skillet, heat oil over medium-high heat. Add salt pork and sauté 5 minutes, transferring dice to a 3-quart flameproof casserole or dutch oven as they are browned.

4. Pat chicken dry. In the same skillet, brown chicken thighs, a few at a time, transferring them to casserole as they are lightly browned, about 5 minutes per side.

5. Pour off half the fat from the skillet. Add onions to skillet; cook over high heat 2 minutes, stirring constantly. Using a slotted spoon, transfer onions to casserole.

6. Deglaze skillet with vinegar. Add 2 cups of the stock and bring to a boil. Skim off scum that rises to the surface. Scrape up all the bits and pieces that cling to bottom of skillet. Pour boiling stock over chicken, onions, and salt pork and cook, covered, over medium-low heat 20 minutes. Set skillet aside.

7. Remove chicken from casserole and remove all the bones and gristle (add to stockpot if you have one on the fire).

8. Strain liquid (reserving salt pork and onions) into a tall, narrow container.

Quickly chill strained liquid and remove the fat that rises to the surface.

9. Mix chicken, onions, and salt pork in a bowl. Return liquid to casserole; reduce to 1 1/2 cups over high heat, if necessary. Add cream and boil down to 1 cup. Pour over still-warm chicken mixture. Let cool, uncovered.

10. Meanwhile, prepare the vegetable. If using fresh salsify, wash well in several changes of water. Using a stainless-steel knife, peel and cut into 2-inch pieces. Immediately drop pieces into water with a little lemon juice added (in the proportion of 1 tablespoon lemon juice to 2 cups water) to keep them from darkening. Cook salsify in 3 cups boiling salted water with the juice of 1/2 lemon until just tender, 8 to 10 minutes. Drain well and dry on a kitchen towel. (Makes about 2 cups.) If using canned salsify, drain, rinse, and drain dry on a kitchen towel.

11. Continue to cook salsify in the same skillet in which the chicken was browned, in 3 tablespoons of the butter, 1 to 2 minutes. Season to taste with pepper. Add the remaining 1/2 cup stock and boil down to a glaze, shaking the skillet often to prevent burning. Sprinkle with snipped herbs and finely chopped garlic. Season with salt to taste.

12. Fold the vegetables into the chicken-sauce mixture. Adjust seasoning, adding a teaspoon or more of strained lemon juice. Allow to cool, uncovered, then cover and refrigerate. *Prepare 1 day ahead to this point.*

13. Preheat oven to 400° F.

14. Butter a 9-inch pie pan. Between sheets of waxed paper, roll out half the dough into an 11-inch circle. Pastry is very thin—about 1/8 inch thick. Fit into prepared pie pan. Prick bottom and sides with a fork; brush a sheet of waxed paper with remaining tablespoon softened butter and place buttered side down on pastry. Fill with rice, beans, or aluminum weights. Bake 10 minutes. Remove weights and paper; lower oven temperature to 375° F. and bake 5 minutes longer. Cool pastry in pan on a rack.

15. Fill pastry-lined pan with chicken mixture. Roll out remaining dough to 9 1/2 inches. Moisten around the edges with water, cover the *tourtière* with dough, and crimp to seal. Chill at least 15 minutes before baking.

16. 1 HOUR BEFORE SERVING, position oven rack on lower-center oven shelf and line rack with a baking stone, quarry tile, or heavy black baking sheet. Preheat oven to 375° F. Make 3 small openings in top of *tourtière* and insert a funnel in each to allow steam to escape during baking.

17. Brush top of dough with beaten egg yolk and set in oven on heated tile or baking sheet to bake 15 minutes. Remove funnels. Continue baking until crust is brown, about 30 minutes. Serve hot or lukewarm. Use a serrated knife to cut *tourtière* into serving wedges.

NOTE TO THE COOK

If substituting parsnips, cook 1 pound fresh parsnips, unpeeled, in boiling salted water until just tender—that is, until it is easy to pierce one with a skewer. Drain and refresh in cold water. Peel and cut into 2-inch pieces. Drain dry on a kitchen terry towel. Add a pinch of sugar to skillet in which chicken was browned before sautéing.

Inspired by a recipe from Lucien Vanel.

CHICKEN BREASTS WITH MUSSELS AND ASPARAGUS FLANS

Suprêmes de Volaille aux Moules et aux Flans d'Asperges

Chicken and mussels may seem a strange combination, but the idea of mixing chicken with shellfish is actually quite common in South-West France. In the Tarn, the chicken is combined with crayfish, and in the Charente with clams. This particular dish is based on an old Landais recipe. Originally the chicken was sautéed and the pan juices were deglazed with the mussel liquor, then the dish was garnished with mussels and asparagus. Though the traditional recipe is easy to execute and full of honest good flavor, I prefer to add such "refinements" as cream, chives, and the asparagus flans—so that a simple rustic dish becomes a sensational party dish. The asparagus flans are patterned in buttered brioche molds to make an attractive presentation. For a more substantial meal, fresh noodles are an excellent accompaniment. For dessert, serve Poached Figs in Raspberry and Red Wine Sauce.

SERVES 8

CHICKEN AND MUSSELS
ACTIVE WORK: 30 minutes
PARTIALLY ATTENDED COOKING TIME: 1 1/2 hours
BROILING TIME: 5 minutes

OPTIONAL ASPARAGUS FLANS AND SPEAR GARNISH
ACTIVE WORK: 30 minutes
COOKING TIME: about 20 minutes

> 4 **pounds mussels, scrubbed and debearded***
> 1/3 **cup chopped onions**
> **Herb bouquet: 3 sprigs parsley, 1 sprig thyme, 1 bay leaf, and 1 sprig celery leaves, tied together**
> 4 **large whole unboned chicken breasts (about 1 pound each)**
> **Salt and freshly ground pepper**
> **Milk**
> 8 **tablespoons unsalted butter**
> 1/3 **cup minced shallots**
> 1/2 **cup dry white wine**
> 3 **small cloves garlic, halved**

Asparagus Flans

> 2 **dozen medium-size asparagus spears (about 2 pounds)**
> 2 **eggs**
> 2 **egg yolks**
> 1/2 **teaspoon salt**
> 1/4 **teaspoon finely ground white pepper**

1/8 teaspoon freshly grated nutmeg
2/3 cup milk
2/3 cup heavy cream

1 1/2 cups heavy cream (for the sauce)
1/2 cup Crème Fraîche
3 tablespoons strained fresh lemon juice
4 tablespoons snipped fresh chives

*Follow instructions for cleaning mussels in Chapter 8, under "Mussels—cleaning mussels" (see Index).

1. Combine mussels, 1/2 cup water, onions, and herb bouquet in a *wide* pan. Cover tightly and cook, shaking pan often until mussels open, about 3 to 5 minutes. (This can be done in a covered roasting pan in a hot oven, if necessary; bake 8 minutes.) Using a slotted spoon, remove mussels from pan 1 at a time, allowing juices to fall back into the pan. Discard any mussels that did not open. Shell the mussels and reserve.

2. Strain mussel liquor through several layers of damp cheesecloth and reserve. (If mussel liquor is excessively salty, use only half and add extra stock or water when simmering the sauce.)

3. Split the chicken breasts. Remove bones and tendons, but do not remove the skin. Crack chicken bones into small pieces. (The bones will be used to make the sauce.)

4. Gently flatten each breast with the side of a cleaver or spatula for uniform thickness. Season with salt and pepper. Soak in milk to cover in refrigerator until 30 minutes before broiling.

5. Make the sauce for the chicken and mussels. Melt 3 tablespoons of the butter in a large skillet over high heat. Add chicken bones and cook until lightly browned, about 2 minutes. Lower heat; add shallots and cook, stirring, until they soften. Tilt skillet; press on shallots with a slotted spoon and blot away released fat with a paper towel.

6. Deglaze with white wine. Boil down to a glaze. Add garlic and reserved mussel liquor, stirring to blend. Raise heat and bring to a boil. Simmer, covered, 30 minutes, while preparing asparagus garnish and flan mixture.

7. Trim tough ends from asparagus and discard. Cut off tips. Blanch tips in boiling salted water until crisp-tender, 2 to 3 minutes. Remove with a slotted spoon to a towel and press to extract excess water. Reserve on a heatproof plate for garnishing the dish.

8. Slice asparagus stalks into small pieces (you need 1 1/4 pounds sliced stalks for the flans). Cook stalks in boiling salted water until tender, about 6 minutes. Drain; squeeze dry to extract as much moisture as possible. Push through the fine blade of a food mill or purée in the jar of an electric blender or food processor. Measure and reserve 2/3 cup purée.

(continued)

9. In a mixing bowl, combine 2/3 cup purée, eggs, yolks, and seasonings. Gently heat the 2/3 cup milk and 2/3 cup cream. Add to bowl, then press through a strainer. Discard asparagus fibers in strainer. Allow to settle 1 minute. Skim off foam. Have ready 8 buttered brioche molds, each with a capacity of 1/3 or 1/2 cup. (Small porcelain ramekins can be substituted.)

10. Strain and degrease cooking juices in skillet. You should have about 1 1/2 cups. Return cooking juices to a clean wide saucepan, add the 1 1/2 cups heavy cream, and bring to a boil; reduce by half, about 20 minutes.

11. Fold shelled mussels into sauce and set aside, partially covered. *If not serving within 45 minutes,* refrigerate when cool. Otherwise set aside in a cool place, partially covered.

12. 45 MINUTES BEFORE SERVING, preheat oven to 325° F. Line a baking pan with 2 or 3 layers of newspaper. Cut a slit through the center of the paper to avoid its expanding when wet. Carefully ladle asparagus mixture into prepared molds. Set in lined pan. Place baking pan on center oven rack. Remove one of the filled molds. Fill pan with enough boiling water to come halfway up sides of molds. Return the filled mold. Bake 20 minutes, or until set. Flans should just puff lightly and barely shudder when lightly prodded with 2 fingers. If the flans are not set, turn off oven heat and continue baking 5 to 10 minutes longer. (Different shaped molds and cups require different cooking times.) Remove pan from oven and let molds stand in the water 10 minutes longer before turning out.

13. Meanwhile, remove chicken breasts from milk. Pat dry with a towel. Arrange skin side up on a broiler rack. Smear 1 tablespoon Crème Fraîche over each breast.

14. Broil chicken breasts about 4 inches from heat for 5 minutes. Do not turn over. Set aside and keep warm.

15. Meanwhile, reheat asparagus-tip garnish by placing plate in a warm oven to warm them up, 2 to 3 minutes. (If you drop them into boiling water they will only become waterlogged.) Asparagus tips can be set in a steamer to be reheated. If flans need to be reheated, see Note.

16. Gently reheat sauce. Cut remaining 5 tablespoons butter into small pieces. Swirl butter into reheated sauce. Adjust seasoning with lemon juice, salt and pepper to taste, and chives.

17. Remove and discard chicken skins. Cut each breast into 4 strips diagonally against the grain. If chicken is not completely cooked, add to the sauce and let the pieces poach gently for 1 minute. Do not allow sauce to boil.

18. Arrange chicken strips, mussels, and asparagus tips on individual serving dishes. Coat with the sauce. To turn out the flans, place a wide spatula over one, invert mold onto spatula, then slide upside-down mold onto the serving plate and remove mold. Repeat with remaining flans. Serve at once.

NOTE TO THE COOK

Though this dish may seem a little complicated to serve for guests, it is actually easy to execute. To make the dish smoothly, the mussels can be cooked 4 to 5 hours in advance; the sauce can be prepared ahead, the mussels kept moist in the sauce. Be careful about the mussels—if they are overcooked they'll become tough. Remember that they will be reheated and thus further cooked in the sauce. Forty-five minutes before serving, cook the flans in the oven for 20 minutes, then preheat the broiler. Five minutes before serving, broil the chicken breasts and reheat the asparagus tips and flans in a warm oven for 5 minutes before unmolding. Asparagus tips and flans can be reheated in a steamer.

CHICKEN IN RED WINE
Poulet au Vin Rouge

A true *coq au vin* should be made with an old, flavorful bird and a strong red wine. The long cooking softens the flesh of the bird and mellows the wine. This dish of young chicken in red wine is a good example of the updating of classic French country cooking using a mixture of modern and traditional methods. The dark, very flavorful sauce results from a technique called *tomber à glace*; a series of reductions of liquid makes the sauce darker, shinier—almost syrupy. If you should make Corn Cakes as an accompaniment, you will have a fine Gascon dinner. Finish with Prune and Armagnac Ice Cream.

SERVES 4

ACTIVE WORK: 15 minutes
COOKING TIME: 1 1/4 hours

2 small chickens (1 1/2 to 2 pounds each), split, or 2 small fresh Rock Cornish game hens,* split
1/2 pound (12–18) small white onions (about 1 inch in diameter)
6 ounces lean salt pork, simmered 3 minutes, drained, refreshed, drained, and cut into 1/4-inch dice
2 teaspoons rendered poultry fat, or 1 tablespoon mixed oil and butter
1 tablespoon tomato paste
2 1/2 cups full-bodied red wine such as a California Petite Sirah (see Note)
1/2 pound fresh mushrooms, halved or quartered depending upon size
3 cups unsalted Chicken Stock, degreased
Salt and freshly ground pepper
3 tablespoons grape-seed, peanut, or corn oil
1/4 cup finely chopped shallots
Chopped fresh parsley

*Avoid frozen hens; when fresh they are closest to a squab chicken.

1. Season chickens with salt and pepper. Loosely cover with plastic wrap and refrigerate until 1 hour before serving.
2. Cut an X in root end of each small onion. Drop onions into boiling water and

cook 2 minutes; drain. Refresh under cool water. Peel, leaving on enough of root and stem ends so onions will not fall apart. Dry thoroughly on paper towels.

3. Place salt pork cubes in wide noncorrodible saucepan with fat or mixed oil and butter; cook, stirring, 2 to 3 minutes. Add peeled onions and cook over medium heat, stirring, 5 minutes. Pour off any fat.

4. Add tomato paste and stir until onions take on a yellow-red tinge. Add 1/2 cup of the wine; bring to a boil, then reduce to a glaze. Add mushrooms and cook over moderate heat, stirring from time to time, until most of the moisture in the pan evaporates. With a slotted spoon, transfer mushrooms to a side dish.

5. Stir in 1 cup of the stock and blend in with the pan juices. Raise heat and cook, uncovered, until stock reduces to 1/4 cup. Add another cup of stock and repeat. Add remaining cup of stock; lower heat and cook gently 15 minutes, or until onions are tender, skimming from time to time. Liquid should have reduced to about 1/2 cup. Stir mushrooms into pan juices. Set aside, uncovered. *Can be prepared ahead up to this point.*

6. ABOUT 1 HOUR BEFORE SERVING, remove chickens from refrigerator to bring to room temperature. Dry chickens well.

7. Place the 3 tablespoons oil in a well-seasoned wide, heavy-bottomed noncorrodible skillet with a tight-fitting lid and set over high heat. When oil is hot, add chickens, skin side down. Cover skillet tightly and cook 5 minutes over high heat without lifting cover. Remove cover and wipe off moisture on lid, being sure that no moisture falls back into skillet. Cover and continue cooking over high heat 1 minute longer. (If your skillet is not large enough to handle all the chicken in 1 layer, brown in 2 batches in the same oil.)

8. Set chickens aside. Pour off oil from skillet and discard. Deglaze pan with 1/2 cup of the wine. Bring to a boil and reduce to a glaze. Return chicken, skin side up, to skillet. Scatter shallots around chicken, add remaining wine, and cook, uncovered, over medium-high heat 20 minutes, or until chickens are just cooked and wine has reduced to a glaze. As soon as chickens test for doneness, remove to a serving platter and keep warm. Continue to reduce wine if necessary.

9. Scrape reserved onions, mushrooms, and reduced stock into skillet; reheat and quickly reduce to a thick and shiny sauce, skimming once or twice. Adjust seasoning.

10. Coat chickens with sauce and serve at once, sprinkled with parsley.

NOTE TO THE COOK
Petite Sirah is very similar to the Madiran of South-West France. If you prefer to use a less expensive wine, see Appendix, "Wines for Cooking," for alternatives.

Inspired by a recipe from André Daguin.

CHICKEN DRUMSTICKS AND THIGHS WITH SOUR GRAPE SAUCE AND GARLIC CLOVES IN THE STYLE OF THE DORDOGNE
Cuisses de Poulet au Verjus à la Dordogne

Verjus is made from sour green grapes that are not yet ripe, puréed and strained. You can make it in advance and freeze it, as described under *"Verjus"* in the Appendix, or you can substitute, as explained at the end of the recipe. The strong acid flavor is very refreshing along with the garlic, which becomes very sweet after cooking.

This is a wonderful dish to serve with a Sarlat Potato Cake. Follow with a Walnut Cake from Masseube accompanied by unsweetened whipped cream.

SERVES 6

ACTIVE WORK: 10 minutes
COOKING TIME: 30 minutes

> 6 meaty chicken legs with thighs attached
> Salt and freshly ground pepper
> 2 tablespoons rendered poultry fat or 2 1/2 tablespoons unsalted butter
> 12 plump cloves garlic, unpeeled (not elephant garlic)
> 1/3 cup dry white wine
> 6–7 tablespoons *verjus* (see Appendix)
> 1 cup well-reduced unsalted Chicken Stock (reduced from 3 cups)
> 2 tablespoons unsalted butter
> 2 dozen sour green grapes (see Note 1)
> 1 1/2 tablespoons chopped fresh parsley

1. Trim away excess fat from chicken pieces. Rub with salt and pepper. Loosely cover with plastic wrap and refrigerate until 30 minutes before cooking.

2. Remove chicken from refrigerator 1 hour before serving to bring to room temperature. Dry chicken well.

3. In a large, deep, heavy-bottomed noncorrodible skillet, preferably a *sauteuse*, heat the fat or butter over high heat. Add chicken, skin side down, and garlic cloves. Brown 1 minute each side, shaking skillet to keep chicken and garlic from sticking.

4. Lower heat, cover skillet tightly, and cook slowly 10 minutes. Uncover skillet, tilt, and degrease juices. Turn chicken. Add white wine; recover and cook slowly 10 minutes.

5. Uncover skillet; add 5 tablespoons of the *verjus* and quickly cover so that chicken pieces absorb all the aroma and flavor. Cook slowly about 5 minutes longer.

6. Add 3/4 cup of the stock; cook 5 minutes. Raise heat; add remaining stock, the butter, and remaining 1 or 2 tablespoons *verjus*. Swirl over heat to combine. Add grapes to warm; adjust seasoning with salt and pepper.

7. Arrange chicken, garlic, and grapes on heated serving platter. Spoon over the sauce (which will be about 1/2 cup). Sprinkle with parsley. Serve hot.

NOTES TO THE COOK

1. The success of this dish depends upon obtaining sour green grapes—however, sometimes that is all that's available in the supermarket! Making *verjus* in early summer with homegrown unripened grapes and freezing, as directed in the Appendix, is ideal.

2. To substitute: add 2 pinches of tartaric acid to the sauce as follows. Boil 1 tablespoon water in a small saucepan, add the tartaric acid, and boil until dissolved. Stir into the sauce for the last 5 minutes of cooking. Tartaric acid is the main ingredient in wine that makes it acidic; it is organic and not dangerous. It is very sour and is often used as a substitute in commercial fruit drinks for a lemon flavor. It is available wherever wine-making supplies are sold, or may be ordered by mail from Milan Home Wines and Beers, New York City (see under *"Verjus"* in Appendix).

RAGOUT OF CHICKEN (OR DUCK) WINGS IN THE STYLE OF THE BÉARN
Alycot Béarnaise

This dish, sometimes called *alicuit* and *alycou* (*aile* for wing; *cou* for neck), is made all over South-West France. This particular recipe is from the town of Pau in the Béarn and is interesting because it uses cinnamon, an atypical spice in French cooking. Here the cinnamon has a moderating influence on the garlic and onion flavor of the sauce.

Although my version uses only chicken wings, it is more typical to include necks and gizzards as well. This dish is excellent with fresh noodles. For a first course I would serve the Sorrel Fritters, which have to be made at the last minute, but the *Alycot* can be done in advance and reheated. For dessert, try a cool dish of Prunes in Sauternes.

SERVES 4 TO 5

ACTIVE WORK: 20 to 30 minutes
PARTIALLY ATTENDED COOKING TIME: 2 1/2 hours

12 chicken (or duck) wings, tips removed at second joint and reserved for stock
    Salt and freshly ground pepper
1/3 cup rendered chicken or duck fat
1 cup roughly chopped onions
1 1/2 ounces *jambon de Bayonne,* prosciutto, or Westphalian ham, cubed (about 1/4 cup)

1 1/2 cups unsalted Chicken Stock or Dark Rich Duck Stock, degreased
 3/4   cup peeled, seeded, and cubed fresh tomatoes (about 1 large tomato) or
        drained canned Italian tomatoes
   2   large cloves garlic, halved
   1   dried hot red pepper or several drops hot pepper sauce
       Pinch of ground cloves
       Pinch of freshly grated nutmeg
   1   piece cinnamon stick (1 to 1 1/2 inches)
   2   bunches scallions with about 3/4 inch of green parts
   3   large carrots, scraped and cut into 1-inch chunks
   1   tablespoon chopped fresh parsley

1. 3 HOURS BEFORE SERVING (or make in advance and reheat gently before serving), pat wings dry with paper towels. Lightly season with salt and pepper. Heat rendered fat in a 4-quart flameproof casserole or dutch oven over medium-high heat. Add wings and cook until lightly browned, about 5 minutes.

2. Add onions and cook until lightly browned, about 5 minutes. Reduce heat to medium, add cubed ham, and cook 2 to 3 minutes, tossing lightly to blend flavors. Remove excess fat by tilting pan and pressing on wings and onions with the back of a slotted spoon. Blot with paper towels.

3. Add stock to casserole and bring to a boil. Reduce heat to very low and simmer 5 minutes, skimming foam from surface. Stir in tomatoes, garlic, hot red pepper or sauce, and spices. Cover and simmer 1 hour.

4. Blanch scallions in large pot of boiling salted water 2 minutes. Drain and rinse under cold water to stop cooking process. Roll in a kitchen towel or 3 thicknesses of paper towel and gently squeeze to remove excess moisture.

5. Add scallions and carrots to casserole; simmer very gently 1 hour.

6. Using slotted spoon, remove wings, scallions, and carrots from saucepan. Arrange in shallow serving dish. Keep warm. Raise heat to high and bring sauce to a boil. Cook until reduced to about 1 1/2 cups, about 20 minutes. Taste and adjust seasoning (sauce should be peppery but still tempered by sweet spices). Remove cinnamon stick. Spoon sauce over wings. Sprinkle with parsley.

VARIATION

Use 6 wings plus 3 necks and 3 gizzards instead of 12 wings. Slip off neck skin and discard. Cut each neck into 3 or 4 pieces. Clean gizzard. Using a thin-bladed knife, cut away and discard the hard yellow peel as well as the white membrane. Discard any yellow-green parts. Toss wings, necks, and gizzards with salt and pepper. Refrigerate until ready to cook.

CHICKEN LIVERS WITH VINEGAR AND ONIONS
Foies de Volaille au Vinaigre de Vin et aux Oignons

Chicken livers are served with long-cooked onions. The sweet onion flavor unexpectedly combined with a subtle amount of anchovy makes this a very special dish. Serve it with a robust white wine.

SERVES 6 AS A FIRST COURSE OR
3 AS A MAIN COURSE
☆ Begin early in the day
ACTIVE WORK: 20 minutes
PARTIALLY ATTENDED COOKING TIME: 3 hours
LAST-MINUTE COOKING TIME: 5 to 20 minutes

> 3/4 **pound chicken livers, picked over**
> 3/4 **cup milk**
> **Salt and freshly ground pepper**
> 3 **pounds large Spanish onions, sliced thin**
> 3 **tablespoons unsalted butter**
> 3 **tablespoons vegetable oil**
> 2 **ounces anchovy fillets, drained (rinse if very salty)**
> 2 **teaspoons sugar**
> 1/2 **cup red wine vinegar**
> **Flour**
> 1/2 **teaspoon finely chopped garlic**
> 1/2 **cup well-reduced Chicken Stock**
> 6 **thin rounds toasted French bread (baguette) rubbed with a cut clove of garlic**
> 1 **tablespoon chopped fresh herbs: parsley and chives**

1. Preheat oven to 325° F.

2. Soak livers in salted milk for a minimum of 3 hours.

3. Meanwhile, place onions, 2 tablespoons of the butter, and 2 tablespoons of the oil in a 3- or 4-quart heavy flameproof casserole, preferably of cast iron or earthenware. Heat on top of the stove until hot, stirring, then cover tightly and cook on the center oven rack 2 hours.

4. Crush anchovies; add to onions and continue cooking 30 minutes.

5. Remove casserole from oven, but do not turn off heat.

6. In a noncorrodible skillet, heat sugar; add 1/4 cup of the vinegar and bring to a boil, stirring. When sugar-vinegar mixture begins to darken, stop the cooking with a spoonful of the liquid that the onions have exuded. Swirl to combine. Add 1/4 cup water to deglaze skillet and return all ingredients to casserole. Cover and cook another 30 minutes in oven in order to blend flavors. Onions should be a deep

golden-brown color. Adjust seasoning with salt and pepper. *Onions can be prepared early in the day up to this point.* When cool, cover and refrigerate until ready to reheat, 20 minutes before serving.

7. 5 MINUTES BEFORE SERVING, drain, rinse, and dry chicken livers, dust lightly with seasoned flour, and cook in a 10-inch skillet with the chopped garlic in the remaining 1 tablespoon butter and 1 tablespoon oil until lightly browned and just barely cooked through, about 1 1/2 minutes per side (they will still be pink inside).

8. Remove livers to a side dish to relax a few minutes. Meanwhile, deglaze skillet with remaining vinegar and boil up to dislodge any pieces that cling to bottom and sides of pan.

9. Add stock and reduce by half to a syrupy glaze. Spoon over livers. Sprinkle fresh herbs over the livers and reheated onions, and arrange decoratively on individual plates. Accompany with slices of toasted French bread rubbed with fresh garlic.

CHAPTER 10

DUCKS, GEESE, AND GAME

DUCKS AND GEESE

There are times when I am traveling through Gascony that I think ducks are to the South-West what steaks are to Texas: the favorite, most reliable mainstay food of the region. The fattening up of so many ducks and geese for the production of foie gras has led to the invention of numerous dishes.

Americans have a set of notions about duck that is, for the most part, incorrect. We order it in restaurants where more often than not it is greasy, stringy, and served with a sticky fruit sauce in dishes such as that old gourmet warhorse Duck à l'Orange. Often only the skin seems worth eating, and sometimes we are even cheated of that when the duck has been steam-tabled. Another American notion is that a duck must be cooked whole. And still another is that it is fatty and fattening, and that it cannot be eaten unless it's been gooey-ed up.

I want to disabuse readers of all these ideas, for every single one of them is wrong. In the first place, ducks need not be greasy or fattening; nearly every duck recipe in this book is essentially free of duck fat (or the fat is so visible that it is very easy to cut away and put aside). What happens to all that fat? You will learn how to render it completely from your ducks and use it for flavor without ingesting in large quantities. Duck fat, like goose fat and pork fat, is a tasty cooking medium, and is used throughout South-West France to flavor food. Ducks are so versatile, so complementary to so many other foods, that they can be used to play off nearly every flavor combination—sweet, sour, salty, or acid. Ducks go well with vinegars, peppers, olives, and vegetables. One can serve a duck breast with lemon or lime sauce, or turnips and chestnuts, or celery-root purée. The legs can be braised and served with onions or prunes and red wine, or grilled and served with a walnut-garlic sauce. Ducks go with nearly anything and are superb, too, simply grilled alone over dried grapevine cuttings or broiled.

Finally (and this is really the crux of the matter), there is no need, no obligation, to cook ducks whole. They are, in fact, much better cut up, the parts used in different ways. That is the method generally used throughout the South-West where thrift and culinary good sense are working mottoes, and where ducks are truly understood.

For instance, a boned duck breast takes about 5 minutes to grill. But to cook duck legs takes about 45 minutes. So it makes perfect sense to separate these components and treat them in different ways. The cutting up of a duck and the use of its separate parts is one of the most popular classes I teach. It sounds complicated but it isn't. Once you have mastered the instructions for cutting up a duck, a wide spectrum of dishes will become available to you—dishes that will truly vanquish your apprehension of the duck.

If you are using only the breasts, you can reserve the legs for *confit* or simply roast and serve them cold, or cook them in any number of ways described on the following pages. Once you have *confit* of duck or goose on hand, there are many things you can do with it. To eat a piece of hot or cold preserved duck or goose is one of the best ways to enjoy either of these birds. (A brief word here about geese: Geese can be prepared like duck for *confit* with one hour's longer cooking time. I especially recommend preserved goose. Goose has an extraordinary flavor, and the breast as well as the legs makes wonderful *confit*. I have included in this book one beautiful Gascon recipe for Goose Stew with Radishes that is totally goose-fat-free.)

When you have mastered the cutting up of a duck, you will discover that it is economically competitive with other meats. You will have use for the fat as a cooking medium or preservative. The neck bone, wings, and carcass will provide excellent stock for soups and sauces. The neck skin, if you're skillful, can be stuffed (see recipe for Stuffed Duck Neck in Brioche). You will be able to sauté, grill, or poach the breasts—and braise, grill, or preserve the legs. Miscellaneous bits and pieces can be used in pâtés and rillettes (these two dishes are not fat-free, of course). The liver can go into flans, stuffings, or salads. You can sauté the heart as a special treat to yourself. (It takes 4 hearts to make one serving, so in France duck hearts are usually reserved for the cook (see Sautéed Duck Hearts with Green Grapes). You can preserve the gizzard or use it in stocks and soups. And if you want to truly embrace the spirit of the South-West, you can use the duck feathers to apply fat to pastry.

HOW TO CUT UP A DUCK

Lay the duck breast side down on a cutting surface.

Pull the neck skin away from the body and, using a sharp knife, remove it in one piece. Pull as much fat as possible from the body cavity and set it aside (1).

Turn the duck over so that the breast side is up. Using a thin, sharp knife, loosen the wishbone surrounding the neck cavity. Pull the wishbone free of the body, cutting through the joint at each end if necessary (2).

Remove the wing tips at the first joint and set them aside for stock. If you wish to have the wings for *Alycot* or *confit*, sever at the ball joint attaching wing to shoulder. To have a *magret*—boneless duck steak from the breast—sever the wing bones at the ball joint attaching wing to shoulder. Then slice along the center line of the breast, cutting through the skin and the flesh down to the breastbone (3).

Slide the knife under one side of the breast. Holding the blade against the carcass, carefully separate the breast meat from the rib cage (4).

Cut the remaining flesh away from the carcass and lift off.

Trim off excess fat surrounding the flesh of this half breast. In the Gascon language this half breast is called a *magret*. (You may remove the skin. I only remove it for some recipes such as Duck Cooked on a String, Duck Breasts with Woodland Sauce, and Old-Fashioned Duck Terrine. But any of the duck breast recipes can be prepared with skinless as well as boneless duck breasts. Cooking time is one minute shorter.)

Repeat with the other half of the breast. If the breast is to be used for *confit*, the rib cage and wing joint should be left attached to the main part of the breast.

Detach the "filet mignon," the narrow strip of delicate meat lying at the back of each half of the breast meat. If you wish to use this for a quick sauté for a salad or a pâté, slide a small knife blade under the white tendon running the length of the fillet and cut it free, keeping the meat intact.

Pull each thigh-leg portion away from the carcass and detach it in one piece. Trim off and reserve all excess fat. This portion can be used in ragouts, grills, salads, pâtés, sautés, and, of course, for *confit* (5).

Cut the carcass into two portions: rib-cage front and back. Cut portions up and use for stock, sauce bases, and soups. (The rib-cage portion, called *demoiselle* ["young lady"], can be roasted and enjoyed as a snack with bread and wine. I have been in small restaurants in Gascony where I have seen platters piled high with roasted carcasses being brought out to other customers. Finally, one day I had a chance to gnaw on one myself. It was spectacular, not unlike the eating of a lobster when you suck out each and every bit of sweet flesh from the carcass. In France the carcass of the lobster is also called *demoiselle*.)

Remove and reserve, for various uses, all skin and fat from the carcass. Reserve the bones, gizzard, liver, and heart.

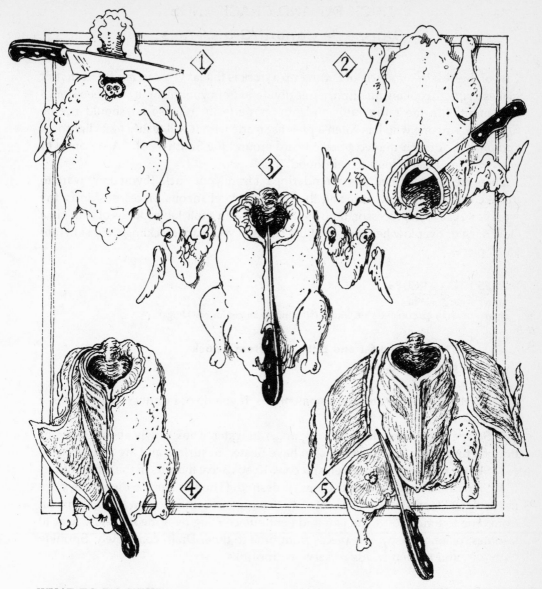

WHAT TO DO NEXT

Lightly salt all the meat and set it in the refrigerator until needed.

Render the fat as directed below if you plan to make *confit* or wish to cook with duck fat.

Soak the liver in lightly salted milk to use it for pâtés, salads, or mousses.

Chop up the bones and set them in a preheated 325° F. oven to brown slowly to make a stock.

Now you are ready to attack any of the following recipes.

DUCK FAT AND CRACKLINGS
Graisse de Canard/Graisserons

One of the best by-products of cutting up a duck is the fat you can render from it. It makes a superb cooking medium, a free dividend from your meat. It will keep from 3 to 4 months in the refrigerator and freezes perfectly. (Goose fat should not be forgotten. Anyone who has eaten a piecrust made with it will testify to its lightness and quality. A much-quoted phrase heard around the South-West: "A spoonful of goose fat can raise a soup to sainthood.")

There are different methods of rendering fat from your duck. If you don't want to make cracklings, simply purée all the fat and miscellaneous pieces of skin in the workbowl of a food processor, then melt it down with a few tablespoons of water in a slow oven or over low heat on top of the stove. If you want cracklings, cut skin into small pieces.

MAKES 1 TO 1 3/4 CUPS
ACTIVE WORK: 5 minutes
MOSTLY UNATTENDED COOKING TIME: 1 hour (40 minutes longer for cracklings)

The reserved fat and fatty skin from 1 duck
2 tablespoons water

1. Cut the skin of the duck into small pieces. If you do not want cracklings, purée fat and skin.
2. Scrape purée into a heavy saucepan. Add water. Cook slowly about 1 hour, or until fat turns clear and pieces of skin have floated to surface and are pale in color.
3. Strain, pour into a container, and cool. Keeps 3 to 4 months in the refrigerator.
4. Skin can be made into cracklings, if desired. (Though hard to digest, they are irresistible!) Slowly reheat pieces of skin 30 minutes or until golden brown, stirring from time to time. Cover the pan and continue cooking over medium-low heat 10 minutes, or until crispy. Stir pieces from time to time. Drain completely. Sprinkle with salt, and toss on salads or serve with drinks.

NOTES TO THE COOK
Pieces of skin and fat must never be melted or rendered at a high temperature because the surface would sear and form a skin, keeping fat in. The ideal temperature for rendering is 170° F.

BROILED DUCK BREAST
Magret de Canard Grillé dans sa Peau

This classic dish of Gascony, called *Lou Magret* in Gascon, is a grilled, sautéed, or broiled boned duck breast served rosy pink with the skin on or removed. After the breast is grilled or broiled it is thinly sliced on the diagonal, much in the manner of a London broil—slices cut this way are much more tender. Slices are served overlapping on the plate. Many Gascons prefer their *magrets* without any sauce. They twist a pepper mill over the slices, devouring them along with a pile of *frites* with the same gusto and delight as we devour a good steak.

When serving duck breasts rosy, it is a good idea to rub them with a salt marinade at least 12 hours before using, which helps tenderize the flesh as well as enhance flavor.

I would suggest serving these delicious breasts with Michel Guérard's Puréed Celery Root with Apples and Red Wine-Cooked Onions. In summer you can serve them with Eggplant Studded with Garlic, and for dessert, Poached Figs in Raspberry-Red Wine Sauce would be sublime.

SERVES 3 TO 4
☆ Begin 1 day in advance
   ACTIVE WORK (DAY 1): 10 minutes
   BROILING TIME (DAY 2): about 5 minutes

2 whole duck breasts, halved, boned with skin intact, fresh or defrosted

Gascon Marinade

   1 1/2 teaspoons coarse (kosher) salt
   1 1/2 teaspoons minced shallots
     1 teaspoon chopped fresh parsley
    1/2 teaspoon crumbled bay leaf
    1/4 teaspoon crumbled thyme leaves
    12 black peppercorns, lightly crushed
     1 clove garlic, thinly sliced
      Freshly ground pepper

1. 1 DAY BEFORE SERVING, trim off all excess fat from the duck breasts. In a noncorrodible bowl combine the salt, shallots, parsley, bay leaf, thyme, peppercorns, and garlic.

2. Roll the duck breasts in the mixture and stack them, skin side down, in the bowl. Cover bowl with a towel or plastic wrap and let stand, refrigerated, 12 to 24 hours, turning breasts over once.

3. 30 MINUTES BEFORE SERVING, wipe or rinse the duck breasts to remove excess seasonings and any liquid that may have exuded during the marinating time.

(continued)

Discard marinade and allow breasts to come to room temperature. Pat ducks dry.

4. To broil, set the broiler rack about 4 inches from heat. Score the skin and place duck breasts skin side down on broiler rack.

5. 8 OR 9 MINUTES BEFORE SERVING, broil 1 minute in order to sear flesh side and melt excess skin-side fat from reflected heat. Turn breasts over and broil about 4 minutes longer. Breasts will "tighten up" and become thicker. With thumb and middle finger, pinch meat from under skin end to flesh side to test for doneness. If the flesh springs back quickly it is rare; if there is some "give" it is medium.

6. Transfer breasts to a carving board and let rest 1 to 2 minutes. To serve, thinly slice meat crosswise diagonally. Sprinkle with freshly ground pepper, then fan each *magret* out on an individual heated serving plate. Serve at once.

DUCK BREASTS WITH PORT WINE SAUCE
Magret de Canard Poêlé au Porto

This is an ideal dish for an elegant dinner. Serve with strips of pan-glazed salsify (see Note 1).

SERVES 3 TO 4
    ACTIVE WORK: 5 minutes
    COOKING TIME: 10 minutes

> 2 whole duck breasts, halved
> Salt and freshly ground pepper
> 1 cup imported ruby port wine
> Juice of 1 orange
> 3 cups unsalted Chicken Stock, completely degreased, reduced to
>   1 1/3 cups
> 1/3 cup heavy cream

1. With a sharp boning knife, lift the duck breast meat from the rib cage without damaging the skin (see How to Cut Up a Duck). Trim away excess fat. Wipe dry; sprinkle with 2 teaspoons salt and 1/2 teaspoon pepper; leave in refrigerator a minimum of 6 hours—even better, overnight.

2. 30 MINUTES BEFORE SERVING, remove breasts from refrigerator. Rinse off salt.

3. 15 MINUTES BEFORE SERVING, preheat oven to 350° F.

4. 10 MINUTES BEFORE SERVING, pat duck dry with paper towel. Score skin at 3/4-inch intervals without piercing flesh. Transfer duck, skin side down, to a heavy, noncorrodible large skillet. Place over medium-high heat and sauté until skin is crisp and brown, about 2 to 3 minutes.

5. Transfer breasts to a baking sheet and set in the oven to finish cooking, about 6 to 7 minutes, or until meat is pink and just firm when pressed with fingertip.

6. Meanwhile, pour off fat from the skillet; blot any remaining fat with paper towel. Add port wine and orange juice to skillet; stir over medium-high heat, scraping up any browned bits that cling to bottom and sides of pan. Boil down until reduced to a glaze. Add the reduced stock and boil down until reduced by half (2 to 3 minutes).

7. Transfer to a heavy-bottomed 2-quart saucepan (see Note 2). Return to a boil; add the cream while the sauce is boiling hard. *Do not stir.* (The cream will be "swallowed up" by the sauce.) Boil vigorously 5 minutes, or until you catch a glimpse of the bottom of the pan. Remove from heat; season to taste with pepper and, if necessary, salt. Set over very low heat while slicing the duck breasts.

8. Remove duck breasts from the oven and place on a carving board. Let rest 1 to 2 minutes. Slice duck breasts diagonally and arrange overlapping slices on individual heated serving dishes. Strain sauce over duck slices and serve at once.

NOTES TO THE COOK

1. Prepare salsify as described in Chicken with Salsify in Pastry. Combine cooked salsify, 1/4 cup water, 2 tablespoons butter, and 1/2 teaspoon sugar in a noncorrodible skillet. Heat over medium heat; simmer, stirring occasionally, until water has evaporated (about 2 minutes). Continue to cook salsify, shaking pan occasionally, until well glazed, about 4 minutes. Hold uncovered in skillet. Just before serving, sprinkle 1 1/2 tablespoons water over salsify and heat until hot. Season to taste with salt and pepper. Garnish with a pinch of *persillade* (parsley chopped with garlic).

2. The sauce can be completed in the skillet, but it is tricky—there is a tendency to overreduce the sauce (it becomes oily). If this happens, add a tablespoon of water and swirl to combine.

Inspired by a recipe from Lucien Vanel.

ALAIN DUTOURNIER'S DUCK BREASTS WITH CAPERS AND MARROW
Magret de Canard aux Capres et à la Moelle

In no other section of France do cooks use as many spices as they do in the South-West. In this dish cinnamon, nutmeg, clove, juniper berries, and an assortment of condiments—mustard, capers, and vinegar—make for a delicious and very spicy duck breast.

Izarra, a Pyreneean liqueur made of a great number of green herbs, may be found in Basque neighborhoods in San Francisco, Nevada, and Idaho. If you can't find it, you can substitute green Chartreuse.

The duck breasts are left to marinate in a spicy paste. If you use fresh duck you can marinate them up to 5 days for an especially tender and flavorful result.

(continued)

As the breasts brown, the spice mixture caramelizes. With the addition of soft, plump marrow and astringent capers, this dish becomes a blazing taste experience.

This dish is at its best with steamed new potatoes. For a first course, I would choose a substantial dish like Sliced Salmon with Fresh Oysters or Leek and Mushroom Pie. A fresh fruit sorbet would be an ideal ending to the meal.

SERVES 3 TO 4
☆ Begin 1 to 5 days in advance
ACTIVE WORK: 20 minutes
PARTIALLY ATTENDED COOKING TIME: 40 minutes

> **2 whole duck breasts, halved, boned, excess fat removed, and skin intact (follow instructions for boning a duck breast in How to Cut Up a Duck)**

Spice Paste

> **1 tablespoon juniper berries**
> **1/2 tablespoon black peppercorns**
> **1-inch stick cinnamon**
> **1/2 teaspoon freshly grated nutmeg**
> **1 clove**
> **1 1/2 tablespoons Izarra or green Chartreuse liqueur**
> **1 tablespoon Dijon mustard**
> **3/4 teaspoon coarse (kosher) salt**

> **Marrowbones to yield 12 inches of marrow (about 4 bones)**
> **1/4 cup red wine vinegar**
> **1/2 cup dry white wine**
> **2 1/2 cups Demi-Glace or Duck Demi-Glace**
> **3 tablespoons unsalted butter**
> **1/3 cup nonpareil capers, drained**
> **2 tablespoons snipped fresh chives**

1. BEGIN 1 TO 5 DAYS IN ADVANCE marinating the duck, soaking marrow, and making the sauce base. Pat duck breasts dry with paper towels. Make the spice paste: In a dry skillet over low heat toast the juniper berries until shiny, about 2 minutes (this brings out their flavor). Transfer to spice mill or mortar. Add peppercorns, cinnamon, nutmeg, and clove; grind to a fine powder. Sift if necessary. You should have about 2 1/2 tablespoons spice mixture. Set aside 4 teaspoons for the sauce. Transfer remaining powder to a wide, noncorrodible bowl. Add liqueur, mustard, and salt; blend to a paste.

2. Rub duck breasts with the spice paste. Stack seasoned duck breasts in the same bowl and cover with plastic wrap. Refrigerate 24 hours or more, turning the duck breasts daily.

3. Rinse marrowbones under cold running water; place in a bowl and cover with warm water. Let stand 3 to 5 minutes. Drain well. Using a skewer, loosen the marrow from the bone, then push marrow out in whole pieces into small bowl of cold salted water. (This helps marrow to rid itself of any blood. Marrow will keep fresh for 2 to 3 days.)

4. Make the sauce: Combine reserved 4 teaspoons spice powder with vinegar and wine in small, noncorrodible saucepan; bring to a boil over medium-high heat. Let boil until reduced by half. Add Demi-Glace and bring to a boil. Boil slowly with pan half off the heat, skimming often, until sauce is reduced to 1 1/4 cups, about 30 minutes. *Sauce can be prepared ahead up to this point*; cool, cover, and refrigerate.

5. 30 MINUTES BEFORE SERVING, preheat the oven to 350° F. Remove duck from refrigerator and dry with paper towel. Score skin at 3/4-inch intervals without piercing flesh.

6. 15 MINUTES BEFORE SERVING, transfer duck, skin side down, to heavy large skillet. Place over high heat and sauté until skin is crisp and brown, about 2 to 3 minutes. Transfer breasts to a baking sheet and place in the oven to finish cooking—about 6 to 7 minutes, or until meat is pink and just firm when pressed with fingertip. Set aside.

7. Meanwhile, pour off fat from the skillet; blot any remaining fat with paper towel. Add reserved sauce to skillet and stir over medium-high heat, scraping up any browned bits that cling to bottom and sides of pan. Strain sauce through fine sieve. Return to skillet and keep below a simmer to avoid evaporation.

8. Cut marrow into 3/4-inch chunks. In small saucepan, bring 1 1/2 cups salted water to a boil. Reduce heat to low, add marrow, and gently poach until pale pink-gray in color, about 2 minutes. Immediately transfer marrow to flat dish to drain. *Do not leave in water or marrow will melt*.

9. Remove duck breasts from the oven and place on a carving board. Let rest 1 to 2 minutes. Meanwhile swirl butter into sauce, 1 tablespoon at a time. Stir in the capers. Taste, and adjust seasoning. Cut duck into thin slices diagonally. Arrange on individual hot serving plates. Spoon some sauce over slices. Top with marrow, dividing pieces evenly among servings. Sprinkle with chives.

DUCK BREASTS WITH WOODLAND SAUCE AND WILD MUSHROOM TIMBALES
Magret de Canard Poêlé au Fumet de Bois et aux Gâteaux de Cèpes

This recipe is a perfect demonstration of how the addition of dried cèpes can greatly enhance a sauce. I learned this sauce from chef Francis Garcia of the restaurant Clavel in Bordeaux—he uses it over a rich concoction of puréed chicken breast, foie gras, and cream. I put it on a simply sautéed duck breast. The mushroom timbales accompanying the breasts are made of cultivated mushrooms, dried cèpes, the soaking liquid, milk, cream, eggs, and herbs. The sauce is a slow reduction of meat stock, dried cèpes, and port wine. Its aroma and flavor are woodsy and intense, and you can also use it with excellent results on veal chops, pork chops, or dark chicken meat. (It can be made a day in advance, covered, and refrigerated.) Or serve the timbales as a first course with the sauce.

SERVES 5 TO 6

ACTIVE WORK: 15 minutes
PARTIALLY ATTENDED COOKING TIME: 2 hours

> 3 pair whole duck breasts
> Salt and freshly ground pepper
> 1 ounce dried cèpes
> 1 quart unsalted Chicken Stock, completely degreased
> 1 teaspoon chopped shallots
> 1/2 cup imported red port wine
> 3 tablespoons heavy cream
> 2 1/2 tablespoons rendered duck fat
> 5 tablespoons unsalted butter
> Wild Mushroom Timbales (recipe below)

1. EARLY IN THE DAY OR THE DAY BEFORE, lift the duck breast meat from the rib cage with a sharp boning knife. (Follow instructions for boning a duck breast in How to Cut Up a Duck.) Cut away *all* fat and skin. Wipe flesh dry. Sprinkle with salt and pepper. Cover loosely with plastic wrap. Keep refrigerated until ready to cook.

2. Render fat from skin if necessary to have 2 tablespoons fat for sautéeing.

3. To make Woodland Sauce base: Rinse dried cèpes under running water to rid them of sand and dirt. Place stock in saucepan, add cèpes, and bring to a boil; lower heat and simmer, uncovered, skimming often, 1 1/2 hours, or until the stock is reduced to 1 cup. Strain the liquid through several layers of damp cheesecloth to eliminate any sand or grit. Set aside this sauce base. (Cèpes can be rinsed again and used for the Wild Mushroom Timbales, stuffings, omelets, or stocks, or frozen for later use.)

4. In a small, noncorrodible pan combine the shallots and port wine; heat, then flame. When the flames die out, reduce to a glaze. Add the reserved strained sauce base and bring to a boil; boil down to 3/4 cup, skimming if necessary. Add 3 tablespoons of the cream to the pan and set aside. (*Can be prepared ahead up to this point.*)

5. 30 MINUTES BEFORE SERVING, remove duck breasts from refrigerator. Rinse off salt and pat dry with paper towel.

6. ABOUT 10 MINUTES BEFORE SERVING, heat duck fat in a wide skillet over moderate heat; sauté the breasts until meat is browned on both sides. Lower heat and cook 2 minutes longer per side. Remove and let rest 1 to 2 minutes before slicing.

7. Meanwhile, reheat sauce base. Swirl remaining butter into reheated sauce 1 tablespoon at a time on and off the heat. Season with salt and pepper.

8. Slice the duck breasts diagonally. Arrange overlapping slices on a heated platter, spoon sauce over slices, and serve at once. Serve, if desired, with Wild Mushroom Timbales.

Wild Mushroom Timbales
Gâteaux de Cèpes

SERVES 6

ACTIVE WORK: 30 minutes
BAKING TIME: 25 to 35 minutes

> 1 ounce dried cèpes, plus the cooked cèpes from the previous recipe, if
>   available
> 6 ounces firm fresh mushroom caps
> 2 tablespoons unsalted butter
> 2 teaspoons chopped shallots
>   Pinch of salt
> 1 cup milk
> 3 whole eggs
> 1 egg yolk
> 1/2 cup heavy cream
> 1/2 teaspoon fine salt
> 1/4 teaspoon finely ground white pepper
> 2 pinches of freshly grated nutmeg
> 2 tablespoons chopped fresh parsley

1. Soak the cèpes in 1 cup warm water for at least 30 minutes. Drain, reserving the liquid. Rinse the cèpes under running water to rid them of sand and dirt.

2. Finely chop cèpes and set aside. Finely chop the cooked cèpes and add to the chopped soaked cèpes.

3. Strain soaking liquid through coffee filter paper or several layers of damp cheesecloth; reserve.

4. One by one, place each fresh mushroom sideways on your work surface, holding it by the stem with one hand, and slice the cap into thin rounds, stopping when you reach the gills. Stack the rounds and cut them into thin julienne strips. Use the stems for some other purpose or add to stock (especially if preparing Duck Breasts with Woodland Sauce). Heat 1 tablespoon butter in a nonaluminum skillet. As soon as the foam begins to subside, add mushroom strips, chopped cèpes, shallots, and a pinch of salt. Sauté over high heat for 1 minute, tossing. Deglaze with the reserved soaking liquid. Bring to a boil, stirring. Simmer slowly until all moisture has evaporated, about 10 minutes. Blot away fat with paper towel. Stir in the milk

and gently heat until just warm. Remove from heat, cover, and set aside.

5. In a small bowl lightly beat eggs and egg yolk. Stir in cream. Strain into a larger bowl. Add milk and mushrooms, salt, pepper, nutmeg, and chopped parsley. Stir gently to combine. Adjust seasoning.

6. Preheat the oven to 325° F.

7. Butter six 4-ounce metal molds or porcelain ramekins and place in a deep baking dish.* Boil water to be poured into baking dish. Ladle equal amounts of timbale mixture, stirring between each addition, to fill each mold.

8. Place baking pan on center oven rack. Remove one mold from pan. Carefully pour enough boiling water into baking pan to come halfway up the sides of molds. Return mold. Bake 25 minutes or until timbales feel firm when lightly prodded with two fingers. If the timbales are not set, turn off oven and continue baking 5 to 10 minutes longer. (Molds and cups of different shapes require different cooking times.) Remove pan from oven and let molds rest in the water 10 minutes longer before turning out.

9. To remove, place a wide spatula over the first mold; invert with spatula holding the timbale in place, and guide it to the warm serving dish. Slip the spatula from underneath, leaving the timbale and mold in place. Lift off the mold. Repeat with remaining molds. Serve warm.

NOTE TO THE COOK
To reheat timbales, place in a warm oven for 5 minutes before unmolding.

DUCK BREASTS BAKED IN SALT
Magrets de Canard au Gros Sel

This method of cooking produces duck breasts that are moist, tender, and delicately pink but without a crisp skin. The flavor is incredibly intense. Cooking times should be followed exactly for pink flesh. A total of 30 minutes includes browning to release excess fat, baking in salt, and resting in salt outside of the oven. Salt is mixed with egg whites for the "cooking jacket," and it is the egg whites that absorb the fat from the duck and keep the flesh moist.

This method works equally well for duck legs: press the legs and thighs together in pairs, flesh side in; tie loosely with string and roast for 1 1/4 hours. Serve the duck with a sauce made from the skillet juices or serve it alone, slightly warm, with just a sprinkling of coarsely ground pepper and accompanied by strips of roasted sweet pepper, marinated in oil and garlic, and slices of toasted French bread spread with Tapenade de Toulouse.

*If molds and baking pan are made of metal, line pan with 2 or 3 sheets of newspaper trimmed to fit neatly. Cut an X in the center of the paper to avoid swelling after the pan is filled with molds and hot water.

SERVES 3 TO 4
ACTIVE WORK: 10 minutes
COOKING TIME: 30 minutes

   2 whole duck breasts with skin and bones intact
     Freshly ground pepper
   3 pounds coarse (kosher) salt*
   6 egg whites (about 3/4 cup)*

*If baking molds chosen to hold the breasts are larger than suggested, increase salt to 4 pounds and the egg whites to 1 cup.

1. 40 MINUTES BEFORE SERVING, pat duck dry with paper towel. Cut off wing tips at first joint. Place each whole breast, skin side down, on work surface; cut along both sides of backbone and remove backbone. (Reserve backbone and wing tips for stock or sauce, if desired.) Place duck breasts skin side up on cutting surface. Flatten duck breasts by striking breastbone with a mallet or pushing firmly with heel of hand. Score skin of breasts in crisscross pattern at 1-inch intervals with sharp, thin-bladed knife. *Do not cut through to flesh.*

2. Heat a large, heavy skillet over medium-high heat. In dry skillet, brown duck breasts one at a time, skin side down, for exactly 3 minutes. Pour off fat. Reserve skillet with brown bits in bottom if you wish to make a sauce.

3. Preheat oven to 450° F.

4. Sprinkle browned breasts with pepper. Place duck breast, skin side down, on work surface. Slide two 12-inch lengths of kitchen string under the duck breast. Reshape the duck breast with hands to original shape before the breast was flattened. Tie tightly with the string at each end to retain the shape. Repeat with second duck breast.

5. Combine salt with egg whites and mix until salt is like damp sand. Make a layer of salt about 1/2 inch deep in bottoms of two 5-cup loaf pans, preferably foil.

6. Place 1 breast, breastbone up, in each pan, and spoon remaining salt around sides and top of duck to pack. Press firmly to completely seal breasts with salt.

7. Roast exactly 17 minutes on center oven rack. Remove from oven; let stand 10 minutes on a rack. Keep oven at 450° F.

8. 10 MINUTES AFTER REMOVAL FROM OVEN, crack salt seal with wooden mallet or back of heavy knife. Wipe off as much salt as possible with paper towels. Cut breasts in half along breastbone. Sever wings at joints and remove. Place wings in small baking dish and return to oven to finish crisping, about 15 minutes.

9. Meanwhile, remove skin and lift off breast meat. Slice duck meat diagonally into thin slices. Arrange overlapping slices in rows and sprinkle with pepper. Serve wings separately.

NOTE TO THE COOK
To double this recipe, use twice as many molds. Do not use 1 larger mold.

DUCK COOKED ON A STRING WITH DEVIL'S SAUCE
Canard à la Ficelle, Sauce Diable

This variation of the famous *Boeuf à la Ficelle* (Beef on a String) is made with boneless, skinless duck breast. The duck breasts are suspended by string and are simply dropped into a boiling spicy broth to sear, then cooked until rare. Duck is a most versatile meat; it beautifully plays off oranges, turnips, chestnuts, apples, celery, radishes, and olives. In this case it resonates with a Devil's Sauce made with capers and pickles. Note that this sauce is "short"—only about a tablespoon of sauce per portion—but it is full of flavor. Here the sauce is used almost like a condiment and thus the dish is low in calories, too.

Use the livers to make a sautéed Duck Liver Salad with Apples and Watercress to start off the meal. A nice accompaniment to the breasts would be the Straw Potato Cake Stuffed with Braised Leeks, but instead of leeks use celery, and deep-fat-fried celery leaves for garnish. Finish with Batter Cake with Fresh Pears from the Corrèze.

SERVES 3 TO 4
☆ Begin 1 day in advance
    ACTIVE WORK (DAY 1): 5 minutes
    ACTIVE WORK (DAY 2): 10 minutes
    COOKING TIME (DAY 2): 20 minutes

    2 boned and skinned duck breasts (follow instructions for How to Cut Up a Duck)
      Coarse (kosher) salt
    3 cups unsalted Chicken (or Duck) Stock, completely degreased
    1 tablespoon freshly cracked black peppercorns
      Wings of the 2 ducks, trimmed of excess fat and chopped into 1-inch pieces
    3 tablespoons unsalted butter
 1 1/2 tablespoons minced shallots
  18 small nonpareil capers, drained but not rinsed
    1 tablespoon minced French cornichons
    2 tablespoons cubed fresh tomato
    3 tablespoons red wine vinegar
    1 tablespoon white wine
    1 teaspoon Dijon mustard
      Garnish: 6 nonpareil capers, 1 teaspoon cubed fresh tomato and 1 teaspoon cubed cornichons

1. Rub duck breasts with 2 teaspoons coarse salt. Thread breasts loosely with an 18-inch length of kitchen string and tie ends together. Set on a flat dish, cover loosely with plastic wrap, refrigerate, and let rest overnight.

2. THE FOLLOWING DAY, bring the stock with the peppercorns to a boil in a saucepan. Cover and simmer 20 minutes.

3. Meanwhile in a noncorrodible skillet brown the chopped duck wings in 1 teaspoon of the butter over medium-high heat. Pour off any fat. Push the wing pieces to one side. Add 2 teaspoons butter and the shallots to the skillet and soften over gentle heat 2 to 3 minutes. Add capers, cornichons, and tomatoes. Cook, stirring, 1 minute. With the back of a spoon, crush the condiments in the skillet.

4. Deglaze with vinegar and white wine and boil down to a glaze. Stir in the mustard and 1 cup of the simmering stock. Cook over low heat 5 minutes. Strain the sauce through a wide sieve. Sauce should be very piquant. Cool, cover, and refrigerate sauce base and 2 1/2 cups peppery stock. *Can be made ahead up to this point.*

5. 10 MINUTES BEFORE SERVING, heat the peppery stock in a 2 1/2-quart saucepan. Remove any surface fat from the sauce base. Gently heat the sauce base in a small saucepan.

6. 5 MINUTES BEFORE SERVING, rinse off the salt and drop the string of chilled duck breasts into boiling stock. Lower heat and simmer 3 1/2 minutes for small duck breasts (weighing about 4 1/2 ounces) and 4 minutes for larger sizes (about 5 ounces); remove and allow to rest 30 seconds. Remove string. Strain the stock and reserve for some other purpose. Slice duck on the diagonal into thin slices. Arrange overlapping slices on a warmed serving platter.

7. Swirl the remaining 2 tablespoons butter into the sauce to thicken it slightly. Fold in the garnish and spoon over the breasts. Serve at once.

NOTE TO THE COOK

Use this method for cooking duck breast when you want to make a cold duck salad.

VARIATION
Languedoc Walnut, Garlic, and Oil Liaison
Sauce Aillade

The original recipe for this dish is called *Alhada Tolosenca* in the dialect of Languedoc. It is made as follows: the duck breasts are poached or grilled over charcoal or grapevine cuttings, and are served with a walnut-garlic sauce *(aillade)* made from a good handful of freshly shelled walnuts. They are pounded with garlic in a mortar, then made into a smooth paste by the addition of cold water. This mixture is seasoned with salt and pepper and a tablespoon of fresh chopped parsley. Then walnut oil is slowly added and beaten in. Finally the flavor is heightened by the addition of a small portion of *verjus* or vinegar.

Languedoc is famous for its pink-hued garlic (le rose d'Albi), which costs five dollars a pound in Paris. This garlic is much sweeter and more aromatic than the white variety. To avoid an excessively acrid taste, be sure to slice the garlic *before* adding to the food processor.

It is not authentic to use egg yolk as a binder, but it works well in a food processor and the sauce comes out a good deal fluffier too.

(continued)

MAKES ABOUT 1 CUP (SERVES 4 TO 6)

    1/2 cup (tightly packed) broken walnut meats
    2 cloves garlic, peeled, halved, and sliced
    1 egg
    1/4 teaspoon salt
    Pinch of freshly ground pepper
    1 cup imported walnut oil (1/4 cup may be French peanut oil)
    1 tablespoon chopped fresh parsley
    Verjus **(see Index) or mild vinegar to taste**

1. Grind the walnuts in an electric blender or food processor for 30 seconds, stopping and scraping down the workbowl twice.

2. Add garlic and two tablespoons ice-cold water and process 5 seconds longer. Add the egg and process to combine, about 5 seconds. Add seasonings.

3. With machine on, add the oil in a slow, steady stream. Fold in the chopped parsley. Add *verjus* to taste. Let stand 1 hour before serving.

4. Poach the duck breasts in flavorful stock as described above for 3 to 4 minutes, depending upon their thickness. Let rest 30 seconds before slicing.

NOTES TO THE COOK

1. This sauce is not worth making unless you use a fresh can of imported walnut oil. (After you open a can of walnut oil, keep it refrigerated to preserve flavor.)

2. If you suspect that your walnuts are not fresh enough, heighten their flavor by toasting them in a 325° F. oven for 10 minutes; cool before using.

DUCK LEGS COOKED IN RED WINE
Salmis de Cuisses de Canard

According to the old Gascon cooks, the secret of a great *salmis* is in the reheating over a 3- or 4-day period. Each day the meat is *slowly* reheated, simmered, cooled, and degreased. The flavors mellow at each reheating. The flesh is not mushy but meltingly tender. Don't be put off by this small amount of extra work. This recipe is one of the finest renditions of *salmis* that I have tasted in the South-West. The flour-based sauce is not to be scoffed at. It holds the wine flavor through all those reheatings and is sensational. (The recipe can be doubled.)

An absolute "must" accompaniment is the fried cornmeal cakes called *armottes* (see Index). The flavors mingle perfectly, making this a very fine rustic dinner. Nothing could be better for dessert than Prune and Armagnac Ice Cream, which has the illusion of seeming very rich in cream but is made mostly with milk. If this seems too heavy, a simple fruit sorbet served in a chilled champagne glass would be delicious. Serve bakery *tuiles* or homemade Madeleines from Dax with a sorbet.

SERVES 4

☆ Begin 3 days before serving
ACTIVE WORK (DAY 1): 30 minutes
UNATTENDED COOKING TIME (DAY 1): 1 hour
UNATTENDED COOKING TIME (DAY 2): 1 1/2 hours
UNATTENDED COOKING TIME (DAY 3): 1 1/2 hours

4 pair duck legs, defrosted if frozen
3 tablespoons Armagnac
5 ounces lean salt pork, simmered 3 minutes in water, drained and cubed
1 3/4 ounces shallots (about 5 large)
1 3/4 ounces garlic (about 10 medium cloves)
6 tablespoons flour
1 bottle full-bodied red wine such as a California Petite Sirah or a French Côtes-du-Rhône (see "Wines for Cooking" in the Appendix for less-expensive choices)
Herb bouquet: 3 sprigs parsley, 1 sprig thyme, and 1 bay leaf tied together
Pinch of sugar
Salt and freshly ground pepper
8–12 rounds of French bread toasted in the oven or browned in poultry fat or olive oil and butter
Finely chopped fresh parsley

1. 3 DAYS BEFORE SERVING, trim the fat from all of the legs and render it. With a thin-bladed knife score the fatty skin without piercing the flesh. In a large skillet over low heat, heat 1 tablespoon rendered fat. Add the legs, skin side down, and allow them to brown in the exuding fat, about 3 minutes per side. Brown the legs in batches if necessary. Pour off all the fat in the skillet.

2. Add 2 tablespoons of the Armagnac; allow it to heat up, then set it aflame. When the flames die out, transfer the legs to a 3-quart earthenware or enameled cast-iron casserole.

3. In the workbowl of a food processor fitted with the metal blade, finely chop the salt pork, shallots, and garlic.

4. Scrape up the bits and pieces clinging to bottom and sides of skillet, and add the finely chopped salt pork, shallots, and garlic. Cook the mixture in the skillet until all is lightly browned around the edges.

5. Stir in the flour and cook, stirring constantly, 1 minute. The flour will turn the mixture into a ball.

6. Gradually add the red wine by cupfuls, stirring to smooth out the flour. This must be done very slowly so that the flour will completely absorb the wine and the sauce will thicken properly. When all the wine has been added and the sauce is smooth, bring the mixture to a boil and pour it over the duck legs.

7. Add the herb bouquet, sugar, and salt and pepper to taste. Cover with a sheet of

buttered waxed paper; cover tightly and cook over very low heat 1 hour. The wine should "shudder." (This can be done in a preheated 275° F. oven.) Allow to cool, uncovered; then cover and refrigerate.

8. THE FOLLOWING DAY, remove all fat from the surface. Let come to room temperature. Place in a cold oven; heat to 275° F. and cook 1 1/2 hours. Cool, uncovered; cover, and refrigerate.

9. THE THIRD DAY, repeat procedure but cook at 225° F. for 1 1/2 hours.

10. JUST BEFORE SERVING, adjust seasoning and stir in the remaining tablespoon of Armagnac. Dip one end of each warm bread round into the sauce, then into a small bowl of chopped parsley. Decorate the serving platter with these bread rounds.

Inspired by a recipe from Roger Duffour.

VARIATION
Duck Legs with Red Wine Sauce
(Modern Version)

You can reach a similar rich, intense taste with body and depth of color by making the Duck Red Wine-Flavored Demi-Glace. Make the Demi-Glace at your leisure and keep it in the freezer. You are less than 1 hour away from enjoying a *salmis*. Accompany this very easy dish with Potato, Celery Root, and Corn Pancakes and watercress.

SERVES 2 TO 4
ACTIVE WORK: 10 minutes
COOKING TIME: 45 minutes

> 2 **pair duck legs with thighs attached, trimmed of excess fat**
> **Salt**
> 1 **cup full-bodied red wine such as California Petite Sirah or French Côtes-du-Rhône, or see Appendix under "Wines for Cooking" for other choices**
> 2 **tablespoons minced shallots**
> 3 **tablespoons white port wine or dry Madeira**
> **Herb bouquet: 3 sprigs parsley, 1 sprig thyme, and 1 bay leaf tied together**
> 1 1/2 **cups Duck Red Wine-Flavored Demi-Glace**
> 1/2 **cup heavy cream**
> **Freshly ground pepper**

1. Season duck pieces with salt. Refrigerate until 30 minutes before ready to cook.

2. In a heavy-bottomed nonaluminum saucepan, slowly reduce the wine and shallots until nearly dry—about 20 minutes.

3. Meanwhile remove the duck from the refrigerator and allow to come to room temperature. Wipe the duck pieces to remove excess moisture. Score the skin with the point of a small knife. Brown the duck skin side down in a wide skillet (to avoid crowding and thus steaming them) over medium heat, about 3 to 4 minutes. If necessary, do this in batches. You want to render out the fat under the skin before proceeding to sear the second side of each piece of duck.

4. Tilt the pan to pour off all the fat. Turn the duck pieces over to sear on the flesh side over medium heat. Remove duck pieces and set aside.

5. Add port or Madeira to the skillet and deglaze; reduce by half.

6. Reduce heat to medium low. Scrape in the red wine-shallot reduction, the herb bouquet, and half the Demi-Glace. Swirl to blend flavors. Spread out duck pieces in skillet so that they all are moistened with the mixture. Cover and cook 30 minutes, turning the duck 2 or 3 times to cook evenly.

7. Tilt the skillet and skim off all fat. Reduce pan juices to a syrupy consistency over high heat, turning the duck pieces so that they glaze on all sides.

8. Add the remaining Demi-Glace and continue cooking over low heat until the duck legs are fork-tender. Remove duck pieces to warm serving dish. Season with pepper.

9. Pour the sauce into a heavy saucepan. Bring to a boil and set saucepan half on the heat. Cook at a slow boil, skimming, 2 minutes. Add the cream and quickly boil down to a coating consistency. Correct seasoning with salt and pepper. *Can be prepared ahead up to this point.* Reheat gently. Spoon over the duck and serve hot.

RAGOUT OF DUCK LEGS WITH WHITE ONIONS
AND PRUNES

Ragout de Cuisses de Caneton aux Petits Oignons et aux Pruneaux

Duck breasts have become so popular that people often wonder what to do with the legs. One solution is to use them in this excellent dish which relies on a good hearty wine for background richness. The slow simmering and the degreasing make this version of the dish much lighter than others. It can be made in advance and gently reheated. The addition of triangles of bread fried in olive oil actually rounds out the flavor of the dish; don't leave them out. This is one of my favorite duck recipes.

(continued)

SERVES 4

ACTIVE WORK: 30 to 45 minutes
UNATTENDED COOKING TIME: 1 1/2 hours

    12 dried extra large pitted prunes
     2 cups hot tea, preferably linden or orange pekoe
     4 duck legs with thighs, each cut at the knee joint
     5 ounces salt pork or pork belly, cut into 2 × 1/8-inch strips (lardons)
     3 cloves garlic, peeled
   1/2 teaspoon salt
   1/4 teaspoon freshly ground pepper
      Pinch dried thyme, crumbled
     1 large red onion, thinly sliced (about 1 cup)
     1 tablespoon red wine vinegar
     1 tablespoon Dijon mustard
  2 1/4 cups full-bodied red wine such as California Petite Sirah, French
       Côtes-du-Rhône, or see Appendix under "Wines for Cooking" for
       other choices
  1 1/2 cups unsalted Chicken Stock, completely degreased
     3 medium carrots, scraped and halved crosswise, then lengthwise
    18 small white onions (about 1 inch in diameter)
     4 tablespoons unsalted butter
  1 1/2 teaspoons sugar
     2 tablespoons olive oil
     4 thin slices white bread, crusts removed, each slice cut diagonally into 4
       equal triangles
      Chopped fresh parsley

1. Soak prunes in hot tea. Let stand 2 hours, uncovered, at room temperature. Drain, reserving prunes and liquid separately.

2. Trim off excess fat from duck; render fat with 2 tablespoons water. Strain, reserving 2 tablespoons for this dish. Keep remainder for some other purpose. Score the skin of the duck with the point of a small knife. Wipe off excess moisture.

3. Blanch lardons in boiling water for 3 minutes; drain.

4. Heat duck fat in heavy noncorrodible skillet over medium heat; add blanched lardons. Fry, turning occasionally, until light brown, about 4 minutes. Remove lardons with slotted spoon; drain on brown wrapping paper or paper towels. Reserve drippings in skillet. Transfer lardons to heavy, flameproof 4-quart casserole.

5. Cook duck pieces in reserved drippings in covered skillet over medium high heat, turning occasionally, until well browned on all sides, about 10 minutes. Remove duck pieces with slotted spoon; drain on brown wrapping paper or paper towels.

6. Add duck pieces to lardons in casserole. Add 2 cloves garlic, salt, pepper, and thyme to casserole; toss to coat all ingredients.

7. Remove all but 2 tablespoons fat from the skillet. Add sliced red onion to reserved drippings in skillet. Sauté, stirring frequently over medium heat, until browned, about 5 minutes. Remove onion with slotted spoon; drain thoroughly on brown wrapping paper or paper towels. Add to the casserole.

8. Pour off fat from skillet; add vinegar and mustard. Whisk to combine; moisten with 1/3 cup of the wine. Heat to boiling, scraping up brown bits that cling to the bottom and sides of the skillet. Reduce to a glaze. Add another 1/3 cup wine and reduce again (this develops a stronger, deeper color).

9. Add deglazing liquid from skillet, remaining wine, and stock to casserole; heat to boiling. Reduce heat and simmer, uncovered, 5 minutes, skimming surface. Add the carrots. Simmer, tightly covered, until duck pieces are tender (about 1 1/2 hours), or cook in a preheated 300° F. oven.

10. Cut an X in root end of each small onion. Blanch 2 minutes; drain. Refresh under cold water until cool enough to handle. Peel the onions, leaving on enough root and stem end so the onion won't fall apart.

11. Combine onions, 1/2 cup water, 2 tablespoons of the butter, and the sugar in medium skillet. Heat over medium heat; simmer, stirring occasionally, until water has evaporated, about 6 minutes. Reduce heat to low; cook onions, shaking pan occasionally, until tender and well browned, about 8 minutes.

12. Heat remaining 2 tablespoons butter and the olive oil in large skillet until very hot. Fry bread triangles, turning once, until golden brown on both sides, about 6 minutes. Drain on brown wrapping paper or paper towels. Rub lightly with cut surface of remaining clove of garlic.

13. 15 MINUTES BEFORE SERVING, transfer duck pieces with slotted spoon to heated serving platter; surround with carrots and onions. Sprinkle lardons over duck; cover loosely with foil tent. Strain sauce through fine mesh sieve into small saucepan; press on solids with back of spoon to extract liquid. Skim off fat that rises to the surface. Bring to a boil and set saucepan half on the heat. Cook at a slow boil, skimming, 10 minutes, or until reduced enough to coat spoon lightly.

14. Meanwhile replace prunes in their soaking liquid in medium saucepan. Simmer about 10 minutes, drain well. Add prunes to platter. Spoon sauce over duck and garnishes. Serve immediately with reheated bread slices.

NOTE TO THE COOK
To save time during final steps of preparation, onions can be done several hours in advance. Just before serving, sprinkle water over onions and heat gently over medium heat until heated through.

Inspired by a recipe from Lucien Vanel.

DUCK SAUSAGE WITH GREEN APPLES AND CHESTNUTS
Boudin de Canard aux Pommes et aux Marrons

A *boudin* is a type of homemade sausage wrapped in pork casing, cooked, then browned in fat to reheat before serving. It is usually either "white"—made with pork, soaked bread, herb, spices, and truffles—or "black"—made with pork blood, pork, onions, and spices.

This giant duck *boudin* is different; it is a light, peppery sausage made with duck meat that is placed in a temporary casing of boilable plastic wrap in order to keep it together while being poached (think of the wrap as a sausage skin). It is cooled, unwrapped, browned, and finished in the oven. It is particularly good with roasted chestnuts and sautéed apples.

SERVES 4

ACTIVE WORK: 30 minutes
COOKING TIME: 1 hour

Boudin

      3 pair duck legs with thighs
      1 tablespoon unsalted butter
      4 ounces thinly sliced mushrooms
1 1/4 teaspoons salt
  1/2 teaspoon freshly ground pepper
      2 eggs
  1/2 cup heavy cream, chilled
      1 tablespoon vegetable oil

The Sauce

      1 medium carrot, halved
      2 small onions, halved and unpeeled
      1 small celery, sliced
  1/2 cup full-bodied red wine
  2/3 cup heavy cream
      3 teaspoons Dijon mustard
      2 egg yolks
2 1/2 teaspoons fresh lemon juice
      Pinch of grated nutmeg
      Salt and freshly ground pepper

Chestnut and Apple Garnish

4 tablespoons unsalted butter
2 tart green apples, peeled, cored, and cut into chunks the size of chestnuts
1 cup whole, unsweetened roasted chestnuts, freshly cooked or vacuum-packed *without brine*

1. Skin and bone the duck legs and thighs as described in How to Cut Up a Duck. Crack the bones and reserve for the sauce. Render fat and skin; reserve 3 tablespoons rendered fat.

2. Melt butter in small skillet over medium-high heat, add mushroom slices, and sauté until all moisture evaporates. Remove mushrooms from skillet; drain off butter and leave mushrooms to cool on a plate.

3. Trim the duck meat of all connective tissue. Grind meat and mushroom slices through the medium blade of a food chopper, or in a food processor using on-off turns, until meat and mushrooms are coarsely but evenly ground. Add salt and pepper. Mix in eggs, one at a time, then gradually beat in the chilled cream. Taste for seasoning. Mixture should be light and fluffy. Chill.

4. Brush lightly with oil a 12 × 18-inch sheet of heatproof plastic wrap (see Note 1). Spread the ground duck mixture into a 5 × 10-inch log. Roll it up into an 8-inch sausage, using the wrap as an aid as you roll. Twist ends to tighten the roll. Add 6 or 7 more layers of wrapping in both directions in order to make the sausage watertight (see Note 2).

5. In a deep skillet heat until hot but not boiling enough water to cover the sausage. Poach sausage in the water 35 minutes, turning midway. *Immediately drop into icy slush to cool down.* Remove when cold. It will keep 2 to 3 days in its wrapping in the refrigerator.

6. Meanwhile make the sauce base. Brown bones and vegetables in 1 tablespoon of the rendered duck fat in a heavy skillet, about 10 minutes. Degrease; deglaze with red wine and reduce over high heat to a glaze. Add 3 cups boiling water, reduce heat, and simmer 20 minutes. Strain into a saucepan, pressing down on ingredients. Degrease juices. Bring to a boil, set saucepan half over the heat and slowly boil, skimming, until reduced to 1/2 cup, about 20 minutes. Cool uncovered, cover, and refrigerate. *Can be prepared 1 day ahead up to this point.*

7. 45 MINUTES BEFORE SERVING, preheat oven to 325° F. Remove sausage from refrigerator and unwrap.

8. 30 MINUTES BEFORE SERVING, heat the remaining 2 tablespoons reserved duck fat in a wide, ovenproof skillet; add the *cold* sausage and brown on all sides, about 6 minutes. Pour off the duck fat. Place *boudin* in the oven to finish reheating in 20 minutes.

9. Heat butter in a second skillet and sauté the apples until soft and golden brown on all sides. Add the chestnuts and toss gently to heat through. Season with salt and pepper. Set in the oven to keep hot.

(continued)

10. Meanwhile reheat the sauce base from Step 6 above in a small, heavy saucepan. Stir in the cream.

11. Whisk together mustard and egg yolks in a small bowl. Off the heat, combine them with the cream. Reheat slowly, whisking. *Do not allow the mixture to boil.* Add the lemon juice and seasonings to taste.

12. Place the sausage on a warm serving dish. Coat with the sauce. Serve at once with chestnut and apple garnish.

NOTES TO THE COOK
1. Saran Wrap is a brand that does not melt when used in cooking.
2. A boilable cooking pouch vacuum-packed by a sealing appliance works as well.

Inspired by a recipe from Lucien Vanel.

DUCK LEG AND SWEETBREAD RAGOUT
Ragout de Cuisses de Canard aux Ris de Veau

A dish created by Lucien Vanel for the thrifty cook!

This fascinating ragout—*two* stews joined together after each has been fully cooked and degreased—has the contrapuntal quality of a great duet: tastes interweave, textures collide, and the whole is greater than the sum of its parts. This is one of those *plat des pauvres* (poor people's food)—wonderful flavors from a bit of this and a bit of that, brought to sophistication. In many ethnic neighborhoods and some supermarkets, sweetbreads are readily available and inexpensive.

Serve with the Straw Potato Cake Stuffed with Braised Leeks. A sorbet or fruit compote would be the best way to finish the meal.

Duck Leg Ragout

SERVES 6
☆ Begin 1 day in advance
ACTIVE WORK: 10 minutes
COOKING TIME (MOSTLY UNATTENDED): 1 hour

        3 pair duck legs with thighs attached
          Salt and freshly ground pepper
        4 tablespoons (1/2 stick) unsalted butter
    1 1/2 cups coarsely chopped onions
        1/4 cup red wine vinegar
          1 tablespoon Dijon mustard
          2 cups dry white wine

    2 cloves garlic, halved
    2 pinches thyme leaves
1 1/2 cups unsalted Chicken Stock

1. Preheat oven to 350° F.

2. Trim away excess skin and fat from the legs and thighs. Season liberally with salt and pepper.

3. Heat the butter in an ovenproof noncorrodible skillet. Add the legs and thighs and brown briefly on both sides. Prick the fatty parts many times without piercing the flesh itself. Continue to sauté the duck 5 minutes longer. Remove pieces to a side dish lined with brown wrapping paper or paper towels. Pour off all but 1 1/2 tablespoons fat from skillet.

4. Add the onions to skillet and sauté until limp. Drain off fat. Add the vinegar, mustard, and wine to the skillet, stirring. Over high heat, reduce rapidly by one third, scraping up all the little bits and pieces that cling to the bottom of the skillet (10 minutes).

5. Stir in the garlic, thyme, and stock; return duck pieces to the skillet and bring to a boil, skimming. Cover with a sheet of buttered parchment or waxed paper, and a lid; set in the oven to cook 45 minutes or until legs are just tender. Cool, uncovered; cover and refrigerate overnight. *The following day,* make the Sweetbread Ragout.

Sweetbread Ragout

ACTIVE WORK: 10 minutes
COOKING TIME: 20 minutes

    3/4–1 pound fresh or frozen sweetbreads
    1 tablespoon wine vinegar
    4 tablespoons unsalted butter
    3 tablespoons minced carrot
    3 tablespoons minced onion
1 1/2 tablespoons minced celery
    2 tablespoons dry vermouth
    1/4 cup imported ruby port wine
    1/2 cup Demi-Glace, or 2 cups unsalted Chicken Stock, degreased and reduced to 1/2 cup
    1 teaspoon tomato paste
    Salt and freshly ground pepper

1 cup heavy cream *for the finale*

1. Soak sweetbreads 2 hours in 2 or 3 changes of acidulated water (1 tablespoon vinegar to 2 cups water). If using frozen sweetbreads, defrost directly in water; add 1 to 2 hours to soaking time. (Sweetbreads are not blanched for this dish.)

(continued)

2. Drain, peel, and cut away connective tube, gristle, and any fatty parts. In a covered 10-inch skillet or wide saucepan, melt butter. Spread out minced vegetables in skillet in 1 layer; cover and sweat vegetables 5 minutes over low heat.

3. Uncover skillet, add sweetbreads, and turn them in the pan juices to moisten. Add the vermouth; cover and gently cook 10 minutes, turning the sweetbreads midway. Add the port; reduce pan juices over medium heat to a glaze. Allow sweetbreads to brown slightly on both sides in the syrupy juices.

4. Add the Demi-Glace or reduced stock and tomato paste; season with salt and pepper. Bring to a simmer, skimming. Swirl to combine pan juices and keep sweetbreads moist. Cover and cook over very low heat 7 to 8 minutes longer, turning sweetbreads once or twice. Cool uncovered. *Can be prepared ahead up to this point.*

TO ASSEMBLE

ACTIVE WORK: 15 minutes
COOKING TIME: 30 minutes

1. 45 MINUTES BEFORE SERVING, preheat oven to 300° F.

2. Lift and discard the chilled fat that formed over duck legs and sauce. Scrape sauce off legs and reserve.

3. Place legs in shallow ovenproof serving dish.

4. Remove sweetbreads to work surface and slice them on the diagonal into 1-inch pieces. Arrange sweetbreads alternately with duck legs in serving dish. Cover and set aside.

5. Skim off fat from sweetbread juices. Scrape reserved duck sauce into sweetbread pan juices; add cream and reduce together, stirring, until sauce has enough body to coat a wooden spoon. Adjust seasoning. Strain sauce over legs and sweetbreads, and gently heat in oven until hot and ready to serve, about 30 minutes.

NOTE TO THE COOK
While the ragout is heating, make the Straw Potato Cake Stuffed with Braised Leeks.

CONFIT OF DUCK AND GOOSE

In some ways *confit* (pronounced *cón-fee*) is less a recipe than a way of life. Logical enough in the context of farmhouse abundance and the annual round of putting up meats for winter, the process needs a certain amount of adaptation for cooks not blessed with constant, taken-for-granted supplies of the right meats and good, home-rendered fats. But after years of experimenting with *confit* in American kitchens, I have arrived at both a satisfactory adjustment of the basic techniques to our somewhat different ingredients and a reasonable compromise with our less leisurely household rhythms.

Put *confit* into cassoulets, garbures, soups, and fava, lentil, and bean dishes. Add them, hot or cold, to a walnut oil-dressed salad of mixed greens. Serve them hot and crispy as a main dish along with French fried potatoes or a plate of Puréed Sorrel, with braised cabbage, with *Cèpes à la Bordelaise*, with Sarlat Potato Cake, with Potatoes in the Style of Quercy, with sautéed apples, with fresh green peas cooked in goose fat along with *jambon de Bayonne* and baby white onions, with marinated strips of roasted red bell peppers, or shredded and sautéed with rice and slices of spicy pork sausage.

The fatty Long Island and Petaluma ducks sold in America are very good for making *confit*, but they are smaller and less meaty than the force-fed birds used in the French strongholds of *confit*-making. On its home territory, too, *confit* was intended to last for months without refrigeration—in fact, meats preserved in this way were sometimes kept the year round, with occasional reheating to prevent spoiling. As a result, with the traditional method the ducks (or other meats) are salted for a longer time than is necessary in this country with our smaller ducks. I have reduced the initial salting period accordingly, while retaining the basic principles of *confit*-making—quite simple principles, but also quite unusual.

As with other preserved meats, a certain amount of time is necessary to allow the chemical changes to take place that will produce the mellow flavor of true *confit*. (People on rushed schedules can taste their *"confit"* within a week or so, or for that matter as soon as it finishes cooking, but what they are eating won't really be *confit* any more than freshly drained curds are ripe cheese.) The amount of salt I suggest for 2 ducks (6 tablespoons, which corresponds to the traditionally used French formula of 22 grams to each pound of trimmed meat) is predicated on a maturing period of at least a week and up to 4 months—enough to allow the salt to react gradually with the meat inside its protective seal of solidified fat. For storage of less than a week, the amount of salt should be halved, since the full ripening reaction won't have time to take place. In either case, the marinated duck pieces are rinsed under running water to eliminate the excess salt before cooking.

I have found that the gentle heat of a Crock-Pot is ideal for making *confit*; if using another vessel, be sure that it is heavy enough to conduct heat steadily and gently. Increase quantities if desired, cooking the *confit* in batches as necessary and putting it up in any convenient-sized vessels; proportionally less fat will be necessary to cook increased amounts of duck. Any leftover fat that will not fit into *confit* crocks will make a delicious sautéing fat for potatoes, apples, or cabbage, or can be used in putting up additional *confit* of any type. Store the fat, refrigerated, in clean covered containers up to 4 months, or freeze it up to 1 year.

A final note on the duck pieces used in this recipe: In the South-West of France, where large numbers of ducks and geese are raised for foie gras and *confit* is put up in vast quantities at a time, there are always enough duck leg pieces—the most desirable part for preserving—to make huge pots of *confit* without using the breasts. Though the breasts can be used, they do not take as well as the rest of the duck in the *confit*-making process, and are generally reserved for other purposes unconnected with *confit*-making—for example, grilling. Because it may not be practical for home cooks in this country to buy extra duck legs, this version is based on two whole ducks, breasts included; however, by all means substitute 4 more duck legs for 2 whole duck breasts if you are able to do so. If you do use the breasts for *confit*, be careful not to overcook them, since they are apt to turn stringy if not handled gently. In the recipes using duck *confit*, supplement the preferred duck legs with the breasts as necessary.

14 DETAILED STEPS TO PERFECT *CONFIT* OF DUCK

MAKES ENOUGH *CONFIT* TO FILL 3
1-QUART OR 1 1/2 TO 2-QUART
CONTAINERS
☆ Begin at least 2 days in advance
  ACTIVE WORK (DAY 1): 20 to 30 minutes
  ACTIVE WORK (DAY 2): 30 minutes
  UNATTENDED COOKING TIME: 3 to 4 hours

2	ducks (each about 4 1/2 pounds) with necks and gizzards, or 4 pair duck legs with thighs attached
3–6	tablespoons coarse (kosher) salt
1 1/2	tablespoons coarsely chopped shallots
1 1/2	tablespoons chopped fresh parsley
2	teaspoons black peppercorns, lightly crushed
1	bay leaf, crumbled
1	teaspoon coarsely chopped garlic
	Pinch of dried thyme, crumbled, or 1 sprig fresh thyme, chopped
4–6	cups good-quality lard or rendered goose fat (see Note 1)
1	whole head garlic
2	whole cloves
	Peanut oil
1/2 to 3/4	teaspoon salt (optional)
	Good-quality lard (optional)

1. 1 DAY IN ADVANCE, trim loose flaps of skin from duck and pull out all loose fat from cavity; reserve. Remove any skin from necks; reserve. Peel off and discard outer covering of gizzards.

2. Using poultry shears or large, sharp, heavy knife, cut up ducks to produce pieces for *confit*: 4 legs (thigh with drumstick attached), 4 wings, and 4 breast pieces. Remove wing tips; reserve backs and wing tips for soup or other purpose. Remove skin from backs; add to reserved pieces of skin and fat.

3. Weigh the trimmed pieces. For every pound use 4 1/3 teaspoons salt for long-term ripening (more than 1 week). Using half the amount of salt if you intend to keep

confit less than 1 week, and the larger amount if you wish *confit* to ripen more fully and last 3 to 4 months, combine salt with shallots, parsley, peppercorns, bay leaf, minced garlic, and thyme in large bowl. Toss duck pieces, necks, and gizzards with the mixture. Cover with kitchen towel or plastic wrap and refrigerate 18 to 24 hours.

4. Meanwhile, cut reserved pieces of fat and skin into small pieces (1/4 inch or less) and render out most of the fat by either oven or stove-top method as follows: For oven method, heat oven to 300° F.; cook duck fat and skin in deep ovenproof bowl for about 1 hour, or until fat turns clear and bits of skin have floated to the surface and are pale golden. For stove-top method, combine duck skin and fat with 3 to 4 table-spoons water in a small, heavy saucepan; simmer, uncovered, over low heat about 1 hour, or to same stage as described above. Strain rendered fat into heatproof container. If not using fat immediately, cool, uncovered, to room temperature; store, tightly covered, in refrigerator.

5. THE FOLLOWING DAY, place rendered duck fat in Crock-Pot or large, very heavy pot such as enameled cast-iron casserole. Add 4 to 6 cups rendered poultry fat or lard—exact amount will vary depending on size and shape of your cooking vessel. Slowly melt the fat. Reserve meat juices for stock or Cornmeal Porridge, using them as part of the liquid.

6. Remove marinated duck pieces from bowl and rinse under cold running water. Let drain briefly (it is not necessary to dry surface completely).

7. As soon as fat has melted, slip in pieces of duck. Fat should cover duck; if there is not enough fat, work in batches. Split head of garlic in half crosswise and stick a whole clove in each half. Add garlic to melted fat.

8. In Crock-Pot or over very low heat, uncovered, bring fat to temperature of 190° F.; this should take about 1 hour in covered Crock-Pot or partially covered casserole (faster heating will result in a stringy-textured *confit*). (See Note 2.) Hold temperature at 190° F., adjusting setting as necessary, until gizzards, neck, wings, and breasts are tender enough to be pierced easily with wooden pick, about 1 hour; Crock-Pot should be partially covered, casserole uncovered. Skin will be pale in color. Remove these pieces with slotted spoon as they are done; keep pieces covered with foil to prevent drying out. Maintain 190° F. temperature another 30 minutes, or until thickest part of thigh tests done. Remove from heat; let duck legs cool in fat 1 hour. Remove duck thighs and garlic with slotted spoon (see Note 3).

9. If Crock-Pot was used, ladle fat to large, very heavy pot. Heat, uncovered, over medium-high heat to almost boiling, skimming off foam that rises to surface. Let bubble 5 to 10 minutes, or until spattering stops and surface of fat is nearly undisturbed. Watch carefully and adjust heat if necessary to avoid burning or smoking; fat that is allowed to reach smoking point will be ruined for reuse. Remove from heat; let cool a few minutes.

10. Have ready a clean, dry container or several containers chosen according to how long you plan to keep the *confit*. *Confit* to be used within a week, rather than being allowed to mellow, can be stored very simply in any convenient-sized bowl or plastic tub; place duck pieces in container and ladle still-warm fat from pot through

fine-mesh sieve to cover *confit* completely. Allow fat to congeal overnight; pour a layer of peanut oil over the top. Store, covered with foil, up to 1 week in refrigerator or cool, dry place; it will not be necessary to seal more completely.

11. *Confit* to be kept longer than a week and up to 4 months requires a somewhat different procedure. For this amount, use three 1-quart or two 1 1/2-quart crocks or jars. (Since pieces will be embedded in solidified fat and cannot be casually removed, it is necessary to use more than 1 vessel in order to separate larger pieces that will be served whole, or in attractive slices, from smaller and bonier ones that are best added to soups or stews.) Heavy, glazed earthenware crocks, taller than they are wide, are excellent (see Note 4). Remember that the narrower the vessel, the less fat will be needed to cover duck pieces; however, pieces should not be crowded against the sides. Line up containers and prepare to fill them. Pour boiling water into each; swirl and discard. Thoroughly dry the containers. Immediately place 1/2 teaspoon salt in bottom of each crock; this prevents meat juices (*salarque*) that may seep from duck during ripening process from turning sour. Examine cooked duck pieces. Bones may have come loose from some pieces; if so, use loose bones to make crisscross platform on bottom of one or all vessels. Reheat fat. Ladle bubbling clear top fat through fine-mesh strainer into each container; be sure not to use the more perishable cloudy fat and meat juices at the bottom (see Note 5). Fill about halfway; slip in still-warm *confit* pieces without crowding. Ladle in additional clear fat as necessary to cover *confit* and leave a generous inch of air space between surface of fat and rim of vessel. Rap containers gently on work surface to tamp out any air pockets. Let cool, uncovered, to room temperature. Store, covered, overnight in refrigerator or in cold cellar or other cool storage area.

12. THE NEXT DAY, seal *confit* by spooning a 1-inch layer of melted lard over surface; since lard is more impenetrable to air than duck fat, this protects against spoilage. (Amount of lard necessary will vary with dimensions of your vessels.) Cover with kitchen parchment secured with rubber band; this is sufficient protection with or without lid placed on top. Store in refrigerator. Do not freeze; freezing inhibits the ripening process and dries out the meat.

13. To use *confit*, set vessel in warm room or place in deep pan of warm water until fat is softened, about 4 hours. Take out as many pieces as you need; set aside. Make sure remaining pieces are well covered with fat; add peanut oil, if necessary. Once seal is broken, *confit* will be more perishable and should be used within a week.

14. The various *confit* pieces require different handling for different uses. However, *confit* should always be heated before serving, even in dishes to be served cold or at room temperature. If crisp skin is not necessary for presentation, steam pieces 5 minutes over boiling water in a steamer or heat slowly in oven. If you want a crispy skin, like Peking Duck, here's how to do it. In the South-West the key is gentle reheating or broiling, allowing a slow cooking to bring the skin to crispness. These techniques simply don't work here, because the skins of American ducks are thinner than those of French ones. I have found that the following method, inspired by James Villas's instructions on how to crisp chicken for Southern Fried chicken in his *American Taste*, works better than any other technique I know. Lift the *confit* pieces

from the crock; scrape fat that clings to pieces into a skillet with a tight-fitting lid. (I use a steel skillet, because it heats fast.) There should be about 2 to 3 tablespoons fat in the skillet for 2 pieces of *confit*. Add 2 tablespoons grapeseed or peanut oil and heat the fat to sizzling but not smoking. (Adding oil allows the fat to "ripple" at a higher temperature.) Add the *confit* pieces (not more than 2 at a time) skin side down; cover tightly and cook over high heat. You will hear much spattering and sizzling. Don't uncover the pan! Cook 2 minutes. Remove lid and carefully wipe off moisture clinging to underside; shake pan to make sure *confit* is not sticking and check crispiness. Cover and continue cooking, if necessary, for 2 to 3 minutes to finish browning. Remove from heat and uncover. Pour off fat and turn each piece skin side up. Cook, uncovered, over low heat about 3 to 4 minutes. Remove to wire racks or brown paper bag to drain.

NOTES TO THE COOK

1. Good-quality butcher's lard, purchased from a pork butcher or other reliable meat store, is ideal for this recipe; do not use packaged commercial lard, which is too strong-tasting. Rendered goose fat, available from some ethnic butchers, is also an excellent choice. French goose fat in 12 11/16-ounce jars, imported by Petrossian, Inc., is sold by Dean & DeLuca (see mail order sources in Appendix). You can also freeze any unused pieces of fresh fat and skin whenever you cook a duck or goose. When you have accumulated several cups' worth, render it according to the directions in Step 4. (Fat before rendering will keep up to 6 months in freezer; rendered fat will keep 4 months in refrigerator, indefinitely in freezer.) Another alternative is to make your own lard from pork leaf lard (see Rendering Pork Fat).

2. Alternatively, *confit* can be cooked, uncovered, in oven. Place duck pieces, skin side down, and melted fat in a deep baking dish; place in cold oven. Turn oven on to 275° F. After temperature of fat has reached 190° F. (1 to 1 1/2 hours, depending on your oven), reduce setting to 200° F. Adjusting oven control as necessary, maintain temperature of fat at 190° F. until duck pieces are tender. Turn off oven; let duck legs cool in fat, in the oven, 1 hour. Ladle off melted fat into heavy saucepan and proceed with Step 9.

3. Although *confit* at this point will not have the excellent flavor of aged *confit*, it can, if desired, be used at once in any *confit* recipe; follow recipe directions for browning or steaming and carving.

   Press garlic through sieve to obtain small amount of an unusually flavorful spread.

4. Stoneware jugs that are glazed on inside only are my first choice. Glass jars can also be used.

5. The cloudy fat can be used as a flavorful sautéing fat; any juices left in pot after all fat has been removed can be saved and added to soups for flavor. Any debris on bottom of pan after fat and juices have been removed can be turned into rillettes, a delicious spread. Scrape up debris and mix well in a small bowl with an equal amount of *confit* fat or fresh unsalted butter. Season liberally with pepper; use as a spread on crackers or toast rounds.

PRESERVED DUCK WITH GREEN PEAS AND HAM
Confit de Canard à la Gasconne

This is an excellent supper dish for spring and early summer when fresh tender peas still in their moist pods are available.

I am not a food snob; I *do* taste the difference between frozen and fresh peas. Because peas play such an important role in this dish, I think one should hold out for fresh peas. Shelling peas is tedious for some people, but I have never minded this chore. I usually turn on the radio, listen to music, and dream away. The time does seem to go faster that way.

Serve this dish in a shallow earthenware pot for rustic presentation.

Start the meal with a Sorrel Omelet and finish with Fresh Strawberries with Peppercorns and Red Wine.

SERVES 2 TO 4
> ACTIVE WORK: 15 minutes
> COOKING TIME: 30 minutes

> 4 **thigh-drumstick portions** *Confit* **of Duck**
> 2 **pounds unshelled green peas (preferably sugar snap peas)**
> **Salt**
> 2/3 **cup cubed** *jambon de Bayonne,* **prosciutto, or Westphalian ham**
> 6–12 **small white onions, peeled**
> 1/3 **cup cubed carrots**
> **Pinch of sugar**
> **Herb bouquet: 3 sprigs parsley, 1 sprig thyme, and 1/2 bay leaf tied in a bundle**
> **Freshly ground pepper**

1. ABOUT 4 HOURS BEFORE BEGINNING MAIN PREPARATION, set out crock of *confit* in warm room or deep pan of warm water to soften fat.

2. Shell the peas. You should have about 2 cups. Blanch peas in boiling salted water 2 minutes; drain and refresh. Set aside. Set aside 2 tablespoons fat from *confit*.

3. Lightly crisp the duck *confit* in a covered skillet in its own fat 5 minutes. Remove to brown wrapping paper or paper towels to drain. Pour off all the fat in the skillet. Do not wash skillet.

4. Add to the skillet 1 tablespoon of the reserved fat from *confit*, the ham, onions, and carrots. Cover and cook 5 minutes. Uncover and cook, stirring, until carrots and onions become light brown around the edges. Add the drained peas, 1/3 cup water, sugar, and herb bouquet. Cover tightly and simmer until peas are almost cooked (depending on the age and size of the peas, this could take from 5 to 15 minutes).

5. Meanwhile reheat and finish crisping the *confit* in a second skillet.

6. When peas are almost cooked, nestle the *confit* in the peas; add the remaining tablespoon duck fat. Simmer together uncovered 5 minutes to blend flavors. Remove herb bouquet; add pepper to taste and, if necessary, a pinch of salt. Serve very hot.

CONFIT OF GOOSE
Confit d'Oie

Throughout South-West France, goose is as often turned into *confit* as is duck. Unfortunately, it isn't easy to find geese in American markets except at Christmas. However, goose is particularly desirable as *confit*. Its taste is richer and rounder than *confit* made with duck, and its fat is even better for cooking. To make *confit* of goose, follow the steps for duck but marinate a 9- pound goose, cut up, for 24 hours. Cook it for 2 to 2 1/2 hours, or until pieces are tender when pierced with a wooden pick. If your pot is not large enough to cook large pieces all at once, cut into smaller pieces or cook in batches. It may be necessary to remove larger bones after cooking to fit *confit* into storage containers.

It is best served in the following traditional ways: hot in garbures, in cassoulets, with sautéed potatoes, with puréed sorrel, and with sautéed wild mushrooms; or cold with a green salad.

Confit of stuffed neck is a delicious dish of the South-West. The neck skin of a goose is stuffed, tied, and cooked in rendered goose fat 1 to 1 1/4 hours, or until it rises to the surface. This is often served in a pot-au-feu or browned in a skillet and served with a salad or puréed sorrel, or with a sauce Périgueux. (See Stuffed Duck Neck in Brioche for an adaptation using the neck skin and serving it wrapped in brioche with a red wine sauce.)

GOOSE STEW WITH RADISHES
Daube d'Oie aux Radis

This is a modern version of a very old Gascon recipe for goose stew. It is totally free of goose fat. For good reason we associate geese with fat, but goose meat itself is lean, especially in the breast. In this recipe the breast meat is actually larded to keep it juicy—the strips of fat are soaked first in Armagnac mixed with chopped garlic and herbs. The addition of radishes is new—they taste like peppery turnips when they are cooked. Salsify, turnips, carrots, and blanched baby onions can be prepared similarly and used as an alternative garnish for this daube. The daube requires long cooking, but the result is rich and satisfying. Noodles make a good accompaniment. Like most good stews, this one is better reheated, so plan to make it 3 to 5 days in advance of serving.

(continued)

SERVES 6 TO 8
☆ Begin 3 to 5 days in advance
ACTIVE WORK (DAY 1): 30 minutes
ACTIVE WORK (DAY 2): 10 minutes
PARTIALLY ATTENDED SIMMERING (DAY 2): 7 to 8 hours
ACTIVE WORK (DAY 3): 20 minutes
PARTIALLY ATTENDED SIMMERING (DAY 3): 2 1/2 hours

1 goose (10 to 11 pounds)*
3 tablespoons Armagnac
1 teaspoon minced shallots
1 teaspoon minced fresh parsley
1/4 teaspoon dried thyme, crumbled
1/4 teaspoon freshly grated nutmeg
1 clove garlic, thinly sliced
6–8 slices lightly smoked bacon or 1/2 pound salt pork, blanched 3 minutes, drained, and cut into thin strips
Coarse (kosher) salt
Herb bouquet: 6 sprigs parsley, 1 sprig thyme, and 1 bay leaf tied together
1 bottle full-bodied dry red wine such as California Petite Sirah or French Côtes-du-Rhône, or see Appendix under "Wines for Cooking" for other choices
2 medium onions, thinly sliced
1 medium carrot, thinly sliced
1 medium leek, white part, thinly sliced
8 1/2 cups unsalted Chicken Stock, totally degreased
1/4 cup unsalted butter
2 teaspoons sugar
3–4 dozen large fresh radishes, trimmed and peeled
Salt and freshly ground pepper
Chopped fresh parsley

*If frozen, defrost goose in original wrapper in refrigerator or soak overnight in water, still in wrapping.

1. 3 DAYS BEFORE SERVING, trim all fat and skin from goose. Render, cool, then store in covered jar in refrigerator.

2. Combine Armagnac, shallots, parsley, thyme, nutmeg, and garlic in large bowl; mix well. Toss still warm strips of bacon or salt pork with mixture. Chill strips in marinade.

3. Meanwhile cut up the goose, using sharp, thin-bladed knife. Cut down the center breast to the bone. Guiding knife along breast, pull meat back and lift from bone. Sever legs and thighs at joints; remove bones and trim meat as necessary. Cut meat into 1 1/2-inch chunks. Set aside.

4. Remove strips from marinade. Cut into small pieces. With a thin, sharp knife, pierce a hole in center of each chunk of meat. Fill holes with strips. Transfer goose meat to marinade. Add 1 tablespoon salt and toss lightly. Let marinate 2 nights in refrigerator.

5. Peel gizzard. Rinse gizzard and heart; transfer to deep, noncorrodible bowl. Crack carcass, wings, and neck into very small pieces. Add cracked bones and herb bouquet to gizzard and heart. Pour wine over all and set in cool place or refrigerator to marinate overnight. Reserve liver for pâté or some other use.

6. THE FOLLOWING MORNING, or one day before serving, make a red wine-flavored demi-glace with the goose bones. Heat 1 1/2 tablespoons reserved rendered goose fat in a large deep pot over medium heat. Add onions and carrot and sauté until browned, about 5 to 10 minutes. Tilt pot and press lightly on vegetables with slotted spoon to release fat. Blot fat with paper towel. Return pot to medium heat. Add leeks, marinated bones, herb bouquet, gizzard, and heart with wine marinade. Slowly bring mixture to boil. Reduce heat to low and cook until liquid is reduced to 1/2 cup, about 3 to 4 hours, skimming often. (Demi-glace can also be done in a Crock-Pot or in the oven.)

7. Add 8 cups Chicken Stock to pot. If necessary, add water to cover mixture. Bring to boil over medium heat. Reduce heat and simmer, skimming frequently, 3 to 4 more hours until stock is reduced to 3 cups. Strain demi-glace stock through sieve. Set in refrigerator until fat hardens on surface. Discard fat.

8. THE MORNING OF SERVING DAY, pat goose meat dry with paper towel. Heat small amount of reserved rendered fat in deep skillet over medium-high heat. Add goose meat in batches and cook about 10 minutes until browned on all sides. Tilt pan and blot all excess fat with paper towel. Add the demi-glace to the goose meat and bring mixture to a boil. Reduce heat and simmer gently until meat is very tender but not falling apart, about 2 to 2 1/2 hours. Remove meat to a side dish. Degrease the demi-glace. Pour demi-glace into a saucepan and bring to a boil. Set saucepan half on the heat and cook at a slow boil, skimming, 10 to 15 minutes, or until thick enough to coat the meat. Pour over the pieces of goose. (*Can be prepared ahead up to this point and refrigerated.*)

9. ABOUT 30 MINUTES BEFORE SERVING, remove any fat from surface of stew. Place goose and sauce in a large, heavy-bottomed skillet. *Slowly* reheat to a simmer.

10. Meanwhile prepare vegetable garnish. Combine remaining Chicken Stock with butter and sugar in a large skillet over high heat. Add radishes, cover and cook until crisp-tender, about 5 minutes; *do not let radishes burn*. Remove cover and shake skillet to glaze radishes. Drain and discard any liquid.

11. Add radishes to stew and simmer 5 minutes. Season to taste with salt and pepper. Transfer to large serving dish or platter. Sprinkle with parsley and serve.

Inspired by a recipe from Jean-Louis Palladin.

GAME DISHES

GRILLED QUAIL
Cailles Grillées

The Gironde is abundant with quail and snipe, both of which should be eaten fresh, not hung. In one Landais cookbook the author quotes her grandfather's motto: "Snipe should be eaten at the end of a gun." In the South-West, quail and snipe are often wrapped in layers of oiled grape leaves, then grilled over dried vine cuttings until done. They are usually eaten right away off hot plates, though they can also be eaten cold.

In a country inn in Gascony I observed the following cooking procedure. A thin sheet of pork was wrapped around each quail, then the pork-wrapped birds were strung on a skewer and grilled over a pan containing country bread that had been rubbed with garlic and arranged to catch the cooking juices. When the birds were done, everything but the gizzards was chopped, doused with Armagnac; softened with butter, and spread on bread. As we ate the quail, the cook toasted the slices of country bread over the embers until they became crusty. In the Landes, bread embellished like this is called *la rôtie*. There are many versions of it, some much simpler but equally delicious. The Roasted Bread (see Index) that is to be served with a salad and Salmon Rillettes is spread with olive oil and mixed herbs, then roasted until it glistens. In the Périgord, frothy egg whites are spread on the toasted bread, which is roasted again to sparkling crispness and used to mop up soup.

Serve Grilled Quail with Cèpes in the Style of Gascony and a crisp green salad. Follow with Preserved Spiced Pears in Red Wine with Armagnac.

SERVES 2
    MARINATION TIME: 2 to 3 hours
    ACTIVE WORK: 10 minutes
    COOKING TIME: 10 minutes

> **2–4 quail depending on size, freshly killed and cleaned**
> **1 large clove garlic, finely chopped**
> **1/2 teaspoon mixed herbs: Herbes de la Garrigue or herbes de Provence**
> **1/2 teaspoon salt**
> **1/4 teaspoon freshly ground pepper**
> **1/2 cup olive oil**
> **2–4 slices thin Country-Style Bread**
> **Lemon wedges**

1. Split quail down the back and gently flatten each with the side of a cleaver.
2. In a bowl, mix garlic, herbs, salt, pepper, and olive oil.
3. Rub quail with marinade and let stand a few hours, turning from time to time.

4. Light vine cuttings or coals, or preheat the broiler. When hot, grill quail with breast side facing heat first, 2 to 3 minutes, basting with oil marinade. Turn every 2 minutes, basting until cooked and golden brown (9 to 10 minutes), or until the breasts feel *slightly* springy when pressed.

5. Brush bread slices with marinade and quail juices. Run under broiler or grill just before serving.

6. Serve quail very hot with lemon wedges.

NOTE TO THE COOK
(Grape-wood) vine cuttings may be ordered through the mail; see Grape Wood entry in Appendix.

PHEASANT BREASTS WITH FOIE GRAS
Suprêmes de Faisan au Foie Gras

An elegant dish for a very special evening. Serve with Michel Guérard's Puréed Celery Root with Apples, or with peeled tart apple quarters sautéed in butter and sprinkled with lemon juice.

SERVES 8
☆ Begin 1 day in advance
  ACTIVE WORK (DAY 1): 20 minutes
  COOKING TIME (DAY 1): 2 hours
  ACTIVE WORK (DAY 2): 30 minutes

> 4 tender young pheasants, cleaned
> Salt and freshly ground pepper
> 4 tablespoons dry white wine
> 3 tablespoons oil, preferably French peanut oil
> 4 tablespoons minced shallots
> 3 tablespoons Armagnac
> 3 tablespoons red port wine
> 5 cups unsalted Chicken Stock, thoroughly degreased and reduced by one half
> 3/4 cup full-bodied red wine such as California Petite Sirah or French Côtes-du-Rhône, or see "Wines for Cooking" in Appendix for other choices
> Pinch of Quatre Épices
> 8 tablespoons unsalted butter
> 1 ounce foie gras

1. 1 DAY IN ADVANCE, lift off the breasts of each pheasant. Set aside the livers and hearts. Salt and pepper the breasts and sprinkle lightly with 2 tablespoons of the

white wine. Refrigerate, covered, overnight, until 1 hour before serving.

2. Chop the carcass into small pieces. Heat the oil in a wide, heavy-bottomed skillet; add the carcass and brown deeply on all sides, about 30 minutes.

3. Add half the shallots; lower heat and allow to soften. Tilt the skillet and spoon off the oil and discard.

4. Add the Armagnac, remaining white wine, and port. Cook down to a glaze. Stir in 1 cup of the reduced stock and slowly reduce to a glaze. Add remaining stock and cook over low heat, covered, 1 hour, skimming often.

5. Add the hearts and livers to the pan and cook 30 minutes longer. Strain into a tall, narrow container and allow to cool. When cool, remove the fat from the surface and discard. Pour liquid back into saucepan and bring to a boil. Set saucepan half on the heat. Cook at a slow boil, skimming, 10 minutes or until reduced to 1 cup.

6. Meanwhile, slowly cook the red wine with the remaining shallots and a pinch of Quatre Épices in a small nonaluminum saucepan to a glaze, about 30 minutes. Combine with reduced sauce base and hold until ready to sauté the pheasants. *Can be prepared 1 day ahead up to this point.*

7. 1 HOUR BEFORE SERVING, remove breasts from the refrigerator.

8. ABOUT 15 MINUTES BEFORE SERVING, heat all but 2 tablespoons butter over medium-high heat in a large, heavy-bottomed skillet. When hot, add the pheasant breasts, skin side down, and brown. Turn over and cook until just tender, about 12 minutes, depending upon size and tenderness.

9. Meanwhile, in a small saucepan reheat sauce base and red wine reduction. Cut each of the breasts into 3 slices across the grain, slightly on the diagonal. Arrange overlapping slices on a heated serving dish. Pour off all fat from skillet and deglaze with the heated sauce base. Remove from heat and blend in pieces of foie gras, and remaining butter. *The sauce must not approach boiling.* Adjust seasoning of the sauce with salt and pepper. Strain the sauce directly over the pheasant. Serve at once.

NOTE TO THE COOK

The dark meat is used for pâtés or can be chopped up and added to the carcass in preparing the sauce. If desired, cook the dark parts in a second skillet 5 to 10 minutes longer, covering them midway so that they will cook up fork-tender.

RABBIT STEW WITH PRESERVED PEARS WITH GINGER
Blanquette de Lapin au Confit de Poires et Gingembre

This combination of mustard-flavored rabbit stew and gingered pears is most unusual and exciting to the palate. Though wild rabbits are particularly flavorful, this recipe will work very well with the fresh or frozen farm-bred variety. I believe that rabbits, like ducks, work best when cut up into parts, then used in different ways. The front part of this animal has little meat, while the saddle and hind legs are abundantly meaty. When I buy frozen rabbit I use only the meaty pieces for this dish, saving the ribs and front legs for a delicious Old-Fashioned Rabbit Soup (see Index).

Begin this winter meal with one of the appetizer salads in Chapter 4. Serve the rabbit with ribbon noodles and finish with the Basque Cake with Pastry Cream Filling.

SERVES 4 TO 6
☆ Begin 2 or 3 days in advance
ACTIVE WORK (DAY 1): 10 minutes
ACTIVE WORK (SERVING DAY): 20 minutes
COOKING TIME (SERVING DAY): 2 1/2 hours

Marinade

1 1/2 cups dry white wine
3 tablespoons olive oil
2 cloves garlic, halved
4 large shallots, halved

1 or 2 fryer rabbits (4 pounds total dressed weight), fresh or frozen; all parts of 1 rabbit or 2 pair hindquarters and saddles cut up for stewing
1/3 cup rendered poultry fat, or substitute 1/2 cup mixed vegetable oil and unsalted butter
5 ounces lean salt pork or mild-flavored slab bacon, blanched in water for 5 minutes, rinsed, and cut into 1-inch cubes
Freshly ground pepper
1/2 teaspoon Herbes de la Garrigue or herbes de Provence
Coarse (kosher) salt
3 yellow onions (about 3/4 pound), thinly sliced
Scant 1/2 cup Dijon mustard
1 1/2 cups dry white wine
2 egg yolks
Pinch of grated nutmeg
1 cup heavy cream
Juice of 1/2 lemon
3 tablespoons snipped fresh chives
Preserved Pears with Ginger (recipe below)

1. Combine ingredients for marinade in noncorrodible bowl; mix well. Add rabbit pieces and turn them over until well coated. Cover with plastic wrap and refrigerate for 2 to 3 days, turning the rabbit pieces once or twice a day. If rabbit is purchased frozen, defrost directly in the marinade.

2. 3 HOURS BEFORE SERVING, remove pieces of rabbit and pat dry with paper towels. Strain marinade, reserving garlic, shallots, and juices.

3. Preheat oven to 300° F.

4. In a large skillet, heat the fat or the oil and butter. Sauté the salt pork or bacon

cubes, transferring them to a 4-quart casserole as they are browned. In the same skillet, brown the rabbit pieces, a few at a time, on both sides, transferring them to the casserole as they are browned. Sprinkle the rabbit and the pork cubes with pepper, herbs, and very little salt.

5. Pour off all but 2 tablespoons fat from the skillet. Add the onions to the skillet along with the reserved garlic and shallots; stirring to avoid burning, sauté over moderately high heat until soft and golden brown, about 6 to 8 minutes.

6. Meanwhile combine 1/3 cup of the mustard with the juices in the bottom of the casserole and stir to blend well.

7. Tilt the skillet, pressing on the onions and garlic to exude excess fat; blot with a paper towel. Using a slotted spoon, transfer onions and garlic to the casserole. Deglaze skillet with strained marinade and bring to a boil, skimming off scum that rises to the surface. Add white wine and return to a boil. Skim again and pour boiling liquid over the rabbit and onions. Cover with buttered parchment or waxed paper and a tight-fitting lid.

8. Set casserole in the oven to cook 2 hours or until the rabbit is meltingly tender. (To avoid stringy rabbit, do not rush cooking time; if rabbit is not tender, let it slowly finish cooking in the oven.) Remove pieces of rabbit to a warm bowl; cover and keep moist.

9. Strain the cooking liquid, pushing down on the onions to extract all their juices. Quickly cool liquid and remove fat that surfaces. Place in a heavy saucepan over medium-high heat and bring to a boil. Shift the pan so that only half of it is over heat. Slowly boil down to 1 cup, skimming often.

10. 5 MINUTES BEFORE SERVING, whisk together the egg yolks, nutmeg, *remaining mustard*, and cream in a small bowl until well blended. Whisk a few tablespoons of the hot reduced cooking juices into the egg-yolk mixture, then whisk the mixture back into the saucepan. Heat gently, whisking until the sauce thickens. *Do not allow sauce to boil.* Add lemon juice and salt and pepper to taste. Stir in the chives. Spoon the sauce over the rabbit and serve hot with the Preserved Pears with Ginger.

NOTE TO THE COOK
You can cook the rabbit in the casserole through step 8 in advance. Leave the rabbit pieces in the sauce. Gently reheat, then remove the pieces of rabbit to a warm bowl and continue to make the sauce as directed above.

Preserved Pears with Ginger
Poires Confites au Gingembre

SERVES 6

ACTIVE WORK: 15 minutes
COOKING TIME: 45 minutes

> **2 tablespoons grated fresh ginger root**
> **1/4 cup sugar**
> **3/4 cup dry white wine**
> **1 cup unsalted Chicken Stock, degreased**
> **3 large Bosc pears (about 1 1/2 pounds)**
> **1 tablespoon unsalted butter**
> **3 tablespoons strained fresh lemon juice**

1. Preheat oven to 375° F.

2. In a noncorrodible saucepan combine ginger, sugar, and wine. Cook, stirring, to dissolve sugar. Slowly cook down to 3 tablespoons. Add the stock and bring to a boil, stirring.

3. Meanwhile, peel, halve, and core the pears. Arrange, cut side down, side by side in a buttered baking dish. Sprinkle with 1 1/2 tablespoons lemon juice. Pour stock mixture over pears.

4. Set on upper middle oven shelf and cook 45 minutes, or until golden brown and glazed. Baste often with the syrupy juices. Sprinkle with remaining lemon juice and serve warm. Can be reheated. Do not refrigerate.

Inspired by a recipe from Lucien Vanel.

CHAPTER 11

CASSOULET

Cassoulet is one of those dishes over which there is endless drama. Like bouillabaisse in Marseilles, paella in Spain, chili in Texas, it is a dish for which there are innumerable recipes and about which discussions quickly turn fierce. As an outsider, I felt I might be able to settle some questions: Which regional version of the dish is really the best, and who serves the best restaurant cassoulet in France?

It did not seem too difficult a task. Waverley Root, the *Larousse Gastronomique*, and the food critics Henri Gault and Christian Millau have all defined the war over the three "genuine" versions of this casserole dish of meats and haricots (dried white beans), one from each of three towns in the Languedoc.

In Castelnaudary, the legend goes, the dish was invented, and therefore a "pure" version is served. The haricots are cooked with chunks of fresh pork, pork knuckle, ham, pork sausage, and fresh pork rind. In Toulouse the cooks add Toulouse sausage and either *confit d'oie* or *confit de canard* (preserved goose or duck—see Chapter 1, under "Confits"), while in Carcassonne chunks of mutton are added to the Castelnaudary formula, and, during the hunting season, an occasional partridge, too. There would be many variations, I knew, but it seemed a simple matter to travel to each of these towns, discover where the best cassoulets were served, taste them, and decide which one I liked the best. What I did not count on was that these regional distinctions are now completely blurred, and that cassoulet, like life itself, is not so simple as it seems.

Take mutton. Not one person in any of the three towns would admit that mutton could go into a local cassoulet. Whether my expert was a chef, a waiter, or just a citizen on the street, he or she would point in some other direction and say: "Oh, they use mutton in Toulouse [or Carcassonne, or Castelnaudary, or some other town that came to mind]. They don't know any better."

Take partridge. Some people said they'd heard of putting partridge in cassoulet, but no one could say he'd actually seen it done. Take bread crumbs. "Never! Impossible!" many people proclaimed, but the woman who cooked the best traditional cassoulet I ate used bread crumbs without a qualm.

And what about breaking the crust—seven times, as some cookbooks proclaim? People laughed, but some agreed the crust could be broken and re-formed twice to get some texture into the sauce. No need to go on. These technical matters diverted me from my mission. When I found the best cassoulet, I'd find out how it was made.

After a few hours' recuperation from jet lag in Paris, I ventured out to Lamazère, a restaurant where cassoulet in the style of Toulouse is a specialty of the house. Though the portion of meat was parsimonious, the cassoulet was very good, the beans enveloped in a thick creamy sauce, the preserved goose superb, put up the traditional way in stoneware jars for a minimum of six months. I returned to my hotel happy at last to have the taste of a good cassoulet in my mouth. Alas, I had not counted on the aftereffects. Requiring heavy doses of Alka-Seltzer to get to sleep, I was reminded of the famous tale of Prosper Montagné—how one day he came upon a sign on the door of a bootmaker's shop in Carcassonne: *Closed on Account of Cassoulet*.

A few days later, on a cold and rainy night in Toulouse, I tried one of that graceful town's better-known cassoulet establishments, called, not surprisingly, Le Cassoulet. Arriving early, I was intercepted by a friendly drunk. "Go someplace else," he warned me; "in ten years they haven't changed the menu here."

My first cassoulet of Toulouse was crusty and wonderful, bubbly and aromatic, very subtle in regard to garlic. The *confit* literally melted in my mouth, and the Toulouse sausage (actually made for the restaurant by a charcutier in Castelnaudary) was extraordinarily fine. The charming and opinionated owner, Monsieur Bonnamy, held forth while I ate. "I'm from Provence, and I tell you that there is more drama here concerning cassoulet than anything I ever saw over bouillabaisse. In Toulouse everyone talks about cassoulet, everyone cooks it, everyone eats it, *but very few make it well*. They use canned *confit*, even canned beans, or sometimes, God help them, they eat the whole dish from a can. Bread crumbs? I never use them! Mutton? It has no place in the dish. Put mutton in a pot with some preserved goose, and the mutton eats the goose alive! You ask me about the cassoulet of Carcassonne? It's just beans with a load of charcuterie! You say Michel Guérard says mutton is indispensable? A comment typical of a person who lives in the Landes—they have so many sheep there they're always trying to think up things to do with them!"

Early the next morning I paid a call on the most famous chef of Toulouse, the kind, brusque, estimable, inventive Lucien Vanel. His restaurant, called simply Vanel, is a magnet for all gastronomic travelers to Toulouse. But Vanel is adamant—he will not cook cassoulet.

"I'm from the Quercy," he says. "This is my adopted town, so I leave cassoulet to the native chefs. There are restaurants here that specialize in it, and I have arranged for a friend to cook you a good homemade version [see Cassoulet in the Style of Toulouse]. But I do have something for you today."

There then appeared a twinkle in his eye as he told me he'd prepared his *cassoulet de morue*, something I thought he'd dreamed up for journalists—his satire on the most famous dish of his adopted town.* His satire must be recounted: in a casserole of white beans he cooks salted cod (his "preserved goose"), a seafood sausage (his "sausage of Toulouse"), and large juicy mussels (his "chunks of pork"). The stock is a saffron-flavored fish soup, bound with mustard, egg yolks, and cream. The dish is a marvelous spoof on a real cassoulet, and, like everything *chez Vanel*, a treat.

I tried more restaurant cassoulets in Toulouse, Castelnaudary, and Carcassonne, then returned to Toulouse for a homemade version arranged for by Vanel. My hostess was Madame Pierrette Lejanou, wife of a potato broker, descendant of an old Toulouse family, gastronome, and an excellent cook who learned to make cassoulet at her grandmother's knee.

What can I say about her version except that it was the best traditional cassoulet I ever ate? Madame Lejanou was so precise in her choice of beans, so careful about her cooking, so firm in her commitment to *andouillettes* (chitterlings), so intent on achieving a crust, so particular about her pork fat being just ever-so-slightly-rancid, and so careful in her selection of meats (she puts up her own *confit*, as a good Toulouse cook always does) that her cassoulet was simply great. A charming woman, effervescent in her approach to food, generous in the tradition of the Languedoc, she feasted me and instructed me until I was overwhelmed. The secret of her cassoulet, I thought, was that it was *made with love*.

It was on account of Michel Guérard that I drove to Robert Garrapit's restaurant in Villeneuve-de-Marsan in the Landes. Guérard had told me of a cassoulet cook-off among the chefs of the Landes. Garrapit had won first prize, and Guérard recommended his cassoulet in the highest terms. I arranged to meet him a few weeks later at Garrapit's restaurant for a feast.

Now, Michel Guérard is a modest man, becoming in so renowned a chef, but on the subject of cassoulet he is as opinionated as anyone else: "Cassoulet," he told me, "was originally a ragout of beans, which was obviously improved by the addition of mutton. To make a cassoulet without mutton is to be banal, and, in my opinion, to commit heresy. Mutton is indispensable in a cassoulet, as indispensable as the bony fish *rascasse* in a bouillabaisse. It is a sophistication of dubious value to add *confit*. Cassoulet becomes too refined when it has a crust. Chefs put a crust on it to make it look better, but in the process they make it heavy and obfuscate its peasant origins.

*I learned later that such a dish actually does exist.

One must keep in mind the history of cassoulet and cook it as the peasants did, with mutton and poor people's food, such things as gizzards and pork skin."

By this time Garrapit has appeared with his chef d'oeuvre. There were carrots in it and I asked him why. "They're pretty," he said, "and they sweeten the mutton, too."

Garrapit's cassoulet was light, his sauce good-tasting and thin. I understood why he had won the cook-off in the Landes, where, on account of Guérard's influence, lightness in cooking is an important goal. And there were interesting things about his dish—his use of preserved gizzards, and huge Tarbes beans that he'd canned fresh so that, most particularly, he would not have to use them dried. It was all very good, but was it a cassoulet? Guérard, of course, insisted that it was nothing less than an authentic version of the dish. I was not so sure. Those very refinements that Guérard deplored (crustiness, a thick creamy sauce) have become, in my opinion, indispensable to a great rendition of the dish. Two years later I discussed all this again with Guérard when we dined together in Auch. He told me that he had changed his mind totally, that he now makes his cassoulet with *confit*, and leaves the mutton out.

All right—I had dined in the best cassoulet establishments in Paris, in the three great cassoulet towns, and also in the Landes. Madame Lejanou's cassoulet was still dear to my heart, but was it the ultimate, or can the great dish of South-West France reach an even higher, more heavenly sphere?

During this visit to the region I'd become friendly with the Gascon chefs, especially their spiritual leader, the handsome, generous, multitalented André Daguin, whose elegant Hôtel de France in Auch is a mecca for gastronomes.

When Daguin learned I was passionate about cassoulet he offered to cook me three different kinds and serve them at a single lunch. Knowing the brilliance of this chef, my tongue quivered with anticipation, even though by this time my stomach had started to rebel.

"Don't worry," said Daguin. "You will taste, not eat." But this proved impossible. Who can merely taste delicious food?

I had come full circle now, from the parsimony of Lamazère in Paris to the plenitude and hospitality of a great Gascon chef. Tasting and cross-tasting, eyed by envious diners at other tables who could not believe the sight of a single woman surrounded by huge casseroles, I ate and ate while Daguin paced by, every so often eyeing me like a sly Gascon fox.

His "normal" cassoulet was robust. The taste of a strong garlic sausage permeated the beans. This was a real country cassoulet but touched by a light hand. Daguin had used broken old beans as a thickening agent, rather than an inordinate amount of pork fat, as is common practice in the Languedoc. There was a lot of *confit* in this casserole (steamed first, interestingly enough). And tomatoes broke up the usual golden champagne color—Daguin's cassoulet was creamy-red.

Next came his cassoulet of lentils—green lentils cooked with duck fat, pork *confit*, and Spanish chorizo sausages. It had a subtlety and mellowness that did not at first announce themselves; it was a quiet, deceptively lazy dish that crept up on me until I could not stop replenishing my plate (see recipe for Pork *Confit* with Lentils and Chorizo Sausages in Chapter 12).

But the best was yet to come: Daguin's famous *Cassoulet de Fèves*, a concoction of preserved duck and fresh fava beans, crisp on the outside, soft and buttery-tender within. The contrast of flavors and textures, the beans so full of spring and the Mediterranean, beans that absorbed the taste of the other ingredients and yet, almost paradoxically, maintained a fresh taste of their own—I could not quite believe what I was eating. It seemed a miracle.

Suddenly all the controversy—Toulouse versus Carcassonne versus Castelnaudary; mutton versus preserved goose; the questions of bread crumbs and partridges and *andouillettes*—became irrelevant. For Daguin's cassoulet of fava beans transcended definitions. As far as I was concerned, the cassoulet war was won.

ANDRÉ DAGUIN'S FAVA BEAN CASSOULET
Cassoulet de Fèves

According to Robert Courtine, the French food authority, before white beans were cultivated in France, fava beans were used to make this dish. In effect, then, Daguin's version *is* the "original" cassoulet.

SERVES 8

ACTIVE WORK: 45 minutes

PARTIALLY ATTENDED COOKING TIME: 3 hours

4 drumstick-thigh portions *Confit* of Duck, split at the joint
8–9 pounds fava beans, in their pods (usually available starting in March)
1 3/4–2 pounds small white onions, peeled
1 1/2 pounds lean fresh pork side or belly, cut into 1 1/2-inch dice, or substitute slab bacon, blanched 10 minutes in plenty of water, rinsed, drained, dried, and diced
Freshly ground pepper
1 tablespoon sugar
6 ounces fresh pork skin with 1/4-inch layer of hard fat attached, or substitute skin from pork side, fatback, or pork belly
1 quart unsalted Chicken Stock, thoroughly degreased
1 leek, trimmed, well washed, and left whole
2 small ribs celery, chopped
6 small ribs celery, tied in a bundle
5 firm cloves garlic, peeled

1. ABOUT 4 HOURS BEFORE COOKING, set out crock of *confit* in warm room or deep pan of warm water to soften fat.

2. Shuck beans and discard pods. You should have about 2 quarts. Slip off and discard the heavy skin of 1 cup of favas; set skinned beans apart. Cut off the tiny shoots on remaining beans, if old. (Because all the favas are not skinned, the cassoulet will turn dark in color; this is as it should be.)

3. Scrape fat off duck *confit* and reserve meat and fat. Sauté onions in 1 cup of the reserved *confit* fat in a large (5- or 6-quart) flameproof casserole 4 or 5 minutes, stirring. Add diced pork or bacon and a light sprinkling of pepper; sauté over moderate heat, stirring often, 5 minutes longer.

4. Stir in cup of peeled fava beans and sugar. (The natural starchiness of the favas will act as a liaison for the cooking juices.) Cover pan tightly and cook beans slowly 10 minutes.

5. Meanwhile, simmer pork skin separately in water to cover until supple, 10 to 20 minutes. Drain it, roll it up, and tie it with string.

6. To the casserole of meat and beans add stock, remaining favas, rolled pork skin, leek, all of the celery, and garlic. Bring to a boil and skim carefully. Reduce heat, cover with a sheet of parchment or foil pricked in 2 or 3 places with the tines of a fork, and simmer 1 1/2 hours.

7. Place pieces of duck *confit* in a colander set snugly over a kettle of boiling water (or use a steamer or couscous cooker). Cover and steam 10 minutes. Remove duck, allow to cool slightly, then remove skin and bones. Set aside, covered with foil to keep meat moist.

8. Preheat oven to 300° F.

9. Remove rolled pork skin from ragout and cut into slices. Unroll slices and line a 3- or 3 1/2-quart earthenware baking and serving dish with skin, fat side down. (The skin side sticks.) Place pieces of duck on top.

10. Discard leek and bundle of celery from ragout. With a slotted spoon, transfer favas to baking dish, leaving cooking juices in pan. Skim off fat. Pour enough of the cooking juices over the duck and favas to cover. Reserve remaining juices. Loosely cover dish with foil and set in preheated oven.

11. After 20 minutes' baking, spoon off all the fat that rises to the top; there will be about 1 cup. Then add enough reserved cooking juices to keep favas moist. After 1 hour's baking, remove foil and allow a crust to form on the top, about 30 minutes. Serve hot.

NOTE TO THE COOK
This is excellent reheated later in the day, or even the next day. The *confit* is salty and will salt the dish sufficiently.

CASSOULET IN THE STYLE OF TOULOUSE
Cassoulet de Toulouse

A great dish is the master achievement of many generations.
— CURNONSKY

This is the recipe given to me by Pierrette Lejanou.

SERVES 10 TO 12
☆ Begin 2 days in advance
ACTIVE WORK (DAY 1): 10 minutes
ACTIVE WORK (DAY 2): 30 minutes
COOKING TIME (DAY 2): 2 hours
ACTIVE WORK (DAY 3): 30 minutes
COOKING TIME (DAY 3): 1 1/2 hours

1 1/2 pounds boneless pork shoulder
2 pounds fresh ham hock or pigs' knuckles
1 pound fresh pork skin with 1/4-inch layer of hard fat attached, cut in 2-inch-wide strips (see Note 1)
Salt and freshly ground pepper
2 pounds dry white beans, or Great Northern, marrow, or pea beans
1/2 pound lean salt pork or unsmoked slab bacon, or substitute Italian *pancetta* (original recipe calls for slightly salted breast of pork called *cansalade*)
5 tablespoons fat from *confit* (see ingredients below)
2 medium onions, peeled and cubed
3 small carrots, scraped and cut into rounds
1 small whole head garlic, unpeeled
6 ounces *jambon de Bayonne,* prosciutto, or Westphalian ham, in one piece
1 small whole red-ripe tomato, peeled (see Note 2)
2 quarts unsalted Chicken Stock, thoroughly degreased
Herb bouquet: 4 sprigs parsley, 2 sprigs thyme, 1 bay leaf, and 3 small ribs celery, tied together
1 pound *andouillettes,* if available, or other spicy cooking sausage (optional)
6 drumstick-thigh portions *Confit* of Duck, split at the joint
1/4 pound fresh hard pork fat or fat salt pork

4 small cloves garlic, peeled
1 pound homemade Toulouse Sausages, fresh garlic-flavored pork
    sausages, *cotechino*, or *Confit* of Toulouse Sausages
2 tablespoons fresh bread crumbs
2–3 tablespoons imported walnut oil (optional)

1. 2 DAYS IN ADVANCE, season pork shoulder, fresh ham hock or pigs' knuckles, and pork skin moderately with salt and pepper. Place in an earthenware or glazed dish, cover, and refrigerate overnight.

2. THE FOLLOWING DAY, sort beans and rinse them under cool running water. Soak them in water to cover for 1 1/2 hours (longer if you suspect they are over 6 months old).

3. Meanwhile, cut pork shoulder into 1 1/2-inch cubes. Reserve. Simmer pork skin in water to cover until supple, 10 to 20 minutes. Drain, roll up strips, and tie them with string. Blanch lean salt pork or bacon 3 minutes in simmering water.

4. In a 5-quart flameproof casserole, heat duck fat and lightly brown cubed pork shoulder. Add onions and carrots and sauté over moderate heat, stirring, until onions are soft and golden, about 5 minutes. Add ham hock (in 1 piece) or pigs' knuckles and blanched and drained lean salt pork or bacon. Raise heat and allow meats to brown a little around the edges, turning pieces occasionally. Add head of garlic, ham, and tomato; cook, stirring, 1 minute. Add stock and bring to a boil; reduce heat, add herb bouquet, and simmer, covered, 30 minutes.

5. When beans have soaked 1 1/2 hours, drain and put in a 4- or 5-quart heavy pan; cover beans with tepid water and slowly bring to a boil. Simmer 10 minutes, then drain and immediately add to simmering ragout. Continue simmering. (See Note 3.)

6. Separately cook *andouillettes* in water to cover 30 minutes. Add to ragout, along with 1 cup of the sausage cooking liquid, and cook 30 minutes longer. (Total cooking time is about 2 hours.) Cool. Lift off some of the fat that has risen to the top and reserve it. Cover ragout and beans and refrigerate.

7. THE NEXT DAY, ABOUT 4 HOURS BEFORE COOKING, set out crock of *confit* in warm room or deep pan of warm water to soften fat.

8. Remove ragout and beans from refrigerator. Blanch fat salt pork 3 minutes, rinse, and drain well (if you're using it instead of fresh pork fat). Grind fat or salt pork to a purée with peeled garlic cloves in a food processor or electric blender. Reheat ragout, add pork purée, and simmer together 30 minutes. Allow to cool slightly. Discard herb bouquet and whole head of garlic.

9. Preheat oven to 275° F.

10. To assemble the cassoulet, remove the roll of pork skin from the ragout. Untie, cut skin into small pieces, and line a large (6-quart or larger), deep ovenproof serving dish with them, fat side down. (The skin side sticks.) Cover with one third of the beans.

11. Remove ham hock or pigs' knuckles and cut meat into bite-size pieces, discarding bones and fatty parts. Scatter these pieces and the pork shoulder cubes on top of

beans. Cut *andouillettes* into 1-inch pieces and place them between pork chunks. Heat *Confit* of Duck separately over low heat and pull out all the bones.

12. Place duck meat on top of pork and sausages. Add another layer of one third of the beans. Cut lean salt pork or bacon and piece of ham into bite-size pieces and scatter on top of the beans. Cover with remaining beans. Taste cooking liquid and adjust seasoning. (There will probably be no need for salt.) Pour just enough cooking liquid over beans to cover them. Be sure there is at least 3/4 inch of "growing space" between the beans and the rim of the dish.

13. Stiffen homemade Toulouse Sausages, garlic sausages, or *cotechino* in boiling water for 2 minutes before broiling. (Make sure sausages are totally dry before browning them.) Prick sausages, brush with fat, and brown them on one side under a hot broiler or in a skillet. Drain, cut larger sausages into 3- or 4-inch pieces, and place, crisp side down, on top of beans. Sprinkle beans very lightly with bread crumbs and drizzle on 2 tablespoons of the reserved fat from Step 6.

14. Set dish in oven and bake cassoulet 1 1/2 hours. The top crust will become a beautiful golden brown. Serve directly from the dish. Sprinkle with walnut oil, if desired (see Note 4).

NOTES TO THE COOK
1. Fresh pork rind is essential to enrich and flavor the beans. If fresh pork skin is not available, use rind from fatback. Blanch 5 minutes, drain, and allow to cool before cutting and adding in Step 1. If only salted rind is available, do not include in the first day's marinade.
2. The acid of tomato in the ragout keeps the beans from cooking too quickly, so that they can absorb more flavors.
3. The blanching of the beans makes them easier to digest. See under "Beans" in Appendix.
4. The addition of walnut oil at the last moment "brightens" the taste of the beans.

CHAPTER 12

MEAT

PORK DISHES

Où il y a un beau cochon, il y a une bonne ménagère.
(Where there is a beautiful fat pig, there is a good home cook.)
—SOUTH-WEST SAYING

"You shouldn't write your book until you see the ritual killing of a pig," said Alain Dutournier. "You must understand how important the pig is to us. It is the basis of our cuisine. When we kill a pig it means we will have food on our table for months: bacon, ham, salt pork, *confits*, sausages. . . . Please go back to the countryside and see how we do the slaughter."

I did not go to see the killing of a pig. I could not bring myself to after so many years of witnessing the ritual slaughter of lambs in Morocco. But the process has been described to me in great detail, and Dutournier is absolutely right about its importance. There is a mystical feeling about these beasts on the farms of the South-West, similar to the way bread is regarded in some other parts of France. The pig itself is held in high esteem. Zette Guinaudeau-Franc remarks that the word *porc* is rarely used: "We always refer to him [the pig] as *le cochon*, or, with respect, *le monsieur*, in patois, *lou moussur*."

The cult of the pig is exemplified in numerous proverbs: "Where there is a beautiful pig, you will find a good soup." "Seven hours of sleep for a man, eight for a woman, and nine for a pig!" "Four legs—four seasons!" signifying that a single pig can provide a family's food for an entire year.

"Nothing is lost with me," says the pig in a fable I have read. In fact, this is true; all the parts are used, from the snout to the tail, including the skin, the feet, the ears, and the blood. There are so many different preparations for the various parts of the pig that in the South-West the art of charcuterie is vast. It includes not only sausages, hams, pâtés, rillettes, *andouilles*, and *boudins* (both black and white), but also a unique regional dish: "the glory of the South-West," the *confit*.

CONFIT OF PORK
Confit de Porc

I believe *Confit* of Pork is one of the best ways to treat the lean pork we have developed so plentifully in the United States. Shoulder makes the best *confit*, but other pieces can be used as well. Some people use pork loin, but I find it too dry.

Cold *confit* of shoulder or butt goes splendidly in a salad of Cold *Confit* of Pork with Green Beans and Cabbage or in a casserole of Pork *Confit* with Lentils and Chorizo Sausage. Snout, ear, and ham hock *confits* are generally used to flavor soups and garbures, while *confit* of pork rind is used in dishes of dried beans.

Even when you serve *Confit* of Pork cold, you should first brown it in its own fat. When it is reheated this way, a flavor slightly reminiscent of hazelnuts is developed on the exterior of the meat while the inside remains moist and aromatic—better than the best roast pork. In summer, the Basques serve lightly browned pork *confit* with pickled cabbage or slice it thin to serve with vinegared grapes or Sweet and Sour Cherries.

MAKES ENOUGH TO FILL 3 (1-QUART)
OR 2 (1 1/2-QUART) CONTAINERS
☆ Begin 2 days in advance
ACTIVE WORK: 30 minutes
MOSTLY UNATTENDED COOKING TIME: 3 1/2 hours

> 3 1/2 pounds pork butt or boned pork shoulder or blade end (see Note 1)
> 2–4 tablespoons coarse (kosher) salt
>   Large pinch of dried thyme, crumbled, or 1 sprig fresh, leaves only
> 1 teaspoon whole peppercorns, lightly crushed
> 4–6 cups good-quality rendered fat (see Note 2)
> 1/2 small head garlic
> 1 clove

1. 2 DAYS IN ADVANCE, cut meat into 7 portions, each weighing about 1/2 pound. Trim away any ragged bits.

2. If planning to use *confit* within 1 week, use lesser amount of salt. Roll pork pieces in salt combined with thyme and pepper. Place in a deep noncorrodible bowl; refrigerate, covered with plastic wrap, 36 hours.

3. When ready to cook *confit*, remove marinated pork pieces from bowl; wipe off salt and exuded juices and pat dry with paper towels. Tie each piece with string to preserve compact shape during cooking.

4. Place rendered fat with 2 tablespoons water in a Crock-Pot (slow cooker) or large, very heavy pot such as an enameled cast-iron casserole; exact amount of fat will vary depending on size and shape of cooking vessel. Melt fat over low heat; as soon as it has melted, slip in pieces of pork. Fat should cover meat fairly well; add peanut oil, if necessary. However, if meat is almost completely covered, enough additional fat will render out in cooking to submerge it. Add the half head of garlic stuck with the clove.

5. At high or medium Crock-Pot setting or over medium-low heat, heat fat to a gentle simmer. Maintain simmer for 3 hours, adjusting setting as necessary; during this period, Crock-Pot should be partially covered, stovetop vessel uncovered (see Note 3). Temperature of fat should never exceed 200° to 205° F.

6. Remove vessel from heat. For best results, let pork cool in fat 1 hour; pork can be removed at once, but there will be some loss of texture. Remove pork pieces and garlic with slotted spoon; set meat aside to cool slightly. Meat will become firmer-textured as it cools.

7. If Crock-Pot was used, ladle fat into large, heavy saucepan, leaving meat juices behind. Heat, uncovered, over medium-high heat to boiling, constantly skimming off foam that rises to surface. Slowly boil 5 to 10 minutes, or until spluttering stops and surface of fat is nearly undisturbed. Watch carefully and adjust heat if necessary to avoid burning or smoking; fat that is allowed to reach smoking point will be ruined for *confit*. Remove from heat; let cool a few minutes.

8. When pieces of pork *confit* are still warm but have firmed up slightly, remove strings (see Note 4). Have ready a container or containers chosen according to how long you plan to keep the *confit*; proceed according to recipe for *Confit* of Duck, Steps 10, 11, and 12. Pork *confit* is best after at least a 2-week ripening; it can be kept up to 4 months, refrigerated.

9. To use, set container of *confit* out in warm room or place in deep pan of warm water until fat is softened. Take out as many pieces as you need; set aside. Make sure remaining pieces are well covered with fat; add peanut oil if necessary. Return remaining *confit* to refrigerator; plan on using it within 1 week. To cook the removed *confit*, scrape fat clinging to pieces into heavy medium-size skillet; add another tablespoon if amount of fat looks insufficient for browning. Heat fat over medium heat to rippling; sauté *confit* pieces until lightly browned on all sides, 5 to 8 minutes. Remove to wire rack or brown paper bag to drain; serve hot, at room temperature, or cold.

(continued)

NOTES TO THE COOK

1. If using shoulder or blade end, request weight of 4 1/2 to 5 pounds before boning and have meat boned in one piece.

2. Rendered fat suitable for this recipe can be any desired combination of butcher's lard from a reliable source, duck or goose fat, or home-rendered lard. (Though it is possible to use all lard, flavor will be somewhat inferior; for authentic flavor, include a good proportion of rendered duck or goose fat.) For preparation of home-rendered poultry fat or lard, see under "Duck Fat and Cracklings," and "Rendering Pork Fat" (immediately following); good store-bought equivalents are available by mail from Dean & DeLuca (see Appendix).

3. Alternatively, place pork pieces, rendered fat, and garlic stuck with clove in deep baking dish; place in cold oven. Turn oven on to 275° F. Leave pork in oven 3 hours, or until meat can be easily pierced with a wooden skewer; check at intervals after about 1 hour to be sure temperature of fat never exceeds 200° to 205° F. Remove from oven and proceed with Step 6.

4. Although pork will not at this point be as rich-flavored as aged *confit*, it can be used at once, if desired, following directions in Step 9 for browning.

Rendered Pork Fat
La Graisse

The term *la graisse* refers to the fat of ducks, geese, and pigs. Pork fat or lard is used in cooking and for storing *confits*, rillettes, pâtés, and stuffed goose necks. It takes longer to render pork fat than the fat of a goose or duck, but the same basic principles are employed. One difference: sometimes a cheesecloth bag of cinnamon sticks, whole cloves, garlic, and pieces of nutmeg is added for flavor.

MAKES 4 TO 6 CUPS RENDERED FAT

ACTIVE WORK: 10 minutes
MOSTLY UNATTENDED COOKING TIME: 3 hours

1. Preheat oven to 225° F.

2. Grind 2 1/2 to 3 pounds cubed unsalted pork fat (leaf lard, the firm white fat that surrounds the kidneys, is best) in the workbowl of a food processor fitted with the metal blade. You can do this in batches.

3. Place fat in a deep, heavy ovenproof saucepan. Add 1/3 cup water. Place saucepan in oven and allow fat to render slowly, about 3 hours, or simmer slowly on top of the stove.

4. Strain carefully and keep refrigerated until needed.

PRESERVED PIG'S OR CALF'S TONGUE
Confit de Langue de Porc ou de Veau

This is a variation on a family recipe from the town of Blaye near Bordeaux. It is done with pig's tongue, but a very small calf's tongue works beautifully. The texture and taste of tongue cooked this way are sensational. Do not be put off by the fat—you only cook with it, you don't eat it.

Serve warm, thinly sliced, with Sweet and Sour Prunes as a first course.

SERVES 4 TO 5 AS A FIRST COURSE
☆ Begin 1 day in advance
   ACTIVE WORK: 10 minutes
   UNATTENDED COOKING TIME: 1 1/2 to 2 hours

    2 pigs' or calves' tongues, each weighing about 10 ounces
    1 tablespoon coarse (kosher) salt
  1/2 teaspoon crumbled thyme
    3 cups mixed fat: preferably goose or duck, but rendered homemade lard can be substituted (have enough to cover tongues)
  1/2 head garlic

1. 1 DAY IN ADVANCE, wash and dry tongues. Slit each tongue down the center, opening it slightly. Roll in salt and thyme. Set in a noncorrodible bowl, loosely covered with plastic, in refrigerator 24 hours.

2. THE FOLLOWING DAY, preheat oven to 300° F.

3. Rinse tongues under running water to remove salt marinade. Place fat in a deep ovenproof bowl or earthenware dish. Place in oven. When melted, add tongues and garlic. Cover and cook 1 1/2 to 2 hours, or until very tender. A thin skewer should enter very easily. Remove from the oven and allow tongues to cool in the fat.

4. When cool, peel off the skin, return to the fat, and store in the refrigerator completely covered with fat until ready to use. Use within 1 week,

5. To serve, bring fat to room temperature. Scrape off fat, and steam tongues to warm and remove remaining fat by heat. Serve at room temperature, or hot or cold, thinly sliced. (For longer storage, follow directions for storing in recipe for *Confit* of Duck, Steps 10, 11, and 12.)

Inspired by a recipe from Jean-Pierre Xiradakis.

PORK COOKED IN MILK
Porc Frais au Lait

There is a Venetian dish called *arrosto di maiale al latte* (pork loin braised in milk), described by Elizabeth David, which is somewhat similar to this one. I'm not sure where the recipe originated, but it appears prominently in Maïté Escurignan's marvelous work on Basque cookery.

Though red meats become more succulent and tender when cooked slowly in liquid, white meats, such as pork or veal, sometimes end up stringy and without much taste. Here is a recipe that solves that problem—a pork loin is submerged in flavored milk and slowly cooked at a very low temperature. The small quantity of butterfat in the milk "swims" through the meat, and the milk keeps the loin totally moist. The pork is *not* browned first, as this would seal the meat off from the milk and inhibit the mingling of flavors. Long, slow simmering in a fatty substance will actually make the meat more juicy than it would be if it were sealed, and, at the same time, the meat will be virtually fat-free when removed from the cooking medium. Only after the cooking do you brown the pork while you are degreasing and finishing the sauce.

Start the meal with Leeks Broiled or Baked in Their Own Juices Under a Bed of Ashes and a creamy garlic vinaigrette. Serve the pork surrounded with glacéed vegetables—onions, carrots, and turnips—and finish with fresh fruit and a goat cheese. Serve a white Graves. Pork and the goat cheese marry especially well with this wine. Leftover pork served cold is delicious.

SERVES 6
☆ Begin 1 to 2 days in advance
ACTIVE WORK: 30 minutes
PARTIALLY ATTENDED COOKING TIME: 3 1/2 hours

> **3–3 1/2 pounds boneless center pork loin or 1 center rib loin (5 1/2 pounds), trimmed of excess fat (see Note for how to bone)**
> **2 cloves garlic, cut into slivers**
> **Coarse (kosher) salt**
> **1/4 cup finely chopped carrots**
> **1/4 cup finely chopped onions**
> **2 tablespoons finely sliced leek (white part only)**
> **2 tablespoons unsalted butter**
> **1 quart whole milk (not low-fat or skim)**
> **1/4 teaspoon ground white pepper**
> **Herb bouquet: 3 sprigs parsley, 1 sprig thyme, and 1 bay leaf, tied together**
> **1 tablespoon chopped fresh parsley**

1. 1 TO 2 DAYS IN ADVANCE, stud pork loin with slivers of garlic. Rub the surface with salt; cover loosely and keep refrigerated.

2. 4 HOURS BEFORE SERVING, preheat oven to 300° F. Remove meat from refrigerator.

3. In a deep 3- or 4-quart pot or flameproof casserole, slowly cook vegetables in butter until soft but not brown. Place pork loin on top of vegetables and set over low heat.

4. In a saucepan, heat milk to almost boiling and pour around pork. Add pepper and herb bouquet. Cover and place on lowest oven shelf to cook 3 hours. Turn meat in cooking liquid at intervals.

5. Remove casserole and raise oven temperature to 375° F. Transfer meat to an open baking dish, fat side up, and return to oven to brown, about 20 minutes.

6. Meanwhile, strain cooking juices into a narrow, deep container, pushing down on the milk solids that have separated out in the cooking. Quickly chill (put in freezer or into a bowl of ice) so fat rises to surface. Remove and discard fat.

7. Return cooking liquid to casserole and bring to a boil with a metal spoon on the bottom to keep liquid from boiling over. Reduce by two thirds, about 15 minutes. Adjust seasoning to taste.

8. Slice meat and arrange overlapping slices on a serving platter; spoon sauce over and sprinkle with chopped parsley.

NOTE TO THE COOK

A 5 1/2-pound center rib roast after boning yields about 3 1/2 pounds. Work with well-chilled meat. Use a boning knife to cut between meat and ribs. Loosen ribs at the base. Slip knife along the chine and cut away meat from each "bump." Remove all bones. Tie up loin at 1-inch intervals. Stud, season, and refrigerate 1 to 2 days.

GARLIC-STUDDED PORK ROAST IN THE STYLE OF THE PÉRIGORD
Enchaud

Here a loin of pork is simmered slowly in a casserole with pig's feet, vegetables, and spices. The result is actually two dishes: primarily the pork, studded with garlic and fresh herbs, served either hot or cold; and secondarily the pig's feet, which can be served up separately any number of different ways.

When the pork loin has cooled in its delicious cooking juices, it is served along with the resulting jelly, nicely chopped, and some slices of French cornichons or tiny pickles. In his book on the Périgord, La Mazille speaks of placing slices of the pork on bread rounds, spreading them with the jellied sauce and a little cooking fat, decorating each open sandwich with a slice of cornichon, and serving them along with wine and grapes to hungry grape-pickers working in the fields. In a super-luxurious version, the pork loin is studded with black truffles instead of garlic. The dish then becomes suitable for a festive occasion such as a Christmas Eve buffet.

Serve with a bitter green salad dressed with walnut oil and red wine vinegar or *verjus*.

As for the pig's feet, you may serve them for lunch the day the pork is to be eaten or save them for use on another day. A regional preparation is to bone them, then roll them in mustard and bread crumbs, and serve them burning hot straight from the broiler or oven with a squeeze of lemon juice. If you're at all squeamish about serving pig's feet, you can use their wonderful, succulent meat (after boning and grinding) in stuffings. An equal amount of pig's foot and pork sausage meat doused with a little Armagnac makes a superb stuffing for chicken, cabbage, eggplant, tomatoes, or whatever. Or try thinly sliced boned pig's feet tossed with a mustard or spicy vinaigrette as part of a cold first course of small salads.

PORK LOIN SERVES 6; PIG'S FEET
SERVES 2 TO 4
☆ Begin 1 day in advance
ACTIVE WORK: 30 minutes
UNATTENDED COOKING TIME: 3 1/2 hours

3–3 1/2 pounds boneless center pork loin, or 1 center rib loin (5 1/2 pounds) (to
    bone meat, see Note in recipe for Pork Cooked in Milk)
1 tablespoon finely chopped garlic
1 tablespoon roughly chopped fresh parsley
  Salt and freshly ground pepper
  Bones from the pork, cracked into small pieces
1 onion, sliced
1 carrot, sliced
2 medium pig's feet, singed and halved (see Note 1)
4 cups unsalted Chicken Stock or water
  Pinch of Quatre Épices (Spice Mixture for Pâtés and Stews)
  Herb bouquet: 3 sprigs parsley, 1 sprig thyme, and 1 bay leaf, tied
    together
  Cornichons (optional)

For serving pig's feet (optional)

  Dijon mustard
  Soft white bread crumbs
2 eggs
2 tablespoons melted butter or oil
  Lemon wedges

1. 1 DAY IN ADVANCE, trim excess fat from pork. Combine garlic and parsley; add 1/2 teaspoon salt and 1/4 teaspoon pepper. Press into a paste. With a sharp knife, make

deep slits in the pork and push some garlic-parsley paste into each slit. Tie up the pork at 1-inch intervals. Rub any remaining mixture over meat. Place in a dish, cover loosely with plastic wrap, and set in refrigerator to rest overnight.

2. THE FOLLOWING DAY, preheat oven to 375° F.

3. Wipe pork to remove excess moisture, then place on a baking sheet. Surround with cracked bones and sliced vegetables. Place on upper-middle oven shelf for 20 minutes and allow meat, bones, and vegetables to turn a golden brown, basting once or twice.

4. Meanwhile, blanch pig's feet in water 5 minutes; drain and tie in pairs.

5. Place bones in a 5-quart flameproof casserole as a bed for the pork loin and vegetables. Place these on top of bones. Add pig's feet and 4 cups stock or water. Slowly bring to a boil on top of stove and skim carefully. Add Quatre Épices and herb bouquet. Lower oven temperature to 300° F. Tightly cover casserole and cook 3 hours.

6. If you want to serve pork hot, remove it, untie strings, and allow it to rest while degreasing and straining cooking liquid. Pour cooking liquid into a saucepan. Bring to a boil and set saucepan half over heat. Cook at a slow boil, skimming, 10 to 15 minutes, or until reduced to a slightly thickened consistency. If you wish to serve pork cold, place it in a deep bowl or an earthenware terrine (the sort used for pâtés is ideal). Strain cooking liquid through a fine sieve over pork loin while meat is still warm; allow to cool completely. Refrigerate so liquid can jell. (The surface fat can be saved for sautéing potatoes.) To serve pork loin, cut into slices. Chop cooking juices, which should be jellylike. Arrange cold pork slices overlapping on serving platter, and garnish with chopped jelly and cornichons.

7. To serve pig's feet, allow them to cool a little, then remove bones. (Do not wait until the feet are cold; it is very difficult to remove the bones unless the feet are warm.) Smear with Dijon mustard, dust with soft white bread crumbs, dip in foamy beaten eggs, and roll in bread crumbs again. Chill in the refrigerator to set. Drizzle a little melted butter or oil over the prepared pig's feet and set in a preheated 425° F. oven to crisp and brown, about 15 minutes. If desired, you can run them under the broiler to further crisp them. Serve burning hot with lemon wedges.

NOTES TO THE COOK

1. If pig's feet have any hairs, they need to be burned (singed) off. Roll pig's feet over a flame, then wash and blanch 5 minutes.

2. To prepare the pig's feet for stuffing, allow them to cool slightly, then remove the bones. Grind roughly in the workbowl of a food processor. Cool completely. Mix with freshly ground pork sausage meat and seasoning. Wrap tightly and save for sausages or stuffings.

PORK *CONFIT* WITH LENTILS AND CHORIZO SAUSAGE
Confit de Porc aux Lentilles et Saucisses

The *Confit* of Pork is as crucial to the taste of this lentil dish as duck or goose *confit* is to a classic cassoulet. It is best to put up the *confit* some weeks in advance and let it ripen to full flavor and heady aroma, but once I tested this dish with pork *confit* made the same day and found it meltingly tender, aromatic, and delicious, though I compensated by halving the salt content of the marinade.

Serve with a mixed green salad, followed by an assortment of cheeses: Cabecou, Chaumes, and Bleu d'Auvergne. A Red Wine Sorbet with Madeleines from Dax will provide a light and delicious finish to the dinner.

SERVES 6

ACTIVE WORK: 30 minutes
COOKING TIME: 1 1/2 hours
REHEATING TIME: 1 1/2 hours

> 1 1/4 pounds (about 2 1/3 cups) green or brown lentils, picked over
> 1 recipe *Confit* of Pork
> 1/3 cup fat from the *Confit* of Pork
> 1 1/2 cups chopped yellow onions
> 1/4 pound unsmoked bacon with rind removed (or blanch mild-flavored smoked bacon 10 minutes in plenty of water; rinse well), cut into 1 × 1/4-inch pieces
> 1/2 pound (about 12) baby white onions, peeled
> 1 1/2 tablespoons tomato paste
> 1/2 cup thinly sliced celery
> 1/2 cup thinly sliced carrots
> 1/2 pound chorizo sausage
> 6 cloves garlic, peeled and halved, 1 stuck with 1 clove
> 1/2 pound fresh pork rind, rolled and tied with a string (see Note 1)
> Salt and freshly ground pepper

1. Wash lentils and leave to soak 1 hour in water to cover.

2. In a 5-quart flameproof casserole (see Note 2), heat fat from *confit*. Sauté onions and bacon pieces 5 minutes, stirring. Add white onions and tomato paste. Cook, stirring, 5 minutes, or until onions take on a yellow tinge.

3. Drain lentils and add to casserole. Moisten with 6 cups water and slowly bring to a boil. Skim off the scum that rises to the surface. Add celery, carrots, whole chorizo sausage, garlic, and rolled pork rind. Bring back to a boil; skim again. Partially cover and simmer gently 1 1/2 hours. Uncover and cool. Do not salt at this time. (The *confit* to be added later is usually sufficiently salty to salt the dish.) *Can be prepared ahead up to this point.* Refrigerate, covered, until 2 1/2 hours before serving.

4. ABOUT 4 HOURS BEFORE BEGINNING MAIN PREPARATION, set out crock of *confit* in warm room or deep pan of warm water to soften fat.

5. 2 1/2 HOURS BEFORE SERVING, remove casserole from refrigerator so it can stand 1/2 hour to come to room temperature. Preheat the oven to 375° F.

6. Remove chorizo and pork rind, and cut into thin slices. Slice pork *confit*. In a 4-quart bean pot, baking dish, or heatproof serving dish, arrange a bottom layer of sliced pork rind, fat side down. (The skin side sticks.) Cover with slices of pork *confit* and chorizo. Spread lentils, onions, and cooking liquid on top; loosely cover with a sheet of foil and set in oven to bake 1 hour.

7. Remove foil, correct seasoning with salt and pepper, and return to oven to bake 30 minutes longer, or until surface is crusted and brown.

NOTES TO THE COOK
1. If pork rind is brittle, simmer in water 10 to 20 minutes, or until supple.
2. For the lentils: do not use an aluminum pot or they will lose their color.

Inspired by a recipe from André Daguin.

Black Sausage
Boudin Noir

When a pig is killed, it is an essential part of the ritual to catch the blood from its severed throat in a bowl to which some vinegar has been added to prevent coagulation. From this blood the South-Westerners make a delicious black sausage (*boudin noir*) perfumed with onions and often flavored with red pepper, cloves, nutmeg, and cinnamon. Cooked, then partially dried, these sausages are wonderful sliced and fried in a little fat, drained, then folded into an omelet—or cut into chunks and fried in butter along with very thin slices of tart green apple. A wonderful accompaniment to drinks would be small brioche pouches filled with this mixture of black sausage and apple. In Bergerac is found a dish called *croquignolles*: deep-fat-fried pastry rounds stuffed with plumped raisins and *boudin noir*.

I have developed a way of cooking *boudins noirs* without having them explode apart after being pierced. I slowly heat them in a skillet half-filled with water, then, when the water is very hot, slip the skillet into a medium-hot oven for 10 to 15 minutes, turning the sausages once. Served with homemade applesauce and good French fries, black sausages make a great home meal.

NOTE TO THE COOK
You can find black sausages in French, German, and Spanish butcher shops.

RED BEANS WITH PORK AND CARROTS
Glandoulat

Red beans have a rich and smooth taste, especially if they are cooked very slowly. This is an old country dish from the Rouergue. The word *glandoulat* refers to the area around the neck and throat where the pork is half fatty and half meaty.

Serve this hearty dish with a simple salad and a country dessert such as the Batter Cake with Fresh Pears from the Corrèze.

SERVES 4 TO 5
☆ Begin 1 day in advance
ACTIVE WORK (DAY 1): 5 minutes
ACTIVE WORK (DAY 2): 45 minutes
UNATTENDED SIMMERING TIME: 4 1/2 hours

    2 **cups small red beans or red kidney beans**
    1 **cup full-bodied red wine, such as Côtes-du-Rhône**
1/4 **pound pork fatback**
    1 **small pig's foot, split (optional)**
    1 **large onion, split and stuck with 2 cloves**
    1 **cinnamon stick**
    1 **large carrot, chopped**
    1 **onion, finely chopped**
    2 **tablespoons goose, duck or pork fat**
    1 **pound boneless pork butt or shoulder, cut into 4 or 5 pieces**
    4 **cloves garlic**
    4 **sprigs parsley**
    1 **imported bay leaf**
1/4 **teaspoon thyme leaves**
1/2 **pound carrots, scraped**
    2 **tablespoons butter**
      Pinch of sugar
      Salt and freshly ground pepper
1 1/2 **tablespoons *eau de vie* or Armagnac**
      Walnut or olive oil
      Red wine vinegar
    1 **teaspoon roughly chopped fresh parsley**
1/2 **teaspoon chopped garlic (chopped by hand)**

1. 1 DAY IN ADVANCE, place beans in colander and rinse under cold water until water runs clear. Drain beans and place in bowl. Add water to cover and let stand overnight.

2. EARLY THE FOLLOWING DAY, rinse and drain beans. Place beans in a 5-quart

flameproof earthenware or enameled cast-iron casserole with wine and enough water to come 1 inch above the level of the beans; slowly bring to a boil.

3. Meanwhile, blanch fatback and pig's foot (if using) 5 minutes; drain and rinse.

4. When beans come to a boil, skim carefully, then add pig's foot, onion stuck with 2 cloves, and cinnamon stick. Lower heat and simmer while preparing vegetables and pork.

5. In a skillet, brown chopped carrots and onions in 2 tablespoons fat. Add pieces of pork butt or shoulder, and brown on all sides. Transfer to beans.

6. In the workbowl of a food processor fitted with the metal blade, grind fatback with garlic, parsley, bay leaf, and thyme to a purée. Add to casserole.

7. Cook beans over very low heat or in a preheated 275° F. oven 2 1/2 hours. Check that pig's foot (if using) is buried in cooking juices. After 2 1/2 hours, uncover beans and cook until liquid is thick, about 1 1/2 hours.

8. Meanwhile, cut the 1/2 pound carrots into 1/2-inch-thick rounds. Place in a heavy-bottomed saucepan with 1 tablespoon of the butter; cover and cook slowly 5 minutes, then uncover and add remaining 1 tablespoon butter and swirl over medium-high heat 1 to 2 minutes, or until carrots take on a little color. Add pinch of sugar and salt and pepper to taste, and swirl for a second, then add carrots to beans in casserole.

9. When pig's foot is tender, remove and allow to cool slightly. Allow bean mixture to cool, then skim off surface fat. When pig's foot is cool enough to handle, remove all the bones and discard. Dice meat and fold back into bean mixture. Set aside. *Can be prepared ahead up to this point.*

10. 1 HOUR BEFORE SERVING, preheat oven to 350° F.

11. Return uncovered casserole to oven and allow top to glaze slightly, then gently stir so that meat and beans on the surface will not dry out. Cook until a light crust forms on the surface, about 30 minutes.

12. 5 MINUTES BEFORE SERVING, stir in *eau de vie* or Armagnac. Adjust seasoning with salt and pepper. Serve hot with a light sprinkling of walnut or olive oil, vinegar, chopped parsley, and chopped garlic.

NOTE TO THE COOK

To avoid drying and breaking the beans, be sure that they are always covered with the cooking liquid or enrobed in the sauce. If necessary, add *boiling* water. Cooking beans in wine keeps them from turning mushy. They need longer cooking but are able to absorb more flavor.

Adapted from Fernand Molinier's Promenade Culinaire en Occitanie.

TOULOUSE SAUSAGES
Saucisses de Toulouse

These pork and garlic sausages, named for the ancient city of Toulouse, are sold all over France but are rarely made properly; imitators use ordinary pork fat rather than hard fatback, add water, and sometimes even use food coloring. No matter—these sausages are simple to make.

Toulouse Sausages are wonderful in cassoulets and garbures. They're also delicious in Toulouse Sausages with Savoy Cabbage or with a Sarlat Potato Cake. Thick country-style sausages will do in a pinch, but Toulouse Sausages are coarser in texture and are flavored with nutmeg or mace. You can substitute Italian and Polish sausages, but the results will not be the same at all.

MAKES ABOUT 1 1/4 POUNDS
☆ Begin 1 to 2 days in advance
   ACTIVE WORK: 30 minutes
   COOKING TIME: 12 minutes

    4 **ounces very lean salt pork without rind, washed to remove surface salt, dried carefully, and cubed by hand**
  12 **ounces pork tenderloin, trimmed of all fat**
    4 **ounces pork fatback at room temperature (if substituting salt fatback, simmer in water 5 minutes, drain, and cool to room temperature)**
    1 **teaspoon fine salt**
 1/2 **teaspoon freshly ground pepper**
 3/4 **teaspoon freshly cracked black peppercorns**
 1/4 **teaspoon grated nutmeg or mace**
 3/4 **teaspoon sugar**
    1 **large clove garlic, finely minced**
     Hog or sheep casing*
    2 **tablespoons rendered lard or goose fat**

***Available in Eastern European, Italian, and German meat markets.**

1. 1 TO 2 DAYS IN ADVANCE, cut pork meat and fatback into dice. Fatback should be warm enough to absorb seasonings. Toss with seasonings and push everything through large blade of a meat grinder. If you do not have a meat grinder, finely cube meat and fatback separately, toss with seasonings, and chop separately in batches in the workbowl of a food processor with an on-off motion. Cover and refrigerate overnight.

2. THE FOLLOWING DAY, unravel a few feet of casing. Soak in lukewarm water for 30 minutes. Slip one end of casing over faucet nozzle and run water through. Check that there are no holes in the casing. If you find a hole, sever at that point and tie a knot. Tie knots at one end of each length after washing and draining.

3. Using a sausage stuffer, follow manufacturer's directions and push the mixture through. Press out all the air, but do not fill the skin tightly. (Skin will burst if too tight.) Twist filled skins at intervals to shape sausages. Secure with string, if desired. If using a small, inexpensive, hand-held funnel sausage stuffer (available by mail from H. Roth & Son; see Appendix), slip all of one length of casing onto stubby end. Using both thumbs, push mixture down funnel and fill casings. Press out the air. Tie at intervals and at other end close to the meat. Or you may shape the sausage into one long coil and leave it to rest on a rack on a flat plate. Brush with fat. If possible, leave sausages overnight to allow flavors to mellow.

4. To cook sausages, prick 3 or 4 times with a needle before dropping into enough simmering water to cover to stiffen and poach for 2 minutes. Drain thoroughly. Brush with melted fat or butter and broil 10 minutes, turning often to brown evenly. To fry sausages, heat rendered pork or goose fat in a skillet. Add "stiffened," drained, and greased sausages, and cook slowly until done, about 12 minutes. If you have made a coil, fasten with 2 crisscrossing skewers to hold securely. As soon as the sausages have cooked, drain on brown wrapping paper or paper towels. Serve as soon as possible.

CONFIT OF TOULOUSE SAUSAGES
Saucisses de Toulouse Confites

Preserved Toulouse Sausages have a unique flavor that goes well with red-wine-cooked beans (in *Confit* of Toulouse Sausages and *Confit* of Duck Cooked with Red-Wine-Flavored Beans) or with braised cabbage (in Toulouse Sausages with Savoy Cabbage), or sliced and added to a garbure or cassoulet. They may be sliced, sautéed, and served with scrambled eggs, or simply eaten along with a sharp mustard. Country-style sausages can be preserved the same way.

SERVES 4 TO 6
ACTIVE WORK: 10 minutes
UNATTENDED COOKING TIME: 1 hour

3 cups Rendered Pork Fat
1 pound uncooked Toulouse Sausages or other fresh pork sausages

1. Bring fat to a simmer over medium heat in a wide saucepan; lower heat and slip in the uncooked sausages to cook very slowly for 1 hour.

2. Pack sausages into clean dry jar(s) with cooking fat to cover. Be sure they are well covered in fat. Cool completely before closing. Store in refrigerator until ready to use. Keep at least 1 week before using. Keeps 1 to 2 months in refrigerator.

3. To remove, gently warm opened jar in a pan of warm water and pull out sausages.

TOULOUSE SAUSAGES WITH SAVOY CABBAGE
Saucisses de Toulouse aux Choux

This buttery, delicious dish is for a cold winter day—perfect for a relaxed, informal meal. It can be prepared ahead and reheated. Serve with steamed potatoes, a robust red wine, and a strong Dijon mustard.

SERVES 4 TO 6
ACTIVE WORK: 20 minutes
COOKING TIME: 45 minutes

> **6 ounces lean salt pork with rind removed**
> **1 savoy cabbage (2 pounds)**
> **1 teaspoon coarse (kosher) salt**
> **1/2 cup diced carrots**
> **1/2 cup diced onions**
> **1/2 cup diced leeks**
> **1/4 cup diced celery**
> **1/2 cup (4 ounces) unsalted butter**
> **2 cloves garlic, finely chopped**
> **1 cup unsalted Chicken Stock, totally degreased**
> **Freshly ground pepper**
> **Pinch of freshly grated nutmeg**
> **1 recipe Toulouse Sausages or 1 recipe *Confit* of Toulouse Sausages**
> **Dijon mustard**

1. Place salt pork in a saucepan of water to cover and bring to a boil. Simmer 5 minutes. Remove with a slotted spoon; refresh in cold water and cut into 1/4-inch dice. Set aside.

2. In a large pot, bring plenty of water to a boil. Meanwhile, remove outer leaves from cabbage. Quarter, core, and remove thick ribs. Separate leaves and shred coarsely. Swish in a basin of water to wash. Drain and squeeze dry. Drop cabbage into boiling salted water, partially cover, and quickly bring back to a boil. Cook, uncovered, for 15 minutes.

3. Drain cabbage and quickly refresh under cold running water and drain well. Squeeze to remove excess water.

4. In a wide heavy-bottomed 3-quart skillet, covered, soften carrots, onions, leeks, and celery in 2 tablespoons of the butter for 5 minutes. Uncover, add diced salt pork, and cook over medium-high heat until vegetables turn golden, about 5 minutes.

5. Unravel cabbage and add to skillet along with garlic. Cook, stirring, 5 minutes to blend. Then add stock and bring to a boil. Cook, stirring with a wooden spoon, over low heat until all the moisture has evaporated. Do not allow vegetables to burn.

6. Raise heat and stir in half the remaining butter. When the vegetables have absorbed the butter, add remaining butter and allow it to be absorbed, stirring

constantly. Adjust seasoning. *Can be prepared ahead up to this point.*

7. 20 MINUTES BEFORE SERVING, reheat cabbage gently. Meanwhile, broil or fry the fresh sausages. If using the *confit*, wipe away most of the fat and slowly brown in a skillet. Drain on brown wrapping paper or paper towels. Nestle the sausages in the cabbage, partially cover the skillet, and cook gently 5 to 10 minutes to blend flavors.

CONFIT OF TOULOUSE SAUSAGES AND *CONFIT* OF DUCK COOKED WITH RED-WINE-FLAVORED BEANS
Confits dans les Haricots au Madiran

Madiran is a "big" red wine, deep in flavor and very dark in color. It is like a full-bodied American Petite Sirah. Although you may have heard that beans should not be cooked in wine or, for that matter, in any other acid, this unusual recipe given to me by André Daguin exploits that prohibition to great advantage. The beans cook very slowly and absorb the flavor of the wine, which loses its acidity on account of the slow cooking, becoming mellow by the time the dish is fully cooked.

SERVES 6

ACTIVE WORK: 35 minutes
MOSTLY UNATTENDED COOKING TIME: about 4 1/2 hours

   6 pieces *Confit* of Duck with 1/3 cup fat
1/2 recipe *Confit* of Toulouse Sausages
   1 pound dried white beans such as Great Northern, pea, or marrow
   1 cup chopped onions
5–6 cloves garlic, peeled
   2 teaspoons tomato paste
   4 cups full-bodied red wine, such as Madiran or Petite Sirah
     Herb bouquet: 3 sprigs parsley, 1 sprig thyme, and 1 bay leaf, tied together
   1 quart unsalted Chicken Stock, completely degreased
   7 ounces unsmoked pork rind (can be cut from salt pork or fatback)
     Salt and freshly ground pepper
 12 baby white onions (about 1/2 pound)
   1 tablespoon sugar

1. ABOUT 4 HOURS BEFORE BEGINNING MAIN PREPARATION, set out crocks of *confit* in warm room or deep pan of water to soften fat.

2. Pick over beans and rinse them under cool running water. Soak them in water to cover for 1 1/2 hours.

3. After 1 1/4 hours, in a 5-quart flameproof noncorrodible casserole, heat 1 1/2 tablespoons of the duck fat from the *confit*. When very hot, add chopped onions and whole garlic cloves. Stir in tomato paste. When onions and garlic are a uniform pink

color, add red wine and herb bouquet. Bring to a boil, lower the heat, and simmer 15 minutes.

4. Put drained beans in a heavy pan, cover with tepid water, and slowly bring to a boil. Boil 5 minutes. Separately bring stock to a boil. Drain beans and immediately add to simmering red wine; immediately pour boiling stock over. Skim simmering liquid 3 to 4 minutes.

5. Preheat oven to 275° F.

6. Meanwhile, soften pork rind, if necessary, by simmering in water 10 minutes. Drain, roll up, and tie with a string. Add to beans.

7. Cover beans tightly and place in oven. Bake 3 1/2 hours, or until beans are tender and wine has lost its acid taste. Season with salt and pepper.

8. In a small skillet, cook the baby white onions in 1/2 cup water until almost tender, 6 minutes. Add sugar and 1 teaspoon duck *confit* fat. Continue cooking over medium-high heat, stirring often, until all the water has evaporated and onions begin to brown on all sides, 2 to 3 minutes. Remove from heat.

9. Raise oven temperature to 350° F.

10. To assemble the dish, remove pork rind and cut into small pieces and line a deep, ovenproof 3 1/2-quart serving dish with them, fat side down. Cover with half the beans. Cut duck *confit* into bite-size pieces; discard bones and skin. Cut Toulouse Sausages into 1-inch pieces. Scatter *Confit* of Duck and sausage pieces on top of beans. Place baby onions on top. Add another layer of beans. Scatter any leftover pieces of pork rind on top. Pour cooking liquid over. Return dish to oven to bake 30 minutes to 1 hour, basting 3 or 4 times with remaining duck fat from the *confit* (4 tablespoons), or until the top crust becomes a beautiful mahogany brown. Serve directly from the dish.

NOTE TO THE COOK
This dish can be prepared in advance and gently reheated.

BARBECUED SPARERIBS, LANGUEDOC STYLE
Coustelou au Feu de Bois

Whether you prepare these ribs over charcoal or in the broiler of your oven, you will find them a unique eating experience and a welcome change from the sweet, glazed effects of standard Chinese rib barbecue. The pork, marinated in herbs, will show its flavor undisguised, and the potatoes, also flavored with herbs and sizzling ham fat, will taste delightfully different.

The old recipes for this dish call for a special implement, the *flambadou*, a perforated wrought-iron cup fastened to a long rod. (In Albi this instrument is called a *capucin*, the word for monk, a reference to the shape of the cup, which is similar to a monk's tonsure.) The *flambadou* is a basting instrument used in charcoal cookery. The cup is made red-hot in the coals; then a piece of country ham fat is placed inside. The fat instantly melts and drips through the perforations; sizzling hot fat dropping onto the meat sears it and gives it a wonderful charred ham flavor. (Chicken is also grilled this way in the South-West.) You can achieve the same effect by rendering some fat from an American southern ham, such as Smithfield ham. If you're cooking out-doors, use a heavy-bottomed small saucepan and a heat-resistant mitt. The recipe is also very good without the ham fat.

Serve the ribs and potatoes with Sweet and Sour Onion and Raisin Relish (recipe follows).

SERVES 3 OR 4
☆ Begin 1 to 2 days in advance
ACTIVE WORK (DAY 1): 5 minutes
ACTIVE WORK (DAY 2): 20 minutes
COOKING TIME: 45 minutes to 1 hour

> 3 pounds pork loin rib ends for barbecue, or 2 sides of meaty
> country-style spareribs (about 4 pounds), divided into serving
> pieces (do not substitute ordinary spareribs)

Marinade

> 1 1/2 teaspoons coarse (kosher) salt
> 1 teaspoon fresh thyme leaves or 1/2 teaspoon dried leaves, crumbled
> 1 bay leaf
> 1/2 teaspoon fennel seed, lightly crushed
> 1/2 teaspoon crushed rosemary
> 6 fresh mint leaves, slivered
> 1 sage leaf
> 4 cloves garlic, finely sliced
> 2 tablespoons olive oil

Herb-Flavored Oil

> 3 sprigs thyme
> 1/2 bay leaf
> 1 teaspoon fennel seed
> 2 sprigs fresh mint
> 2 sage leaves
> 1/2 cup olive oil

> 4–6 medium potatoes
> Freshly ground pepper
> Vegetable oil for grill
> Chopped fresh herbs for garnish: thyme, mint, and parsley
> 2–3 tablespoons fresh lemon juice
> 1/2 cup cubed ham fat (optional)

(continued)

1. 1 TO 2 DAYS IN ADVANCE, marinate pork ribs in marinade. Place in a noncorrodible container; cover loosely with plastic wrap and refrigerate.

2. Make herb-flavored oil and set aside to mellow in flavor.

3. 2 HOURS BEFORE GRILLING, remove ribs from refrigerator; wipe off excess marinade.

4. Peel potatoes and cut into 1-inch-thick slices. Brush potatoes with a little of the herb-flavored oil.

5. If you are using a charcoal grill, the grill should be about 9 inches above the embers, which should be ash-white. Brush grill with plain vegetable oil, then arrange ribs flat on the grill. Every 10 minutes, turn and baste meat with herb-flavored oil. Add potatoes after the first 10 minutes. Baste potatoes as well. Meat should be cooked well done, 45 minutes to 1 hour. Serve hot with a sprinkling of pepper, herbs, and lemon juice. If you plan to flavor meat with rendered hot ham fat, simmer ham fat in 3 tablespoons water over very low heat 15 minutes. When all the moisture has evaporated and there are only cubes of fat and rendered fat in the pan, spread them on spareribs and potatoes the last 5 minutes of grilling. Ribs can also be roasted on a rack in a preheated 375° F. oven about 1 hour 15 minutes, turning them every 15 minutes and basting them frequently.

Sweet and Sour Onion and Raisin Relish
Oignons aux Raisins Secs

This is a version of *oignons à la monégasque*; it is an excellent relish to serve with rich meats. The natural flavor of the pearl onion is retained, but there's a wonderful marriage of flavors, and the final sprinkling of olive oil just before serving enhances the sweetness of the onions.

MAKES ABOUT 2 CUPS
☆ Begin 2 to 3 days in advance
   ACTIVE WORK: 25 minutes
   UNATTENDED COOKING TIME: 1 hour

> 1 sweet red bell pepper
> Zest of 2 oranges
> 1 pound baby white onions, about 1/2 inch in diameter
> 2 tablespoons sugar—or more to taste
> 1/4 cup red wine vinegar—or more to taste
> 2 1/2 tablespoons olive oil
> 2 large tomatoes, peeled, seeded, and chopped (about 1 cup chopped)
> 1/3 cup golden raisins
> 1/4 cup currants
> 1 tablespoon tomato paste

1/4 teaspoon cayenne pepper
Salt
3/4 cup dry white wine

1. Heat broiler. Roast red pepper, turning frequently, until skin is charred and blistered on all sides, about 10 minutes. Place in paper bag until cool enough to handle, about 20 minutes. Peel off and discard skin. Remove stem, seeds, and thick veins. Cut into 1/8-inch-wide strips.

2. Remove zest from oranges with swivel-bladed vegetable parer. (Reserve fruit for another purpose.) Cut zest into 1/16-inch-wide julienne strips. Blanch in boiling water 2 minutes. Drain; refresh and drain on paper towels.

3. Cut an X in root end of each small onion. Blanch 2 minutes; drain. Refresh under cold water until cool enough to handle. Peel; trim root and stem ends with small sharp knife. Dry thoroughly on paper towels.

4. Melt sugar in small noncorrodible saucepan over very low heat. When sugar is light brown, about 5 minutes, remove from heat; carefully stir in vinegar. Return to heat; stir until caramel is dissolved; set aside.

5. Preheat oven to 375° F. Heat 1 1/2 tablespoons of the oil in a 2-quart flameproof noncorrodible casserole. When oil ripples, add onions; sauté over medium heat, shaking pan frequently, until onions are lightly glazed, about 3 minutes. Add red pepper, orange zest, tomatoes, raisins, currants, tomato paste, cayenne, salt to taste, and vinegar mixture. Add wine and enough water to cover ingredients; slowly bring to a boil. Cover pan.

6. Bake on lowest shelf of oven until onions are very tender, about 1 hour. There should be just enough liquid to coat vegetables. If there is more, strain liquid into small saucepan and reduce enough to coat spoon lightly. Adjust seasoning; add more vinegar or sugar to taste. Cool uncovered, cover, and refrigerate. Onions can be stored, covered, in refrigerator up to 5 days.

7. Remove from refrigerator 2 to 3 hours before serving. Serve at room temperature. Sprinkle with remaining 1 tablespoon olive oil just before serving.

BEEF DISHES

STEAK BORDELAISE WITH MARROW AND SHALLOT GARNISH
Entrecôte à la Bordelaise

This is, of course, the great specialty of Bordeaux. Alcide Bontou in his excellent book on Bordelaise cooking, *Traité de Cuisine Bourgeoise Bordelaise*, explains that the true original version is simply a grilled rib steak garnished with a mixture of "four shallots, a nice piece of firm bone marrow, and a small amount of parsley all chopped together. This mixture is spread over the side of the steak that has been grilled first; then a large wide-bladed knife is heated to melt the marrow. When the second side has been grilled, care must be taken that the topping doesn't fall off." Bontou goes on to explain that at one time, when "gourmets" descended to the wine cellars to try the famous steaks, they discovered that the wine-masters burned old wood from chestnut barrels that was said to impart an excellent flavor to the meat. Now the "gourmets" of Bordeaux will tell you to add dried grapevine cuttings to the cooking fire, too.

When I lunched at Château LaBrède, about twenty kilometers outside of Bordeaux, the steak was prepared in the following way: the caterer cooked the meat in an open fireplace over a fire of dried vine cuttings, then served it with a cooked marrow and shallot garnish that was juicy enough to be called a sauce. The vine cuttings imparted a delicious flavor and aroma to the meat.

SERVES 4
ACTIVE WORK: 10 minutes
COOKING TIME: 20 minutes

2 (2-inch-thick) boneless rib eye beef steaks (about 2 pounds in all), well trimmed
Salt and freshly ground pepper to taste
2 tablespoons grape-seed, French peanut oil, or unflavored vegetable oil
36 small to medium shallots (about 6 ounces)
1 tablespoon red wine vinegar
1/4 cup dry white wine
1 turn of the pepper mill
1/4 bay leaf
1/4 cup well-reduced meat or poultry stock or Demi-Glace

Marrow from 4 (1-inch) veal or beef marrowbones, pried out, soaked in salted ice water overnight or until whitened, then drained just before using

1 tablespoon finely chopped fresh parsley mixed with some chives, if available

1. Lightly season meat with salt and pepper; rub with oil. Cover loosely with plastic wrap and refrigerate until ready to cook. Remove from refrigerator 1 hour before cooking. Dry meat. Brush with fresh oil.

2. Blanch shallots in boiling water 1 minute. Drain and refresh under cold running water (this makes them easier to peel and milder in flavor). Peel and coarsely chop shallots. You should have about 1 cup.

3. In a small saucepan, simmer wine vinegar, wine, salt, pepper, bay leaf, and stock or Demi-Glace, 5 minutes. Remove from the heat. Remove bay leaf. Fold in chopped shallots and set aside until just before serving. *Can be prepared ahead up to this point.*

4. Broil or grill steak to desired degree of doneness. Broil 2-inch-thick steaks 3 inches from the heat, 8 minutes on the first side and 6 minutes on the second side for rare. To grill over embers, use grapevine cuttings for best flavor (see under "Grape Wood" in Appendix for mail order source). Grill about 5 inches from heat. After meat is turned, spread 1 or 2 tablespoons of drained shallot mixture on top of the steak, then cover steak and shallots with a *cold* plate or pot lid. Continue grilling steaks on the second side. (The flavor of the shallots will penetrate the meat, giving it added flavor.) Remove steak to rack and let stand 5 minutes to rest before slicing.

5. Meanwhile, cube marrow and poach it separately in lightly salted water, without boiling, until it turns pink-gray; then add to the reserved shallots. Toss marrow over low heat with shallots and liquid in the saucepan until well blended and hot. Adjust seasoning, add herbs, and serve as a garnish with the steak.

NOTE TO THE COOK

A little trick I learned from André Guillot: lightly salt the meat the minute you bring it home. If you do this, you won't need to salt later, and in the end you'll use half as much salt as you would normally. Lightly salted meat will tenderize and mature in flavor when stored overnight in the refrigerator. Though some blood will run out, it is insignificant. Guillot also suggests that meat be coated lightly with grapeseed oil to keep it from drying out; he prefers grapeseed because it smokes at a much higher temperature than other oils. (I often mix grapeseed oil with a little poultry fat to combat the very *slight* aftertaste it often leaves on meat; some grapeseed oils contain herbs or other flavorings, but there is a type without flavoring under the Bénédictine label available in many grocery stores.)

WHITE BORDEAUX WINE SAUCE FOR STEAKS AND ROASTED VEAL KIDNEYS
Sauce Bordelaise au Vin Blanc

J.-E. Progneaux in his *Recettes et Spécialités Gastronomiques Bordelaises et Girondines* gives seven versions of the famous wine and shallot combination known worldwide as *sauce bordelaise*. A true *sauce bordelaise* must be made of Bordeaux wine, but interestingly enough, not all of the versions offered by Progneaux employ red wine. Since red wine recipes have been published so widely, I offer here my adaptation of a recipe by Curnonsky using a dry white Graves. Serve hot with steak or kidneys.

MAKES ABOUT 3/4 CUP (SERVES 4)

TOTAL PREPARATION TIME: 45 minutes

> 1 1/2 cups white Bordeaux wine
> 3 fresh white mushrooms
> 1/4 cup dried cèpes, well washed
> 2 tablespoons thinly sliced shallots
> 1/2 teaspoon freshly ground pepper
> Herb bouquet: 3 sprigs parsley, 1 sprig thyme, and 1/2 bay leaf, tied together
> 2 cups unsalted meat stock
> 1 to 2 teaspoons arrowroot
> 1 tablespoon mixed chopped fresh herbs: parsley, tarragon, chives, chervil

1. In a noncorrodible saucepan, combine wine, mushrooms, cèpes, shallots, pepper, and herb bouquet. Simmer slowly until reduced to a glaze, about 30 minutes.

2. Add 1 cup of the stock and reduce slowly to a glaze, about 15 minutes, skimming often.

3. Add remaining stock and simmer slowly 10 minutes, skimming often. Strain through several layers of damp cheesecloth lining a strainer. Squeeze cheesecloth to extract all the good flavor. Return to clean saucepan and set saucepan half over the heat. Cook at a slow boil, skimming, 5 minutes, or until reduced to 3/4 cup.

4. Combine 1 1/2 tablespoons water and arrowroot, mixing until smooth. Bring sauce base to a boil; whisk in arrowroot mixture. Cook over medium-low heat until thickened. Fold in chopped fresh herbs. Serve hot with grilled or broiled steak, or Veal Kidneys Garnished with Shallot *Confit*.

STEAK WITH SHALLOTS IN RED WINE SAUCE
IN THE STYLE OF ALBI
Entrecôte à l'Albigeoise

The "steak Bordelaise" served in restaurants around the world is not the marrow-and-shallot-sauce version given in the recipe for Steak Bordelaise with Marrow and Shallot Garnish but a steak with a red wine, shallot, and marrow sauce. This Albigeoise variation also combines red wine and shallots. The recipe was given to me by the top gastronomic personality of Albi, Jacques Rieux, whose father, Louis, wrote the definitive book on Albigeoise cooking.

SERVES 4

ACTIVE WORK: 20 minutes
PARTIALLY UNATTENDED SIMMERING TIME: 1 hour

 2 (2-inch-thick) boneless rib eye beef steaks (about 2 pounds in all), well trimmed
   Salt and freshly ground pepper
 3 tablespoons grape-seed, French peanut, or unflavored vegetable oil
24 small to medium shallots (about 4 ounces), peeled
 1 large head garlic, halved crosswise and unpeeled
 2 cups full-bodied red wine such as Burgundy or an Algerian Dahra (see Note 1)
 1 tablespoon sugar
   Herb bouquet: 3 sprigs parsley, 1 sprig thyme, and 1/2 bay leaf, tied together
1 1/2 tablespoons sherry wine vinegar or red wine vinegar
 1 cup rich unsalted meat stock, degreased
 2 tablespoons unsalted butter
 1 tablespoon mixed chopped fresh herbs: parsley and chives

1. Season steaks with salt and pepper; rub with 2 tablespoons of the oil. Cover loosely with plastic wrap and refrigerate until ready to cook. Remove from refrigerator 1 hour before cooking. Dry steaks with paper towels.

2. In a noncorrodible 2-quart saucepan, combine shallots, garlic, red wine, 1 1/2 teaspoons of the sugar, 1/4 teaspoon pepper, and herb bouquet. Simmer, uncovered, 1 hour, or until wine (excluding the shallots, herb bouquet, and garlic) is reduced by three quarters. Remove from the heat; discard herb bouquet and garlic. Scrape liquid and shallots into a small bowl and hold until ready to finish the dish. *Can be prepared ahead up to this point.*

3. Sear steaks in a very hot, well-greased or oiled, heavy noncorrodible skillet 2 minutes per side. Using tongs, transfer steaks to a cake rack and let them rest while finishing sauce. Blot out any fat in the skillet.

(continued)

4. Add vinegar to skillet, bring to a boil over high heat, and cook until reduced to a glaze, 2 to 3 minutes. Add 1/2 cup of the stock and boil down to a syrupy glaze. Scrape in the shallot–red wine reduction. Add 1 1/2 teaspoons sugar and cook, stirring, 1 minute, or until sauce begins to glisten. Add remaining stock and bring to a boil. Pour sauce into a small saucepan; boil down to 3/4 cup and reserve. Wipe out skillet with paper towel; rub inside with remaining 1 tablespoon oil and set aside. *Can be prepared ahead up to 15 minutes before serving* (see Note 2 below).

5. Heat greased skillet and return steaks to skillet to finish cooking to desired degree of doneness, turning once, over medium-high heat (about 3 minutes per side for medium-rare). Transfer steaks to slicing board.

6. Reheat reserved sauce. Swirl butter into the sauce, 1 tablespoon at a time. Season with salt and pepper to taste. (Makes almost 1 cup sauce.) Set sauce aside while slicing steak and arranging slices on heated platter. Spoon shallots and sauce over steak. Sprinkle with chopped fresh herbs and serve at once.

NOTES TO THE COOK

1. You want a heavy red wine with a strong alcoholic content so that it will reduce to a rich consistency. I find that Burgundies and Algerian wines do this better than Bordeaux wines. When they reduce to a glaze, the color is very deep as well.

2. Steaks can be completely cooked just before serving and the sauce finished while steaks rest before slicing. Brown the meat over medium-high heat 8 minutes; turn and finish on the second side, 6 minutes, or until desired degree of doneness. Remove steaks to rack to rest 5 minutes. Wipe out excess fat; complete the sauce, but do not transfer it to a small saucepan as directed in Step 4.

FILLET OF BEEF WITH ROQUEFORT SAUCE AND MIXED NUTS
Filet de Boeuf au Roquefort

This combination is a specialty of the town of St.-Juéry in the Tarn. The brilliant sauce is the creation of Gascon chef André Daguin.

The benefits of salting meat and rubbing it with oil far in advance of cooking are explained in the Note to the Cook in the recipe for Steak Bordelaise with Marrow and Shallot Garnish. The method of cooking and racking the fillet is my way of handling roasts and thick steaks. I happened on this method while preparing twenty pounds of beef fillet for a benefit in La Jolla, California. I wanted to be able to present all the fillets at once, perfectly cooked, *hot*, and at just the moment when my sauce was right. At eleven in the morning I started searing them, in pairs, in a mixture of near-smoking grapeseed oil and duck fat (grapeseed oil takes a high temperature without burning and breaking down; duck fat gives wonderful flavor to beef).

So far I was following a normal professional kitchen procedure. The difference came when the fillets had been seared and I was looking for a place for them to rest before their final cooking in the oven two hours hence. Most cooks I know place the seared meat on an upside-down plate set atop a larger dish; any juices that run out collect in the lower dish and are used later in the sauce. The fallacy of this procedure is that the side of the meat that rests on the plate tends to soften and the beef crust tends to crack, thus releasing quite a bit of juice. I found that when I placed fillets on wire racks, so that air could flow underneath them as well as above, their crusty exteriors remained intact, and out of my twenty pounds of seared fillets less than half a teaspoon of meat juice was released!

Later, of course, I finished their cooking in the oven, and then, too, no juice was lost. In fact, all the juice remained suspended in the fibers of the beef, keeping it moist, tender, and delicious until the fillets were finally carved.

When ordering a fillet, ask the butcher to give you a center piece so that the thickness will be even from one end to the other. Have him remove all the fat and sinews. Do not have him bard the meat, but do ask him to tie it at one-inch intervals.

· SERVES 4 TO 5

ACTIVE WORK AND COOKING TIME: 1 hour

     1 center piece beef tenderloin (2 pounds; trimmed weight 1 3/4 pounds)
     Salt and freshly ground pepper
     Grape-seed oil, French groundnut oil, or good peanut oil
     1 teaspoon rendered poultry fat or clarified butter (for the latter, see Appendix)
     1 tablespoon minced shallots
     3 tablespoons dry Madeira wine or ruby port wine
  1/2 cup Demi-Glace, or 1 1/2 cups unsalted, degreased meat stock reduced to 1/2 cup
     2 ounces creamy Roquefort cheese
  4–5 tablespoons unsalted butter
     3 tablespoons Crème Fraîche or heavy cream, whipped until stiff
     2 tablespoons lightly toasted pine nuts
     2 tablespoons lightly toasted walnut pieces
     2 tablespoons lightly toasted sliced blanched almonds
     1 tablespoon chopped fresh parsley

1. Lightly sprinkle meat with salt and pepper. With your finger, rub a little oil on the beef. Keep meat refrigerated, loosely covered with plastic wrap, until 1 hour before cooking. Pat beef dry with paper towels.

(continued)

2. In a large heavy-bottomed skillet, preferably of enameled cast iron, heat 2 teaspoons oil and the fat until very hot. Sear the meat on all sides, about 4 minutes total. Transfer meat to a wire rack or grid; let rest a minimum of 20 minutes.

3. Throw out cooking fat. Add chopped shallots and Madeira or port to the skillet; reduce to a glaze. Add the Demi-Glace or reduced stock and bring to a boil. Reduce to a syrupy consistency. Scrape into a smaller skillet, if desired. Set aside.

4. In the workbowl of a food processor fitted with the metal blade, combine the Roquefort and 4 tablespoons of the butter; process to a smooth, creamy paste. Taste the mixture; if too salty, add another 1/2 to 1 tablespoon butter. Separate the mixture into 4 or 5 chunks and keep refrigerated.

5. ABOUT 30 MINUTES BEFORE SERVING, preheat oven to 450° F.

6. Finish beef fillets in the oven: 17 minutes for "blue"; 18 for rare; 19 for medium-rare.

7. Meanwhile, gently reheat the syrupy sauce in the skillet; swirl in the cheese-butter pieces one by one. For added enrichment, fold the Crème Fraîche or whipped cream (see Note) into the sauce, off the heat.

8. Spoon sauce onto heated serving platter. Slice meat and arrange, overlapping. Surround with nuts mixed with parsley. Serve at once.

NOTE TO THE COOK

Adding 3 tablespoons of homemade Crème Fraîche or whipped cream to a sauce in order to thicken it sounds rich, but compared to butter enrichment, it isn't. Three tablespoons of heavy cream or homemade Crème Fraîche is equal in butterfat to about 1 tablespoon butter. It is the consistency of the cream that thickens the sauce. To beat up that small amount of whipping cream may sound ludicrous, but with the new hand-held battery whisks that fit into a small cup, it is a simple chore of 30 seconds.

OXTAIL DAUBE
Daube de Queue de Boeuf

Consider a perfectly cooked prime-grade porterhouse steak. We know it is the marbling in the meat, the streaks of fat, that make it so succulent and delicious. We know it isn't healthy to eat much meat fat, but for flavor's sake we do. Here is a dish which uses fat to enhance its flavor but which is served virtually fat-free because it is double-degreased. In fact, when you read the recipe, you will see that I have actually added fat for extra flavor, but that is eliminated, too, before the dish is served. The result is a very soft, fleshy oxtail daube of incredible lightness and flavor.

The secret is long, slow cooking in a closed pot. During this time the meat is *never* moved, and the juices are *never* allowed to boil. (If they did boil, the fats would bind with the wine and the sauce would be muddy.) Through long, slow cooking the meat renders out all of its fat; the meat and sauce retain the flavor of fat, which is water-soluble, but not the fat itself.

This dish, like many stews and daubes, benefits from being made one day in advance. In fact, some of the *salmis* (stews of wild birds and domestic barnyard fowl) and daubes of tough cuts of meat of the South-West are slowly reheated and cooled each day for a period of four or five days so that, with each reheating, the flavors grow stronger and deeper. For our cuts of meat this is not possible—one would end up with a mushy, tasteless stew.

Serve with noodles and a bitter green salad.

SERVES 5 TO 6
☆ Begin 1 day in advance
ACTIVE WORK (DAY 1): 1 hour
MOSTLY UNATTENDED COOKING TIME (DAY 1): 4 1/2 hours
ACTIVE WORK (DAY 2): 20 minutes
MOSTLY UNATTENDED COOKING TIME (DAY 2): 1 1/2 hours

41/2–51/2 pounds oxtail, cut into pieces
     1 calf's foot, split
     1 slab (3/4 pound) lean salt pork
     1 tablespoon vegetable or French peanut oil
      Salt and freshly ground pepper
     5 medium onions, coarsely chopped
     1 bottle full-bodied red wine such as Petite Sirah (see "Wines for Cooking" in the Appendix for less expensive choices)
      Herb bouquet: 3 sprigs parsley, 1 sprig thyme, and 1 bay leaf, tied together
     2 cloves garlic, whole and peeled
     2 ounces *jambon de Bayonne*, prosciutto, or Westphalian ham, cut into cubes (1/2 cup cubed)
   3/4 ounce dried cèpes

1. 1 DAY IN ADVANCE, preheat oven to 275° F.
2. Trim off all excess fat from the pieces of oxtail.
3. Blanch calf's foot and salt pork 3 minutes; drain. Slice off and reserve rind from salt pork. Cube pork and divide into 2 batches. In a heavy noncorrodible skillet, heat the oil and slowly cook half the salt pork, stirring often, until the cubes turn golden brown and a great deal of their fat has rendered out, about 10 minutes. Line a flameproof earthenware or enameled cast-iron 5- or 6-quart casserole with pork rind, fat side down. (The skin side will stick.) Transfer browned cubes to casserole, set over low heat. (Use a heat diffuser if using earthenware that may not be flameproof.)
4. Brown oxtail pieces in the skillet in batches. Transfer to the casserole. Sprinkle meats with pepper. Stir over low heat; tilt casserole and spoon off any fat that has accumulated.

(continued)

5. Remove and discard half the fat in the skillet. Cook onions in remaining hot fat until golden brown. With the back of a slotted spoon, press on the onions and spoon away all the fat that is exuded. Add onions to casserole.

6. Deglaze skillet with 1 cup of the wine. Boil down to a glaze. Add the remaining wine and 1 1/2 cups water. Bring just to a boil and skim carefully. Pour over the meats. Add calf's foot, herb bouquet, and garlic. Cover tightly and place in oven to cook very slowly for 3 hours without disturbing.

7. Carefully remove oxtail to a deep bowl; cover and keep moist. Strain cooking liquid into a tall, narrow container so that the fat will quickly rise to the surface. Set container in bowl of ice to speed process. Degrease carefully.

8. Meanwhile, remove the meat from the calf's foot while still warm and place in the workbowl of a food processor fitted with the metal blade. Add the batch of salt pork cubes that has *not* been cooked, cooked pork rind, and ham. Grind to a purée.

9. In a saucepan, bring strained and degreased cooking liquid to a boil, lower heat, and cook, skimming from time to time, until reduced by one third.

10. Wipe out the casserole. Carefully return the pieces of oxtail to it and spread the purée on top. Pour the reduced liquid around. Cover and set in a 275° F. oven 1 1/2 hours without disturbing. Uncover and cool. Cover and refrigerate overnight.

11. 2 1/2 HOURS BEFORE SERVING, remove casserole from refrigerator and lift off all congealed fat. Let stand at room temperature 30 minutes.

12. Preheat oven to 275° F. Meanwhile, place dried cèpes in a fine strainer. Wash carefully under warm running water. Add to the casserole. Cover and reheat slowly in oven, 1 1/2 hours.

13. To serve, remove oxtail pieces one by one and set on heated shallow, wide serving dish, side by side. Cover and keep warm in turned-off warm oven. Strain sauce, pressing down on solids, into a small saucepan. Bring to a boil and cook at a slow boil, half over the heat, skimming, until sauce lightly coats a spoon, about 20 minutes. Adjust seasoning. Pour over meat and serve hot.

Inspired by a recipe from Lucien Vanel.

DAUBE OF BEEF IN THE STYLE OF GASCONY
Daube de Boeuf à la Gasconne

Maurice Coscuella, a Gascon chef from the town of Plaisance-du-Gers, taught me the secret of this beef stew: "It should be made with a mixture of meats: gelatinous pieces such as shin; deep, flavorful pieces such as short ribs; and firm pieces such as chuck or bottom round." All the pieces should be large chunks lest you end up with a crushed meat stew such as the Daube de la St.-André.

This version of a Gascon dish, traditionally served on All Souls' Day, is always started at least four days in advance. Ideally, it is made with red wine produced that year (a violet-colored liquid called *vin bourret*), but you may substitute any young red wine.

Serve with Fried Cornmeal Porridge Cakes in the Style of Gascony.

SERVES 6 TO 8
☆ Begin 3 to 4 days in advance
  ACTIVE WORK (DAY 1): 10 minutes
  ACTIVE WORK (DAY BEFORE SERVING): 45 minutes
  UNATTENDED SIMMERING TIME (DAY BEFORE SERVING): 6 hours
  COOKING TIME (SERVING DAY): 30 minutes

5–6 pounds mixed cuts of beef in large pieces: 2 1/2 pounds chuck pot roast and/or bottom round, trimmed of fat, mixed; 1 1/2 pounds beef short ribs or short ribs for flanken, and 1 beef shin with marrow
  Salt and freshly ground pepper
4 small carrots, scraped and cut into thin rounds
3 medium onions, thinly sliced
1 head garlic, halved
1/2 teaspoon Quatre Épices (Spice Mixture for Pâtés and Stews), plus an extra grating of fresh nutmeg
2 herb bouquets: each containing 6 sprigs parsley, 2 sprigs thyme, 1 small bay leaf, 2 celery leaves, tied together with string
1/2 pound celery root, peeled and cut into thin slices, or substitute 1 celery heart, thinly sliced
4 cups red wine, such as Petite Sirah of the current year or a young, full-flavored Burgundy
4 tablespoons poultry fat or oil
3/4 pound fresh or salted pork rind,* blanched 5 minutes and cut into strips
1 small veal knuckle or pig's foot, split, blanched 5 minutes, and drained (optional)
1/4 cup Armagnac
3/4 cup flour
1 teaspoon oil

*Pork rind can be cut off from either fatback or lean salt pork, or purchased separately from a pork butcher. Do not use bacon rind, which is smoked.

1. 3 OR 4 DAYS IN ADVANCE, cut chuck and bottom round into 18 pieces of approximately equal size. Season meat with salt and pepper. Place all the meat in a large noncorrodible bowl. Add carrots, onions, and garlic. Add the Quatre Épices, one of the herb bouquets, and celery root or celery. Pour wine over to cover. Cover bowl with plastic wrap, and let meat marinate 2 to 3 days in refrigerator, stirring mixture twice a day.

(continued)

2. 1 DAY BEFORE SERVING, preheat oven to 250° F. Remove meat and dry with paper towels. Discard herb bouquet.

3. Heat fat or oil in a heavy-bottomed skillet. *Lightly* brown meat in batches in hot fat, about 5 minutes for each batch. Line an 8- or 9-quart enameled cast-iron casserole or *daubière* with pork rind, fat side down. (The skin side sticks.) Place browned meat on top of pork rind.

4. Strain marinating liquid through a fine strainer into a bowl. Press down to extract all juices from the vegetables. Add vegetables to the skillet and brown them over high heat 5 minutes, stirring. Using a slotted spoon, transfer vegetables to the casserole.

5. Brown the veal knuckle in remaining fat. Add veal to casserole. Sprinkle meat and vegetables with Armagnac. Tuck in the second herb bouquet.

6. Wipe out fat in skillet; add 1 cup marinating liquid and bring to a boil. Deglaze skillet, scraping up all the bits and pieces that cling to the bottom. Skim carefully. Boil down to a glaze. Add another cup marinating liquid and reduce to a glaze. Add remaining marinade and simmer, skimming, 15 minutes. Add 3 cups water and bring to a boil. Pour hot contents of skillet over meat and vegetables. Cover casserole.

7. Make a paste of flour, water, and oil; seal the casserole or *daubière* with a ribbon of the mixture. Set in oven to cook 6 hours.

8. Break seal and discard it. Carefully remove meat to a large bowl. Cover and keep meat moist.

9. Meanwhile, strain cooking liquid and quickly chill. Push out the marrow from the knuckle (if using) and the shin. Purée one third of the vegetables, all the loose meat, and the marrow in the workbowl of a food processor fitted with the metal blade. Strain over meat. Discard remaining vegetables. Bone warm pig's foot (if using) and discard bones. Cut meat into dice. Add to other meat. Cool, cover, and refrigerate.

10. Degrease cooking liquid and pour into a heavy saucepan. Bring to a boil and set saucepan half over the heat. Cook at a slow boil, skimming, 10 minutes, or until reduced and very flavorful. Cool, cover, and refrigerate.

11. ON SERVING DAY, remove any additional fat that surfaced. Reheat sauce, pour over meat, and reheat slowly in oven or on top of stove. The fresh pork rind and the meat from the shin and the knuckle (if using) can be cut into small dice and served with the other meat. Adjust seasoning. Serve hot.

JELLIED BEEF IN THE STYLE OF THE GIRONDE
Terrine de Boeuf à la Girondine

This old recipe for jellied beef is a good dish for picnics and warm summer night buffets. A dry white wine is used, and the dish benefits from being made a few days in advance. Choose either bottom round or sirloin tip or the midsection of the rump. It must be larded with hard fatback flavored with herbs, brandy, and lots of chopped garlic so that while the beef cooks it is nourished and flavored from within (see Note).

The meat is cooked in its marinade, then sliced and layered in a terrine to be sliced like a pâté. Its own delicious natural jelly is poured over. The jelly is never clarified for this sort of country dish. A Creamy Shallot Vinaigrette (recipe follows) makes a good sauce. A good accompaniment would be a salad of extra-thin green beans and a platter of thinly sliced red-ripe tomatoes. Follow with the delicious Fruit Terrine.

SERVES 8

☆ Begin 2 or 3 days in advance
ACTIVE WORK (DAY 1): 30 minutes
ACTIVE WORK (DAY 2): 45 minutes
UNATTENDED SIMMERING TIME (DAY 2): 5 hours

9 ounces firm white pork fatback with rind
1/4 cup chopped fresh parsley
1 teaspoon finely chopped garlic
1 tablespoon *eau-de-vie*, Armagnac, or brandy
1/4 teaspoon Quatre Épices (Spice Mixture for Pâtés and Stews)
1 piece lean beef, bottom round or sirloin tip or midsection of the rump,
(4 1/2 to 5 pounds), trimmed of all fat
Salt and freshly ground pepper

Marinade

2 cups dry white wine, such as a white Graves or Sauvignon Blanc
Herb bouquet: 4 sprigs parsley, 1 sprig thyme, 1 bay leave, 3 celery
leaves, 2 cloves, 1 small cinnamon stick, and 2 cracked allspice
berries, tied together in cheesecloth
1 cup thinly sliced carrots
1 cup thinly slices onions
1/4 cup white wine vinegar
3 tablespoons olive oil
2 tablespoons *eau-de-vie*, Armagnac, or brandy

1 calf's foot or 2 small pig's feet, split
1 tablespoon rendered poultry or pork fat
1 tablespoon grapeseed or corn oil
1 leek, split and well washed, or 6 shallots, peeled and sliced
1 medium tomato, peeled, seeded, and chopped, or 1/2 cup canned
tomatoes, drained
3 cloves garlic, halved
1/2 tablespoon lightly cracked peppercorns
3 cups unsalted chicken, veal, or beef stock, or a mixture

Creamy Shallot Vinaigrette

(continued)

1. Place pork fatback in cold water; bring to a boil and simmer 3 minutes. Drain, rinse, and sever rind from fat. Reserve both. Cut the fat, while still warm, into thin strips. Toss with chopped parsley, garlic, brandy, and Quatre Épices (warm fat absorbs flavors better). Refrigerate until the fat hardens so that you can easily lard the meat. Cut pork rind into strips and set aside.

2. Meanwhile, rub beef with 1 teaspoon salt and 1/2 teaspoon pepper. Place marinade ingredients in a noncorrodible bowl and set aside. Use half the seasoned strips to lard the beef *with the grain*, keeping the spacing even. Use remaining strips to lard *on the diagonal* throughout the meat (like a porcupine's quills). (When fat melts during the cooking, it passes through the "capillaries" of the meat, keeping it moist and flavorful.) Tie meat to keep its solid shape. Soak larded meat in marinade 24 hours, turning meat 2 or 3 times. Refrigerate, loosely covered with plastic wrap.

3. Blanch calf's foot or pig's feet 5 minutes. Drain, rinse, and drain again.

4. Preheat oven to 250° F.

5. Remove beef from marinade. Set aside herb bouquet. Dry beef thoroughly. Strain marinade, reserving vegetables (and any fatback strips) and liquid separately. In a large heavy skillet, heat fat and oil until hot. Lightly brown meat on all sides, about 10 minutes. Do not sear the meat. Set aside. Pour off fat; add marinade vegetables and allow them to brown over medium heat, about 10 minutes.

6. Meanwhile, line a casserole large enough to hold all the ingredients with the strips of pork rind, fat side down. (The skin side sticks.) Place meat on top of rind. Add calf's foot or pig's feet. Add browned vegetables and herb bouquet. Add leek or shallots, tomato, garlic, and peppercorns. Pour the stock over.

7. Deglaze skillet with strained marinade liquid and bring to a boil. Simmer 2 to 3 minutes. Strain over meat. Discard scum in strainer. Cover casserole with waxed paper and a tight-fitting lid. (If desired, seal hermetically with a ribbon of flour, water, and a teaspoon of oil mixed together.) Cook 5 hours in the oven.

8. Remove casserole from oven. Break seal and let stand 1 hour, uncovered. Remove calf's foot or pig's feet and bone while still warm. Use bones for stock or discard. Degrease liquid. Cube calf's or pig's feet meat.

9. Lift out meat and remove strings. Strain liquid and chill for thorough degreasing. Boil down to 3 cups clear jellylike liquid. Adjust seasoning. Strain through well-dampened cheesecloth. Slice meat and arrange overlapping slices in a 5- to 6-cup terrine. Scatter cubed calf's or pig's feet on top. Pour liquid over meat and chill. Wrap well; it will keep 3 to 4 days in refrigerator. Serve from the terrine, slicing carefully.

NOTE TO THE COOK
There are many types of larding needle on the market, each of which requires a slightly different larding technique. Follow manufacturer's instructions. I use a *boeuf à la mode* larding needle, available by mail order through the Bridge Company, 214 East 52nd Street, New York, NY 10022. Whichever you use, be sure the fat is well chilled for easier handling. If you do not have a larding needle, drill holes with a skewer in the meat and push cold strips into incisions.

Creamy Shallot Vinaigrette

2 tablespoons white wine vinegar
1/2 teaspoon salt
1 teaspoon Dijon mustard
6 tablespoons olive oil
1/4 teaspoon freshly ground pepper
1/3 cup heavy cream
1 tablespoon chopped shallots (chopped by hand)
1 teaspoon chopped fresh parsley

1. Whisk vinegar, salt, and mustard until well blended. Slowly beat in the oil to make a smooth emulsion. Beat in the cream.
2. Just before serving, stir in the shallots and herbs. Serve with jellied beef.

TRIPE AND PIG'S FEET STEW
Tripes au Safran

This extraordinary dish is popular in Albi, where it is alleged to have been invented for the famous Toulouse-Lautrec family. Two foods of superb and varying texture— succulent, gelatinous nuggets of pig's feet and moist, chewy slices of tripe—carry the perfume of saffron, the strong earthy flavor of garlic, the saltiness of country ham, and the piquant taste of capers.

As in so many recipes of the South-West, slow cooking is the secret to its succulence. The tripe and its flavorings are sealed in a large pot and set in a slow oven (210° F.) to cook for at least 12 hours. The tripe softens, the liquid never boils, the flavors mingle, and the sauce base becomes highly aromatic. Since tripe is relatively tasteless (I like tripe for its texture and ability to carry other tastes), this is one of the few times when the sauce should dominate the meat.

When you buy tripe (beef stomach lining), it varies in texture enormously; choose a honeycomb or weave pattern with small holes. Pieces with a larger weave will need an extra hour or two of cooking time to soften. The tripe and the sauce base can be prepared days in advance. The dish can then be finished just before serving. Present on very hot plates with plenty of crusty French bread.

SERVES 6
☆ Begin 2 days in advance
   ACTIVE WORK (DAY 1): 10 minutes
   ACTIVE WORK (DAY 2): 30 minutes
   UNATTENDED SIMMERING TIME (DAY 2): 12 hours
   ACTIVE WORK (DAY 3): 30 minutes

(continued)

        4 fresh pig's feet
          Coarse (kosher) salt
        1 teaspoon Herbes de la Garrigue or herbes de Provence
        2 pounds ready-to-cook tripe
        3 tablespoons wine vinegar
    1 1/2 cups sliced carrots
    1 1/2 cups sliced onions
      3/4 cup well washed sliced leeks
      1/4 cup sliced celery
          Herb bouquet: 3 sprigs parsley, 1 sprig thyme, and 1 bay leaf,
            tied together
        1 bottle dry white wine
        1 tablespoon tomato paste
      1/4 teaspoon saffron threads
      3/4 cup flour
        1 teaspoon oil
      1/2 pound *jambon de Bayonne*, prosciutto, or Westphalian ham, with fat,
            cut into 1/3-inch cubes (about 1 1/4 cups cubed), rinsed, drained, and
            dried
    1 1/2 tablespoons finely chopped garlic
        3 tablespoons chopped fresh parsley
        3 tablespoons drained nonpareil capers
          Tabasco or other hot pepper sauce
      1–2 teaspoons arrowroot (optional)

1. 2 DAYS IN ADVANCE, singe (set over flame to burn off hairs), scrub, and dry the pig's feet. Rub with 1 tablespoon salt and the mixed herbs. Cover loosely with plastic wrap and refrigerate overnight.

2. THE FOLLOWING DAY, soak tripe 1 hour in 3 cups water and the vinegar. Rinse and drain. Place tripe in a deep kettle, cover with cold water, and bring slowly to a boil. Simmer 15 minutes. Drain, cool, and cut into 1 1/2-inch pieces. Set aside.

3. Preheat oven to 210° F. ("low"). Place vegetables in a 7- to 9-quart pot, preferably of earthenware or enameled cast-iron. Add herb bouquet, tripe, wine, tomato paste, and saffron. Rinse pig's feet, drain, and add to the pot. Add enough water to cover. Add 1/2 teaspoon salt and cover pot. Make a paste of flour, water, and oil. Seal pot with a ribbon of mixture. Place pot on center oven shelf to cook 12 hours.

4. 12 HOURS LATER OR THE FOLLOWING MORNING, strain contents. Discard all bones, vegetables, and herb bouquet. Bone pig's feet while still warm, making sure you catch all the little foot bones. Discard bones. Cut into small pieces. Place tripe and boned pig's feet in deep bowl.

5. Allow fat to rise to surface of cooking liquid. Skim off and discard all fat. Place degreased liquid in a deep saucepan and boil, skimming, until reduced to 3 cups. Pour liquid over tripe and pig's feet; set aside to cool. When cool, cover and

refrigerate until 45 minutes before serving. *Can be prepared 1 to 2 days ahead up to this point.*

6. 45 MINUTES BEFORE SERVING, gently reheat tripe and cooking liquid.

7. In a large, deep, covered skillet, cook the ham over low heat 10 minutes, shaking the skillet frequently. Add garlic and parsley; cook, covered, 2 to 3 minutes longer. Add tripe and cooking liquid. Simmer, uncovered, 30 minutes, stirring often. Add capers. Adjust seasoning, adding 1/4 teaspoon hot pepper sauce or more to taste. If sauce is too thin, mix arrowroot with 1 1/2 tablespoons cold water until well blended. Stir into the sauce and bring to a boil. Simmer, stirring, until thickened. Ladle meat and sauce into heated individual soup plates.

CRUSHED MEAT DAUBE FOR EARLY SEPTEMBER
Daube de la St.-André

This daube, traditionally eaten in early September during the first cold days of autumn, employs farmhouse methods that result in a melting, delicious, flavorful stew that can be eaten hot or cold. The meat, which is very lean, is sliced, layered with ground fat and flavorings, and cooked very slowly for hours in an aged red wine cooking liquid. It is totally degreased the next day, a process during which all the ground fat which was put in to keep the meat moist and succulent, and which was rendered by slow cooking, is removed from the surface. This is slow, effortless cooking. You need a solid piece of meat (with no muscle separations) that will slice into 1/2-inch-thick slices. Use either top round or bottom round, and cut the slices against the grain.

The original recipe calls for the slices to be very thin, which means the meat would have to be chilled before slicing. Such thin slices will be quite fragile when cooked and will tend to fall apart upon serving. Actually, in some homes in the South-West, that is *exactly* how the dish is served. The meat and sauce are cooked overnight in the fireplace, degreased, cooked again, and degreased again and then the meat is crushed with a fork into the sauce so that the dish becomes, in effect, a very rich, thick meat sauce. (Its appearance is similar to that of a Georgia Brunswick stew.)

In the old days this type of crushed meat stew was served with the cornmeal-and-flour-based fried cakes called *armottes*. Today these cakes are usually replaced by the *baguette*, a sad evolution. In my opinion the cornmeal porridge of the South-West, which is similar to Italian polenta, makes the best accompaniment to a red wine–based meat stew, and so I recommend you serve this dish with *Armottes* (Fried Cornmeal Porridge Cakes in the Style of Gascony) and glacéed carrots.

SERVES 6

☆ Begin 1 day in advance
    ACTIVE WORK (DAY 1): 30 minutes
    UNATTENDED COOKING TIME (DAY 1): 6 hours
    ACTIVE WORK (DAY 2): 10 minutes
    UNATTENDED COOKING TIME (DAY 2): 1 hour

    3–3 1/4 pounds bottom or top round of beef, trimmed of all fat, cut into
            1/2-inch-thick slices
            Freshly ground pepper and salt
      1 pound fresh or salted pork fatback with rind, blanched 5 minutes,
            rinsed, drained, and dried
      1/4 cup chopped fresh parsley
      1/4 cup chopped shallots
  1 1/2 tablespoons chopped garlic
      2 cups full-bodied red wine, at least 5 years old
      1/2 onion, stuck with 1 clove
      1 bay leaf
      1 sprig thyme
      1/2 teaspoon sugar
      Pinch of Quatre Épices (Spice Mixture for Pâtés and Stews)

1. 1 DAY IN ADVANCE, preheat oven to 225° F. Rub the meat with pepper and very little salt (see Note).

2. Slice rind off fatback; cut fat into 10 or 12 chunks and grind in food processor, using an on-off motion, or push through the medium blade of a food chopper (makes 1 cup). Mix ground fatback with parsley, shallots, garlic, pepper, and very little salt to make a loose paste.

3. Line a 3- or 4-quart casserole, preferably of enameled cast iron or earthenware, with pork rind, fat side down. (The skin side sticks.) Layer beef slices with alternate layers of fat mixture. In a nonaluminum saucepan, bring wine to a boil, simmer 15 minutes to evaporate alcohol, then pour hot over the meat. Add remaining ingredients. Cover with a sheet of parchment and a tight-fitting lid. Set on middle oven shelf to cook 6 hours.

4. Allow to cool, uncovered, then cover and refrigerate overnight.

5. THE FOLLOWING DAY, carefully degrease. Heat oven to 250° F. Cover and cook 1 hour in the oven.

6. Allow to cool completely and remove the fat that surfaces. Lift each slice of meat and arrange overlapping slices in a shallow baking dish. Strain juices to eliminate remaining fatback and rind, as well as any other debris. If there is too much cooking liquid, reduce by boiling until flavorful and lightly thickened, skimming often. Pour over meat. *Can be prepared hours in advance up to this point.*

7. Reheat gently and serve hot. If desired, crush the slices in the cooking juices.

NOTE TO THE COOK
Omit salt if using salted fatback.

VEAL DISHES

VEAL CUBES BRAISED WITH ONIONS IN THE STYLE OF THE BÉARN
Veau à la Béarnaise

The secret of this simple, tasty family dish is in the cutting of the onions: *they must be hand-diced.* (If they are chopped in a food processor they will end up acrid and mushy.) Diced by hand, they retain their body while slowly exuding their sweet moisture. It is this liquid that provides the cooking medium for the cubed lean veal.

The onions and ham slivers are first sweated in a small amount of fat on top of the stove; then the veal and crushed anchovies are stirred in, and the casserole tightly covered. Once the ingredients are hot they are placed in a slow oven to cook for two hours without further attention. This method is ideal for cooking *lean* tender veal: the morsels of meat turn succulent; the onions, soft but still distinguishable, provide the sauce; the anchovies and ham provide added flavor.

This dish is good with rice, scalloped potatoes, or noodles.

SERVES 3 OR 4
ACTIVE WORK: 30 minutes
PARTIALLY ATTENDED COOKING TIME: 2 1/2 hours

1 1/4–1 1/2 pounds onions, peeled
    1 tablespoon rendered ham, duck, goose or chicken fat
1 1/2 ounces *jambon de Bayonne*, prosciutto, or Westphalian ham, slivered
    (about 1/3 cup)
1 3/4–2 pounds boneless lean veal, cut from loin or rump
    4 anchovy fillets, rinsed and crushed to a purée
    Freshly ground pepper to taste
    Salt (optional)
    1 tablespoon finely snipped fresh chives

1. Preheat oven to 325° F.
2. To dice onions, halve lengthwise, then place each half cut side down. Make even vertical cuts from the root end. Make several horizontal cuts, then slice downward into 1/3-inch pieces. Do not chop in any sort of machine, even a hand-operated "onion chopper." Makes about 5 cups chopped.
3. Heat fat in a 3-quart flameproof earthenware or heavy-bottomed enameled cast-iron casserole until hot. Add onions and ham; toss with a spoon to mix well. Immediately cover and set over medium-low heat 10 minutes to sweat.
4. Meanwhile, trim veal of excess fat and cut into 1-inch cubes.

(continued)

5. Add the veal, anchovies, and pepper to taste to casserole. Cover tightly and return to heat 5 minutes longer. Set on middle oven shelf to cook 2 hours without disturbing. After 1 hour, lower oven temperature to 300° F.

6. After 2 hours cooking, the meat will be done. Strain cooking juices into a saucepan. Return meat and onions, uncovered, to oven to keep hot. Degrease cooking liquid, then boil down by one third. Taste the sauce for seasoning; add salt, if necessary. Pour sauce over veal and onions. Serve at once with a sprinkling of chives.

NOTE TO THE COOK

The best method I have found to avoid tears when chopping onions is to *lightly* sprinkle the sliced onions and the work surface with vinegar.

VEAL WITH ORANGE SAUCE
Veau à l'Orange

This Toulouse dish originally called for the bitter Seville orange, *bigarade.* To compensate for that special tanginess I have used plenty of strained lemon juice. This dish is good with rice. For dessert, serve the Walnut Cake from Masseube with a creamy vanilla ice cream.

SERVES 4
ACTIVE WORK: 30 minutes
COOKING TIME: about 2 hours

> 1/3 cup diced fatback or salt pork, blanched 3 minutes, rinsed, drained, and dried
> 2 tablespoons vegetable oil
> 4 pounds veal riblets or 1 1/2 pounds boneless veal shoulder, cut into 1 1/2-inch chunks
> 1 or 2 veal bones, cut into very small pieces (optional)
> 2 cups dry white wine
> 1 1/2 cups rich veal or Chicken Stock
> 2 medium yellow onions, thinly sliced
> 4 cloves garlic, halved
> Herb bouquet: 3 sprigs parsley, 1 sprig thyme, 1 bay leaf, 1 sprig celery leaves, and a few pieces green of leek, tied together
> 1 1/2 teaspoons tomato paste
> Salt and freshly ground pepper to taste
> 1/2–2/3 cup freshly squeezed and strained orange juice
> 1/4 cup freshly squeezed and strained lemon juice
> 2/3 cup heavy cream
> Zest of 1 medium orange

2 teaspoons minced fresh chives
1 teaspoon minced fresh parsley

1. In a skillet, sauté fatback in hot oil until golden and lightly crisp. Transfer to a flameproof heavy casserole large enough to hold all the ingredients. Trim veal of excess fat. Add a few pieces of veal to the hot skillet and brown on all sides. Do not crowd the skillet; brown the pieces in batches. As each piece browns, transfer it to the casserole. Lightly brown veal bones (if using) in the remaining fat.

2. Pour out fat and deglaze the skillet with white wine. Pour pan juices over veal. Add stock, onions, garlic, herb bouquet, tomato paste, and salt and pepper to taste. Cover and simmer 1 1/2 to 2 hours, or until veal is very tender. Test meat for tenderness by piercing with the point of a sharp knife; it should penetrate the meat easily.

3. Remove meat and cover to keep moist. Discard herb bouquet and bones. Strain juices; chill quickly and degrease completely.

4. Add 1/2 cup of the orange juice and the 1/4 cup lemon juice to pan juices. Bring to a boil and reduce to 2 cups, skimming. Add cream, bring back to a boil, and reduce to 1 1/2 cups. Adjust seasoning. Add more orange juice, if desired. Fold meat into sauce and reheat.

5. Meanwhile, remove any white pith from the orange zest. Cut zest into fine julienne strips; simmer 5 minutes in boiling water. Drain; refresh under cold running water and drain again. Add zest and herbs to sauce. *This dish can be prepared in advance and reheated.*

VEAL KIDNEYS GARNISHED WITH SHALLOT *CONFIT*
Rognons de Veau Poêlés au Confit d'Échalotes

This recipe of Bordeaux chef Christian Clément treats the shallots as if they were pieces of duck or goose, cooked very slowly for a long time in rendered goose or duck fat. When they have become soft and translucent, they are caramelized in a skillet or in the oven at high heat. The juicy kidneys are served not with a sauce but with the soft, sweet shallots. This dish is especially good with potatoes sautéed in goose fat.

SERVES 4 TO 6
ACTIVE WORK: 25 minutes
UNATTENDED COOKING TIME: 1 1/2 hours

1 cup rendered goose or duck fat, fresh or canned
1/2 pound large shallots, about 1 inch in diameter, whole and peeled
2 light-colored, very fresh veal kidneys (about 12 ounces each)
Freshly ground black pepper
Coarse (kosher) salt

(continued)

1. Reserve 3 tablespoons of the poultry fat for cooking kidneys. In a small heavy saucepan, warm remaining fat and 3 tablespoons water over very low heat to body temperature. Slip shallots into warm fat and simmer slowly about 1 1/2 hours, or until they become translucent and very soft. Carefully remove from the pan and set aside; reserve 2 tablespoons of this fat. (Remaining fat can be used for potatoes or *confit*.)

2. With a sharp knife, remove as much of the fat and membrane covering kidneys as possible, leaving them whole. In a heavy medium-size skillet, place the 3 tablespoons reserved fat over moderately high heat. Add kidneys and sauté 4 minutes. Turn and cook 3 to 4 minutes, until the kidneys are firm but not too resistant to pressure; they should be very pink inside. (Kidneys that weigh 1 pound cook in 10 minutes, 4 1/2 to 5 minutes per side.) Remove kidneys to a wire rack set over a plate to catch any juices. Cover loosely with foil to keep warm.

3. Wipe out skillet with paper towels (do not wash). Add the 2 tablespoons reserved fat from the shallots and place over moderately high heat. Add shallots and cook, tossing frequently, until browned and caramelized on all sides, 5 minutes.

4. With a sharp knife, cut kidneys slightly on the diagonal into thin slices. Arrange the slices overlapping in a flowerlike ring on warm serving plates. Season lavishly with freshly ground pepper, and salt lightly. Place the shallots in center of kidneys and serve hot. Discard any kidney juices caught in the plate.

NOTE TO THE COOK
If a sauce is desired, make the White Bordeaux Wine Sauce for Steaks and Roasted Veal Kidneys.

FRICASSÉE OF VEAL KIDNEYS AND ARTICHOKES
Fricassée de Rognons de Veau aux Artichauts

This recipe comes from Alain Dutournier, chef of Le Trou Gascon restaurant in Paris. An easy and light lunch dish, it employs an excellent Demi-Glace as a sauce. Serve with buttered noodles, if desired.

SERVES 2
TOTAL PREPARATION TIME: 35 minutes

> 1 **veal kidney (3/4 pound)**
> **Coarse (kosher) salt**
> 2 **large artichokes or 1 (9-ounce) package frozen artichoke hearts,**
>   **defrosted**
> 1 **lemon, cut in half**
> 1 **large carrot, scraped and sliced into 1/4-inch-thick rounds**
> **Freshly ground pepper**
> 1 **cup Demi-Glace**

**1 1/2 tablespoons rendered poultry fat or 1 tablespoon each olive oil and
butter**
1/3 cup heavy cream
1 sprig fresh tarragon (optional)

1. Remove membrane and fat from veal kidney. With a sharp knife, cut kidney lengthwise and remove inner core. Deeper sections can be removed with a pair of scissors. Cut kidney into 1 1/4-inch chunks. Sprinkle very lightly with salt and set aside.

2. Pull off tough outer leaves of each artichoke. With a sharp knife, cut off about one third of each top. Cut off stem. Using a small stainless-steel paring knife, trim outside of artichoke bottom. If artichokes are very large, cut them into eighths; otherwise cut them into quarters. Scoop out fuzzy center choke. Leave tender inner leaves intact. Rub any cut surfaces with the cut lemon to prevent discoloration.

3. In a deep saucepan, steam artichokes over 1 1/2 inches boiling water 10 minutes; add carrots and steam 5 minutes longer, or until almost tender. Drain vegetables on a kitchen terry towel. Sprinkle with salt and pepper to taste. *Can be prepared ahead up to this point.*

4. Put the Demi-Glace, artichokes, and carrots in a 2-quart saucepan. Simmer, uncovered, until vegetables are tender.

5. Meanwhile, in a 10-inch skillet, heat fat or oil and butter until a drop of water sizzles and bounces. Wipe kidneys dry and add to skillet. Sauté over moderately high heat, tossing and turning them until browned on all sides. The kidneys must not cook longer than 3 minutes, or they will be tough. The surface juices should be pink. Transfer kidney chunks to a colander to drain. Discard pan juices. Sprinkle kidneys with pepper. Arrange in shallow serving bowl.

6. With a slotted spoon, transfer cooked carrots and artichokes to bowl and mix with kidneys; keep warm while finishing sauce.

7. Bring sauce in the saucepan to a vigorous boil. Add cream and cook over high heat, without stirring, until small tight bubbles completely cover the surface. To tell whether sauce is ready, stir with a wooden spoon: when you see glimpses of the bottom of the pan, remove from heat. The process usually takes 6 to 8 minutes over high heat. The sauce is thin; it barely coats the spoon. Adjust seasoning and pour sauce over kidneys and vegetables. If available, roughly chop fresh tarragon leaves and sprinkle over all. Serve at once.

CALF'S LIVER AS PREPARED IN THE VALLEY OF OSSAU
Foie de Veau à la Vallée d'Ossau

This is a personal book, a book of food that pleases me. I've always been seduced by dishes off the beaten track—odd ways of doing things that result in the expected taste plus a twist. This dish is one of my favorites, and it fits the description of such a dish. And it's a wonderful one, too.

It was the late Roland Casau, chef at Chez Pierre in Pau, who first showed me how the Ossalois (people from the valley of Ossau) prepare calf's liver. I was immediately enchanted—the recipe was intriguing, using a variant on the technique of *confit* to create a silky-smooth texture, juicy and delicious. It is a dish hard to forget; I never enjoyed liver so much.

In cities like Bordeaux and Bayonne large chunks of calf's liver are often roasted with delicious results. But the Ossalois apply two intermediate steps, first marinating the liver to enhance its flavor, then poaching it in a liquid that Casau called *la mère*. This expression—literally "the mother"—is used to describe a poaching liquor used over and over for many different items, picking up the flavor of each and imparting it to the next. It is the classic poaching liquor for foie gras in Quercy, where I met a woman who used the same liquor for cooking pig's feet for over a year. In the Landes, Pepette Arbulo used the word to describe the base stock of her garbure in which she poached her stuffed cabbage and her duck breasts. The *mère* in this case is a stock filled with pork rinds that have rendered out all their fat and flavor. The liver is tightly wrapped in cheesecloth, allowing the flavors of the stock to enter the flesh but still holding the fragile meat together. The large amount of fat in the stock keeps the texture of the liver silky—the way poultry and pork cook in a *confit*. After poaching, the liver is allowed to firm up by cooling down. Then it is unwrapped, lightly rubbed with oil, and set in a very hot oven to brown just before serving. This is excellent with Sautéed Peppers in the Style of Béarn or Red-Wine-Cooked Onions.

SERVES 5 OR 6

ACTIVE WORK: 30 minutes
SOAKING AND MARINATING TIME: 7 hours
UNATTENDED COOKING TIME: 2 hours

> 1 center piece calf's liver (2 1/2 pounds)
> 2 cups milk
> 1/2 pound fresh or salted fatback
>   Freshly ground pepper and salt to taste
> 1 tablespoon chopped fresh parsley
> 1 quart unsalted Chicken Stock, degreased
> 1/2 onion, cut into thin slices
> 1 sprig thyme
> 1 tablespoon chopped young celery leaves
> 1/2 bay leaf

1/4 teaspoon Quatre Épices (Spice Mixture for Pâtés and Stews)
6 tablespoons vegetable oil
1/2 pound thinly sliced *jambon de Bayonne*, prosciutto, or Westphalian ham, cut into small pieces
4 tablespoons wine vinegar or *verjus* (see Appendix)
3 tablespoons *hachis*: 1 tablespoon finely chopped garlic (chopped by hand) and 2 tablespoons finely chopped fresh parsley

1. Have the butcher remove the thin membrane surrounding the liver, or do it yourself with a thin-bladed knife. Cut out all pieces of fat and hard parts and discard.

2. ABOUT 8 1/2 HOURS BEFORE SERVING, soak liver in milk a minimum of 3 hours.

3. Meanwhile, simmer fatback 3 minutes. Drain, rinse, and drain again. Remove rind and set aside. While fatback is still warm, cut 12 strips 4 inches × 1/2 inch; sprinkle with pepper and 1 teaspoon of the chopped parsley. Chill the strips.

4. Cube remaining fatback and rind; combine with chicken stock. Simmer stock 1 to 1 1/2 hours so that rind and pieces of fatback are totally rendered and stock is very fatty. Set aside. *Can be prepared 1 day ahead up to this point.*

5. Remove liver from milk, rinse, and dry thoroughly. Use a larding needle to lard the liver with chilled strips at equal intervals (see Note to the Cook). Marinate liver in a mixture of onion, thyme, celery leaves, bay leaf, Quatre Épices, and 4 tablespoons of the oil. Let stand a minimum of 4 hours.

6. 1 HOUR BEFORE SERVING, tightly wrap liver in a single layer of cheesecloth or stockinet and slip liver into simmering (206° F.) stock. (Add marinade to simmering stock for added flavor.) Simmer 25 minutes (or exactly 10 minutes to the pound) for rosy liver. The temperature of the poaching liquid *must* remain at 206° F. Use a fat thermometer; do not allow liver to boil or it will harden and overcook. Carefully remove liver to wire rack; unwrap and pat dry carefully.

7. 20 MINUTES BEFORE SERVING, preheat oven to 550° F. Grease a shallow 10-inch baking dish with 1 tablespoon of the oil and scatter chopped ham over the bottom. Brush "bone-dry" liver with remaining 1 tablespoon oil and place over ham. Set in oven to brown and crisp, 6 minutes. Transfer liver to a slicing board.

8. Scrape ham onto a warmed serving platter. Quickly deglaze pan with vinegar or *verjus*, then add 1/2 cup water and set over very low heat for an instant.

9. Thinly slice liver (2 1/2 pounds from the center yields 12 slices) and arrange overlapping slices over the ham on the heated serving platter. Scatter garlic and parsley *hachis* on top. Swirl the juices in the pan, scraping up all the brown bits that cling to the bottom. Spoon juices over the liver; sprinkle lightly with salt (if the ham is not too salty) and with some pepper. Serve at once.

NOTE TO THE COOK
Follow manufacturer's instructions for larding needle technique. I use a *boeuf à la mode* larding needle; if you do not have a larding needle, drill holes with a skewer in the meat and push cold strips into incisions. Be sure the fat is well chilled for easier handling.

BRAISED SWEETBREADS WITH MARROW
AND TRUFFLES
Ris de Veau Braisé à la Moelle et aux Truffes

This is a "modern" dish that is both elegant and sublime. It isn't for everyday eating
and it requires a few last-minute touches to make it perfect. If you have carried home
from France one of those little glass jars with one whole black truffle in it, this is a
recipe that will do it justice.

True sweetbreads are the throat glands (thymus). Sometimes butchers will substitute the cleaned pancreas or the testes. These organs, though edible, are not considered choice and should be avoided. When you shop for sweetbreads, look for very
fresh, white, swollen-looking lobes, soft to the touch. If they look leathery and gray
in color, don't buy them. Frozen sweetbreads are a lot better than you might think
(provided they are the round ones). Though sweetbreads should be soaked for
several hours in several changes of water, they do not need to be blanched for this
dish if they are fresh or frozen-fresh. The sweetbreads can be bought fresh, cooked in
the vegetable stock, and kept refrigerated for 2 to 3 days before making the dish.

SERVES 4 TO 6
☆ Begin 2 or 3 days in advance
ACTIVE WORK: 30 minutes
UNATTENDED SIMMERING TIME: 20 minutes

2–3	**veal or beef marrowbones**
	Salt
1 1/2–2	**pounds fresh or frozen sweetbreads**
	Vinegar
2	**medium carrots, scraped and chopped**
1	**medium white turnip, peeled and finely chopped**
1	**rib celery, finely diced**
1	**medium onion, finely chopped**
1	**white of leek, quartered lengthwise, well washed, and cut into very thin slices**
7	**tablespoons unsalted butter**
	Herb bouquet: 3 sprigs parsley, 1 sprig thyme, 1 sprig celery leaves, and 1 bay leaf, tied together
1/2	**teaspoon roughly cracked peppercorns**
3	**tablespoons port wine**
2 1/2	**cups rich unsalted Chicken Stock, degreased and reduced to 1 1/4 cups**
1 1/2	**tablespoons truffle juice**
1	**small truffle, cut into thin slices**

1. 1 TO 3 DAYS IN ADVANCE, wash marrowbones under running water; place in a bowl, cover with warm water, and let soak 2 to 3 minutes. Drain. Using a skewer, loosen marrow from each bone. Push marrow out in whole pieces and drop them into a bowl of cold salted water. Refrigerate overnight, changing the water often or until clear. (This will allow the marrow to rid itself of any blood.)

2. EARLY IN THE DAY, OR 2 TO 3 DAYS IN ADVANCE: soak sweetbreads in several changes of lightly acidulated cold water (1 tablespoon vinegar to 3 cups water) for at least 1 1/2 hours.

3. Cut away hard pieces of fat and cartilage, but do not peel at this time.

4. Soften vegetables in a covered heavy skillet or wide saucepan in 3 tablespoons of the butter 5 minutes over low heat. Uncover skillet and cook vegetables 2 to 3 minutes longer, or until the beads of moisture evaporate without burning.

5. Wrap herb bouquet and peppercorns in cheesecloth and add to skillet. Add sweetbreads and turn them in pan juices to moisten. Cover and cook gently 5 minutes longer, turning them over midway. Add port wine and reduced stock. Cover with buttered parchment and a tight-fitting cover. Simmer sweetbreads gently 20 minutes, turning them midway. Immediately remove from heat; uncover and allow sweetbreads to cool in the broth. *Sweetbreads can be kept in this broth under refrigeration 2 to 3 days.*

6. When ready to finish sweetbreads, remove surface fat from broth and discard. Strain broth into a wide saucepan or deep skillet. Peel sweetbreads and cut into 1/2-inch slices. Gently reheat sweetbread slices in the broth without boiling. With a slotted spoon, remove and arrange overlapping slices on a warm serving dish; cover and keep hot.

7. Reduce skillet juices to 1/2 cup. Off heat, swirl in the remaining 4 tablespoons butter. The sauce should be just thick enough to coat a spoon lightly. Stir in the truffle juice.

8. Meanwhile, drain marrow and cook in barely simmering salted water 1 minute. Drain, cut into thin rounds, and place over sweetbread slices.

9. Adjust seasoning and spoon the very hot sauce over the marrow and sweetbreads. Decorate with truffle slices and serve at once.

Inspired by a recipe from Jean-Louis Palladin.

LAMB DISHES

Mutton or lamb is the most succulent meat of the whole range the butcher can offer. It is wholesome, strengthening; an aid to digestion and even slightly aphrodisiac. There are very few that are not all the happier and healthier for having dined on it.
—FULBERT-DUMONTEIL (a Périgourdin writing over eighty years ago in Paris)

ROAST LEG OF LAMB IN THE STYLE OF BORDEAUX
Gigot à la Bordelaise

"To truly sear meat, immerse it in boiling oil," says André Guillot.

Some Périgourdins do something similar with a leg of lamb: they dip it in boiling water for a minute to seal the surface. Perhaps a more practical method of sealing is to massage the exposed flesh of the meat with lots of seasoning and fat or oil. When the meat is exposed to a very high temperature in the oven, it will quickly create a crust. Massage the lamb with garlic, salt and pepper, and the fat or oil the day before you plan to cook it, to deeply flavor and nourish the flesh as well.

The flavor of shallots and vinegar makes this roast leg of lamb delicious. Artichokes and Potatoes au Gratin goes particularly well with the lamb.

SERVES 6
ACTIVE WORK: 30 minutes
ROASTING TIME: about 1 hour

> 1 leg of lamb (5 1/2 pounds)
> 2 large cloves garlic, peeled and cut into thin slivers
> 1 teaspoon coarse (kosher) salt
> 1/2 teaspoon freshly ground pepper
> 2 tablespoons rendered goose or duck fat
> 2 tablespoons grape-seed or French peanut oil
> 3/4 cup red wine vinegar
> 2 tablespoons finely chopped shallots
> 3/4 cup unsalted Chicken Stock, degreased

1. Trim off excess fat and tough outer skin from lamb, leaving a thin layer of fat. Make about 10 incisions near leg bone and insert garlic slivers. Rub meat with salt and pepper, then coat with fat and oil. Massage into the meat. Refrigerate, loosely covered with plastic wrap. Remove from refrigerator 2 to 3 hours before roasting.

2. 1 3/4 HOURS BEFORE SERVING, preheat oven to 500° F.

3. Place lamb on grid or rack in large open roasting pan. Set pan on upper-middle

oven shelf. Roast lamb, fat side up, 25 minutes. Remove from oven. Let lamb relax 30 minutes.

4. Meanwhile, in a small noncorrodible saucepan, combine vinegar and shallots; bring to a boil. Simmer slowly about 20 minutes, or until reduced to 1/3 cup. Strain, reserving shallots (*can be done in advance*).

5. Degrease roasting pan. Add vinegar solution and 1/2 cup water to pan juices. Lower oven temperature to 350° F. Return meat to oven and roast 30 minutes longer, basting with vinegar-flavored pan juices every 5 minutes. (Total roasting time should be about 10 minutes to the pound for medium-rare, or 135° to 140° F. on meat thermometer.)

6. Remove lamb from oven. Add stock and reserved shallots to pan drippings (usually there is not much more than a glaze) and deglaze the pan. Boil up and season lightly. Let lamb rest 5 to 10 minutes. Slice lamb. Serve with shallot sauce.

LAMB CHOPS WITH PORT WINE AND TARRAGON
Côtelettes d'Agneau à la Sauce d'Estragon

Tarragon is a wonderful flavoring for lamb, and a change from rosemary or mint. Chef Francis Garcia of Bordeaux freezes fresh tarragon leaves with great success, then uses them in their frozen state. To prepare fresh tarragon for freezing, drop the sprigs into boiling water. Remove at once and refresh in a bowl of ice-cold water. Drain, pat dry, and place dry sprigs on sheets of paper towel. Roll towels into cylinders. Pack in plastic bags and freeze. Frozen tarragon will keep several months.

Garcia's method with lamb is interesting: he sears the chops to seal in their juices, then allows them a short rest off the heat while the sauce is being made. After a simple deglazing with port wine and meat stock, the sauce is finished with butter, and fresh tarragon leaves are added. The chops are then finished over medium heat.

SERVES 2

ACTIVE WORK: 15 minutes
COOKING TIME: 8 to 10 minutes

> 2 loin lamb chops, each about 1 1/3 inches thick, trimmed of extra fat
> 1 clove garlic, halved
> 1/3 cup chopped onions
> 1/2 cup chopped carrots
> 1/3 cup chopped celery
> 4 tablespoons unsalted butter
> Salt and freshly ground pepper to taste
> 1/4 cup ruby port wine, preferably imported
> 2 teaspoons fresh or frozen tarragon leaves
> 1/4 cup Demi-Glace
> 1 1/2 teaspoons grape-seed or French peanut oil

(continued)

1. ABOUT 30 MINUTES BEFORE SERVING, rub lamb with garlic and set aside.

2. In a covered 9-inch heavy-bottomed skillet, cook onions, carrots, and celery in 1 tablespoon of the butter over low heat 5 minutes. Uncover, raise heat, and allow moisture beads on vegetables to evaporate. Push vegetables to one side. Add lamb chops to the skillet. Sear 2 minutes to a side. Season at once with salt and pepper.

3. Using tongs, remove chops and let them relax at least 5 minutes. Meanwhile, degrease by blotting the skillet and vegetables with paper towels. Moisten with port wine and reduce to a glaze. Add 1 teaspoon of the tarragon leaves and the Demi-Glace. Simmer over low heat 1 minute. Strain into a small saucepan, pushing down on vegetables and tarragon to extract all the good flavor. Discard vegetables. Keep warm.

4. Return skillet—without washing it—to stove. Add oil and heat until smoking; finish chops to desired degree of doneness, about 2 minutes more per side for medium-rare. Blot and place chops on serving dish.

5. Swirl remaining 3 tablespoons butter into sauce in saucepan. Adjust seasoning and spoon sauce over lamb. Decorate with remaining tarragon leaves.

ROAST SHOULDER OF LAMB WITH ANCHOVIES
Épaule d'Agneau aux Anchois

This shoulder of lamb is stuffed with anchovies and garlic and left to marinate overnight. The salty anchovies flavor from within as well as help tenderize the flesh. Despite the seemingly large amounts of anchovy in the dish, at the end the flavor is haunting and the taste of anchovy is hardly perceptible. Serve with Eggplant Studded with Garlic.

SERVES 6 TO 8
☆ Begin 1 day in advance
   ACTIVE WORK (DAY 1): 35 minutes
   PARTIALLY UNATTENDED SIMMERING TIME: 1 to 2 hours
   ACTIVE WORK (DAY 2): 10 minutes
   ROASTING TIME (DAY 2): 35 minutes

    10 **anchovy fillets***
     3 **tablespoons olive oil**
     2 **cloves garlic, halved and unpeeled**
 1/4 **teaspoon dried thyme, crumbled**
     1 **shoulder of young spring lamb (about 4 pounds), boned, bones reserved and cracked into 2-inch pieces**
     2 **tablespoons vegetable oil**
     2 **cups unsalted Chicken Stock, degreased**
 1/4 **cup red wine vinegar**

1 tablespoon Dijon mustard
3 tablespoons Crème Fraîche (optional)
Salt and freshly ground pepper

*If using salt-packed Italian or Greek anchovies, rinse off salt from 3 anchovies. Soak in plenty of cold water for 2 hours; drain. Remove fillets and cut in half lengthwise. Two and one-half salt-packed anchovies equal 10 canned anchovy fillets.

1. 1 DAY IN ADVANCE, rinse anchovies under cold running water; pat dry with paper towels. Cut fillets in half lengthwise; place in small bowl with olive oil, garlic, and thyme. Let stand at room temperature, covered, 2 to 3 hours.

2. Place lamb shoulder, fat side down, on work surface. Use small knife to remove tendons and hard cartilage. Make shallow slits in flesh about 1 inch apart for anchovies. Drain anchovies, reserving oil. Slip halved anchovy fillets into slits. Place any remaining anchovy pieces in creases between large portions of flesh. Roll shoulder tightly into a sausage shape. Tie securely with butcher's string at 1 1/2-inch intervals. Rub surface of roast with reserved anchovy oil; wrap in plastic wrap. Refrigerate for 6 hours or overnight.

3. Heat vegetable oil in large heavy skillet over medium-low heat until rippling; add lamb bones. Sauté, turning occasionally, until well browned, about 15 minutes. Pour off fat from skillet; deglaze with 1/2 cup of the stock, scraping up brown bits that cling to bottom and sides of pan. Add remaining 1 1/2 cups stock; heat to boiling. Reduce heat; simmer, partially covered and skimming often, until rich broth develops, 1 to 2 hours. You should have about 1 1/2 cups of broth for sauce base. Strain sauce base through fine-mesh sieve into medium bowl; discard bones. Cool sauce base. Refrigerate, covered, overnight.

4. ABOUT 2 1/2 HOURS BEFORE SERVING, remove lamb from refrigerator. Let stand 1 hour to come to room temperature.

5. Preheat oven to 500° F. Place lamb on rack of roasting pan just large enough to hold it snugly. Roast in top third of oven 15 minutes. Remove lamb from pan; let stand on rack set over plate to collect juices 30 to 45 minutes. Lower oven temperature to 425° F.

6. Meanwhile, degrease drippings in oasting pan, Place pan over medium heat. Add vinegar and deglaze pan, scraping up brown bits that cling to bottom and sides of pan. Transfer to small heavy saucepan; reduce over medium heat to 2 tablespoons. Whisk in mustard. Remove from heat.

7. Remove and discard fat from surface of reserved sauce base; whisk sauce base into vinegar-mustard reduction. Add to sauce any juices that have accumulated under the roast. Set sauce aside.

8. 25 TO 30 MINUTES BEFORE SERVING, return lamb to rack in roasting pan; return to oven. Roast until instant-reading meat thermometer inserted into thickest part of lamb registers 135° F. for medium-rare, about 20 minutes. Transfer roast to cutting board; let stand while finishing sauce.

(continued)

9. Degrease any roasting pan drippings and deglaze roasting pan with 2 tablespoons water. Scrape into sauce. Boil down to 1 cup, skimming. Swirl in Crème Fraîche (if using); heat to boiling. Remove from heat; adjust seasoning with salt and pepper, if necessary. Slice shoulder into 1/2-inch slices. Arrange overlapping slices on heated plates. Spoon sauce over and around lamb. Serve immediately.

Inspired by a recipe from Lucien Vanel.

LAMB WITH GARLIC AND WHITE BEANS
Épaule d'Agneau à la Catalane (en Pistache)

Here is a superb version of cassoulet called in Catalan *en pistache*, as served in the central Pyrenees. If you like the combination of lamb and garlic (and who doesn't?—Lucien Vanel once told me one should fall to one's knees before such a beautiful affinity of tastes!), you will adore this dish.

Buy "choice" lamb rather than "prime"—it is less fatty, and lamb fat is not particularly delicious. The method of cooking the lamb in its own juices with a small quantity of wine and aromatics was devised to bring out the true flavor of the meat. With the dish, pass a small bowl of pickled walnuts.

SERVES 8

ACTIVE WORK: 1 hour
PARTIALLY ATTENDED SIMMERING TIME: 2 1/2 hours
BAKING TIME: 1 hour

1 pound dried white beans such as Great Northern or pea beans
10 ounces lean salt pork
1 boned lean shoulder of lamb (3 to 3 1/2 pounds), cut into 2-inch cubes
1 head plus 4 cloves garlic
Salt and freshly ground pepper
Granulated sugar
2 tablespoons peanut or olive oil
1 1/2 cups chopped onions
1 cup dry white wine
3 tomatoes, peeled, seeded, and chopped
1 tablespoon tomato paste
1/2 ounce dried cèpes
1 piece orange rind
2 carrots, sliced
1 onion stuck with 2 cloves

Herb bouquet: 3 sprigs parsley, 1 sprig thyme, 1 bay leaf, and 2 celery leaves, tied together
1 pound garlic sausage, or homemade Toulouse Sausage flavored with cinnamon, cloves, marjoram, and cayenne pepper, or *cotechino*, or chorizo, or kielbasa

1. ABOUT 7 HOURS IN ADVANCE OR THE DAY BEFORE (see Note 3), soak beans 1 1/2 hours in water.

2. Meanwhile, with a thin-bladed knife, remove rind from lean salt pork. Cook both pieces in simmering water 3 minutes. Drain, rinse under cold running water, and dry. Cut lean salt pork into small cubes. Set aside cubes and whole rind.

3. Cut away as much fat as possible from each cube of lamb. Peel 4 cloves of garlic and cut each clove into slivers. With a small paring knife, make a slit in each cube of meat and insert a sliver of garlic. Rub the meat with a little salt and pepper and sprinkle very lightly with sugar so the lamb will have a nice brown glossy color when browned.

4. In a flameproof 3-quart heavy-bottomed casserole, heat oil over high heat and brown lamb on all sides in batches. Avoid too high a heat, but do sear the lamb cubes. Transfer each batch to a plate to make room for the next batch.

5. When all the lamb has been browned, wipe out the fat in the bottom of the casserole. Add cubes of salt pork. Lower heat, cover, and cook 5 minutes, shaking the casserole often so cubes will not stick. Uncover, add onions, and cook gently, stirring once or twice, until soft and golden. Tilt casserole and press on onions and pork cubes with the back of a slotted spoon to extract excess fat. Use a paper towel to blot up fat.

6. Deglaze the casserole with wine. Return lamb pieces and any juices that have exuded on the plate. Add tomatoes, tomato paste, cèpes (washed—not soaked), and the orange rind. Bring to a boil, then simmer, tightly covered, 2 hours, or until tender.

7. When beans have soaked 1 1/2 hours, drain and put in a 4- or 5-quart heavy pan. Cover with tepid water and slowly bring to a boil. Boil beans 5 minutes.

8. Meanwhile, bring a kettle of water to a boil. When beans have boiled 5 minutes, drain and return to pan. *Immediately* pour enough boiling water over to cover. (This little extra step eliminates a great deal of the gas that causes some bean eaters to suffer.)

9. Add carrots, onion stuck with 2 cloves, blanched pork rind, and herb bouquet. Reduce heat to low, cover, and simmer 2 hours. Midway add 1 teaspoon salt.

10. When lamb has finished cooking, set aside, uncovered. Spoon off any fat that rises to the surface.

11. Prick sausage or sausages 3 or 4 times. Add to beans after they have cooked 1 1/2 hours. Continue cooking beans, uncovered, 30 minutes.

12. Remove and discard carrots, onion stuck with cloves, and herb bouquet.

13. Separate remaining garlic head into cloves. Cook cloves in their skins in a small saucepan with water to cover 10 minutes. Drain and peel (see Note 1). Set aside.

14. Preheat oven to 325° F.

(continued)

15. Line a 5 1/2-quart earthenware or stoneware bean pot with the pork rind, fat side down. (The skin side sticks.) Using a slotted spoon, transfer about one third of the beans to make a layer over the rind, then add a layer of about half of the lamb. Cut the sausage or sausages into 8 slices of approximately equal size; place between lamb chunks. Scatter peeled garlic cloves on top. Cover with another layer of beans, then add remaining lamb, then remaining beans. Pour all the meat cooking liquid over the beans and add just enough of bean cooking liquid to moisten. Set pot in oven to bake 1 hour, or until a crust forms on the surface. Serve directly from earthenware dish.

NOTES TO THE COOK
1. Parboiling the garlic cloves, then peeling and tossing them with the beans, makes for a pleasant surprise, since the peeled cloves and the white beans look alike.
2. You can make your own Catalan sausage for this dish by following the recipe for Toulouse Sausage and seasoning the meat with pinches of ground cinnamon, ground cloves, crumbled marjoram, and red-hot cayenne, while leaving out the nutmeg. Or substitute a mildly spicy Italian, Spanish, or Polish sausage.
3. Dish can be prepared 1 day in advance. Poke holes in bean crust, add 1/2 cup water, and bake 1/2 hour to reheat in a 350° F. oven.

CHAPTER 13

DESSERTS

SKILLET DESSERTS

While researching this book I came upon a great number of desserts that are made in a heavy black skillet—not just simple crêpes, but crêpes flavored with tantalizing combinations of aromatics, as well as other things that I have collected and filed under the category "skillet desserts." In the South-West the most common flavoring for crêpes is anise, but many skilled home cooks have their own secret preparations for "perfuming" crêpes, waffles (*gaufres*), sponge-type cakes (*massepain*), and the famous *gâteau Basque*. I collected recipes for these, but found that much depends upon the right kind of brandy, the right brand of orange flower water, and the right flavor and color of rum, so I must warn that some of these combinations—when made with inferior ingredients—are not as enchanting as they are in France. For this reason I have included only two simple recipes.

Some charming and simple skillet desserts are: *les daudines* in the Périgord (called *pain perdu* elsewhere) which is nothing more than French toast—slices of stale bread bathed in sugared milk flavored with rum or orange flower water, dipped in beaten eggs, then fried in butter, and served with currant jelly or honey; *cruchades* (in the Landes) or *millas* (in the Languedoc), which is simply leftover cornmeal porridge that is fried, then sprinkled with sugar.

But there are other, more esoteric skillet desserts such as *pescajoun aux fruits*, a crêpe batter made with part buckwheat and part wheat flour and fresh diced fruit soaked in liqueur—the batter is lightened with beaten egg whites. Also *clafouti poêlé*, a crêpe batter studded with Italian plums mixed with muscat raisins and scented with rum or *eau-de-vie* or the Limousin version of black cherries or cubes of sugared pumpkin. In the old days this dish was baked in a skillet that was placed, covered, in the embers, and the top covered with more embers; today it is baked in the oven in a baking pan or a skillet.

MIXED FRAGRANCES
Parfums Mélangés

For those who enjoy mixing aromatic concoctions, I offer the following two formulas for use in crêpes, cakes, and pastry cream. The first is a family "secret" of a pharmacist who lived in the Lot-et-Garonne. It is a very delicate combination of Armagnac, anise, lemon essence, orange flower water, and rum. Though the pharmacist gave me this recipe in cubic centimeters, the original required a special cone-shaped glass with a foot for use as a measure. It called for some of the ingredients to be placed in the glass, for sufficient rum to coat the insides of this glass, which was then to be filled to the top with orange flower water, after which the mixture had to be stirred.

The second combination is a simple, straightforward Basque mixture.

1/4 teaspoon lemon essence* or 1 teaspoon lemon extract
1/4 teaspoon anise essence* or 1 teaspoon anise extract
1 tablespoon Armagnac
2 teaspoons vanilla extract*
3 tablespoons dark rum
3 ounces French orange flower water*

*Available by mail from Dean & DeLuca (see Appendix).

Mix ingredients in a clean jar, cover tightly, and keep in a cool cupboard or refrigerator.

Basque Aromatic Mixture

2 tablespoons orange flower water
2 tablespoons anisette
2 tablespoons dark rum
1/4 cup Armagnac

1 teaspoon almond extract
1 strip untreated lemon or orange peel

Mix ingredients in a clean jar, cover tightly, and keep in a cool cupboard or refrigerator.

CUSTARD AND FRESH FRUIT BAKED IN A SKILLET
Clafouti Poêlé aux Fruits Frais

The easiest and homiest of desserts, this *clafouti*, when lukewarm, can be slipped out of the baking pan or skillet for an attractive presentation, if desired (see Note 1). It can be served lukewarm or cold.

SERVES 4
(MADE IN 8-INCH SKILLET OR
BAKING PAN)*
ACTIVE WORK: 20 minutes
BAKING TIME: 40 minutes

1 pound small cherries or apricots, or about 14 black Italian plums, washed and carefully dried
1 tablespoon unsalted butter
1 1/2 tablespoons unbleached all-purpose flour
Pinch of salt
2 tablespoons granulated sugar
2 eggs
1 egg yolk
1 cup milk, heated and kept warm
3/4 teaspoon vanilla extract
2 tablespoons *eau-de-vie*, Armagnac, or dark rum
Confectioners' sugar

*For a 9 1/2 or 10-inch baking dish or skillet, use 1 1/2 times the fruit and double the remaining ingredients. Bake 5 minutes longer.

1. Preheat the oven to 350° F.
2. Stem and, if desired, pit the cherries, or halve and pit the apricots or plums. Roll fruit in kitchen towel or paper towels to dry.
3. Butter skillet or baking dish. Arrange fresh fruit in 1 layer. Plums or apricots can be slanted and overlapping if desired.
4. In a mixing bowl, combine flour, salt, and sugar. Combine eggs, egg yolk, and milk, whisking to blend thoroughly. Gradually stir into the flour mixture until well

blended. Add flavorings. Strain over the fruit and set skillet in the oven. Bake 40 minutes or until set.

5. Cool on a rack until ready to serve. *Do not unmold until lukewarm.* Turn onto a flat sheet, then invert onto a serving platter. Lightly dust with confectioners' sugar just before serving.

NOTES TO THE COOK
1. If substituting juicy red or black plums, do not unmold.
2. One of my favorite combinations in summer is 1/3 cup muscat raisins soaked in Armagnac mixed with pitted and halved red plums. I mix half the sugar with the butter in a heavy black skillet, allow the fruit to lightly caramelize in it, then strain over the custard mixture. I serve the *clafouti* directly from the skillet.

SOUFFLÉ OMELET WITH FRESH FRUITS
Soufflé Poêlée aux Fruits

One of the lightest and simplest skillet desserts is a soufflé omelet. One starts out as if making a standard soufflé omelet, shaking the skillet over the heat as the bottom of the omelet cooks. But when the omelet begins to rise around the sides, it is strewn with assorted fresh fruits, and then placed in the oven where it continues to rise like a soufflé. It will rise in about five minutes in a rustic, wavy manner. It is neither omelet nor soufflé, but rather an extremely light dessert, excellent when served with a scattering of fruits.

Almost any sort of fruit can be used, depending on the season: apples macerated with sugar and rum; prunes cooked in a thick black syrup laced with Armagnac after being plumped in lukewarm tea; strawberries heated with sugar, allowed to caramelize, then flamed with kirsch; or oranges caramelized in butter and sugar, then flamed with Grand Marnier.

SERVES 2 OR 3
ACTIVE WORK: 10 minutes
COOKING TIME: 6 minutes

    3 tablespoons unsalted butter
4 1/2 tablespoons sugar
1 1/4 cups peeled, diced, or sliced fresh fruit: oranges, pears, peaches,
        assorted berries, drained and juices reserved (do not use pineapple)
    2 tablespoons Grand Marnier, dark rum, kirsch, Cognac, or Armagnac
    3 egg yolks at room temperature
    4 egg whites at room temperature
      Pinch of salt
      Confectioners' sugar

1. 30 MINUTES BEFORE SERVING, preheat oven to 425° F.

2. In a small skillet, heat 1 tablespoon of the butter over medium heat; add 1 tablespoon sugar and stir to blend. When the butter and sugar begin to caramelize, add the fruit and toss gently to coat. Cook 30 seconds. Add 1 tablespoon of the liqueur and ignite, shaking pan gently until flames subside. Remove skillet from heat and set aside. (*This can be done in advance and reheated*.)

3. With an electric beater, beat the egg yolks with 2 tablespoons sugar until thick and whitened, not less than 5 minutes. Add remaining tablespoon liqueur and beat 1 minute longer.

4. Separately—and preferably at the same time—beat the egg whites with a pinch of salt until foamy. Gradually add 1 1/2 tablespoons sugar, and continue beating until whites are stiff but not dry.

5. Whisk 1 heaping tablespoon of whites into the yolk mixture, then gently fold in the remaining whites. Blend gently but thoroughly. The mixture should be firm but foamy.

6. In a 9- or 10-inch ovenproof skillet, preferably of copper, melt remaining 2 tablespoons butter over medium heat until sizzling. Scrape in the egg mixture and let it set for an instant. Gently smooth the surface with a spatula. Lower heat and cook 2 minutes, shaking pan gently back and forth so that the bottom turns golden brown but does not stick. When the omelet begins to rise slightly in the skillet on top of the stove, scatter the fruit on top.

7. Quickly reduce the fruit juices in the small skillet to 2 to 3 tablespoons; sprinkle over the top. Place omelet on upper center oven shelf and bake 5 minutes, or until puffed and golden brown. Dust with confectioners' sugar and serve at once.

NOTE TO THE COOK

Success with this dessert depends upon your pan. You must find one that can go into a hot oven and can also withstand stove-top heat. It must be attractive enough to serve in, too. A copper skillet will do beautifully; a good heavy black iron skillet will appeal to those who like the homespun look. Do not use a pan with wooden handles.

BATTER CAKE WITH FRESH PEARS FROM THE CORRÈZE
Flaugnarde

"It's our best dessert," says Albert Parveaux, proprietor of the Château de Castel Novel. He is speaking of the *flaugnarde* of Corrèze, a superb soufflélike fruit cake similar to a German apple pancake. "But," he adds, "its simplicity is misunderstood by some of our guests who think complexity is the same thing as excellence." He explained the true secrets of a successful *flaugnarde:* "First, never put sugar into it the way they do in the Périgord, because it won't rise on account of the extra weight. Second, be sure to use a metal dish since metal heats up quicker and thus will give the batter a better rise. Third, only fill the pan to one third of its height—the *flaugnarde* will thus have room to rise, and it will in fact fill the pan when baked."

You must eat this *flaugnarde* while hot, though it will hold its rise as long as 10 minutes. When serving, slip it out of its pan onto a serving plate; then dust heavily with granulated sugar. You can substitute a straight-sided skillet to cook this.

SERVES 4

ACTIVE WORK: 20 minutes
BAKING TIME: 45 to 50 minutes

> **3 eggs**
> **7 ounces (about 1 1/2 cups) unbleached all-purpose flour, or 1/5 cake flour and 4/5 unbleached all-purpose flour**
> **Pinch of salt**
> **1 cup milk, warmed**
> **1 tablespoon dark rum**
> **2 tasty sweet pears such as Comice or Anjou**
> **2 1/2 tablespoons unsalted butter**
> **Superfine sugar**

1. 2 TO 3 1/2 HOURS BEFORE SERVING, lightly beat the eggs in a mixing bowl. Sift the flour and salt; add to the eggs, stirring. Add 2 tablespoons warm milk and mix until the egg-flour mixture is completely smooth. Gradually stir in the remaining milk and rum; strain through a fine sieve and let stand 1 to 2 1/2 hours.

2. 1 HOUR BEFORE SERVING, preheat the oven to 450° F.

3. Peel, core, halve, and thinly slice the pear (the 3 mm slicing disk attachment of a food processor is perfect for the job). Lavishly butter a straight-sided 8- or 9-inch cake pan (use half the butter). Pour in the batter and delicately lay fruit slices on top, then scatter bits of remaining butter over all. Bake on lower oven shelf 15 minutes, then lower oven heat to 400° F. and bake 30 to 35 minutes, or until well puffed and golden brown.

4. Use a spatula around the edges and under the *flaugnarde* to loosen. Lift out onto a serving dish. Sprinkle lavishly with sugar and serve within 5 minutes.

FARMHOUSE CRÊPES WITH SOUTH-WEST FRAGRANCE
Crêpes Fermières

Crêpes in the South-West are flavored with any one of the various fragrances popular in the region: orange flower water, anisette, rum, lemon, Armagnac, prune *eau-de-vie,* cherry laurel leaves, Cognac, vanilla, almond, or combinations.

For light crêpes, allow the batter to rest a few hours before cooking. Perfect crêpes are thin, light, and dry, yet supple enough to roll. The secret of these Farmhouse Crêpes is to strain the batter so that it is perfectly smooth.

A country method for greasing the crêpe pan is to skewer half a potato or apple flat side out, dip it into melted fat, and use it as an applicator.

SERVES 4 TO 6
(MAKES 2 CUPS BATTER, ENOUGH TO MAKE ABOUT 18 CRÊPES)
ACTIVE WORK: 15 minutes

    4 1/2 ounces (about 1 cup) unbleached all-purpose flour, sifted
      3 whole eggs
    3/4 cup milk
      2 tablespoons unsalted butter, at room temperature
    1/8 teaspoon fine salt
      3 tablespoons mixed fragrances: combine 2 tablespoons Pernod, 2 1/2
          teaspoons French orange flower water, 1/2 teaspoon almond extract,
          and finely grated rind of 1/2 lemon
 1 1/2 tablespoons superfine sugar
      1 tablespoon clarified butter (see Appendix) or rendered fat
          Granulated sugar and lemon wedges, or homemade jams, and 3/4 cup
          crushed walnuts, blended with enough sweetened whipped cream to
          make a sauce

1. 3 1/2 HOURS BEFORE SERVING, With an electric beater or with a hand whisk, slowly blend flour and eggs.

2. Meanwhile gently heat milk with the butter until butter is melted. Add salt, flavorings, and superfine sugar to the warmed milk. Slowly add milk to the egg-flour mixture. Mix until well blended, then strain so that it will be absolutely smooth. Let rest at least 3 hours in a cool place.

3. Heat a 5- or 6-inch iron crêpe pan or a nonstick omelet pan and grease with butter or fat. Wipe out with a paper towel, leaving only a film of shiny grease. With a ladle or a large spoon, stir up the batter to recombine. Add about 2 1/2 tablespoons of the batter to the hot pan. Lift and tip pan so that batter covers the bottom completely. Shake out excess. Cook over medium heat until underside is lightly browned and the edges become almost transparent. (Be careful, because crêpes made with sugar can burn rather than brown.) Flip or use a small, thin-bladed spatula to turn crêpe over; cook on the second side. As the crêpes cook, stack and keep warm on a plate set over simmering water. Cover with foil and keep hot until ready to serve.

4. To serve, sprinkle each crêpe with granulated sugar and serve with lemon wedge, *or* spread with homemade jam and roll up and sprinkle with sugar, *or* serve stacked with layers of crushed walnuts mixed with sweetened whipped cream. Serve this last version cold, sliced in wedges. (To make ahead, stack in piles of 8 with sheets of waxed paper in between. Keeps 1 to 2 days wrapped in foil in the refrigerator. Reheat, wrapped in foil, in a 300° F. oven 10 to 15 minutes.)

COVERED PIES AND CAKES
CROUSTADES, *PASTIS*, *TOURTIÈRES*

The pastry-covered pie, called croustade in Languedoc and Guyenne, *pastis* (*postis* in dialect) in Quercy and the Périgord, and *tourtière* in Tarn and the Landes, is basically the same dish: paper-thin sheets of pastry brushed lightly with clarified butter or goose fat and wrapped about a sweetened fruit filling, shaped according to the custom of the region, then baked.

The different shapes are interesting. In Quercy the *pastis* is rolled up like strudel, then shaped into a serpentine coil. (In Languedoc the same cake shaped in this fashion is called *en cabessal*—the word means the strip of cloth wound into a spiral and placed flat on a woman's head to enable her to carry pitchers of water or baskets of grapes.) In the Landes a *tourtière* is a flattened disk (a *pastis*, in this region, refers to a kugelhupf-style cake). And in Gascony the croustade (or *pastis* in patois) is shaped like "a giant overblown tea rose," a description coined by the food writer Anne Penton in *Customs and Cookery in the Périgord and Quercy*.

The names can mean very different things in different regions. *Pastis* in Gascony and Quercy may be an apple cake in strudel-type dough, but in the Landes it is a brioche-type cake flavored with anise and rum. And *tourtière* in the Landes is an apple cake in a strudel-type dough, but in Quercy it is a chicken and salsify pie in a *pâte brisée*-type dough made with pork fat taken from around the kidneys.

Whatever it is called, the pastry is considered so intricate and awesome that few regional bakers, including professionals, ever bother to make it. Local women guard the secret carefully, selling their homemade version to bakeshops, charcuteries, and personal clients. In fact, the pastry is exactly the same as strudel dough (Greek phyllo dough—available frozen or, better yet, fresh nearly everywhere in the United States—makes a fine substitute). If you want to make your own, using the food processor, see Index for recipe for Croustade Dough. It really isn't difficult at all.

How did these fragile pastry leaves come to be made in France? French gastronomic historians insist they are related to the pastry in the Moroccan *bisteeya* or *pastilla*, the magnificent pie of pigeon meat, almonds, lemons, eggs, cinnamon and myriad other spices introduced to Spain during the time of the Moorish conquest and brought into France as far as the gates of Poitiers. There are many other evidences of Moorish culinary influences in South-West France: the preserving of meat as *confit* (the Moroccans preserve red-fleshed meat in exactly the same way and call it *khlea*); anise-flavored bread; orange flower water flavoring for cakes; the use of cinnamon and nutmeg in chicken dishes; saffron-flavored tripe and poultry dishes; small almond-flavored cookies; prunes and quince in rich meat stews; fish with spices, onions, and raisins; and meat, fish, and poultry dishes smothered in onion marmalade.

The best Gascon croustade (*pastis*) I ever tasted was made by a woman from the Gascon town of Eauze. She mixed cooked apples with prunes that had been marinated in Armagnac for six months. This created the following recipe. If the decoration of "petals" atop the croustade seems too complicated, simply wrap the fruit in the dough, bake it, and call it a *tourtière Landaise*. Serve it lukewarm. In Gascony long, thin scissors are used to cut this cake into wedges.

PASTRY CAKE FILLED WITH APPLES AND PRUNES IN ARMAGNAC
Croustade de Pommes et de Pruneaux à la Gasconne
(Pastis Gascon)

SERVES 6 OR 7
ACTIVE WORK: 20 minutes
COOKING TIME: 20 minutes
BAKING TIME: 35 minutes

   2 1/2 **pounds Granny Smith or Pippin apples, pared, cored, and thickly**
         sliced
   1/2 **cup plus 6 tablespoons granulated sugar**
     1 **vanilla bean, split**
     2 **thin pieces lemon peel**
       Orange flower water
       Armagnac
    30 **Prunes in Armagnac* (see Index), plus about 5 tablespoons**
         prune-Armagnac syrup
     1 **recipe Croustade Dough, or 9 or 10 strudel or phyllo leaves (see Note 1)**
   1/3 **cup clarified butter, melted**
       Confectioners' sugar
*Preferably prunes that have soaked in Armagnac at least 15 days.

1. In a heavy 4-quart pot or casserole cook the apples, covered, with 1/2 cup sugar, vanilla bean, and lemon peel over very low heat until soft, about 20 minutes (see Note 2).

2. Pit the prunes. Cut into small pieces and let soak in 4 tablespoons of prune-Armagnac syrup until ready to use.

3. Mix 2 tablespoons butter with 1/2 teaspoon orange flower water, 1 tablespoon sugar, 2 teaspoons prune-Armagnac syrup, and 2 teaspoons Armagnac. Set aside to flavor and sprinkle the "flowers." *Can be prepared 1 day ahead up to this point.*

4. 2 TO 3 HOURS BEFORE SERVING, assemble and bake the cake. Place baking stone or heavy baking sheet on lowest oven rack. Preheat oven to 400° F. Lightly brush a 15-inch round pan (preferably with black finish, but a pizza pan will do) with a tablespoon of the remaining butter.

(continued)

5. If using homemade Croustade Dough, cut into 9 equal-sized leaves; stack them. Unroll strudel or phyllo leaves in front of you and cover with a damp towel. Working quickly (pastry dries out fast when exposed to air), brush top leaf lightly with melted butter. Fold in half lengthwise and brush each side lightly with butter. Place one end of folded leaf at center of pan, extending leaf over side of pan (1). Repeat with remaining leaves, placing them spoke fashion so that inner ends are stacked in a hub and outer ends barely touch (2 and 3).

6. Sprinkle dough extending over edge of pan very lightly with some of the reserved scented butter liquid. Place drained pitted prunes in a 10-inch circle in center of pastry. Top with drained cold apples.

7. To enclose filling, start with the last leaf placed on the pan. Lift end of leaf up and bring toward center of filling. Holding end with both hands, twist the leaf end once so that underside faces you. Form end of strip into cup-shaped "petal." Place petal on top of twist, pressing lightly into filling (4). Repeat with remaining leaves in order, placing petals close together to cover top of cake. (Do not worry if a little filling shows through petals.) Sprinkle top very lightly with remaining scented butter liquid, drizzle with remaining butter, and dust with 3 tablespoons granulated sugar (5).

8. Place pan in oven on hot baking stone or baking sheet; bake 12 minutes. Reduce oven temperature to 350° F. Bake 20 to 25 minutes longer, until cake is golden and crisp. Slide cake from pan onto wire rack; sprinkle with 2 tablespoons granulated sugar. Cool to lukewarm. Just before serving, dust with confectioners' sugar.

NOTES TO THE COOK

1. Strudel leaves are stronger and fewer to the pound than phyllo leaves. They do a better job of keeping the "petals" rigid after shaping, but if you can buy only the thinner phyllo leaves, that won't lessen the rustic charm of this wonderful, easy cake. You can order strudel leaves by mail from Dean & DeLuca (see Appendix).

If you prepare the cake early in the day and wish to prevent the bottom layer of pastry from becoming too wet, use stale sponge cake or crustless white bread grated in the food processor between the bottom leaves of the pastry. This makes an excellent foil for absorbing the moisture of the fruit fillings. If the crumbs are soft, toast lightly in the oven or brown in butter until golden and crisp. Mix 1/2 cup stale sponge cake crumbs or dried bread crumbs with 2 tablespoons sugar and sprinkle 1 1/2 teaspoons of this mixture between each pastry layer after buttering. Scatter remaining crumbs over the top leaf. Add the prunes and apples and finish assembling the cake.

2. For an intense apple flavor: Slice apples and mix with sugar and lemon peel. With a small sharp knife, scrape vanilla seeds from bean and add to apples. Vacuum-pack in a boilable pouch (see Appendix—"Notes on Equipment"). Cook 20 minutes in boiling water to cover. Remove and drop into icy slush until cold. Keep apples in pouch 1 to 2 days in refrigerator, if necessary. Drain off liquid before using.

CROUSTADE WITH QUINCE AND PRUNES
Croustade de Languedoc

This croustade, an enclosed pie with a rich, intensely flavored filling of quince and prunes, originates in Languedoc, where it is subtitled *en cabessal* because its shape resembles the coil of cloth that market women wear to carry baskets or jugs on their heads. The pastry, made of strudel-type dough, is brushed lavishly with melted butter and oil so that when it is curved into a coil it will not crack or break.

In my version I have substituted a light, flaky, thin pastry dough for the strudel type, and have shaped the croustade into a simple round. If you want to make a coil with large sheets of commercial strudel dough or homemade Croustade Dough, you will find special directions below.

This croustade is beloved in the Languedoc for its special aroma and taste. Quince preserve (rather than jelly) is full of flavor and texture. The taste of quince is tangy and balances the sweetness of the prunes.

SERVES 6 TO 8

☆ Begin 1 day in advance
  ACTIVE WORK (DAY 1): 15 to 20 minutes
  COOKING TIME (DAY 1): 20 minutes
  ACTIVE WORK (DAY 2): 20 minutes
  BAKING TIME (DAY 2): 40 to 45 minutes   *(continued)*

     1 recipe Pastry for Country-Style *Tourtes* and *Tourtières*
   3/4 pound pitted sweet prunes
     2 cups tea, preferably linden or orange pekoe
   3/4 cup granulated sugar
     1 teaspoon vanilla extract
     1 tablespoon strained fresh lemon juice
   1/2 teaspoon grated lemon rind
1 1/2 tablespoons prune *eau-de-vie*, slivovitz, or Armagnac
     1 cup quince preserve, homemade or Tiptree or Hero brand
       Egg glaze (1 egg yolk mixed with 1 tablespoon milk)
       Confectioners' sugar
       Crème Fraîche or unsweetened whipped cream

1. 1 DAY IN ADVANCE, make the pastry. Soak the prunes in tea until soft; drain. Discard the tea. Make a syrup with sugar and 1 1/2 cups water in a deep saucepan. Bring to a boil, stirring until sugar dissolves; boil 5 minutes. Add the drained prunes. Lower heat and simmer 20 minutes. Remove from heat and cool. Add the vanilla, lemon juice, and lemon rind and let stand until cold.

2. Drain the cold prunes, reserving the liquid. Chop prunes in workbowl of a food processor fitted with the metal blade. Stir in the brandy. Gently heat the quince preserve in a small saucepan until just melted. Stir in one quarter of the prune cooking liquid, mixing well. Allow to cool.

3. EARLY THE FOLLOWING DAY, divide the *tourte* dough into two equal parts. Place each part between two sheets of lightly floured waxed paper. Roll out 1 piece of dough into 11-inch circle. Lift paper from time to time to allow dough to stretch. Peel off top paper. Prick surface all over with the tines of a fork. Turn *upside down* onto a 9- to 10-inch fruit tart pan or into cake pan. Peel off paper. Chill pastry-lined pan while rolling out other half of pastry between waxed paper. Chill second circle of pastry. Discard waxed paper.

4. Spread the cold quince preserve over the bottom of pastry-lined pan, leaving a 1-inch border all around. Brush exposed edges with egg glaze. Top the quince preserve with the prunes in an even layer. Cover the fruit filling with second circle of dough. Crimp the edges to seal.

5. Preheat the oven to 425° F.

6. Brush the top of pie with egg glaze. Decorate with crisscrossing lines and make a few holes on top with the point of a sharp knife so that steam can escape during baking.

7. Bake on lower oven rack 15 minutes. Lower temperature to 350° F. and place pan on upper middle rack; bake 35 minutes longer, or until the pastry is crisp and brown.

8. 10 MINUTES BEFORE THE PASTRY IS DONE, dust top with confectioners' sugar. Continue baking until top is shiny and glazed. Cool on a wire rack. Serve lukewarm or cold with Crème Fraîche or unsweetened whipped cream.

To make the pastry coil with your recipe for homemade strudel or my recipe for Croustade Dough, follow these directions:

1. Place a sheet or tablecloth on a large table; lightly rub with flour. Pull dough on floured sheet as directed in recipe for Croustade Dough.

2. After the dough has dried, brush a mixture of melted butter and oil over all the surface. Fold in half crosswise, then brush the dough again.

3. With a damp spatula spread the prune-quince filling evenly over a strip 2 inches wide and the length of the longer side of the sheet, leaving a 2-inch border at either end.

4. With the aid of the sheet, roll the dough from the long side into a thin jelly roll. Pinch one end to make it small and narrow. Flatten the end slightly, then shape the whole long sausage shape into a coil and tuck in the end. Lavishly brush the exterior of the pastry with melted butter and oil so that it will not crack. Slip onto a buttered baking pan.

5. Preheat the oven to 425° F.

6. Bake 5 minutes. Lower oven temperature to 375° F. and bake 25 minutes longer. Remove from the oven and gently slide onto a rack.

NOTE TO THE COOK
You cannot make this shape with commercial phyllo dough; the sheets are too small. But you can make individual coils. Bake 15 minutes at 375° F.

BASQUE CAKE WITH PASTRY CREAM FILLING
Gâteau Basque

There are as many versions of *Gâteau Basque* as there are people who bake it, and the Basques like nothing better than to sit around and discuss the relative merits of one baker's recipe versus another's. It's like listening to Toulousains talk about cassoulet, Provençals arguing about bouillabaisse, or Alsatians quarreling over choucroute. A combination cake and pie, *Gâteau Basque* is stuffed with pastry cream flavored with almonds, anise, rum, orange flower water, and Armagnac. The town of Itxassou along the Nive River is famous for its black cherries, which make for a most delicious variation. Hero, a Swiss brand of black cherry preserves, is a particularly good substitute.

The dough is a little tricky to make because at first you think you are making a cake batter, then all of a sudden you discover you are making a pie. Actually, if you know how to cream butter with sugar until it is very pale in color and fluffy, and how to roll out a piece of delicate dough, you should have no trouble at all.

SERVES 6 TO 8
☆ Begin 1 day in advance
ACTIVE WORK (DAY 1): 30 minutes
ACTIVE WORK (DAY 2): 20 minutes
BAKING TIME: 45 to 50 minutes

(continued)

> Pastry Cream (recipe below) flavored with 2 tablespoons Basque
>   Aromatic Mixture, chilled
>   6 ounces (about 1 1/4 cups) unbleached all-purpose flour
>   3 ounces (2/3 cup) cake flour
>   1/8 teaspoon salt
>   1 teaspoon double-acting baking powder
>   9 tablespoons unsalted butter, at room temperature
>   9 tablespoons sugar, preferably superfine
>   2 eggs, lightly beaten
>   1 1/2 tablespoons Basque Aromatic Mixture
>   1 teaspoon milk

1. 1 DAY IN ADVANCE, prepare Pastry Cream. To make the dough, sift flours, salt, and baking powder into a bowl. Set aside. With a wooden spoon or an electric mixer, cream the butter until fluffy. Gradually add the sugar by spoonfuls. Cream together until very light and fluffy. The mixture must not feel granular.

2. Set aside 2 tablespoons beaten egg for glazing the gâteau. Add the remaining eggs to butter and sugar by spoonfuls, beating well between additions to blend completely. If using an electric mixer, add eggs at low speed. Add the Basque Aromatic Mixture *and one quarter of the sifted flour.* Fold in remaining flour and gather into a ball. Do not overmix or knead the dough. It will be very sticky and soft. Dust lightly with flour and invert into a wide soup bowl. Wrap in waxed paper. Let rest overnight in the refrigerator.

3. EARLY THE FOLLOWING DAY, divide the dough into 2 unequal parts, one slightly larger than the other. Roll out the larger portion into a 10-inch round between sheets of lightly floured waxed paper. (Loosen paper from time to time to facilitate rolling.) Remove top sheet of paper and invert dough into 8-inch cake pan; line bottom and sides. Peel off paper; if pastry tears, use edges to repair or pinch torn pastry together. Trim edges and fill with pastry cream. Roll out smaller ball of dough into an 8-inch round. Remove paper and invert onto filling; crimp edges. Chill completely.

4. Preheat oven to 425° F. Place a baking sheet or tile on lowest oven rack.

5. Brush pastry with reserved beaten egg diluted with 1 teaspoon milk. Make crisscrossing marks on top with the back of the tines of a fork. Make 3 slashes for escaping steam. Place on heated baking sheet or hot tile. Immediately lower oven temperature to 375° F. and bake 45 to 50 minutes, or until cake is a light golden brown.

6. Remove to a rack and let cool 10 minutes. Invert out of pan and invert again onto a rack to cool completely. The cake will harden as it cools. Serve at room temperature, cut in wedges.

VARIATION I

Itxassou version: Substitute 12 ounces (1 jar) black (bing) cherry preserves (preferably Hero brand) for Pastry Cream.

VARIATION II

Mixed Pastry Cream and preserves: Place 1 1/3 cups Basque Aromatic Mixture-flavored Pastry Cream on pastry; cover with layer of black cherry preserves (about 1/2 cup, gently heated in order to spread easily over the Pastry Cream).

Inspired by a recipe of Rosalie Muruamendiaraz of the Restaurant Euskalduna in Bayonne.

Pastry Cream
Crème Pâtissière

MAKES 1 1/3 CUPS

ACTIVE WORK: 20 minutes

> **1 cup milk**
> **3-inch vanilla bean, split, or 1/2 teaspoon vanilla extract**
> **Pinch of salt**
> **3 1/2 tablespoons superfine sugar**
> **3 egg yolks**
> **4 teaspoons cornstarch**
> **2 tablespoons heavy cream**
> **1 tablespoon unsalted butter**
> **1 tablespoon flavoring (use Basque Aromatic Mixture for *Gâteau Basque*)**

1. Bring the milk to a boil with the vanilla bean, if using, in a small saucepan. Cover and set aside.

2. Place salt, sugar, and egg yolks in a mixing bowl; beat until pale yellow and thick. Beat in the cornstarch and vanilla extract, if using; beat until smooth.

3. If using vanilla bean, remove it from the hot milk. Gradually beat the hot milk into the egg yolk mixture. Pour into clean saucepan, set over medium heat, and cook, stirring constantly, until boiling. Continue to stir vigorously until the custard is no longer lumpy, about 1 to 2 minutes. Remove from heat and continue to beat vigorously 30 seconds longer. Pour through a strainer into a bowl.

4. Stir in cream, butter, and flavoring. Stir from time to time as the Pastry Cream cools. Place a sheet of buttered waxed paper directly on the cream to inhibit the formation of a skin. Chill.

WALNUT CAKE FROM MASSEUBE
Tarte aux Noix à la Masseube

Provence, the Savoy, and Dauphiné all have their regional walnut cakes, as do the Périgord and the Dordogne. This rich, rustic version comes from the Gascon town of Masseube. The walnuts are cooked in a toffeelike mixture and baked in a sugar crust that appears to be wavy rather than flat. Plain granulated sugar is sprinkled on top. This cake keeps about a week if well wrapped in foil and kept in a cool, dry place (not the refrigerator). It is excellent with vanilla ice cream, unsweetened Crème Fraîche, and sliced fresh fruit or berries. This cake is extremely rich—plan on serving very thin slices. The filling can be doubled for a thicker cake. The cake improves in flavor, so make it at least 3 days in advance.

SERVES 10

ACTIVE WORK: 30 minutes
BAKING TIME: 35 minutes

> 1 **recipe Sugar Crust**
> **Flour**
> 1 **cup plus 1 1/2 tablespoons granulated sugar**
> 1/2 **cup milk or light cream, heated**
> 1/2 **pound walnuts, fresh shelled or from a vacuum-packed can, chopped**
> **to the size of small blueberries and warmed 5 minutes in a dry skillet**
> **or the oven before using**
> 7 **tablespoons unsalted butter, at room temperature**
> **Egg glaze (1 egg yolk mixed with 1 tablespoon milk)**
> **Granulated sugar for the topping**

1. Make the Sugar Crust dough; divide into two unequal parts, one slightly larger than the other. Chill a minimum of 3 hours—even better, overnight.

2. Roll out the larger round between two sheets of lightly floured waxed paper. (Loosen paper from time to time to facilitate rolling.) Peel off top paper and fit dough round into a 9- or 9 1/2-inch tart pan with a removable bottom. Pastry will be thin. Set in the freezer for 1 hour. Roll out remaining round between sheets of lightly floured waxed paper to make a perfect round 11 to 12 inches in diameter. Place on flat sheet and keep chilled in the refrigerator until ready to use.

3. Preheat the oven to 450° F.

4. In a heavy, deep 4-quart pot, preferably stainless steel-lined copper, aluminum, or a copper preserving pan, heat the sugar and 1/3 cup water; bring to a boil over medium heat, stirring until sugar dissolves. Raise heat and cook, covered, 2 to 3 minutes; then lower heat, uncover, and cook without stirring until light caramel. Gently swirl the pan from time to time to even out the color as it develops, about 10 minutes. Then immediately remove from heat.

5. As soon as it stops boiling, gradually stir in the hot milk (be very careful because mixture bubbles up considerably). When all the milk has been added, stir in the warm walnuts and butter. Return to medium heat and cook, stirring, at a slow boil for 4 to 5 minutes. The temperature of the mixture should remain at 240° F. on a candy thermometer.

6. Meanwhile line a baking sheet with foil, shiny side down, and set on the lowest oven rack. Remove the now nearly frozen shell from the freezer. Carefully pour the hot walnut mixture into the shell. Immediately brush edges with egg glaze and place the reserved cold second pastry round on top. Press all around to seal. Top will be bubbly and become wavy. Brush it lightly with egg glaze; pierce once or twice in the center and set on the hot baking sheet in the oven. Immediately lower oven temperature to 400° F. and bake 15 minutes.

7. Remove the cake from the oven and brush a second time with glaze. Sprinkle very lightly with granulated sugar and lower oven temperature to 300° F. Bake 20 minutes longer or until top is golden brown. Remove and cool on a rack at least 4 hours before wrapping. Keep wrapped in foil in an airtight container.

NOTE TO THE COOK
When Annie, the then pastry chef at André Daguin's restaurant, first gave me this recipe I was a little apprehensive about pouring a hot walnut mixture onto raw pastry dough. Seeing my disbelief, she very kindly decided to teach me the three important tricks for success. Once you know them, it's a cinch to make: (1) the milk must be *hot* when you add it to the caramel; (2) the filling must cook to the soft-ball stage on a candy thermometer (234°–240° F.); and (3) the pastry dough must be ice-cold when the hot walnut filling is added to it.

MADELEINES FROM DAX
Madeleines de Dax

These soft, spongy, buttery madeleines are not the same as the *madeleines de Commercy*, which one finds elsewhere, or the *génoise* type that appear in so many cookbooks, or, for that matter, the dunking type described so vividly and nostalgically by Marcel Proust. These lovely South-West-style madeleines are more like little cakes, in the traditional shape (like a shell on one side; with an adorable hump on the other), flavored with lemon rind or orange flower water. These are delicious served with sorbets, homemade jams, and fruit compotes, or simply eaten without any accompaniment at all.

The patron saint of the Landais town of Mont-de-Marsan is Ste. Madeleine, and in the neighboring town of Dax madeleines have been famous for many years. Both towns hold madeleine bake-offs, and recipes vary widely. At Michel Guérard's Eugénie-les-Bains establishment, the madeleines served for breakfast are actually closer to slices of orange-flavored chiffon cake.

(continued)

I learned this recipe from a young male baker who gave me the recipe in "egg weights"—the old way of setting culinary proportions. ("Egg weights" are determined by weighing an egg, then weighing out the flour, sugar, and butter using the weight of the egg as a constant. If you visualize an old-fashioned fulcrum-type balance scale, the method makes more sense.)

MAKES ABOUT 18 3-INCH CAKES OR
24 2-INCH CAKES
☆ Begin 1 day in advance
   ACTIVE WORK (DAY 1): 10 minutes
   BAKING TIME (DAY 2): 12 to 15 minutes

> 2 "large" eggs
> Pinch of salt
> 7 tablespoons superfine sugar
> 1 1/2 teaspoons orange flower water
> 1 teaspoon pure vanilla extract
> 5 1/2 tablespoons unbleached all-purpose flour plus 5 1/2 tablespoons cake flour, combined and sifted twice
> 3/4 teaspoon double acting baking powder
> 5 tablespoons clarified butter (see Appendix), melted and cooled
> 2 tablespoons heavy cream
> 1 tablespoon softened unsalted butter

1. 1 DAY IN ADVANCE, in a mixing bowl combine the eggs, salt, and sugar. Beat with a whisk until thick and light. Add the orange flower water and the vanilla extract; whisk to combine.

2. Sift the flours with the baking powder. Gradually stir into the egg-sugar mixture. *Do not overbeat.* Add the butter and the cream; stir gently until smooth. Cover with plastic wrap and let stand in the refrigerator overnight.

3. THE FOLLOWING DAY, preheat the oven to 425° F.

4. Coat the ridged hollows of the madeleine pan with softened butter using a pastry brush. (It is not necessary to dust with flour.) Use a teaspoon and a small spatula to barely fill each hollow with batter—about two thirds full. Tap the mold on the table to allow batter to settle. (It is not necessary to smooth the surface or fill the bottom of each hollow.)

5. Bake on upper middle oven rack 5 minutes. Lower oven temperature to 325° F. and bake 7 to 10 minutes longer.

6. When the madeleines are golden and just turning brown around the edges, remove from oven. Use the tip of a knife at the base of each to turn out onto wire racks to cool. Serve warm and freshly baked with fruit compotes, sorbets, and granitas. Leftover madeleines may be stored in an airtight tin and reheated gently before serving.

NOTES TO THE COOK

The batter *must* be made a day in advance so that the proteins in the flour can relax, and the madeleines will be very tender when baked.

You can bake a batch of fresh madeleines each day (storing the unused batter in the refrigerator), or cook them in relays if you have only one mold with 6, 8, or 12 shapes.

Madeleine pans should never be scrubbed with harsh abrasives. Harshly abrased pans cause madeleines to bake up very pale on the ridged sides.

FRUIT

ROAST FIGS IN THE STYLE OF THE PYRENEES
Figues Rôties

During September and October, when small purple figs are available, you can transform them into these cool, sweet, peppery delights—crunchy on the outside, softly melting on the inside.

SERVES 6

ACTIVE WORK: 10 minutes
BAKING TIME: 30 minutes

 1 tablespoon unsalted butter
18 small purple figs, slightly overripe
 4 tablespoons plus 1 teaspoon sugar
1/2 cup shelled walnuts
 1 tablespoon honey
   Juice of 1 lemon
 2 or 3 turns of the pepper mill
   Crème Fraîche

1. Preheat the oven to 400° F.

2. Butter a shallow, flameproof baking dish. Place figs in it side by side, stems up. Sprinkle with 4 tablespoons of the sugar and 1 tablespoon water. Bake on center oven rack 20 minutes, basting figs from time to time with the syrupy juices in the dish.

3. Add the walnuts and sprinkle with remaining 1 teaspoon sugar. Lower oven temperature to 300° F. and bake 10 minutes longer.

4. Carefully transfer figs and walnuts to serving dish. Add honey to cooking juices. Set on top of stove and cook, stirring, over low heat to blend. Spoon syrup over figs. Sprinkle with lemon juice and pepper. Serve cold with Crème Fraîche.

FRESH STRAWBERRIES WITH PEPPERCORNS AND RED WINE

Fraises au Poivre et au Vin Rouge

I found this dessert described in a little Landais cookbook. The recipe called for a touch of cinnamon. I have substituted freshly ground black pepper—not a modern conceit, since the combination of fruit with peppercorns is traditional in the South-West (see Index for Preserved Spiced Pears in Red Wine with Armagnac).

SERVES 4 TO 6
ACTIVE WORK: 10 minutes

2 pints fresh strawberries
Granulated sugar
Red wine
Squeeze of lemon juice
4–6 turns of the pepper mill

1. Wipe the strawberries if they are sandy. Hull and sprinkle with sugar; let stand 2 hours in a serving dish at room temperature.
2. Sprinkle with red wine and more sugar. Let stand 20 to 30 minutes longer.
3. Just before serving, add a sprinkling of lemon juice and fresh pepper with a few turns of the pepper mill for all.

PRUNES IN SAUTERNES

Pruneaux au Sauternes

Though prunes cooked in red wine is a more famous preparation, prunes in Sauternes is more delicious and requires less sugar. The luscious, nectarlike fruitiness and enormous fullness of Sauternes, combined with the flavor of prunes, make this an exceptional dessert. Served with Madeleines from Dax, it makes a spectacular yet understated ending to a meal.

The flavor improves enormously if this dessert is prepared two to three days in advance. A great Sauternes is not needed to make this special dessert.

SERVES 4
☆ Prepare 2 to 3 days in advance
ACTIVE WORK: 5 minutes
COOKING TIME: 10 minutes

12 ounces sweet pitted prunes
2 cups Sauternes wine

1/2 **vanilla bean, split down one side**
  2 **tablespoons sugar**
    2-inch piece lemon rind
  1 **cinnamon stick**

1. 2 TO 3 DAYS BEFORE SERVING, soak the prunes in the wine for half a day.

2. Scrape seeds from vanilla bean. Rub seeds with the sugar to separate. Simmer prunes in the wine with the vanilla-sugar, the scraped vanilla bean, lemon rind, and cinnamon stick for 10 minutes. Cool completely; chill.

3. Serve cool.

POACHED FIGS IN RASPBERRY AND RED WINE SAUCE
Figues Pochées au Vin Rouge et au Coulis de Framboise

A cook I know once told me there is a wine for every fruit to bring out its flavor; there is Riesling for nectarines; Sauternes for prunes, and red wine for red berries, pears, and black fresh figs.

SERVES 6
ACTIVE WORK: 20 minutes

    1 **pint fresh raspberries, or 1 package frozen unsweetened raspberries, thawed**
2 1/2 **tablespoons strained fresh lemon juice**
  3/4 **cup superfine sugar**
    1 **bottle red wine, preferably a Bordeaux**
12–18 **slightly underripe small black mission (purple) figs**
    1 **orange**

1. In the workbowl of a food processor fitted with the metal blade, purée raspberries with lemon juice and 1/3 cup of the sugar for 2 minutes. Remove and push through a sieve. Discard seeds.

2. Place purée in a wide, nonaluminum saucepan. Add red wine and remaining sugar; bring to a boil. Lower heat and cook, stirring constantly, until sugar is completely dissolved.

3. Poach figs in raspberry-wine syrup over low heat, uncovered, 4 minutes, turning them every minute or so as they cook. Remove figs with a slotted spoon and arrange them in a shallow bowl, stem side up. Reduce poaching liquid to about 1 1/4 cups. Spoon over figs and chill.

4. Make a garnish with the rind of 1 orange. Cut rind into julienne strips. Boil 3 minutes in water; drain and refresh. Drain and pat dry. Decorate the top of each fig with a few strands of orange rind.

NOTE TO THE COOK

The months of September and October are the time that you will find fresh, violet-hued figs at fine greengrocers. It is certainly worth trying this very easy and elegant dish during that time. If figs are not available you can substitute 12 small, peeled, whole peaches. Garnish with a few whole fresh raspberries.

FRUIT TERRINE

Terrine de Fruits à la Mousse de Crème d'Amandes

This dessert is the creation of Firmin Arrambide, a young Basque chef working in St.-Jean-Pied-de-Port, a town of fewer than two thousand people deep in the Pyrenees. Here I learned to make one of the best of the recent "terrines," a jewel-like mosaic of bright fresh fruits arranged in an airy almond cream. The whole is enclosed in a thin casing of Génoise. It is served with two sauces, a thin raspberry sauce and a light Crème Anglaise. The vanilla-flavored Crème Anglaise acts in counterpoint to the tart puréed raspberries. This dessert is not complicated, but you should begin two to three days before serving to allow the flavors to meld and to facilitate slicing. The Génoise for the outside can be baked ahead or even ordered from a local bakery and kept frozen until ready to use. It must be frozen or stale so it can be sliced thin without breaking. The cake slices line the bottom and long sides of a loaf pan, and after the filling is in place, another slice goes on top. If there are any holes or tears, simply patch bits and pieces of Génoise into place; this will not harm the final presentation at all.

When you start to layer the terrine, have your design in mind; choose fruits and their arrangement with consideration for both color and flavor balance. Remember to keep the emphasis on what is seasonal; apart from peaches and apricots, canned or frozen fruits are not suggested. Both the terrine and the sauces can be kept in the refrigerator for two or three days. The colorful drama of the presentation and ease with which this special dessert can be prepared ahead make it perfect for any important dinner.

SERVES 10

☆ Begin 3 days in advance
   ACTIVE WORK (DAY 1): 20 minutes
   BAKING TIME (DAY 1): 25 minutes
   ACTIVE WORK (DAY 2): 1 hour

    Génoise, store-bought or homemade (recipe below)
  3 cups small fresh strawberries, rinsed and dried*
  2 kiwi fruits, pared
  4 poached or canned yellow cling peach halves, drained

Unflavored vegetable oil
Almond Cream (recipe below)
Crème Anglaise (recipe below)
Raspberry Sauce (recipe below)

*Fresh raspberries or blackberries can be substituted for the strawberries. Pears, apricots, and nectarines—all pared, poached, chilled, and drained—and peeled seedless green grapes are other fruit alternatives for the kiwis and peaches.

1. AT LEAST 3 DAYS BEFORE SERVING, make Génoise. Wrap in plastic wrap and freeze, or let stand at room temperature, unwrapped, overnight or until firm enough to slice easily without tearing.

2. 2 TO 3 DAYS BEFORE SERVING, assemble terrine. Hull strawberries. Berries should be of uniform size, less than 1 inch from base to tip. If berries are uneven or larger in size, trim at base. Cut each kiwi lengthwise into 6 even wedges; pat dry with paper towels. Cut each peach half lengthwise into 4 wedges; pat dry with paper towels.

3. Lightly oil an 8 1/2 × 4 1/2 × 2 5/8-inch loaf pan (6-cup). Line bottom and long sides of pan with a sheet of plastic wrap, leaving a 5-inch overhang on each side. Lightly oil the plastic wrap.

4. Cut Génoise in half to make 2 pieces, each 8 × 4 inches. With large, sharp knife shave off brown crust from all surfaces of cake and discard. Carefully slice each piece horizontally into 3 thin even layers, each about 1/4 inch thick. Choose 4 best layers; reserve remaining 2 layers for another use. Place 1 layer of Génoise in bottom of lined loaf pan; trim layer if necessary to fit snugly in pan. Use 2 more layers to line sides of pan, extending about 1 inch above top. Reserve fourth layer for top. (Short sides of pan are not lined with cake.)

5. Make the Almond Cream.

6. With a rubber spatula, spread 2/3 cup Almond Cream in bottom of Génoise-lined pan. Arrange half the strawberries stem side down in a single layer over the filling, making short, even rows. Spoon 2/3 cup of the Almond Cream over the berries; pack gently to fill spaces and smooth top. Top with kiwi wedges and peaches arranged lengthwise in a single layer. Cover with 2/3 cup Almond Cream. Arrange remaining strawberries on top, stem side up in a single layer. Top with remaining Almond Cream; pack gently to fill spaces and smooth top. Cover with the fourth layer of Génoise; press lightly into cream. Fold up overhanging plastic wrap to cover tightly. Refrigerate at least 1 day to set.

7. Make Crème Anglaise.

8. Make Raspberry Sauce.

9. 20 MINUTES BEFORE SERVING, unmold terrine onto platter; peel off plastic wrap. Remove Crème Anglaise and Raspberry Sauce from refrigerator. Let stand 15 minutes to develop flavors. Just before serving, with a long, sharp, thin-bladed knife cut terrine crosswise into 1/2-inch slices. Place slice flat in center of large individual dessert plate; ladle spoonfuls of Raspberry Sauce and Crème Anglaise around sides of slice. Pass remaining Crème Anglaise separately.

Génoise

MAKES ONE 9-INCH-SQUARE LAYER,
ABOUT 1 INCH HIGH

ACTIVE WORK: 20 minutes
BAKING TIME: 25 minutes

Unsalted butter and all-purpose flour for the pan
4 large eggs, at room temperature
1/2 cup superfine sugar
3 tablespoons clarified unsalted butter, cooled to tepid
1 1/2 teaspoons vanilla extract
1/2 teaspoon grated lemon zest (optional)
2 ounces (1/2 cup) sifted all-purpose flour
3 tablespoons sifted cake flour

1. Preheat the oven to 350° F.

2. Lightly butter a 8 1/2 × 8 1/2 × 2-inch cake pan. Line bottom with waxed paper, then lightly butter and flour pan; tap out excess.

3. Place eggs and sugar in large metal mixing bowl. Whisk to break up yolks. Set bowl over hot—not boiling—water over very low heat. Stir often with whisk until eggs are warm (100°) to the touch, about 5 minutes. Remove bowl from over water. Beat eggs and sugar with electric mixer at high speed until mixture begins to thicken, then reduce speed to medium. Beat until mixture is cooled, tripled in volume, and forms slowly dissolving ribbon when beater is lifted from bowl (4 to 6 minutes; electric hand mixer will take up to 10 minutes).

4. Transfer a spoonful of the egg mixture to a small bowl. Add clarified butter, vanilla, and lemon zest; stir until well blended. Set aside.

5. Mix all-purpose and cake flours. Sift flour, one third at a time, over remaining egg mixture, folding gently with flat spoon or spatula after each addition while rotating bowl until flour is no longer visible. Quickly but gently fold reserved butter-egg mixture into batter. Do not overfold or mixture will deflate, but be sure no spots of flour remain.

6. Pour batter into prepared pan. Tap pan lightly on work surface to settle batter. Bake until cake is springy and golden and edges are beginning to pull away from sides of pan, 20 to 25 minutes. Cool cake in pan on wire rack 10 minutes. Remove from pan; peel off paper. Cool cake on rack.

Almond Cream

MAKES ABOUT 3 1/2 CUPS

ACTIVE WORK: 10 to 15 minutes

3/4 cup plus 2 tablespoons heavy cream, cold
3/4 cup unsalted butter, at room temperature

1 1/3 cups sifted confectioners' sugar
1 1/2 cups (6 ounces) blanched almond meal* or finely ground blanched almonds
    1 tablespoon plus 1 teaspoon Grand Marnier or Cointreau
  1/4 teaspoon pure almond extract

*Blanched almond meal, which yields a fluffy, smooth-textured cream, can be purchased in specialty food shops, or packaged in supermarkets in some areas. Or order by mail from H. Roth & Son (see Appendix).

1. In chilled small bowl of an electric mixer with chilled beater, beat cream until stiff.

2. Beat butter in large bowl until light and fluffy. Gradually beat in sugar until mixture is airy and almost white in color. Beat in almonds, liqueur, and almond extract until blended.

3. Whisk one fourth of the whipped cream into the almond butter with large wire whisk to lighten mixture. Very gently fold remaining whipped cream into almond-butter mixture until just blended. (Do not overfold.)

NOTE TO THE COOK
Whole or slivered blanched almonds can be finely ground manually in a nut grinder. Processing or blending nuts is not recommended because too much oil is extracted, which results in a heavy filling.

Crème Anglaise

MAKES 2 1/2 CUPS
ACTIVE WORK: 15 minutes

  1/2 vanilla bean, split lengthwise, or 1 1/2 teaspoons vanilla extract
    6 tablespoons sugar
    2 cups milk
    1 piece lemon zest (optional)
    5 egg yolks
       Pinch of salt

1. Scrape seeds from vanilla bean. Rub seeds with 1 tablespoon sugar to separate. Set aside.

2. Scald milk with scraped vanilla bean and lemon zest (if using) in heavy-bottomed medium saucepan. (If using vanilla extract rather than bean, stir in *after* custard cools to lukewarm.)

3. Beat egg yolks, vanilla-seed sugar, and remaining sugar in mixing bowl until pale and mixture forms a ribbon when whisk is lifted. Whisk in a pinch of salt.

4. Remove vanilla bean from milk and rinse. (Bean can be left to dry and used to flavor sugar bin.) Discard the lemon zest.

(continued)

5. In a second heavy enameled saucepan, heat the egg mixture over very low heat, stirring constantly. Gradually add the *hot* milk, stirring constantly with a wooden spoon. Cook over low heat, stirring, until the mixture thickens, the back of the spoon is well coated, the froth on the surface has disappeared, and the mixture registers about 165° F. on a candy thermometer (about 10 minutes). *The mixture must not be allowed to boil.* Immediately remove from heat.

6. Strain through a fine sieve into a chilled mixing bowl set over ice. Cool down quickly, stirring constantly. Add vanilla extract, if using. When cold, cover surface with plastic wrap. Refrigerate until needed.

Raspberry Sauce

MAKES ABOUT 1 CUP
ACTIVE WORK: 10 minutes

> 1 1/2 cups fresh raspberries, or 2 (10-ounce) packages frozen raspberries, thawed and drained (reserve juices)
> 2 tablespoons superfine sugar
> 1–2 tablespoons fresh lemon juice

1. Purée raspberries in blender or food processor fitted with metal blade. Press purée into small bowl through sieve with back of spoon to remove seeds.

2. Stir in sugar and lemon juice to taste. Stir until sugar dissolves. Dilute with reserved juice, if desired. Refrigerate, covered.

SORBETS AND ICED DESSERTS

MELON-ANISETTE ICE
Sorbet au Melon et à l'Anisette

This combination is inspired by the Catalan dessert *Melon con Anís*. This is best served the day it is prepared.

SERVES 4 TO 6
ACTIVE WORK: 20 minutes

> 1 cup superfine sugar
> 1 1/2 to 2 pounds ripe cantaloupe
> 3–4 tablespoons strained lemon juice
> 5–8 tablespoons anisette

1. EARLY IN THE DAY make the sugar syrup: In a medium saucepan combine sugar with 1 1/2 cups water over medium heat, stirring. Cook until syrup is clear and sugar is dissolved. Remove from heat and cool completely.

2. Peel and seed the melon. In a workbowl of a food processor fitted with a metal blade, purée flesh of melon. Strain through a sieve. Makes about 2 cups purée.

3. Stir in sugar syrup. Add lemon juice to bring up flavor and offset sweetness.

4. Pour into a sorbet machine and freeze according to directions, or pour into a shallow metal pan and set in the freezer compartment until mixture is mushy but beginning to set around inside rims, about 2 hours. Beat with an electric mixer until smooth and return to freezer until almost frozen. Repeat beating after 2 hours. Stir in anisette to taste. (Different brands are of different strengths; I use 1/4 cup Marie Brizard.) Return to freezer until firm.

5. Pack into a freezer container. Cover and keep in the freezer until ready to serve. Serve the same day. Spoon a teaspoon or two of remaining anisette over each serving.

GREEN IZARRA SORBET
Sorbet à la Vieille Liqueur du Pays Basque: Izarra

It is not always easy to find Izarra, the old liqueur of the Basque Country, except in Basque neighborhoods in San Francisco, Nevada, and Idaho. Sometimes Sherry-Lehmann Wines and Spirits sells it in New York City and Safeway Liquor Barn carries it in San Francisco. *Izarra* means star. There are two types, yellow and green; the yellow is lighter in flavor, while the green is lustier and drier in taste. Izarra is prepared from an ancient secret formula using exotic plants from the Pyrenees, herbs, honey, Armagnac, and spices including saffron. The yellow type is made from as many as thirty-two plants; the green from forty-eight. When I visited the Izarra distillery in Bayonne I saw such things as mint, coriander, anise, cardamom, star anise, caraway, angelica, vanilla, nutmeg, bitter almonds, dried celery, all laid out in boxes as they are sometimes in health food stores.

Tradition has it that in the Pyrenees Izarra was sprinkled on snow, then eaten—a forerunner, perhaps, to this sorbet.

If Izarra is absolutely unobtainable, try the variation made with Chartreuse listed at the end of this recipe; it's not authentically South-West, but it's good.

SERVES 10
☆ Begin 1 day in advance
ACTIVE WORK: 20 minutes

>   2 cups minus 2 tablespoons superfine sugar
>   1/4 cup green Izarra plus 1 tablespoon to pour over each serving
>   1/3 cup strained orange juice
>   1/4 cup strained lemon juice
>   Green food coloring (optional)
>   1/2 cup heavy cream

(continued)

1. 1 DAY IN ADVANCE, dissolve sugar in 4 cups water over medium heat, stirring. If sugar crystals appear on the inner sides of the pan, brush down with a brush dipped in cold water. Boil undisturbed 5 minutes. Remove from heat. Cool slightly, then add the Izarra. (A little bit of warmth develops the fragrance of green Izarra, but it must be cold to be eaten or drunk.) Cool completely.

2. Combine syrup, fruit juices, and use coloring, if desired, to obtain a mint-green hue.

3. Pour into sorbet machine and freeze according to directions, *adding cream just before it freezes*. Or pour into shallow metal trays and set in freezer compartment until mixture is slushy but beginning to set around inside rims, about 2 hours. Beat with an electric mixer until smooth and return to freezer until almost frozen. Repeat beating after 2 hours. Stir in cream, and freeze until firm.

4. Pack into a freezer container. Cover and allow mixture to ripen overnight.

5. Serve with 1 tablespoon Izarra spooned over each serving.

NOTE TO THE COOK
If the sorbet crystallizes, thaw slightly then beat in a food processor until smooth. Refreeze.

VARIATION
Green Chartreuse Sorbet

Make the same simple syrup. Substitute 1/2 cup green Chartreuse for the Izarra, and use 2/3 cup orange juice and 1/4 cup lemon juice. Stir in 1/2 cup heavy cream just before it freezes.

Inspired by a recipe from Bernard Cousseau.

RED WINE SORBET
Sorbet au Vin Rouge

In a Bordelaise cookbook, I read a description of a fruit soup made with cherries and a St.-Emilion wine, spiced with cinnamon and cloves. I thought it would be fun to adapt the recipe to make a true sherbet (not a slushy granita) with red wine and fresh fruit.

When fresh fruit is out of season, I have found better-quality frozen raspberries than cherries. (If you do use frozen cherries, add a little kirsch to bring up their flavor.) I add a little *eau de framboise* to frozen raspberries, a colorless *eau-de-vie* or *alcool blanc* produced from many pounds of fresh fruit—expensive but worth it. (Avoid fruit-flavored brandies, which will only give this sherbet a cheap taste.)

SERVES 6
☆ Begin 1 to 2 days in advance
ACTIVE WORK: 15 minutes
COOKING TIME: 15 minutes

        1 cup superfine sugar
    1 1/2 cups fruity red wine such as Zinfandel or Chiroubles
        1 pint fresh raspberries, or 1 (10-ounce) package frozen (if packed in
            sugar syrup, use 2 tablespoons less sugar in sugar syrup)
        1 cinnamon stick
        1 clove
      3/4 teaspoon pure vanilla extract
        Juice of 2 oranges
        4 tablespoons strained lemon juice
    1 1/2 tablespoons *eau de framboise*

1. 1 TO 2 DAYS IN ADVANCE, combine sugar and 1 2/3 cups water in a medium saucepan. Cook, stirring, over medium heat until syrup is clear and sugar is dissolved. If sugar crystals appear on the inner sides of the pan, brush down with a brush dipped in cold water. Boil undisturbed 5 minutes. Remove from heat and cool completely.

2. Meanwhile, in a noncorrodible saucepan simmer wine with raspberries and spices 15 minutes. Remove from heat and cool completely.

3. Combine sugar syrup, spiced wine, vanilla, and fruit juices in a glass or stainless steel container. Cover and refrigerate. Allow to ripen 1 to 2 days.

4. EARLY THE DAY OF SERVING, strain the liquid; discard spices and raspberry seeds. You should have about 1 quart liquid. Pour into a sorbet machine and freeze according to directions or pour into a shallow metal pan and set in the freezer compartment until mixture is slushy but beginning to set around inside rims, about 2 hours. Beat with an electric mixer until smooth and return to freezer until almost frozen. Repeat beating after 2 hours. Stir in the *eau de framboise* just before sorbet hardens completely.

5. Pack into a freezer container. Cover and keep in the freezer until ready to serve. Serve the same day.

NOTE TO THE COOK
If the sorbet crystallizes, dump it into the workbowl of a food processor and process 5 seconds. The sorbet will only be better and lighter for this last-minute *truc*.

PRUNE AND ARMAGNAC ICE CREAM
Glace aux Pruneaux à l'Armagnac

This is a variation of a marvelous creation by André Daguin. It is perhaps the most
elegant ice cream I know. It should be made with prunes that have been soaked in
Armagnac for at least 2 weeks. To give an illusion of extra richness but not too many
extra calories, I add a little heavy cream when the ice cream has nearly solidified. This
way the butterfat in the cream will "glide" into the chilled ice cream, endowing it
with a satiny texture.

MAKES 2 QUARTS/SERVES 10 TO 12
☆ Prepare 1 day in advance
ACTIVE WORK: 25 minutes

> 1 **quart milk, heated**
> 1 **small piece vanilla bean, split down one side, or 1 1/2 teaspoons pure**
>   **vanilla extract**
> 10 **egg yolks**
> 1 **cup plus 1 tablespoon superfine sugar**
>   **Pinch of salt**
> 30 **Prunes in Armagnac (see recipe), pitted, plus 1/4 cup of the syrup**
> 1/2 **cup heavy cream**
> 1 **plump Prune in Armagnac per serving for garnish (optional)**

1. 1 DAY BEFORE SERVING, in a heavy enamel saucepan scald the milk with the vanilla
bean; set aside, covered. (If using vanilla extract, add in Step 4.)

2. In a mixing bowl, beat egg yolks and sugar together until thick and a ribbon
forms when the whisk is lifted. Whisk in a pinch of salt.

3. In a second heavy enamel saucepan, heat the beaten eggs over very low heat,
stirring constantly. Gradually add the *hot* milk, stirring constantly with a wooden
spoon. Cook over low heat, stirring, until the mixture thickens, the back of the spoon
is well coated, the froth on the surface has disappeared, and the mixture registers
about 165° F. on a candy thermometer. *The mixture must not be allowed to boil.* Immediately remove from heat.

4. Strain through a fine sieve into a chilled mixing bowl set over ice. Cool down
quickly, stirring constantly. Add vanilla extract, if using. Pour mixture into container
of an electric ice cream maker and freeze according to directions.

5. In the workbowl of a food processor fitted with the metal blade, chop the prunes
fine with an on-off motion. When the ice cream is half frozen, add the prunes and the
Armagnac syrup.

6. When *almost* frozen, add the cream. When the ice cream is done, pack into a
2-quart ice cream mold and set in freezer overnight.

7. 30 MINUTES BEFORE SERVING, transfer the ice cream to the refrigerator to soften
slightly. Invert onto a serving plate. To help loosen the ice cream, soak a kitchen towel

in hot water, wring out, and wrap around the mold. If necessary tap the mold lightly with your fingers and shake it to loosen. If the surface needs a little patching up, smooth it with a spatula dipped in hot water. Return the ice cream to the freezer for 5 minutes to firm up. Place a whole soaked prune on top of each portion and drizzle with a teaspoon or so of the syrup.

MOLDED MINT PARFAIT STUFFED WITH
CHOCOLATE MOUSSE
Parfait à la Menthe et au Chocolat

I learned this rich, smooth, irresistible dessert from Lucien Vanel. The quality of mint syrup is important. Some brands are overwhelming. One I like is the Léotard brand from Provence, available by mail from H. Roth & Son (see Appendix).

SERVES 10 TO 12
☆ Begin 1 day in advance
  ACTIVE WORK: 1 hour (plus 15 minutes for Crème Anglaise)

      2 cups milk
  1 3/4 cups granulated sugar
     12 egg yolks, at room temperature
      1 tablespoon concentrated mint syrup
      1 cup heavy cream, cold
        Crème Anglaise
      1 ounce semisweet chocolate
      4 tablespoons unsalted butter
    1/4 cup unsweetened imported cocoa
        Pinch of salt
      3 egg whites, at room temperature
    1/3 cup superfine sugar
        Fresh mint sprigs (optional)

1. 1 DAY IN ADVANCE, place mold or molds in freezer (see Note 1).

2. EARLY THE FOLLOWING DAY, place milk and 1/2 cup of the granulated sugar in a small saucepan. Heat to boiling, stirring to dissolve sugar. Remove from heat.

3. Beat egg yolks and remaining 1 1/4 cups granulated sugar until thick and very pale in color; mixture should form a dissolving ribbon when whisk is raised.

4. Gradually stir milk mixture into beaten yolks; blend well. Transfer to clean saucepan and cook over low heat, stirring constantly, until mixture reaches 189° F. on a candy thermometer, about 10 to 15 minutes. Mixture should be thick enough to coat a spoon.

5. Transfer custard mixture to large bowl of heavy-duty electric mixer. Beat at medium speed 5 minutes, then decrease mixer speed to low and beat until thick and

foamy, about 15 minutes longer (see Note 2). The mixture should be cool. Gently fold in mint syrup. You should have about 5 to 6 cups beaten custard mixture.

6. Beat cream in chilled bowl with chilled beater until very soft peaks form. Do not overbeat (this would create crystals in the parfait).

7. *Custard mixture and cream must be the same temperature before combining.* Carefully fold one fourth of whipped cream into custard mixture to lighten. Gradually and gently fold remaining whipped cream into custard until thoroughly blended.

8. Carefully spoon parfait mixture into molds, filling about seven eighths full; set on tray and return to freezer. To allow parfait molds to be filled with a total of 2 cups chocolate mousse mixture later, create an indentation in each parfait by using smaller-size molds or containers (see Note 3). When parfait mixture is very cold and thick, place smaller container in center of parfait, pressing down until parfait mixture rises up around smaller mold but does not overflow into it. Leave smaller container in place. Cover with plastic wrap and freeze for at least 6 hours or overnight.

9. Make Crème Anglaise.

10. To prepare chocolate mousse mixture, melt semisweet chocolate and butter in a small, heavy saucepan. Stir in cocoa and salt. Mix until smooth and well blended; transfer to medium bowl. Rinse a clean bowl with hot water to warm it; dry with paper towels. Add egg whites and beat with large whisk until soft peaks form. Gradually beat in superfine sugar until whites are stiff and shiny.

11. Fold one fourth of chocolate mixture into whites until completely blended. Gently fold egg white mixture into remaining chocolate until completely incorporated. Cover mousse mixture and refrigerate until ready to use.

12. JUST BEFORE SERVING, pour a small amount of very hot water into small mold pressed into each parfait, and quickly and carefully lift mold out. Spoon chocolate mousse into indentation, leveling off surface. Place warm towel around outside of mold for a few seconds and immediately unmold onto chilled serving plate. If unmolding small molds, place unmolded parfaits in freezer while unmolding remaining parfaits (see Note 4).

13. To serve individual parfaits, ladle a small amount of Crème Anglaise on serving plate surrounding base of parfait. To serve large parfait, ladle Crème Anglaise onto individual serving plates and place slice of parfait in center of each. Garnish with fresh mint sprigs, if desired.

NOTES TO THE COOK

1. Choose one of the following for parfaits: one 10-cup mold, two 5-cup molds, or ten 10-ounce individual molds. If you do not have individual molds, substitute glass custard cups, porcelain soufflé dishes, or foil baking cups. For the large or medium-sized molds, substitute stainless steel bowls; these are excellent because the metal reacts to temperature change readily and makes the unmolding easier.

2. Custard mixture should be beaten very, *very* slowly (heavy-duty electric mixer will give best results for this). If preferred, mixture may be beaten by hand with a balloon whisk; this will take about 25 minutes of very slow beating. If custard is overbeaten, it will begin to deflate. (If this happens, the custard can still be used but the parfait will not be quite as smooth and creamy.)

3. A 2-cup container can be used to make an indentation in a 10-cup parfait; a 1-cup container in a 5-cup parfait; and a 3-ounce foil candy cup in each 10-ounce parfait.
4. The parfait molds can be unmolded and stored in freezer, but only for a short time before serving, as chocolate mousse should not be allowed to freeze.

PRESERVES

Everyone's cooking reference library should include a book on making preserves (a good one is *Putting Food By* by Ruth Herzberg, Beatrice Vaughan, and Janet Greene). But I didn't feel my book on South-West French food would be complete without including some of the famous regional recipes for preserving fruits.

Most of these recipes involve preserving in alcohol; remember that the fruits must always be completely covered by the liquid. Check your shelf of preserves from time to time to see if any of the fruits inside have swollen up above the liquid line. If they have, add some *eau-de-vie* or brandy until the fruits are again submerged. (Not necessary with peaches, pears, or prunes preserved in red wine and Armagnac; once these processed jars are opened they must be refrigerated and their contents used.)

PRUNES IN ARMAGNAC
Pruneaux à l'Armagnac

This is an essential recipe since the prunes are used in Prune and Armagnac Ice Cream, the Gascon Pastry Cake Filled with Apples and Prunes in Armagnac, and various fruit flans and omelets. They are excellent, too, eaten alone, after which one should drink off the thick, dark, aromatic syrup as slowly as possible, the longer to savor it.

In the South-West there are the world-famous prunes of Agen. Our California prunes are the same variety and as luscious, and have been cultivated in America since the early nineteenth century. Hadley's outside Palm Springs offers the most delicious prunes by mail: Hadley's Fruit Orchards, Cabazon, CA 92230.

MAKES 1 1/2 QUARTS
☆ Begin at least 15 days in advance
   ACTIVE WORK (DAY 1): 5 minutes
   ACTIVE WORK (DAY 2): 10 minutes

     2 pounds extra large prunes, unpitted
     3 cups brewed tea, preferably linden or orange pekoe
     1 cup superfine sugar
     Armagnac to cover (about 3 cups)

(continued)

1. ONE DAY IN ADVANCE OF PREPARING THE PRUNES, soak the prunes overnight in tea so that they will swell.

2. THE FOLLOWING DAY, drain; discard tea. Roll each prune in paper towels to dry well. Place prunes in very clean 6-cup glass preserving jar with tight-fitting lid.

3. Make a syrup with sugar and 1/2 cup water; bring to a boil, stirring. Boil undisturbed 2 minutes. Remove from heat and allow to cool. Pour over the prunes. Completely cover the prunes with Armagnac; stir. If prunes rise above the line of liquid, add more Armagnac. Let soak a minimum of 15 days in a cool, dark place or the refrigerator. Use clean wooden tongs or wooden spoon to remove prunes as needed. Keeps up to one year.

NOTES TO THE COOK
1. In the South-West they soak prunes in linden tea to bring out the full flavor of the fruit.
2. If prunes become uncovered, add more Armagnac to cover.

SWEET AND SOUR CHERRIES
Cerises à l'Aigre-Doux

These pickled cherries and the pickled prunes following make an ideal accompaniment to pâtés, *confits*, foie gras, or any rich daube in this book. This recipe has been adapted to use the cherries available in the market when they are not too sweet.

MAKES 1 QUART
☆ Prepare 3 months in advance
   ACTIVE WORK (DAY 1): 40 minutes
   COOKING TIME (DAY 1): 10 minutes
   COOKING TIME (DAY 2): 20 minutes

     1 1/2 pounds (about 1 quart) firm, not too sweet cherries
       1 cup granulated sugar
       3 cups white wine tarragon vinegar
       2 cloves
       1 piece mace or 1/4 teaspoon ground mace
       90-proof vodka or *eau-de-vie*

1. Carefully inspect, wash, and dry each cherry. Discard any that are bruised. Prick each once or twice with a needle. Trim each stem, leaving about 1/2 inch attached.

2. In a nonaluminum saucepan, combine sugar and vinegar. Cook, stirring until sugar is dissolved. Add cloves and mace; boil 1 minute. Remove from heat and allow to cool. Add the cherries and let stand 1 day.

3. THE FOLLOWING DAY, sterilize two 1-pint canning jars and their rubber rings:

cover with warm water in a pan, bring to a boil, and boil covered 10 minutes. Drain upside down on kitchen towels.

4. Meanwhile, drain cherries (reserve liquid) and place in the clean jars. Bring liquid to a boil and boil 7 to 8 minutes. Cool completely, then pour over the cold cherries. Add vodka or *eau-de-vie* to cover. Seal and *let stand in a cool, dry, dark place for 3 months before serving.*

NOTE TO THE COOK

The cherries will lose their bright color; according to some old cookbooks, this is the sign that the cherries are ready to be eaten.

SWEET AND SOUR PRUNES
Pruneaux à l'Aigre-Doux

These are absolutely delicious with terrines, pâtés, and *confit* of pig's tongue.

MAKES 2 CUPS
☆ Prepare at least 6 weeks in advance
ACTIVE WORK (DAY 1): 10 minutes
COOKING TIME (DAY 1): 10 minutes
ACTIVE WORK (DAY 2): 15 minutes
COOKING TIME (DAY 2): 6 to 8 minutes

    12 **ounces large prunes with pits**
       Tea, preferably linden
1 1/3 **cups granulated sugar**
   2 **cups tarragon white wine vinegar**
   1 **cinnamon stick**
   2 **cloves**
     Vodka

1. Simmer the prunes in tea 10 minutes. Let stand 2 to 3 hours.

2. Meanwhile, in a nonaluminum saucepan, slowly cook the sugar and vinegar, stirring until dissolved. Add the cinnamon and cloves: simmer 10 minutes. Remove from heat and let stand until cold.

3. Drain prunes. Roll in paper towels to dry. Prick each 2 or 3 times with a pin. Place in a bowl, and strain the vinegar-sugar solution over them. Let prunes rest 24 hours.

4. THE FOLLOWING DAY, strain the vinegar solution into the same pan and slowly boil 6 to 8 minutes. Cool completely.

5. Place the prunes in a very clean 1-pint glass preserving jar. Cover with the cold vinegar solution. Add enough vodka to cover the prunes. Seal and *place in a dry dark place for at least 6 weeks.* Refrigerate after opening.

RASPBERRIES IN ARMAGNAC
Framboises à l'Armagnac

These raspberries can be served within two weeks of being soaked in Armagnac, and should be eaten within a month. Otherwise, leave them for four to six months, strain them, and use the liqueur with Champagne in an evening aperitif, a *"kir royale"* South-West style.

MAKES ABOUT 2 CUPS
☆ Prepare at least 2 weeks in advance
  ACTIVE WORK: 20 minutes

> **1 dry pint perfect, but not too ripe, red raspberries**
> **3/4 cup superfine sugar**
> **1 1/2 cups Armagnac or more to cover**

1. Wipe each raspberry very gently with a damp paper towel, then drop one by one into a very clean bottle. Add the sugar, then enough Armagnac to cover.

2. *Let stand in a cool dark place for at least 1 month.* Shake gently from time to time to help the sugar dissolve. Serve chilled in small glass cups. For a raspberry-flavored Champagne aperitif, leave raspberries in Armagnac *for at least 4 months* (longer is better). Strain through coffee filter into a clean bottle. For each drink: Put 1 ounce liquid in a glass; fill with chilled dry Champagne.

PRESERVED SPICED PEARS IN RED WINE
WITH ARMAGNAC
Poires au Poivre et à l'Armagnac

This delicious dessert, invented by André Daguin, is based on the Gascon tradition of using pepper to heighten the flavor of fruits.

SERVES 8 (BUT CAN BE MADE IN
MUCH LARGER QUANTITIES BY
DOUBLING OR TRIPLING THE RECIPE)
☆ Prepare at least 3 months in advance
  ACTIVE WORK: about 30 minutes (a few minutes longer if tripling the recipe)
  COOKING TIME: 1 hour 15 minutes

4 perfect, but not completely ripe, pears
1/2 lemon
3 1/2 cups full-bodied red wine such as Madiran, Petite Sirah, Algerian Dahra, or Spanish Rioja
1 1/2 cups sugar
1 scant tablespoon black peppercorns, rinsed and patted dry
1/2 cup Armagnac

1. For 4 pears, wash and drain two 3 1/2-cup glass preserving jars with lids and new rubber rings. Place in a pan of water and slowly heat to boiling. Drain upside down on a clean kitchen towel.

2. Peel and drop pears into a bowl of water acidulated with the juice of 1/2 lemon.

3. In an enameled or stainless steel saucepan, heat the wine and sugar, stirring with a clean wooden spoon until the sugar is dissolved. Bring to a boil and boil 1 minute. Drain the pears and add to the wine syrup; simmer 2 to 3 minutes.

4. Pack 2 pears in each clean, hot jar. Bring the wine syrup to a boil and boil 4 to 5 minutes to intensify flavor. Add the peppercorns and Armagnac, return to a boil, and pour boiling syrup over the pears, filling to within 1/2 inch of the top of the jar, or until the indicated level. Do not overpack jars. (If there is any leftover juice, freeze for a tiny granita—see Note.)

5. Use a clean wooden spoon to stir the fruit gently to let any air bubbles escape. With a paper towel, wipe the mouths of the jars clean of any syrup. Set the new rubber rings in place and seal the jars at once. Gently lower onto a rack set in a deep pot or water canner filled with enough lukewarm water to cover the jars by at least 1 inch. Bring to a boil. Cover the pot and boil vigorously 1 hour. *Don't be tempted to reduce the cooking time—the wine must be fully cooked.* Let the jars cool in the water before removing. Using tongs, transfer the jars to a rack to rest overnight.

6. THE FOLLOWING DAY, test for a full seal by loosening the clamps and holding the jars from the top. If they don't open, the seals have been completed. (Be sure to have your other hand underneath to catch a jar, if necessary.) If there is a bad seal, do not plan to store the fruits. Instead, refrigerate and use within the week. Label fully sealed jar or jars and *store in a cool place for 3 months before opening*.

7. THE DAY BEFORE YOU PLAN TO SERVE THE PEARS, open the jars and stir 1/4 cup uncooked red wine into each. Chill overnight. Serve 1/2 pear per serving, with a little of the syrup. Serve with an extra grinding of fresh black pepper. If too sweet, add a dash of lemon juice.

NOTE TO THE COOK
Leftover juices make a delicious granita. Add orange and lemon juice to taste (about 3 tablespoons orange juice and 1 tablespoon lemon juice for each cup leftover red wine syrup). Simply freeze until slushy. Break up mixture in food processor, return to freezer, and freeze until hard.

GREEN FIG AND WALNUT JAM
Confiture de Figues Vertes aux Noix

This delicious jam is wonderful with fresh cheese. To Alain Dutournier the combination brought back memories of his childhood; when he described it to me his eyes filled with tears.

MAKES 1 QUART
☆ Prepare 1 month in advance
   ACTIVE WORK: 20 minutes
   COOKING TIME: 2 1/4 hours

> **2 pounds (about 16) fresh, slightly underripe green figs**
> **2 large lemons, preferably home grown or purchased at a store selling organically produced fresh fruits**
> **1 1/2 pounds sugar**
> **3/4 cup shelled fresh walnuts**

1. Wash and remove stem tips if they are hard. Halve the figs. Set aside.
2. Rinse lemons; remove rind and cut into fine julienne strips. Cut away all the white pith and thinly slice the lemon. Remove seeds and put them into a small cheesecloth bag.
3. In a heavy-bottomed saucepan, cook sugar with 1 1/4 cups water, stirring until dissolved. Cook syrup undisturbed until it reaches a temperature of 220° F. Immediately add the figs, lemon rind, lemon slices, and seed bag. Return to the boil, then lower the heat. Cook slowly until setting point is reached, about 2 hours. The setting point is determined by dipping a spoon into the liquid and letting a few drops fall onto a saucer; if they set quickly, it is done. Remove seed bag. Use a spoon to remove any scum on the surface. Add the walnuts and cook 5 minutes longer.
4. Sterilize jars, rings, and lids: Cover with hot water, bring to a boil, and boil 10 minutes. Drain upside down on a kitchen towel. Fill hot, dry jars, leaving a 1/2-inch headspace. Cool and seal. Keep the jam in the refrigerator after opening.

ORANGE RATAFIA
Ratafia d'Orange

Ratafias are liqueurs produced by steeping fruits and peels in Armagnac. Oranges are especially enhanced with the perfume of France's oldest brandy.

This wonderful recipe comes from L'Estanquet in Gastes in the Landes. Pepette, the young woman chef, makes many different fruit and brandy concoctions. She claims this one is especially good for digestion as well as for enlivening the appetite.

MAKES ABOUT 1 1/2 QUARTS
☆ Prepare at least 2 months in advance
ACTIVE WORK: 10 minutes

> **6 large juice oranges (preferably home grown or purchased at a store selling organically produced fresh fruits) to yield 2 cups freshly squeezed orange juice, strained**
> **1 cup granulated sugar**
> **4 cinnamon sticks**
> **1 liter (about 1 quart) Armagnac**

1. Wash 2 of the oranges to remove any chemicals. Using a zester or a swivel-bladed vegetable peeler, remove the outer rind—zest only, without any white pith—and cut the zest into very thin strips to make about 1/3 cup.

2. Combine orange juice and sugar in nonaluminum medium saucepan and bring to a boil, stirring to dissolve sugar. Let stand until completely cool.

3. Combine juice and sugar mixture, zest, cinnamon sticks, and Armagnac in a porcelain crock, pitcher, or glass jug. Cover and let stand 1 month at room temperature, stirring from time to time with a clean wooden spoon. Strain through coffee filter papers into bottles. Cover tightly and let stand at least 1 month before serving.

PASTRY PREPARATIONS USING FOOD PROCESSOR

SUGAR CRUST (FOR WALNUT CAKE FROM MASSEUBE)
Pâte Sucrée

> **8 1/2 ounces (2 cups) unbleached all-purpose flour, a brand with 11 grams of protein per cup (see "Flour" in Appendix)**
> **1/3 cup granulated sugar**
> **Pinch of salt**
> **9 tablespoons unsalted butter, chilled and cut into tiny dice**
> **1 egg, lightly beaten with 3 1/2 tablespoons heavy cream and 1/2 teaspoon pure vanilla extract**

1. Combine flour, sugar, and salt in the workbowl of a food processor. "Sift" by turning machine on-off once. Scatter butter bits on top, and with a series of 5 or 6 on-off motions, turn the mixture into small beads.

2. Add remaining ingredients and process 5 seconds; dump into a bowl. Break off

nuggets and flatten forward with the heel of your hand or a dough scraper to distribute fat and flour evenly. Reshape into two balls of unequal size, one a little bit larger than the other. Wrap in waxed paper and chill in refrigerator at least 4 hours or overnight.

CROUSTADE DOUGH
Pâte à Croustade du Sud-Ouest

"Covered Pies" (see Index) explains the use of this very unusual (for France) pastry dough in the South-West. Layered with butter, this strudel-type dough bakes into a crisp, parchmentlike pastry that makes a wonderful wrapping for all kinds of sweet and savory fillings. In the Périgord the dough is used to wrap up duck *confit* and apples, and in Gascony, prunes marinated in Armagnac and fresh fruits.

Sheets of phyllo dough can be substituted, but they are often obtainable only frozen and tend to be difficult to work with. For full flavor and tenderness, I prefer making my own South-West croustade dough. If you like working with dough, chances are you'll enjoy making this recipe. It is magical to watch the soft, elastic dough—made from just one packed cup of flour—stretch into a paper-thin, 3-foot-by-3-foot expanse. If you try my simple food processor technique, I think you'll find it a rewarding addition to your pastry repertoire.

The art of stretching this dough across a table once called for Old World expertise. Now, anyone who enjoys working with his or her hands can learn to make it easily. Two developments have simplified the process: the national availability of standardized flour brands and the machine power of the food processor.

My recipe calls for an all-purpose unbleached flour, available in supermarkets, that contains eleven grams of protein per cup. Be sure to check the sides of flour packages for the protein content; the exact figure is important for the processor technique that follows. I find this flour much easier to work with than any other, including strudel flour, which contains fourteen grams of protein per cup. And it is the only flour that makes this dough bake up tender.

The processor kneads the dough powerfully, activating the gluten in the flour to the point where it develops enormous stretching power. This special elasticity, which is the essence of South-West croustade-strudel-phyllo pastry, was traditionally obtained by giving the dough a heavy beating, or "workout," by hand. Now the processor will do it for you.

Heat is another factor in activating the gluten strands in the flour. When making your dough, be sure to use warm water, rather than the cold water normally used in pastry-making. The dough is allowed to rest in a warm, turned-off oven, rather than in the refrigerator, before being rolled and stretched. You will have even greater success if you make sure the room you're working in is warm and free of drafts.

After you've made this dough several times, you'll begin to notice subtle variables, such as the difference humidity can make. On a clear day the leaves will dry very quickly, and you'll have to work fast to prevent any cracking. On a rainy day your dough may stretch much more easily.

MAKES APPROXIMATELY 1
STRETCHED SHEET AT LEAST 3 FEET
SQUARE
ACTIVE WORK: 45 minutes to 1 hour

> 5 1/2 ounces (about 1 packed cup) unbleached all-purpose flour, a brand with 11 grams of protein per cup*
> 1/4 teaspoon salt
> 1 large egg
> 1 tablespoon plus 1 teaspoon clarified butter, melted and cooled to room temperature, or substitute an unflavored oil (avoid margarine)
> 1 scant teaspoon strained fresh lemon juice or vinegar
> 3–3 1/2 tablespoons warm water
> Vegetable oil
> 1 recipe filling for Pastry Cake Filled with Apples and Prunes in Armagnac or 1 recipe filling for Duck *Confit* with Sautéed Apples
> 1/2 cup clarified butter, melted
> 1 tablespoon orange flower water (omit if using Duck *Confit* with Sautéed Apples)
> 1/4 cup sugar (omit if using Duck *Confit* with Sautéed Apples)

*I use Gold Medal unbleached all-purpose flour, which is a nationally available brand that contains 11 grams of protein per cup. The amount of flour is most accurately measured by weighing. You should have 5 1/2 ounces or 155 grams. If you do not have an accurate scale, the cup measure will do.

1. Place the flour and salt in the workbowl of a food processor fitted with the metal blade. Turn machine on and off to blend.

2. You will need half an egg yolk for the dough. Crack the eggshell and separate the egg in the usual way. Use half the shell to scoop half of the yolk from the other half of the shell. If you have difficulty with this, beat the yolk lightly and use 1 1/2 teaspoons of it. You will not need the other half of the yolk.

3. In a small bowl, combine the egg white, the half egg yolk, the clarified butter, and the lemon juice. Have the warm water at hand. Turn on the processor and pour the egg mixture all at once through the feed tube. With the machine running, immediately add 3 tablespoons of the water, 1 tablespoon at a time, and continue to process until the dough forms a mass, usually in 15 seconds. (On a humid day, this can take 5 seconds longer.)

4. Feel the dough; it should be slightly sticky but soft and dry. If it is very wet and sticky, sprinkle it with 1 teaspoon flour. If it is very dry, add another 1 to 1 1/2 teaspoons water, 1/2 teaspoon at a time. Turn the machine quickly on and off to

incorporate such adjustments. (On humid days the dough will be slightly softer than on dry days.)

5. *Kneading the dough:* Process the dough 1 minute. (If your machine should stall, knead the dough by turning the machine on for 15 seconds and then off for 10 seconds 4 times.) During this time the dough will slap against the side of the workbowl, sticking at first, then it will begin to form a mass and no longer adhere to the side. Do not overprocess, or the gluten in the flour will break into ropy strands. The kneaded dough will feel soft, warm, and pliable. (On humid days it will feel slightly sticky.)

6. *Relaxing the dough:* With lightly floured hands, remove the dough from the processor and smooth it into a ball. With the palm of your hand, flatten the ball into a thick disk. Brush both sides with vegetable oil.

7. Set the dough on a well-oiled porcelain or glass plate, cover with plastic wrap, and place in a 100° F. oven for 35 to 45 minutes (but not longer than 1 hour). If your oven does not have a warm pilot light or cannot reliably be set at 100° F., set the covered dish over a pan of hot water and cover them both with towels to retain the warmth.

8. While the dough relaxes, prepare croustade filling so that it will be cooled before placing on the stretched dough.

9. *Preparing the work space:* Use a large (at least 3-foot-square) freestanding table. A countertop will not do because you have to walk around the table to pull the dough evenly. A round table or a square or rectangular table with rounded edges will be easier to work on.

10. Cover the table with a cloth or sheet large enough to hang at least 6 inches over the edges of your table. Choose one that has a printed pattern so that you can use the pattern to gauge the thinness and evenness of your dough. Sprinkle the sheet lightly with flour or rub the flour into the cloth.

11. Remove all jewelry from fingers and wrists. A short-sleeved shirt is advised. Close the windows to make sure the room is free of drafts. Once you begin stretching the dough, you must work quickly without stopping.

12. *Rolling and stretching the dough:* Place the relaxed dough in the center of the table and sprinkle it lightly with flour. Roll out the dough into a 10- to 12-inch round. Brush the top lightly with vegetable oil. If the round starts to snap back to a smaller size, cover it with plastic wrap and let it relax 5 minutes.

13. To stretch the dough, lift it and drape it over floured hands—palms down and fingers bent loosely underneath, so that your nails do not make any holes. Most people find it easiest to work with their arms bent at the elbows. Coax the dough to stretch by carefully rotating your hands one after the other, first sideways, then forward. Gently stretch the dough from the center outward, rotating the entire mass of dough as you work.

14. When the dough stretches up to your elbows and becomes difficult to manage, place it on the table. Continue to stretch the dough to paper thinness, using the pattern on the sheet as a guide for evenness. Stretch out thicker portions of the

dough by slipping your hands, palms up, under the area and gently coaxing the dough to stretch. Continually work around the table and pull the dough outward, letting the thick edges hang over the sides of the table. Always stretch from underneath and avoid anchoring a hand on top of the dough as you pull. For more traction, slide the cloth toward you so that a good portion of the dough hangs over the edge of the table, and gently pull at the edges with your fingers to stretch it. Then return the cloth to its centered position. Repeat with other portions of the dough if necessary. Look for thicker patches and lines in the dough, and try to pull those thin. The very edge will remain rather thick.

This recipe will make an approximately square sheet of dough at least 3 feet by 3 feet, or a rectangle or circle of equal area. The dough will then be so thin that you can read fine print through it. Small holes are likely to occur. Do not worry about them, but try to avoid them in the first step of stretching. If holes do appear as soon as you start to stretch, re-form the dough into a ball, let it relax, and start over. Holes around the edge won't affect the croustade at all. Small holes in the center can be pinched together or patched with melted butter and some dough from a thick edge.

15. *Drying the dough*: Leave the stretched dough on the table to dry. Croustade dough usually dries in about 8 minutes, or a bit longer on damp days. Lift the dough once or twice to let air circulate underneath. If any areas pucker and begin to turn brittle, brush them with melted butter to avoid cracking. An open window on a hot summer day or a portable hair dryer set on low and held 2 or 3 feet away can help dry the dough evenly. The dough is dry enough when the unbuttered sections no longer feel tacky to the touch. (If it is still tacky when you fill and roll it, it will bake up tough.)

16. Cut off the thick edges with a scissors or tear into the thick edge and wind it around your index finger, like thread on a bobbin. Discard.

17. *Assembling the croustade:* When the dough is evenly dried, brush with melted butter. Using the sheet to help lift the dough, fold 2 opposite sides together to make a rectangle. Lightly brush folded sides with butter. Sprinkle with sugar. Using sheet to help lift dough, fold in half to form a square. Slide onto a buttered baking sheet. Place filling in the center. Trim edges and fold over to cover filling, leaving ends loosely arranged so that there is an "overblown tea rose" effect.

PASTRY FOR COUNTRY-STYLE *TOURTES* AND *TOURTIÈRES*

MAKES PASTRY FOR 1 COVERED 10-, 11-, OR 12-INCH
TOURTE OR *TOURTIÈRE*

ACTIVE WORK: 20 minutes

> 12 ounces (about 2 2/3 cups) unbleached all-purpose flour, a brand with 11 grams protein per cup
> 1 teaspoon salt
> Pinch of sugar
> 1 stick plus 5 tablespoons (6 1/2 ounces) unsalted butter, well chilled and cut into small pieces
> 1 small egg, lightly beaten
> 1 tablespoon rum or lemon juice
> 3 tablespoons ice water—an extra tablespoon may be necessary with some flours.

1. AT LEAST 4 HOURS BEFORE BAKING, place flour, salt, and sugar in workbowl of a food processor fitted with the metal blade. Sift by turning machine on and off once. Scatter the butter over the flour. Turn machine on and off 4 or 5 times, or until the mixture resembles coarse oatmeal. Combine the egg, rum, and water; with machine on, add to the flour-butter mixture. Stop the machine before the dough forms a ball around the blades.

2. Dump onto a work surface covered with a sheet of waxed paper. Pastry dough should not be too crumbly; if it is, sprinkle with droplets of cold water—just enough to mass the dough together; don't let it get at all damp. Pat out into an 8 × 12-inch rectangle, pressing the pieces together. Cover the pastry with a second sheet of waxed paper and roll the dough to make a larger rectangle, about 10 by 18 inches. Lift off top sheet and fold pastry dough into thirds. Wrap tightly and chill at least 2 hours.

3. When ready to roll out, separate into two parts, one slightly larger than the other. If dough is very cold, allow it to stand a few minutes until malleable. Roll out the larger piece of dough between sheets of floured waxed paper to make a large, thin round. Dough should be very thin, less than 1/8 inch. Remove the top sheet of paper, flip dough over into the mold, and peel off the bottom sheet of paper. Fit pastry into mold. (If pastry is too soft at this point, simply let it chill in the refrigerator 10 minutes before lifting off paper.) Repair cracks or tears with overhanging pieces of pastry; trim off the excess with a thin-bladed knife or by rolling the rolling pin over the edge. Let the pastry rest 1 hour longer in the refrigerator.

4. Meanwhile, roll out the remaining pastry between sheets of floured waxed paper. Roll as thin as possible. Keep covered with plastic wrap in the refrigerator until ready to assemble.

NOTES TO THE COOK

1. Dough can be made 1 day in advance. The part to be used for the bottom of the *tourte* can be rolled out, fitted into a mold, covered tightly with plastic wrap, and refrigerated overnight.

2. The top crust can be made extra flaky by the addition of extra butter folded in as if one were making puff pastry. Dice an extra 4 tablespoons unsalted butter. Roll out the smaller piece of dough to a rectangle and dot the butter over two thirds, beginning at one narrow end. Beginning with the unbuttered third, fold the dough into thirds as if you were folding a letter. Rotate the dough so the short end faces you, then roll into a rectangle. Fold the dough in thirds again. Wrap in plastic wrap and chill thoroughly. Roll out to a circle to fit the *tourte*. Keep chilled until ready to bake.

BRIOCHE DOUGH

I spent an entire autumn working up brioche recipes—trying different methods, consulting with bakers and chefs, thinking and rethinking ways of achieving a perfect all-purpose dough. I hate to think of how many pounds of butter I used, how many dozen eggs, how many packages of yeast, how much oven cleaner! The smell of yeast-risen dough filled my New York apartment. Neighbors sniffed as they passed my door. My children rebelled and demanded "normal bread." But finally (and I say this with my characteristic modesty à la Henry Kissinger), I came up with something that I think is very special because of four unusual things. Actually, none of these things is that unusual in itself—it's the combination that is unique.

1. The lightness and fluffiness of this brioche I attribute to an early nineteenth-century method of initiating the first thrust of the yeast. In this method, known as "sponging," the yeast is mixed with milk, one quarter the total amount of flour, *and an egg*. This mixture is left to rise under a blanket of the remaining flour for 1 1/2 to 2 hours. This stage may be considered as an extra-long rise.

2. The trouble with a lot of brioche recipes is that they force the rising of the dough with too much yeast and end up sacrificing flavor. As a result, the brioche tastes too "yeasty." No matter how fluffy or buttery or light it is, it doesn't taste "natural." My solution is a long, slow rise using a small amount of yeast; this results in a superb natural flavor and a crumb with a better structure.

3. The buttery quality of brioche has traditionally been the result of a messy workout of the dough in which the butter was cut into the dough with a great deal of effort. If there was anything that turned off home cooks contemplating making their own brioche, it was the anticipation of this laborious task. *Food processor to the rescue!* We are now able to achieve perfect absorption of the butter with no manual effort and without any mess at all.

4. The classic technique of making brioche always entails the "knocking down" process (or, as the French say, "waking up"), a deflating and folding of the dough mass to redistribute the yeast cells. Too many recipes call for kneading at this stage, and I couldn't disagree more. It's very important that the redistribution be done *gently*, and you will find precise instructions in my master recipe. *This is the key to the explosion of the dough into a light, spongy cake*. Bakers tell me that you can do everything correctly up to this point but your brioche may fall short of perfection if you do not properly execute this stage.

(continued)

MAKES 1 1/4 POUNDS DOUGH
☆ Prepare up to 3 days in advance
ACTIVE WORK: 15 minutes
UNATTENDED RISING TIME: 5 to 6 hours

        3 tablespoons milk, scalded then cooled to warm
   1 1/2 teaspoons (1/2 package) dry yeast, or 2 packed teaspoons fresh
            compressed yeast
        8 ounces (about 1 2/3 cups) unbleached all-purpose flour, a brand with 12
            to 13 grams protein per cup, or substitute bread flour
        3 eggs, at room temperature
   3 or 4 tablespoons sugar
      3/4 teaspoon salt
       10 tablespoons (1 1/4 stick) unsalted butter, melted but not hot

1. *Making the sponge:* Place milk and yeast in the workbowl of a food processor
fitted with the metal blade. Process on and off to combine. Add 1/3 cup flour and 1
egg. Process 2 to 3 seconds. Scrape down sides of bowl. Sprinkle remaining flour
over the mixture; do not mix in. Cover and let stand 1 1/2 to 2 hours at room
temperature in the workbowl. (If you need your workbowl, scrape the mixture into a
mixing bowl and sprinkle the remaining flour on top.)

2. *Kneading the dough:* Add 3 tablespoons sugar (4 tablespoons if you are making a
dessert), salt, and the 2 remaining eggs to the workbowl. Process 15 seconds. With
the machine on, pour in the melted butter in a steady stream through the feed tube.
Process 20 seconds longer. If the machine stalls (this happens when the butter is
added too quickly), let the machine rest 3 minutes. Meanwhile check that the blade is
not clogged.

3. *First rise:* Scrape the resulting "cream" into a lightly greased 3-quart bowl.
Sprinkle the top lightly with flour to prevent a crust from forming. Cover airtight
with plastic wrap. Let rise at room temperature about 5 hours in warm weather, 6
hours in cold weather, or until dough is light, spongy, and almost tripled in bulk.
Refrigerate 20 to 30 minutes without deflating.

4. *Deflating and redistributing the yeast cells:* Using a plastic scraper, deflate the
dough by stirring it down. Turn out onto a lightly floured board. With floured hands,
gently press the dough into a rectangle, then gently fold into thirds. Dust with flour.
Wrap well and refrigerate. Allow dough to harden and ripen overnight. Punch down
once or twice if necessary. The dough will keep 3 days in the refrigerator if well
wrapped and weighted down, or it can be frozen for 1 week. (Dough doesn't freeze
well for longer than 1 week.) To defrost, thaw overnight in the refrigerator.

APPENDIX

A FEW WORDS ABOUT THE LOCAL WINES

The wines of the South-West include some of the greatest and most illustrious ever produced, as well as hundreds of brands never seen beyond the bounds of their domains. Bordeaux wines are readily available in the United States and are the classic accompaniments to many dishes in this book. For full and excellent treatment of the great whites and reds of Bordeaux, I refer readers to *Alexis Lichine's Guide to the Wines and Vineyards of France* (1979, Knopf).

Madiran is the true wine of Gascony—rustic, solid, dark, and very tannic. This wine keeps very well and improves with age. It is just now coming on the American market and goes wonderfully with the rich, hearty food that is described in this book. When a Madiran is unavailable try the California Petite Sirah, which is very similar in style. I have a very special feeling for the Gascon white, Pacherenc du Vic-Bilh, which I drank every night at the Hôtel de France in Auch, along with my evening bowl of garbure.

Cahors, the famous "black wines" from Quercy, are wonderful on picnics. They are very tannic, go beautifully with rillettes, goat cheeses, and charcuterie, and as they age become acceptable mates for rich meat dishes, mushroom dishes, game, and fowl.

The Béarn country produces a soft, velvety, sweetish wine called Jurançon, quite similar (but with more flavor and less fruit) to an American Chenin Blanc. The legend, which everyone who lives around the area will be quick to tell you, is that when Henri IV was born, his lips were rubbed with garlic and moistened with a few drops of this wine.

In the Landes there is a special appreciation of the aromatic, very dry white Tursan, which has the reputation of being able to "knock you to your knees." And there is a curious and barely known Landais light red, smelling of violets and tasting "meaty," that is grown in sandy soil—the *vin de sable* from the Domaine de Mallecare.

The Basques produce both reds and rosés called Irouléguy, which are full-bodied and acceptable with the local food.

For travelers in the region, there will always be some local wines to try with the local cuisine. The vineyards of the Périgord are at least as old as those of Bordeaux, but far less known. The best among the reds are the Bergeracs. Look for the Domaine du Haut Pécharmant. The white sweet Monbazillac from the Dordogne is called the "Sauternes of the poor." Look for the Château Ladesvignes. On the left bank of the Garonne, on the hillsides west of Agen, are grown some of the new "star" wines of the South-West, the Bordeaux-style Côtes de Buzet. Look for the Château de Padère.

For information on cooking with wine, see "Wines for Cooking" in the following section, Notes on Ingredients.

Notes on Ingredients

Years ago it was necessary to give pages of mail order sources because of the lack of available specialty items. Today there are many shops throughout the United States that sell almost everything called for in this book.

Here are some idiosyncratic views on some of the common and exotic ingredients mentioned in the recipes in this book. For ingredients not available locally, consult the entry for Mail Order Sources.

Beans. There is a method of cooking white beans that I learned from my friend Huguette Melier in Auch, a way of making the beans feel less heavy in the stomach. It requires an extra change of water—a small amount of extra effort considering the discomfort that most diners will be spared. When beans have soaked 1 1/2 hours they are drained, placed in a pot, covered with tepid water, and slowly brought to a boil. Meanwhile a kettle of water is also brought to a boil. The beans are boiled 5 minutes, drained, and returned to the pan. Immediately enough boiling water is added to cover.

Capers. I prefer the tiniest ones. The large, fleshy variety are usually nasturtium buds. Real capers always have the word "nonpareil" on the jar label.

Cèpes. Canned French cèpes are expensive, but are available in many grocery stores. The German *steinpilze* are an especially good variety. A 10-ounce can will serve 4 people. Drain canned cèpes, give them a quick rinse in a colander, dry them on a towel to press out excess water, then cook as if they were fresh. Cook the caps in oil to render their water; they are ready when the oil is clear, in about 15 minutes.

Dried cèpes (similar to porcini in Italian markets) are available in almost every city and are very reasonably priced in ethnic markets. The best are from France and Italy; the Polish and German ones are acceptable. I would avoid the Chilean ones.

There are many recipes involving dried cèpes in this book. They always require soaking for thirty minutes, and it will not harm them to soak longer than that. You can enhance their flavor by adding a pinch of salt to the soaking water and also a dash of Armagnac. Keep the soaking water after straining it through a paper filter or several damp layers of fine cheesecloth to remove the grit; it can be added to the reconstituted cèpes as they sauté in place of the water that exudes from fresh cèpes. The cèpes, too, should be rinsed after soaking, then blotted dry and sautéed.

Chestnuts. Roasted whole chestnuts, vacuum-packed in jars, are available in fine food stores and by mail from Williams-Sonoma. Fresh chestnuts are available in early winter. They taste best when "shown the flames." A chestnut-cooking pan—a long-handled pan with large perforations—is available from Dean & DeLuca. The Basques are the only people who have solved the problem of easily double-peeling chestnuts: they drop them into boiling oil—in and out just once.

To prepare fresh chestnuts without a fireplace and a perforated skillet or cauldron of boiling oil, slash them and set them in a 400° F. oven for 8 to 10 minutes. While they are still hot, peel off their shells and inner skins. They are then ready to be cooked. One method I learned for cooking peeled chestnuts to ensure that they won't break apart is typical of the shrewd approach to cooking developed in South-West France. Peeled chestnuts are wrapped in a thick layer of blanched cabbage leaves, then set in a deep pot with a small quantity of water flavored with stalks of celery or fennel—vegetables that go well with chestnuts and tend to enhance their flavor. The pot is tightly covered and set to cook slowly for 45 minutes. The chestnuts are then unwrapped and served bathed in milk or sautéed in butter. Or they are left to cool for use in salads. When you want to purée chestnuts, simmer them in flavored water until tender. Fresh chestnuts may be cooked up to one day in advance. Keep them in the refrigerator, covered, until 15 minutes before use.

Chickens. To the people of the South-West, yellow-fleshed chickens, raised on corn instead of wheat, are as delectable as white-fleshed chickens raised on wheat are to northern Europeans. Truly yellow chickens (not those fed carotene or marigold petals for coloring) *do* taste different and are preferred by people from Mediterranean countries. In some parts of the United States settled by northern Europeans there is a real prejudice against yellow chickens—an unfortunate prejudice, I think. In any case, you can use a chicken of either hue to make the recipes in this book, but if real corn-fed chickens are available where you live, I hope you will try them for the sake of flavor and authenticity.

Chocolate. It was the exiled Jews from Spain who brought the art of making chocolate to Bayonne, whose chocolate has been famous ever since. The Bayonne chocolate of the seventeenth century was heavily spiced with cinnamon and cloves and had an almost diabolical reputation. Madame de Sévigné wrote about it with great distrust in one of her letters: "Chocolate eventually seduces you, then you are inflicted with a fever which leads to death."

In Bayonne's famous chocolate shop Cazanave, under the Arceaux du Port-Neuf, I drank a cup of hot chocolate called *chocolat mousseux* (frothy chocolate). It was extraordinarily rich-tasting and most unusual, rising somewhat like a soufflé an inch above the top of the porcelain cup. The proprietress told me she made all her chocolate candies by hand every day. She served my cup, not as in Spain with a glass of cold water to clear the palate, but with two huge slabs of buttered toast.

In traditional South-West cooking, chocolate is rarely used in desserts. (The only important chocolate dessert I know of is the Gâteau de St.-Émilion, which, to my amazement, is barely known in St.-Émilion.) But in various regions, particularly in the Landes, chocolate is used much as it is in a Mexican *mole*, in sauces for rabbit and for fish dishes of eel, lamprey, or trout. The fish are cooked and covered in a red-wine sauce with glazed onions, leeks, or prunes. A small amount of chocolate is then added to enrich and thicken the sauce, as in Fish Fillets with Red Wine.

Clarified Butter. Clarification rids butter of its milk solids and some of its excess water as well as any other impurities. To clarify butter without making it indigestible (many recipes call for long, slow boiling, which does just that!), melt the butter in a bowl set over another pan of hot, but not boiling, water. Let the butter melt slowly—about 15 minutes for one stick (1/4 pound) of butter. The milky residue will sink to the bottom. Spoon off the clear yellow liquid and strain it. To store any excess clarified butter, put it in a covered jar or bowl and refrigerate it. The butter will solidify and should be melted gently over warm water before use. It will keep up to 3 months in the refrigerator.

Crème Fraîche. Delicious and thick with round, nutty flavor, this is a staple in my house for broiling and cooking. It is sweet heavy cream that is naturally thickened with the lactic bacteria—the *good* bacterial part of cream, which is killed by pasteurization—restored.

You can make it easily with the freeze-dried Solait starter (available by mail from Williams-Sonoma). Homemade Crème Fraîche made with the freeze-dried lactic bacteria will stay fresh for 3 weeks in my refrigerator. It makes the best-tasting product—even better than the commercially produced Crème Fraîche now available in some parts of the country (some American-made commercial versions contain preservatives and gum for thickening). To use the starter, mix it with 1 tablespoon cold water until thoroughly dissolved, then combine with 1 quart heavy cream that has been heated to 100° F. Let it rest in the "cooker" made by Solait, or under pillows and blankets just the way the Turks used to make yogurt. *Do not use an electric yogurt maker.* Let it rest 18 hours, or until it sets (this can sometimes take up to 24 hours). Then place it in the refrigerator to set further. Chilling will make it thicker. It keeps a few weeks under good refrigeration.

To make Crème Fraîche with buttermilk, combine 1 cup heavy cream and 2 tablespoons active-culture buttermilk in a large jar. Cover and store in a warm place away from drafts 12 to 18 hours, or until thickened. Stir and refrigerate, covered. Keeps 1 week or longer.

VARIATION

Crème Fraîche can be made with light cream. In this case, it should not be used for broiling or thickening sauces but can be used as an accompaniment to desserts such as Walnut Cake from Masseube, as a tenderizer for chicken, and as part of a sauce in a dish such as Squab Chicken or Rock Cornish Game Hen with Lemon-Garlic Sauce.

Save about 2 tablespoons of Crème Fraîche to use as a starter for your next batch. It will keep a week and will make more Crème Fraîche in half the time.

If you want double-thick Crème Fraîche, it is very easy to make. Simply drain your Crème Fraîche in a drip coffee funnel lined with a paper filter and set over a jar. The whey separates through to the jar below, leaving the thickened Crème Fraîche in the filter. This process usually takes about 3 hours. (If you let it go longer, you will end up with fresh cheese.)

Don't discard the separated whey. According to Barbara Kafka, whey has special cooking uses as well as nutritional value. She suggests using it to make lighter and flakier pastry. Use it also in fish and vegetable stocks, where it quickly draws out the flavor of the ingredients. Whey will keep fresh for about a week in the refrigerator.

Ducks. In South-West France the popular duck is the mullard, which has a breast nearly twice as heavy as that of the American Long Island-type duck known as the white Pekin. The mullard is a cross between the mallard and the muscovy. Mullards cannot reproduce, and since they are relatively scarce here, I did not test any recipes with them. All the recipes in this book were tested with our juicy and readily available white Long Island-type Pekin ducks—raised on Long Island, in the Midwest, and in North Carolina. I have had some difficulties with the California Petaluma ducks—they have great, meaty legs, but the Pekins have a bigger, juicier breast.

Because the Pekins are fatty they take well to freezing, so don't shy away from frozen ducks—some brands will give you excellent results. However, *don't refreeze parts of a totally defrosted duck.* The people from the C & D Duck Farm in Wisconsin assured me that if portions are partially frozen as you cut them up, these pieces can be refrozen *if immediately rewrapped.* But use them as soon as possible.

Duck livers. Chinese and Hungarian markets sell them loose. Look for the palest ones, since color indicates how they were fed. I was once shown a chicken that had been fed only rice; its liver was almost white. In the South-West, where chickens and ducks are fed primarily on corn, their livers are "blond."

Essences. Essences—of lemon, anise, and almond—are four times stronger than extracts. They are used in making aromatic mixtures such as the Mixed Fragrances (see Index). Mail order source is Dean & DeLuca.

Flour. For cakes, cookies, and piecrusts I prefer an *unbleached* all-purpose flour with a low gluten content. I tested these recipes with the Gold Medal brand, which has 11 percent protein (gluten). Look on the side of the package for this information. Bread flour without bromates—Hecker's or Cerasota brand—makes the best brioche and Country-Style Bread.

Foie Gras. Imported top-quality foie gras from France is available by mail from Petrossian and D'Artagnan (see Mail Order Sources). It keeps six months in the refrigerator. At the time of this printing, a few U.S. farms have started hand-feeding mallard ducks in order to enlarge their livers. Chefs in this country such as Jean-Louis Palladin acclaim the results. American-produced terrines of *foie gras mi-cuit* and duck breasts and legs are to be mass-marketed within a year.

Game. Fresh quail bred in New Jersey were used in testing for this book. Order fresh and frozen game from Iron Gate Products (see Mail Order Sources). I have had excellent results with frozen quail; on the other hand I have never been excited by the frozen pheasant. Freezing seems to accentuate the dryness of the flesh.

I am always amazed to discover, as I teach around the United States, how many people have hunters in the family and want recipes for pheasant. See my recipe for Pheasant Breasts with Foie Gras. Young, tender partridge breasts can substitute for the pheasant. Fresh mature partridge can be substituted for the *salmis* of duck legs (Duck Legs Cooked in Red Wine).

Garlic. California elephant garlic, though very mild in flavor and aroma when fresh, gets an odd taste when cooked, so it is not recommended for these recipes.

Robert Landry, a French writer on herbs and spices, offers a *truc de trucs* for neutralizing the effect of raw garlic upon the breath: chew three cardamom seeds for four minutes.

I am a great advocate of hand-chopping garlic (or any other bulb from the genus *Allium*—onions, shallots, and leeks) when you intend to eat it raw. To quote food and wine writer Matt Kramer: "Garlic is a member of the Allium family (chives, garlic, leeks, onions), all of which contain various amounts of sulfur. However, garlic has its unique properties. A scientific explanation goes as follows: The pungent aroma of garlic is contained in an *odorless* compound called 'alliin.' When the garlic clove is intact, this compound is stable. But when the clove is chopped or crushed it comes in contact with an enzyme which hangs around in another part of the clove.

"This enzyme converts 'alliin' into three parts: ammonia, another sulfur compound, and pyruvic acid (which resembles acetic acid or, in the vernacular of the street, vinegar). It is the sulfur compound which is ultimately responsible for the characteristic odor of garlic. In short, chopping brings less of the alliin into contact with the enzyme which sets all this into motion; crushing creates a more intimate mingling, the result being an unpleasantly strong garlic flavor and aroma."

On the other hand, if you cook any allium, the strong odor and taste disappear. One of the most fascinating tests to try is in the peeling: take two cloves of garlic; slam one Chinese style with a knife or cleaver to peel it, and cut the other one in half delicately. Smell and taste the difference. Since the Chinese always cook their garlic, it's perfectly okay for them. But the *hachis* (hand-chopped garlic and parsley) that is so often strewn over South-West food is raw and needs more delicate handling; otherwise it would overwhelm the food.

In winter many garlic heads have a green shoot protruding from each clove. This shoot, or "germ" as it is called in France, is thought by many garlic eaters to cause indigestion. If you ask a good cook from the Mediterranean if he takes it out, nine times out of ten he will tell you he does. Does it work? I don't know, but I try to remove it whenever possible as a sort of Pascal's wager in the kitchen.

Geese. We have excellent geese in this country; finding them outside of the Christmas season is the greatest problem. Goose can be prepared like duck for *confit*; it has a different flavor and unlike the breast of duck, the breast of goose makes an extraordinary *confit*.

Goose fat. French goose fat comes in jars, obtained by mail from Dean & DeLuca and Petrossian. Many German and Hungarian butcher shops sell rendered goose fat in the winter. You can also freeze any unused pieces of fresh fat and skin whenever you cook a duck or goose and then, when you have accumulated several cups' worth, render it according to directions in Chapter 10. I use a mixture of grape-seed oil and goose (or duck) fat to brown meats and poultry. It actually makes food taste better and doesn't burn as quickly as butter and oil. And because rendered goose fat is pure, you end up using less of it than butter.

Grape Wood. The famous *sarments de la vigne*, or dried vine cuttings, are used for barbecuing small birds, boneless duck breasts, and steaks in the South-West. Available by mail from North Coast Valley Co., "Grapesmoke," Box 1752, Santa Rosa, CA 95402.

Ham. Salt-cured, air-dried ham flavors many dishes of the South-West. This rosy pink, soft-textured ham is not smoked; it is also not available in the United States. Bayonne ham, a version of *jambon de Bayonne*, is now being produced in the United States by Americans of Basque origin. Purchase by mail order from Oakville Grocery, 1555 Pacific Avenue, San Francisco, CA 94105. Otherwise, the Citterio or John Volpi prosciutto or Westphalian ham can be substituted.

Herbs. Fresh *French* tarragon plants can be ordered from Williams-Sonoma. Fresh herbs are available at fine food stores including many supermarkets throughout the United States.

HERBES DE PROVENCE. This mixture is available by mail from Dean & DeLuca, packed in small and large earthenware jars. It is used to flavor fish, meats, and Roasted Breads (see Index). Herbs include thyme, rosemary, savory, sage, lavender, and basil.

HERBES DE LA GARRIGUE can be prepared with fresh dried herbs according to the recipe (see Index). It is lustier than the Provençal version and includes fennel seeds and the same herbs but in different proportions.

Mail Order Sources.

Dean & DeLuca
110 Greene Street, Suite 304
New York, NY 10012
(212) 431-1691

Williams-Sonoma
Mail Order Department
P.O. Box 7456
San Francisco, CA 94120
(415) 652-9007

Petrossian, Inc.
20 West 64th Street
New York, NY 10023
(212) 496-9088

Todaro Brothers
Bel Canto Importers
555 Second Avenue
New York, NY 10016
(212) 689-4433

D'Artagnan
399–419 St. Paul Avenue
Jersey City, NJ 07306
1-800-DARTAGNAN

Iron Gate Products Co., Inc.
424 West 54th Street
New York, NY 10019
(212) 757-2670

Mint syrup. Léotard mint syrup from Provence is delicious and can be used for drinks as well. It's worth searching out; other mint syrups can be disastrous.

Nuts. Finely ground blanched almond meal is sold in the Sacramento area, the home of the Diamond Almond Company, in every supermarket. Store it airtight in the freezer.

Fresh shelled walnuts are available from Hadley's Fruit Orchards, Cabazon, CA 92230. Keep walnuts in the freezer. Out of season I always buy them vacuum-packed at the supermarket. In the old days in the South-West, housewives resuscitated walnuts by burying them overnight about twelve inches underground, then using them right away. Another *truc* of the South-West is to soak them in milk. I resuscitate them by a gentle warming in the oven with a sprinkling of sugar.

Oils. French peanut oil—*huile arachides*—is a marvelous light cooking and salad oil. Quality brands are available by mail from Dean & DeLuca.

Grape-seed oil—unflavored Bénédictine or Gesundheit brand—is imported from France in 30-ounce jars. It is a light, easily digestible cooking oil, smokeless and odorless as well as low in cholesterol.

Walnut oil—*huile de noix*—is available by mail from Dean & DeLuca in 1/2-liter cans. Soft, fragrant, and green-hued when fresh; keep in the refrigerator.

There are still old mills in the South-West that make stunningly delicious walnut oil. Try M. Jossana, Salle-d'angle near Cognac, and M. Debord at St.-Pierre-de-Cole near Thiviers if traveling in the region. One of the oldest mills—more than 100 years old—is in St.-Nathalene, about 6 miles outside of Sarlat. It produces 150 quarts a day twice a week. The mill is operated by a stream that cracks open the walnuts by gentle crushing. The crushed walnuts are placed in a wooden cauldron and heated to about 120° F. before being pressed; then the oil is collected directly into bottles. In Bordeaux you can buy this oil at M. Gouraud, 7 place des Capucines, telephone (56) 91 65 31.

Orange flower water. This fragrant water distilled from orange flowers comes from France in a small blue plastic bottle. Avoid the Indian and Lebanese varieties as well as those from the drugstore. The first two often contain artificial flavoring and preservatives, and the third is overwhelmingly strong. A small bottle costs less than two dollars; orange flower water is produced in Vallauris. It is available through Williams-Sonoma.

Pork rind and fatback. Pork rind gives body to sauces. Cut if off fresh or use salted fatback or lean salt pork; blanch for three minutes before using. Fatback is best fresh, but often I have simply blanched the salted variety from the supermarket (be sure to cut down on salt in the rest of the dish).

Quatre Épices can be prepared with first-quality spices according to the recipe (see Index).

Sauce bases. In fine food stores in many parts of the United States you can find a wonderful time-saver called Saucier: frozen concentrates of beef, chicken, and fish and lobster. They keep for a year in the freezer, where you can always have them on hand, and are not exorbitantly expensive when you consider the time it takes to make glazes. Other sauce bases such as Minor's (available in the Chicago area) contain so much salt that I can't recommend them for any dish that calls for reducing a sauce to a napping consistency.

Sea salt. Available in 3 grades—fine, medium, and large crystals—from Dean & DeLuca and Williams-Sonoma. I grind sea salt once a week in my spice mill. It has a fresher taste than the free-flowing variety, and if you tried a taste test between them you would notice that the fresher-ground salt tastes saltier. The flavor of various salts is different, depending upon algae in the sea, dead plant life from rock-salt beds, and geography. You will need much less of a truly tasty salt. Sea salt is an absolute must when cooking fish.

Sausages. Toulouse Sausage can be made at home (see Index), but you can find good substitutes in ethnic markets. In Italian markets ask for *cotechino*; in French markets buy a boiling garlic sausage, and in Polish butcher shops a fresh, not smoked, kielbasa. I have used them all in cassoulets at one time or another and have also turned them into *confit*. Even the little sweet Italian sausage in the supermarket is good for making a *confit* of sausage (see Index for *Confit* of Toulouse Sausages).

Snails. Ethnic fish markets carry purged snails from Morocco. They need about six hours cooking in a rich court bouillon. Periwinkles, which cook in less than three minutes and are delicious, can be flavored with hot peppers and melted ham fat to make a variation of the Catalan *cargolade* (see Index for Snails with Country Ham and Garlic). Canned snails can often be dirty-tasting, but I have had no problems with UGMA brand. Rinse snails under running water, if necessary, before cooking. If buying a large can, look for snails from Taiwan. I think they taste better because they have eaten in marshes (as opposed to French woodland snails).

Tomatoes. Everyone knows about our "tomato problem": except for the months of August and September, it is nearly impossible to find an American tomato with any taste. Yes, everyone knows about it, everyone moans and groans about it, but nobody does anything about it—most likely because there's not much one can do. I have come up with a partial solution for dry, cardboardlike, winter-waterlogged tomatoes. It won't turn them into August tomatoes, but it will help resuscitate something resembling a true tomato taste.

Peel the tomato. Quarter lengthwise and remove the *entire* interior, then lay the remaining flesh (which will look like four petals) on a plate and sprinkle with salt, sugar, and vinegar. (A reasonable formula would be 1/2 teaspoon coarse salt, 1 teaspoon vinegar, and 1/4 teaspoon sugar for 1 pound winter tomatoes.) The salt draws out the winter water, the vinegar heightens the taste, and the sugar tempers the acidity. After one hour you will have something usable, easily cubed, ready for cooking or use in salads. (Don't leave it too long or they will turn to mush.) Again, it won't taste like an August tomato, but it won't taste like cardboard either. Canned sliced tomatoes such as those produced by Contadina are excellent in winter. San Marzano packed Italian peeled tomatoes make good sauces when simmered for a time with flavored stock (see Index for Tomato Sauce). This kind of winter tomato sauce keeps well and has a hearty, deep flavor.

Truffles. Jarred or tinned by mail from Petrossian, and fresh at Christmas at choice food markets.

Vanilla. Top-quality vanilla beans and vanilla extract from Madagascar are available in fine food stores and by mail from Williams-Sonoma. When in Paris go to the Les Halles area and purchase fresh "fat as your thumb" vanilla beans from the spice merchant Izraël, 30 rue François Miron.

For the most effective use of the seeds, split the beans and scrape the seeds onto a plate. Mix with a tablespoon of granulated sugar. Rub with your fingertips to separate.

Verjus. Summer and fall are the times to eat dishes made with the condiment *verjus*—a specially made sour grape juice. *Verjus* has a delicious, subtly sharp, thoroughly refreshing taste and enhances the flavor of chicken, green salads, foie gras, green beans, partridge, rabbit, trout, and stewed wild mushrooms. It can be used in sauces, too.

In old regional cookbooks, up until the end of the last century, *verjus* played a prominent role, but today it is rarely mentioned and there is no commercial variety available. The grapes—the *bourdelois*, the *gressois*, and the *farineau*—are no longer grown. Some types can make the process a little tricky. If the grapes are picked too ripe, their liquor will be too watery; if too green, the *verjus* will not taste good. We want grapes in the middle of their ripening, whose juice can be allowed to ferment slightly.

To make *verjus*, choose the sourest green grapes available. Holding on to the thick stem, dip them in bunches into boiling water for three seconds to kill the yeasts. Remove at once and drain on a towel. Roll the bunches, one by one, in the towel while removing the grapes from the stems. Discard any blemished grapes. When dry, place grapes in workbowl of food processor and process 10 seconds; then strain, pressing down on them to extract all the juice. Let stand for 10 minutes, then ladle juice into a sieve lined with a damp cheesecloth and strain again. Use at once, or freeze in plastic ice cube trays. Store the cubes in a plastic bag in the freezer. Use frozen or immediately upon defrosting for maximum flavor. Keeps 3 months.

Some people add alcohol to their *verjus* along with vinegar and sugar so it will keep, but this distorts the flavor. Another way to obtain the sour taste of *verjus* is to add a pinch of tartaric acid, which one can find at a wine-making shop. Don't go over 2 pinches, it is really strong. To quote Tom Stobart in *The Cook's Encyclopedia* (Harper & Row, 1981): "It is very sour—much sourer, weight for weight, than cream of tartar. It can be used in homemade soft drinks and makes a passable substitute for lemon juice." Tartaric acid sounds ominous, but actually it is nothing but the organic chemical that gives a sour quality in grapes. To use tartaric acid in sauces see Index for recipe for Chicken Drumsticks and Thighs with Sour Grape Sauce. A mail order source for tartaric acid: Milan Home Wines and Beers, 57 Spring Street, New York City, New York 10012.

Vinegar—sherry wine. Available at fine food stores and by mail from Dean & DeLuca and Williams-Sonoma.

Wines for Cooking. When a recipe calls for a red wine I usually use a California Petite Sirah or a French Côtes-du-Rhône. On the other hand, I know that in many recipes the wine is considerably reduced (to concentrate color and flavor) and therefore you may want to use less expensive varieties. I suggest: Algerian Medea or Dahra; a Spanish Rioja; a California Zinfandel; a full-flavored Cabernet Sauvignon; or a hearty Burgundy.

When a recipe calls for a white wine use a dry or medium-dry Graves, or, in chicken dishes, a California Sauvignon Blanc. You can substitute white vermouth when cooking fish if a Chablis or Riesling is suggested.

French Sauternes is very expensive. It can be replaced with a California Sauterne (spelled without a final *s*); a Semillon; or a sweet Johannisberg Riesling. The only exception is the recipe for Prunes in Sauternes.

NOTES ON EQUIPMENT

I decided, when I sat down to write this book, not to assume that it would be the only French cookbook my readers would own. Thus I eliminated the need to include that old warhorse list of equipment that has been published and republished so many times: *la batterie de cuisine.*

There is nothing special you will need to make these dishes beyond what you ordinarily own, assuming you are serious and reasonably well equipped. The only possible exception is a slow electric cooker sold under the names slow-cooker or Crock-Pot. Actually such a cooker is not necessary, but it can be economical and convenient. Many of the recipes in this book are to be prepared ahead, calling for long, slow cooking with a simple reheating just before they are served. You can do this well in any large pot, preferably one of earthenware or enameled cast iron with a tight-fitting lid. But if you have a very large oven as I do, you will use up a lot of gas or electricity cooking for so many hours. Thus I have made good use of an electric cooker with a removable glazed earthenware inset. I've used it for *confits*, stews, cassoulets, and for making stocks, and have felt secure leaving it on all day even when I am away, knowing that the temperature regulator is precise and there is no chance of overcooking or accident. Another advantage of such a cooker is that one can remove the insert, cool it, and place it in the refrigerator, allowing the fat to rise and congeal and thus be easily removed. A gentle reheating and the dish is ready to serve, with very easy cleanup of the cooking vessel, too.

To feel more in the spirit of the South-West, you may want to start cooking many different dishes in earthenware. I am particularly partial to the products of Sassafras Enterprises, Inc., Evanston, IL 60204. They make a Superstone roasting pan that cooks very evenly and makes food taste especially good. They also make a domed cover (called La Cloche) that I use to make my Country-Style Bread, the crustiest bread I have ever made at home.

For preserving *confit* I like to use stoneware jugs that are glazed on the inside only (available in department stores).

In case you do not have various sizes of terra-cotta porcelain deep dishes, a lasagna pan works well for many of the dishes in this book, especially cassoulet.

It was in the South-West that I first learned to cook in vacuum-sealed plastic bags. The French chef Francis Garcia of the Bordeaux restaurant Clavel showed me how to prepare fish using a five-thousand-dollar professional vacuum sealer from Switzerland. I adapted his ideas to our own American products—Saran Wrap and boilable plastic pouches—wrapping the food airtight and poaching it. (See recipe for Steamed Salmon with Cooked Egg Sauce.) Flavor, juiciness, and nutrition are all retained better than in any other method I know for preparing chicken breasts, mussels, shrimps, salmon, and white-fleshed fish. When these are cooked under plastic in a microwave, the plastic is pierced; here, no vapors can leave the package. A food journalist writing about my experiments with water-immersion cooking called it "the gastronomic equivalent of stereophonic sound." The idea of food cooked in its own moisture is very similar to another South-West gastronomic triumph, the mussel dish *Éclade*, where mussels are packed together so tightly they can barely open during cooking. This forces them to absorb their own juices. It is the most spectacular mussel dish that I have ever tasted. You can produce the same effect by vacuum-packing the mussels and cooking them in simmering water about 3 minutes. Because very hot water is a fast conductor of heat—much hotter than hot air—the cooking is faster too. In the last two years a machine has arrived on the market that does the job better than the cumbersome wrapping until watertight: the Vacuum Seal-A-Meal III produced by the Dazey Seal-A-Meal Co. It is available in houseware stores as well as most department stores across the United States. A more expensive but more effective machine is Vacuum Fresh, available at Hammacher Schlemmer and Nieman Marcus. To avoid any bacterial buildup, remove cooked food from the bags at once.

Another aid that I have come across to help the cook (me included) is the electric polenta machine for preparing Las Pous. This wonderful unlined copper pot with an electric paddle stirs the cornmeal continuously without any effort on the part of the cook. The pan can also be used to make Green Fig and Walnut Jam and the filling for Walnut Cake from Masseube. Available by mail from Todaro Brothers.

Preserving jars, madeleine molds, and assorted pots and pans made in thick copper are available from Williams-Sonoma.

In the French South-West, fifty minutes' drive from Toulouse, I discovered a wonderful copper source for pots and pans—French copper *pastis-tourtière* pans (top and bottom) in the style of the Lot, and other assorted pots and pans made in thick copper:

M. J. Bonnafous
Société Fonderies et Martinets
81110 Durfort
Dourgne, France

BIBLIOGRAPHY

BOOKS CONSULTED IN PREPARATION OF THIS BOOK:

Barberousse, Michel. *Cuisine Basque et Béarnaise.* Paris: Barberousse, no date.

Brown, Michael and Sybil. *Food and Wine of South-West France.* London: Batsford, 1980.

Bontou, Alcide. *Traité de Cuisine Bourgeoise Bordelaise.* 7th ed. Bordeaux: Feret et Fils, 1977.

Boulestin, Marcel. *What Shall We Have Today?* London: William Heinemann, 1931.

Carreras, Marie Thérèse. *Les Bonnes Recettes du Pays Catalan.* Paris: Presses de la Renaissance, 1979.

Couffignal, Huguette. *La Cuisine des Pays d'Oc.* Paris: Solar, 1976.

Courtine, Robert. *Grand Livre de la France à Table.* Paris: Bordas, 1979.

de Croze, Austin. *Les Plats Régionnaux de France.* Paris: Montaigne, 1928.

Daguin, André. *Le Nouveau Cuisinier Gascon.* Paris: Stock, 1981.

David, Elizabeth. *French Provincial Cooking.* London: Penguin, 1972.

Dubarry, Gabriel. *Cuisine et Poésie, Vieilles Recettes Gasconnes.* Gimont: Published privately, 1975.

Dumonteil, Fulbert. *La France Gourmande.* Paris: Librairie Universelle, 1906.

Dupouy, L. *En Chalosse, Recettes d'Hier et d'Aujourd'hui.* Aire sur l'Adour: Published privately, 1977.

de Echeverria, Juan. *Gastronomia Vasconum.* Bilbao: Izquierdo, 1979.

Escurignan, Maïté. *Manuel de Cuisine Basque.* Bayonne: Harriet, 1982.

Galan, Alain. *Au marche de Brive-la-Gaillarde.* Brive: René Dessagne, no date.

Guillot, André. *La Vraie Cuisine Légère.* Paris: Flammarion, 1981.

———. *La Grande Cuisine Bourgeoise.* Paris: Flammarion, 1976.

Guinaudeau-Franc, Zette. *Les Secrets des Fermes en Périgord Noir.* Paris: Serg, 1978.

La Mazille. *La Bonne Cuisine du Périgord.* Paris: Flammarion, 1929.

Molinier, Fernand. *Promenade Culinaire en Occitanie.* Albi: privately printed, no date (about 1930). Reprint 1978.

Palay, Simin. *La Cuisine du Pays.* 8th ed. Pau: Marrimpouey Jeune, 1978.

Penton, Anne. *Customs and Cookery in the Périgord and Quercy.* Newton Abbot, Devon (England): David & Charles, 1973.

de Pesquidoux, Joseph. *Chez Nous en Gascogne.* Paris: Plon, 1921. Reprint 1981.

Philippon, Henri. *La Cuisine du Quercy et du Périgord.* Paris: Denoël, 1979.

Progneaux, J.-E. *Recettes et Spécialités Gastronomiques Bordelaises et Girondines.* La Rochelle: "Quartier Latin," 1969.

Rieux, Louis. *Au Pays de Cocagne, le Livre de Cuisine Albigeoise.* Albi: Privately published, 1913.

de Rivoyre, Éliane and Jacquette. *La Cuisine Landaise.* Paris: Noël, 1980.

St.-Martin, Paul. *Mes Secrets de Cuisine.* Mont-de-Marsan: Jean-Lacoste, 1964.

INDEX